RESEARCHING DANCE

EVOLVING MODES OF INQUIRY

Edited by Sondra Horton Fraleigh
and Penelope Hanstein

DANCE BOOKS

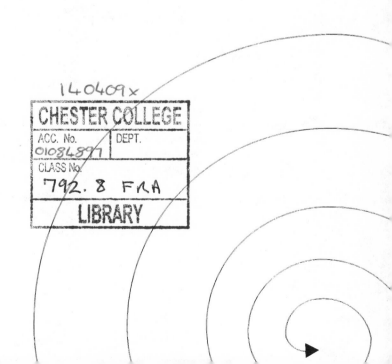

Published by Dance Books Ltd., 15 Cecil Court, London WC2N4EZ

Copyright © 1999, University of Pittsburgh Press

Manufactured in the United States of America

Printed on acid-free paper

10 9 8 7 6 5 4 3 2 1

ISBN 1 85273 067 6

Figure 9.1 is from *Participant Observation* by James P. Spradley, copyright © 1980 by Holt, Rinehart and Winston. Reproduced by permission of the publisher.

A CIP catalog record for this book is available from the British Library.

CONTENTS

PREFACE

Researching Dance: Evolving Modes of Inquiry introduces students to research methods in dance. This book is addressed primarily to graduate students and is particularly useful as a textbook for dance research classes. It will also appeal to advanced undergraduate students who are becoming acquainted with the subject matter and processes of dance research. Researchers and scholars will find the book valuable as well, since there are few published materials that explore modes of inquiry in dance research. As a survey of resources and methods, *Researching Dance* fills a gap because, for the first time, major areas and topics of concern are gathered together in one volume.

In part 1, the editors introduce dance research as evolving. In "Family Resemblance," Sondra Fraleigh raises issues of definition and naming. "We name things and then we can talk about them" is how Ludwig Wittgenstein put this essential first step of identification and definition. Dance is defined contextually in view of its intrinsic participatory values, its developmental aspects, and its purposes from art to ritual. Penelope Hanstein takes the reader through the steps of the research process in "From Idea to Research Proposal: Balancing the Systematic and Serendipitous." Her final chapter in part 1, "Models and Metaphors: Theory Making and the Creation of New Knowledge," explores the role of theory in research. Hanstein examines the function of research in generating and testing theory and defines research as a creative process.

In parts 2 and 3, ten dancer-scholars examine qualitative and quantitative inquiry and delineate the most common approaches for investigating dance. They also contribute study questions, research exercises, and suggested readings, which appear at the end of each chapter. These are in various formats as appropriate to the respective mode of inquiry and focus of the individual chapters.

Quantitative research is based on scientific traditions that had their genesis in the Enlightenment and that seek some measure of predictability. The quantitative researcher wants to know what is "true" for a given population or phenomenon, and under what circumstances. In broader terms, Science seeks a research basis for understanding change itself, as one study supplants another in a chain of revisions.

Qualitative research studies qualitative values (it stands to reason). These are experiential values concretely defined as: educational, social, cultural and cross-cultural, developmental, linguistic, aesthetic, mythological, symbolic, and so on. Because of the broad range of qualitative lenses for looking at dance, it is not easy to distinguish the few overviews that are most inclusive. We have tried in the chapter selections here to indicate some places to begin.

Jill Green and Sue Stinson analyze differences in quantitative and qualitative models in their chapter on postpositivist research. They then present the features of some postpositivist (qualitative) models. It is for this reason that the methodological section of our text, part 2, commences with this chapter. Postpositivist research in dance provides a framework for understanding strategies that respect the qualitative nature of dance. In this chapter, the authors question claims to objective truth. Can there be a value-free truth, particularly in the study of human behaviors? Is reality found through experiment, or is it socially constructed? How shall we regard expectations of reliability and objectivity in research? What are the data of qualitative research? What are some postpositivist approaches and their goals?

As Steven Chatfield takes a closer look at science in chapter 5, part 2, we see that its discoveries have been the products of qualitative leaps of imagination, as well as the results of quantitative research. Creativity operates to further science as well as art. Chatfield explores commonly used experimental research designs and their benefits for dance. We see through his presentation that problem solving in science is not a fixed and lock-step procedure, but an adventure to discovery.

Qualitative methods are particularly applicable to dance in its multivalent nature. Dance is qualitatively constituted in movement and experience, although it can be subjected to quantification through scientific methods and various forms of movement analysis. Even these tools, however, serve larger research purposes and are not ends in themselves. They bring selected aspects of dance processes into sharper focus. Fundamentally, dance is made up of movement qualities that are also human qualities. These imply our living body, its biology and aesthetics, its history and culture.

What are some styles of reporting findings that respect qualitative dimensions of dance? What are inherent limitations of qualitative research? The two methodological approaches that admit qualitative and interpretive grounds in their essential operations are philosophy and hermeneutics. This book therefore considers them next.

Hermeneutics is a field of inquiry involving both philosophy and literary theory (sometimes sociology, psychology, and religion as well). Concerned primarily with interpretation and the unfolding of significance, hermeneutics explores qualitative contextualization per se. As a particular kind of qualitative research, it studies the interface of interpretation with meaning—or how texts become meaningful.

Dances can be considered texts even though they are not written texts. Should this make a difference? Are there obvious limits to a consideration of dance as text? We know that dancing is not words, nor is it writing. Part of the distinguishing character of dance is that it is "nonverbal" in essence, yet in a broad sense, dances bear some similarities to texts. So the hermeneutic problem becomes one of understanding what kind of texts dances are. What are their inherent textual capacities (and limitations)? In what manner may movement performance be seen as a text? We know, for instance, that dances will bear the inscriptions of culture, history, gender practices, and even political persuasions. All of these contribute to the "con-textualization" of dance. Fuller meanings emerge in the textual writings about dance that create a hermeneutic circling of meaning. The theorist, critic, choreographer, performer, and reader all participate (and sometimes do battle) in the creation of signification. Janet Adshead-Lansdale takes up the issue of dance as textual battleground in "Patrolling The Boarders: The Dance Text as Exclusion Zone," *Proceedings, Society of Dance History Scholars,* Toronto, Canada (May 1995): 109–15.

In "Dance In the Hermeneutic Circle," Joann McNamara outlines the two branches of hermeneutics: "positivistic" and "anti-objectivist." The latter emphasizes understanding the essence of the text in its contextual character. This is the approach most often employed by dance writers and scholars, she says. Hermeneutics is a crossroads where many contemporary strains of thought merge. McNamara applies this methodology to dance. Dance is an interpretive activity as it translates human movement in many different contexts and often merges texts syncretically. Consequently, dance and qualitative dance research are already in the "hermeneutic circle."

In "Witnessing the Frog Pond," Sondra Fraleigh establishes a philosophical/ aesthetic context for dance, made explicit in terms of aesthetic theory and its historic tie to beauty and art. She explores aesthetic (perceptual) value across the boundaries of art and ritual. She also investigates how qualitative values arise in perception (aesthetics) and influence judgment (criticism). Can we speak of aesthetic truth? Such truths as aesthetics and history may claim are at least variant, as are those of science. Truths arise in context; we are not merely passive recipients of pre-established truths. Contextual, relational, and situational views assert that we are a part, and maybe the most part, of the truth we find. The terms of aesthetics have broadened beyond beauty and art with the evolution of modern aesthetics. Now they also encompass ritual, entertainment, play, therapy, and nature, to name just a few. In this chapter, Fraleigh examines the term *aesthetic* as basic to dance.

Her chapter introduces some gender issues that have consequences for discourse in dance aesthetics and phenomenology of the body in dance. In both phenomenology and feminism, the personal is political. Problems of intentionality enter into discussions of dance and the body, since dance flows from human agency. We choose to dance: thus, dance embodies our freedom and exercise of intention. Because dance is of the body, it also involves the body's relationship to nature. Questions are posed concerning the reciprocity of nature and culture in dance. As in the chapter on hermeneutics, once more a concern for interpretation is introduced, now in relativist terms. Fraleigh develops phenomenology as a philosophical method for researching dance that aims to validate experience.

In her chapter, "The Sense of the Past: Historiography and Dance," Shelley Berg delineates the discipline of historical scholarship as threefold: "requiring both research and writing, with the act of interpretation forming a critical link between the two." The historian seeks to evoke the past and becomes involved in an interactive process. "The act of historiography is . . . an active engagement in the performance of history." Berg considers the role of the dance historian, discusses questions of methodology, and offers examples of dance historiography in the making. She sees revision of the orthodoxies of historical inquiry continually taking place, producing a "new historicism" and "poetics of culture" with more flexibility across disciplinary boundaries.

As Joan Frosch traces "the weave of dance in the fabric of culture" in her chapter, "Dance Ethnography," she distinguishes the contributions of practitioners of dance anthropology, the anthropology of human movement, ethnochoreology, and dance ethnology. She holds that the practice of ethnography is cyclical in nature, unlike other social science research. It explicitly positions self-biases and allows for a multiplicity of interwoven voices. Frosch sees its hallmark practice of participant observation as well suited to dance study. As an ethnologist, Frosch asks what the research is for and who will benefit, and she addresses how the research could advance the goals or answer the needs of the community. Her chapter further explains what the dance ethnographer does and introduces ethical issues specific to this field of research. She discusses the value of notation, film, and video as research tools. Frosch also provides research resources and a brief history of the study of dance in cultural contexts.

Another element of dance research is its movement basis. Dance is made up of movement. We could say bodily movement is its basic material. We can see movement structures in choreographic and ritualistic aspects of dance, even in its improvisatory examples. Thus dances can be analyzed according to their movement structures and properties: use of space, efforts, time, and rhythm. We can also consider how components of movement contribute to image, symbol, and meaning in dance. Historically, dance analysis is not new. Verbal description, pictures, and symbols as well as poetry detailing past dance forms have been handed down for centuries. What is new are attempts to bring order to the study of movement through systematic analysis, that we might develop tools for looking at movement that could serve the broader purposes of dance research. In the first chapter of part 3, Mary Alice Brennan presents the features of movement analysis and its research application in "Every Little Movement Has a Meaning All Its Own."

Matters of gender have gradually entered the field of dance research, recognized finally in the theme of a conference of the Congress on Research in Dance entitled "Engendering Dance/Engendering Knowledge: Dance, Gender and Interdisciplinary Dialogue" (Texas Woman's University, 1994). Dance is an intimate art of the human body, the symbolic meanings or exemplifications we generate in movement. Thus questions of sex and gender can never be far from the surface. Every kind of dance will project the sexual/gendered body in the particular form and purpose of the dance itself. In other words, we can observe the matters and manners of sex and gender as part of the constitution of the dance form in both choreography and performance.

In her chapter, "Engendering Dance: Feminist Inquiry," Jane Desmond explains that ideologies of gender differences operate to produce the normative. She explores how what is accepted as normal becomes historically instantiated. She implies that questions for research could begin with this recognition. Our very understanding of ourselves through the terms *man* and *woman* is embodied in our dancing. Desmond outlines particular issues concerning sexual identification and gender relevant to dance research.

Scholarship is beginning the search for more inclusive approaches to an understanding of dance in its multicultural (or polycultural) context. In his chapter, "Cultural Diversity and Dance History Research," John O. Perpener III looks at specific concerns of historians involved in African American dance, providing an example for researching areas where issues of cultural diversity play an important role. He discusses concerns for recounting histories that have been marginalized or overlooked. He calls for balance, suggesting a methodology that "guards against dance becoming a mere exemplar of underlying social or political situations" while synthesizing a wide array of historic, aesthetic, social, and political information. Perpener envisions artists, critics, and researchers who could be "new cultural workers" (a concept he develops from philosopher and theologian Cornell West). These proponents of change would "realign" themselves to move across typical divisions of gender, race, age, sexual orientation, and the boundaries of disciplines to create "a more accurate and representative record of America's cultural and artistic heritage."

In our editorial conception of the book and in our own chapters, we raise basic issues for dance research and lay out the research process in detail. We propose no definitive formulas for the very fluid topics of dance research but hope to provoke the serious student to questions (and dances) that expand the text of the present work and move beyond it. We are grateful to our contributors for sharing their expertise with us in the process of bringing this book to realization. As demonstrated by their biographies at the end of the book, the depth of scholarship and experience they bring to this work is enormous. In every chapter, the academic arguments of the book are enhanced by voices of dancer-scholars who have *gone through* the process. This book is a tribute to their knowledge, creativity, and experience.

PART ONE

CONTEXT, PROCESS, AND THEORY

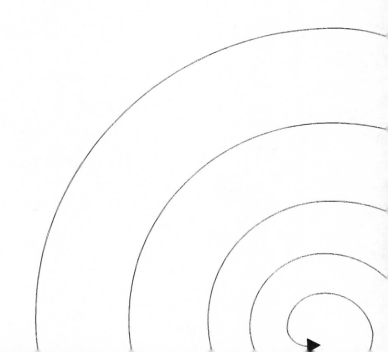

❙ FAMILY RESEMBLANCE

Sondra Horton Fraleigh

We name things and then we can talk about them.

Ludwig Wittgenstein, *Philosophical Investigations*

ANYTHING (MATERIAL OR NONMATERIAL) can be the object of our awareness, attention, or questioning mind. Whenever we ask "what is this?" we enter into an inquiring frame of mind. When we research something, we formalize this intuitive process to establish a definition for qualitative discourse or quantitative testing. We define the thing we seek to know more about. Then we have a basis for communicating the findings. The results of the research will rest on our basic understanding and definition of the thing we are investigating. The activity of defining underlies all other aspects of research.

Naming things is at root a philosophical endeavor, even though the framework or lens for investigation may be oriented aesthetically, biologically, sociologically, or historically. First comes an understanding of the phenomenon—the thing—and in dance this is not a material thing that can be positioned apart from ourselves. Dance derives from human movement and consciousness. It is an activity that ensues from our nature as moving beings and speaks of that nature in its environment and culture. I believe that movement is a part of our nature, which does not mean that we have no choices to make about what movement, where, and when. Nor does it mean that we are doomed to move all the time, like the maiden who makes the mistake of trading her soul for red shoes and has to dance forever.

3

We can be still (although children may have trouble with this). If we could not, we would not know movement. (Whoops! I'm beginning to define movement.) We know things partly through contrast—just as stillness gives us a perspective on movement and thus the possibility of naming it. Dance contains movement and stillness (and more). The "more than movement" aspects of dance point toward context: aesthetic, historical, cultural, kinesiological, and so on, which we explore throughout this text.

What would be the opposite of dance? Lassitude? A loss of dynamic tension between movement and stillness? Would it be "not dancing"? As I sometimes tell my students: "you're not dancing yet." What do I mean? Well, I might mean "you could do better" (enhance or refine performance), or "you're not doing the intended movement yet," or "the movement lacks something (maybe flow)," or "you're doing all the moves, but *you* are missing." These are matters of consciousness, my understanding or tacit definition of dance, as I name its features for the students in response to their performance. My teaching them how they might do better will further shape their understanding of what dance is, assuming they trust me and are paying attention. The dance arises intersubjectively in the interval between us. Our conscious interaction will be reflected in the movement event that we call dance. The concrete product began with our engagement toward a common outcome. This manner of describing experience in order to identify phenomena (the contents of consciousness) was initiated by Edmund Husserl, who hoped to return philosophy to a basic naming of essences, "the things themselves."

Dance is often spoken of as though it were a singular thing, but we know we have various "things" in mind when we say it. It may seem curious to call dance (or dancing) a thing, an object. Yet the moment we bring ourselves to ask, "what is this?" our attention formulates the object of the question, bringing it into sharp relief. And necessarily so, to make the question clear. Our answer will further define the thing we have in mind (at least for the time being).

Thus there is a basic process of definition that is part of our fundamental consciousness of things. As we distinguish one thing from another, the pluralistic world of distinct objects arises, be these material objects, bodily activities (the things we do), or thoughts (the things we think).

But we rightly speak of dance as a subject also, particularly when we make it a topic or theme of inquiry. In this book dance is the central subject. Furthermore, it is the focal point for exploring a variety of research methods and modes of inquiry. Thus we locate the terms of dance in various contexts. Furthermore, we are establishing an entire field of inquiry as we consider the emerging methods for researching dance. This is a field in flux because it flows from studied and critical contributions that define dance at ever deeper levels over time. We could say this is an objectifying process because it produces written texts and other records such as notation and video documents that expand our understandings of dance as a discipline—a researched branch of knowledge. At root is the subjective thematic or experience. We commonly speak of dance as a subjective experience, a part of our sentient life, sometimes synonymous with our subjectivity. This is the dance as perceived in action, not a matter for reflection or study but manifest in the flow of being.

A Family of Meanings

Dance is not a precise concept or singular activity; it is richly diverse. But this does not mean, as is sometimes claimed, that dance cannot be defined. Rather, there are changing perspectives we take on the things we call dance. Dance already has concrete definitions in its various manifestations. Ask anyone what dance is, and they will give you an example. More abstract matters of definition revolve around new examples and whether they fit (or stretch, or contradict) existing understandings. There will always be particular examples or aesthetic movements that challenge existing definitions, but it is in relation to some basic understanding of a phenomenon that new examples can be included. They would bear at least "a family resemblance," as Wittgenstein explores in his philosophy of language.[1]

Human beings are inventive creatures, and they are constantly inventing new ways to dance in bodily means and matters of movement. In addition, intentionality and interpretation enter into the picture. Our reasons to dance and the significance we find therein become part of the definition. We can move spontaneously and suddenly recognize a dancelike quality in the movement or observe the movement around us in a dance framework; but even this presupposes that we have an idea about what dance is.

If I say "I am eating," it is easy enough to visualize the activity; only the circumstances vary. If I say "I am dancing," visualizations of that activity could be infinitely varied. The word has been used to cover a wide range of behavior, from intricately formulated movement vocabularies performed in spectacular settings, as in the classical ballet, to the subtle and dangerous dynamic equilibrium of a tightrope dancer. A child's creative play may be interpreted as dance. Dance therapists consider the whole movement character of a person to be his or her dance. People in wheelchairs dance, and otherwise functional populations also seek the therapeutic of dance and related somatic processes. In order to develop movement therapeutics or integrative movement/dance lessons, a somatic or dance therapist may utilize personal movement patterns as dance. The field of dance is thus wide-ranging, extending from clinical and personalized therapeutic perspectives to historically preserved cultural and traditional forms.

Dance grows out of culture and feeds back into it. We can mistakenly suppose that culture is something that only anthropologists study, and that the study of dance as a matter of ethnic identity applies only to cultures outside the contemporary Eurocentric network. Anthropologist Joann Kealiinohomoku's breakthrough article, "An Anthropologist Looks at Ballet as a Form of Ethnic Dance,"[2] is still relevant in this respect. It is a reminder that all dance is essentially cultural and as such has ethnicity.

The most basic meaning of culture is "to till the earth." All people till the earth of their own identity. That is: we create culture in the creation of our dances, be they for the purposes of art, ritual, fun, or therapy. When we study dance, we are studying culture. When we research dance, we are researching culture, whether as an ethnologist, aesthetician, sociologist, or historian. Only the focus of inquiry varies. Culture is how we dance and dress and cook, how we worship and call upon transpersonal powers, how we paint and write ourselves into history. Culture contains aesthetic values and social-historical processes. Culture is not something we put on or take off, nor is it some higher valuation (even if we do "wear it on our sleeve"). The word *culture* may be used pejoratively, but this is an acceleration of its basic meaning. Culture is created from all of our doings and sayings, our buildings and holdings. In the case of dance, it is created in our movement and the values we create and experience in the particular kinds of dances we do. All people are culturally identified in their dances; all dance has ethnicity, and aesthetic, social, and historical essence.

Creativity Is Apparent in All Dance

Creativity is apparent in all dance from the magic invoked in ritual to the varieties of theater dance that clear a "seeing place" where one may identify with a staged presence. (Our word *theater* is derived from the Greek word *theatron*, which means "seeing place.")[3] Dance is not just any movement, but movement that has been created for some particular purpose. Although we may lose track of the creative origin of traditional dances, all dance is the product of human invention. This is not to say that animals do not dance, nor the cosmos for that matter, just to delimit the phenomenon of human dance.

Aesthetic Value Belongs to All Forms of Dance

Dance movement is also aesthetically constructed. All forms contain the aesthetic impulses that motivated their creation. They appear in the special qualities or properties of the movement—whether the movement stamps, stalks, flows, or freezes. Since we can identify and name such properties, we sometimes call them objective. From *aisthesis* (the Greek word for sense perception) the aesthetic is also the subjectively affective, that which influences sentient life and change. Objectification and naming of aesthetic properties is predicated on subjectively lived aesthetic values in dance. The first gives us the details, the second, the dance. Aesthetics gives us fragrance and also the flower.

Many other movement activities are aesthetically constructed and perceived, but dance is movement that is primarily marked by its aesthetic character (its qualitative dimensions). At best, aesthetic theory stops short of prescriptions, and one enters its objective-subjective loops somewhere in the dance. Not charged with sight, smell, touch, and sound, dictionary definitions can be immobilizing and disappointing.

In what sense is it right that we hold ritual and aesthetics in separate categories? In ritual, attention is also given to qualitative movement. I am thinking about the carefully executed, smooth, and formal movements of the Japanese tea ceremony that I witnessed in Tsuchiura, Japan—quite a dance, but still a ritual ceremony. The Haitian ceremonial dance *Yanvalou,* while intended to invoke healing spirits, is nevertheless aesthetically constructed, as its sinuous flow of body shows. *Yanvalou* presents patterned actions that are part of a cultural expression. The dance's aesthetic style is contextualized ceremonially using music, singing, mythology, and religion, as explained by Joan Hamby Burroughs. Edith Turner also describes a "stylistic" (aesthetic) feature of Inupiat Eskimo dance and culture in northern Alaska that is seen repeatedly: "the slow start, full force climax, and unexpected ending."[4]

Aesthetic value belongs to all forms of dance; it is inherent in movement patterns and qualities, sometimes accentuated by jewelry, costumes, or props, and often contextualized in stories, rituals, myths, or religion. Traditional dances and classical forms (as lasting over long periods of time) produce aesthetic values that identify a people and contribute to their cultural values. Thus we can understand that the properties of South Indian *bharatanatyam* represent classically transmitted religious and theatrical aesthetics, or that American square dance proceeds from rustic folk aesthetics. Aesthetic characteristics of individual performers or instances of particular performances can also be marked.

Dance Always Appears in Context

It is difficult to identify a "pure" or intrinsic dance, but there may be a way to consider this (as I take up shortly). This is because dance always appears in context. Dance is entertainment, play, art, and ritual—sometimes all at once—as in Garth Fagan's syncretic polycultural dance theater. This is apparent in *River Song: From Earth Eagle First Circle* (1995), inspired by the aesthetic freedom of modern dance and tribal traditions in Africa and Native America and cast in an eclectic jazz style infused with ballet virtuosity. The whole emerges in relation to Fagan's movement aesthetics, the feathered costumes of Linda King (Salish and Kootenai Tribe), and the jazz/Indian score (Don Pullen's African-Brazilian Connection and the Chief Cliff Singers).[5]

Dance Always Has Style

Dance always has style. Style is the "how" of dancing, its aesthetic character. It arises in the viewer as a matter of perception and interpretation in relation to the dance event. *Style emerges from intention.* This includes the intentions of the choreographer or the group, the purpose or purposes embodied in the dance event as a specific kind of cultural event, and the individual intentionality of the dancers (their own quality of movement and presence). We can think of style in two senses: the embodied characteristics of the dance, and the dancer's individual qualities as personal signature.[6]

Intentions are clues toward the revelation of design. *Intention* here means "done by design," as an aspect of voluntary motion. It is not a future projection of something that might happen. When we isolate and categorize elements of dance such as style and intention, our view will be partial, because analysis singles out certain elements for attention. But analysis is nevertheless a part of the whole picture. It presents the possibility that the whole exists and may be perceived in its parts.

Meaning Depends on Context

A coherence of parts establishes context, that which makes meaning possible. Meaning depends on the contextualized whole. *Context is the weaving or joining together of elements to produce a whole.* Its first use concerns written text and how words are understood in relation to one another, but it also applies to movement significance. Neither words nor movement makes meaning when perceived out of context. Rather, we come to understand dance and to define it in terms of context, an inner coherence of movement elements according to purpose. Context is also integral to the setting in which the dance is performed or viewed. Ice dancing, for instance, has dramatic aesthetic qualities that contextualize it as theater and entertainment. However, it is often performed in sporting competitions, and in sports arenas, which creates a crossing of contexts (and thus performing intentionality).

Dance Is Both Art and Entertainment

Dance is ubiquitous as entertainment and commonly used for socializing. We do not usually term these forms art; but when forms of entertainment or social dance attain excellence, we do not hesitate to call them art. Fred Astaire and Ginger Rogers have been much admired, for instance. Their art was constituted through combining tap dance and ballroom social dances in movie musicals. Art is another word for excellence, and it also has an institutional meaning, as it designates culturally valued works. For example, the ballroom, Hollywood tap dance of Astaire and the lesser-known vernacular tap dance of Bill Robinson could qualify on both counts. Robinson was no less an artist than Astaire, but the full spectrum of his dancing was not so widely popularized. Because of Robinson's race, acclaim came belatedly.

As art, dance can also be understood in its institutional aspects. We name some arts "fine arts" and institutionalize them in fine arts schools and university departments, a widespread practice in America. We also combine the terms *art* and *entertainment* in various ways. Entertainers are sometimes called artists, and we also speak of the entertainment arts. As an entertainment art, the Broadway musical is an institution that blends dance, music, and drama in total theater events. This blend has produced unique commentaries on contemporary life and its rhythms—from Leonard Bernstein's *West Side Story* (1957) to George C. Wolfe's *Bring in 'Da Noise, Bring in 'Da Funk* (1996). The latter grew out of Wolfe's idea of Savion Glover as a living repository of rhythm. As such it is dance history in the making. Wolf states in the program:

> There are these old black tap dancers, who were taught by the old black tap dancers, and so on. All of those guys passed that information on to Savion, and it landed in his feet, and his being, and his soul.
>
> My interest in tap springs from my passion for folk art. . . . Only a great folk art form can tell all our stories—and tap is one of the greatest folk arts we have.
>
> I wanted to see how tap could not just tell stories, but how it could really convey really complicated emotion. Jazz dance does this, as do modern dance and ballet, but tap wasn't being mined for its emotional content. It was lopped off as

an art form that's just exuberant and fun and playful. With this show, I wanted to see how we could use tap to convey desires and drives—how it could become a source of delight, intensity, rage, or power.

Broadway is not the only institution for blending art forms. Theatrical melds that bear a family resemblance appear in several forms and use other names. Opera uses total theater elements, as do some mixed media and performance art. What we call musical theater in America is called pantomime in Jamaica. The meaning of pantomime as extracting and exaggerating realistic gesture is bypassed in favor of the root *pan,* suggesting an encompassing of elements—and emphasizing dramatic entertainment to music.

Dance Is Often Used as an Educational Medium

Dance is often used as a means to educate: "to draw forth," to *educe* (or lead forth, as a river). Dance may be a vehicle for drawing out individual responses to movement (creative dance) and establishing group cohesiveness (folk forms). There is transmission of group and individual bodily lived values in the educational processes of dance. With this in mind, educators such as Sue Stinson and Jill Green look at student interpretations of their dance classes, and they question educational processes to uncover destructive practices based on control and manipulation that engender poor body images.[7] What goes on under the name of education is not always or necessarily in the best interests of students, as research into dance education may begin to establish.

Dance Is Used for Therapeutic and Healing Purposes

Dance evolved from the therapeutic of ritual and in many traditions is still used to call forth healing spirits. The healing capacities of dance derive from its intrinsic (experiential) values: pleasure in movement and the affective link between motion and e-motion. Dance therapists learn how to elicit the pleasure and power of movement as they use dance processes for therapeutic and healing purposes.

Somatic teacher-therapists draw upon these same experiential values and processes with their modalities of *movement and touch* (as explored in a recent article).[8] Somatic practitioners may attune to the aesthetics of healing in a dance-like manner. They often weave dance processes with somatic practices for body-mind integrity, psycho-physical (emotional) release, physical improvement, and dynamic alignment. The 1996 Conference of the Congress on Research in Dance at the University of North Carolina at Greensboro, *Dance and the Body,* dealt thematically with the relationship of dance and somatics. Movement aesthetics is the root of somatics education and therapy, dance in all of its forms, and dance therapy. Dance crosses over naturally into therapeutic fields through its aesthetic component, "aisthesis" (as we just mentioned), or "aesthetikos," the Greek root of aesthetics, meaning sense perception.[9] The basis for aesthetic perception and appreciation (valuation) lies in sentient life and its ever-present affective dimensions. Affectivity (in art and therapy) presupposes a multitude of stimuli that influence feelings, emotions, and movement: an innerscape, if you will, constantly in flux.

Similar concerns for sense perception and the affective motivate studies of infancy and developmental movement (developmental and cognitive psychology). Daniel Stern studies types of feeling experience involved in *categorical affects* (happiness, sadness, anger, and so on), *vitality affects,* those kinetic terms that indicate intensity and degrees of animation (fading, exploding, pulsing, and the like), and *relational affects* involving interpersonal sharing (feeling esteemed or ineffective, for instance).[10] *All such affects appear in various dance contexts.* They are aspects of experience influencing our perceptions and valuations. Affects color all movement and carry somatic thresholds as they rise to attention. We can become aware of and appreciate the affective in human movement, what philosopher Susanne Langer called "forms of feeling" in her aesthetics: form and feeling. We can describe these forms as they appear in movement. We might deem them beautiful, expressive, exciting, soothing, or—on the other hand—repulsive. Displeasure is also in the affective/aesthetic range of possibility. In such descriptions, we acknowledge the affective. Affectivity is not something added to movement. Human movement cannot be separated from its felt (somatic/affective) basis. Thus the affective permeates and colors all movement. Affective qualities are aesthetically distilled in all dance (playful, ritual, or presentational) and in the therapeutic processes of somatic and dance therapy. As we identify aesthetic qualities in the observable properties of movement to objectively *name* them, we draw upon our subjective experience.

Dance Is a Source for Self-Knowledge and Human Development

As self-directed movement, dance is also a source of self-knowledge. Thus dance studies may be designed around concerns for human development. In their study of perception and movement affectivity, cognitive psychologists articulate concerns for "the self" that could enrich research in dance therapy and dance somatics. A good case in point is Ulric Neisser's "Five Kinds of Self-Knowledge."[11] He describes the person "here in this place, engaged in this particular activity" with respect to the physical environment, as "the ecological self." This would be the dancer oriented in time/space, somatically alive to her experience of moving. What cognitive psychology calls "the interpersonal self" would more appropriately describe the dancer's perception of herself engaged with others in a folk dance, for instance, or in relation to an audience (if she is performing)—engaging them emotionally or conveying nonverbal signals.

Self-knowledge has a basis in sense perception including proprioception, the movement sense. All our movement is constantly being somaesthetically processed in the interweave of our senses, perceptions, and emotions. An essential insight of cognitive psychology beginning with J. J. and Elanor Gibson is that the senses function together *through movement* and not in isolation.[12] When we give conscious attention to our movement experiences, we make somatic processes and sense perceptions concrete. We do this in the act of self-awareness—always available through dance, made more explicit in somatic movement "self-awareness" explorations and in dance therapy through "authentic movement," initiated through the work of Mary Whitehouse. In such work, dance is a source for self-knowledge and human development.[13]

The work of Ellen Dissanayake on human development bridges ethnography and aesthetics, suggesting that *multi-sensory performance* is our earliest art form, based cross-culturally in the mother-baby relationship and "baby talk" rhythmic play. Participation in creative arts and performance, from the first years of life and throughout life, is crucially important to human well-being. Dissanayake's work *What is Art For?* (1988) and *Homo Aestheticus* (1992) is in the center of today's discussions about the role of the arts in the evolution of culture and human survival. Her approach is ethological—that is, she views the arts as biologically evolved or adaptive propensities of human nature. *What is Art For?* considers why the arts evolved in the first place, and *Homo Aestheticus* looks at some naturally aesthetic aspects of human thought and cultural behavior. Her recent work in preparation, *Rhythm and Modes in Love and Art,* finds that precursors of the "arts of time," dance, music, and dramatic performance, appear spontaneously in the earliest interactive relationship between mothers and infants. Babies possess a precocious capacity to respond to "rhythms and modes"—patterned vocal, visual, and kinetic signals that arise in play with loving adult partners. Rhythms and modes, Dissanayake says, "create and sustain love," as they also give rise to the arts.[14]

Dance Often Intersects with Religion

Dance often intersects with religion. It is a means of worship—although in the West, dance has had a love-hate relationship with formalized religion, depending on the prevailing attitudes toward the body. Joann Keali'inohomoku tells us that in the European Christian world, dance was rejected by the church even as this meant its relinquishment over control of the dancers. "The legacy of the separation of dance from the church is seen to this day as the received attitude toward dance as trivialization, denigration, and secular specialization. Today in the Western world serious dance is presided over by a secular priesthood."[15]

It is sometimes difficult to separate dance from religion in traditional societies, however. Parul Shah, a master teacher of *bharatanatyam*, one of India's seven classical dance forms, says that *bharatanatyam* originated in Hindu temples as a solo for *devadasis* (female temple dancers), but as a dynamic living tradition the dance form continues to evolve. Its name derives from *Bharata Natya Shastra*, Bharata's book (written between 200 B.C. and 300 A.D.), and the movements of the dance as presently performed go back about three hundred years. Now it is performed in theaters and sometimes in group choreography, Shah says. There is room for creativity in this form, even as its sacred source is recognized.[16]

Dance Is a Broad Category of Human Activity

Dance is a broad category of human activity embracing tradition even as it evolves new forms. Dance also overlaps the other arts and other movement forms. Gymnastic dance, for instance, is both a competitive sport (in its competitive and quantifying mode) and a dance form (when its primary intent is founded in the qualitative dimensions of the movement and the enjoyment of performer and spectator). Since competition is not essential to dance, we can establish that, nevertheless, dance often appears in competitive contexts. There are ballroom competitions and ballet and modern dance competitions, not to mention highly competitive auditions of all kinds. Dance can be competitively contextualized, but it is not competitive in essence (intrinsically).

In contrast, we have explored that *cultural values* are present in all forms of dance, and that *aesthetic values of movement and the living body*, as well as *historical values*, are in the nature of, or intrinsic to, dance. We have also considered that the (ever-present) *affective values* of movement lend dance its aesthetic and healing powers and its potential for instilling self-knowledge. We have only mentioned *ritual* but have not asked if ritual is an essential element of dance.

Ritual Often Sustains Dance Practices

As repetitive enactments, ritual elements often sustain dance practices. These are evident in daily dance classes that ritualize the experience of learning, for instance. But dances that found culture, that proclaim a people's identity and sometimes their religion and magic, are validated *as ritual.* They are often public rites of renewal and passage; they are not dance in a narrow sense. Ritual dances are usually total events that incorporate music and costumes as artifacts that cannot be divorced from the dance movement. Dance is ritualized in its repetitive enactments and cultural practices. When it becomes commensurate with culturally instantiated rites and beliefs, *dance becomes ritual* as cultural repository. Ritual dances are often passed down for generations and thus become bearers of a people's history.

Cultural rituals and ceremonies extend space and time beyond the ordinary sense, and as such they are transformative on both personal and communal levels. As they embody myths and cosmologies they interpret and integrate culture. There is also the potential for new rituals to emerge, as Kealiinohomoku points out: "dance rituals are always being invented, retrofitted, or re-invented either through revival or syncretism."[17]

Entire systems of belief may be reinvented in ritual dances and translated from the past to the present. Brook Medicine Eagle, who was raised on the Crow reservation in Montana, speaks of "primary people," those who sustain a spiritual connection to the earth, even as she creates new rituals from old ones and gathers Native Americans with other Americans to focus their energies through the great buffalo drum. A simple circular dance pattern and her chanting of ritual songs further unifies the group, as I experienced at the yurt of Linda Herrinwind in Victor, New York, in 1996.

Dance Is a Theater Art

Dance is further contextualized as theater and often called art. The latter may intone personal taste or critical acceptance. Theater arts are established communally and critically through shared values. Dance often comes mixed with other theatrical elements: scenes that imbue time/place and delineate space, costumes that sharpen or soften body lines or dictate period, music integral to rhythms and atmosphere, and spoken text. Is theater a necessary condition of dance, then? I would say no, since theater supposes the gaze of the other, the audience. Theaters are "seeing places" first. They require community, or at least a gathering of viewers. Dance may thus become the means for communication and art making, but its intrinsic character does not require this.

Intrinsic Dance

Dance can be pleasurable and therapeutic. I call this experiential essence *the intrinsic dance*. It is the root of all dance, whether the dance is performed for others or not. As intrinsically valuable, dance is first of all body-for-self. Likewise, the dancer's performance begins with herself. It is she who imbues form, traversing an intentional making and doing that inscribes the movement. She may also repeat or replicate forms (rhythms, dynamics, motifs, actions, or sounds), but these are just parts of her project. She is most concerned with embodying movement holistically, shaping and pouring it through the lived time of her performance.

Performance can indicate something internal to movement—although I realize that performance often means a performance for others, posing questions concerning the "audience effect" in the performer-audience transaction. To perform means to intentionally execute, to carry out a plan or move through a form, to follow through with skill, to finish something. All of these are desirable, at one time or another, in dancing. To perform also means "to show off," or "to show off a skill." This sometimes happens in dance, particularly in recitals that are planned as "smilers" for mommy and daddy, and in adult virtuoso dancing (followed by immediate applause). But we know this is not a necessary condition of dance performances. When the dancer's attention shifts from the intrinsic dance to show the self rather than the dance, the dance is lost, as is also the promise that the performance may carry the performer beyond self-limits (self-focus, self-consciousness). This is a question of awareness. *Dance is performed* as skillful, or playful, or expressive, or the like, within a wide range of intentionality. It is the performer's intention and purpose that makes dance "more than movement."[18] One might argue that trance dances are outside the range of conscious intentionality and therefore not performed. But there is some basic intention for inducing trance and a purpose (usually healing or transpersonal communication) in the trance dance. Related to this would be the kind of dance that taps into the subconscious, such as the improvised "Dansing" performances of Christian Swenson, whose body-voice shimmers on the borderline of shamanistic voyage and performance. Here performance intention is mixed. It derives from his blurring of theatrical presence with phylogenetic quest.

Intrinsic dance is performed as body-for-self, not as body-for-other as in theatrical contexts, but looking inward to the experience. Logically speaking this would not be a type of dance, but a shift of attention. Phenomenologically, the dancer performs the dance in his or her particular manner. The dance can be consciously projected toward another in an act of communication, or more personally absorbed. The dancer's dialogue with her dance and its aesthetic qualities, her purpose, the play of sensation with intention is the irreducible element at the intrinsic level. In value theory, *intrinsic value* is that upon which all other values depend. Moreover, it is an aspect of experience perceived *as valuable* (or it would not be called a value).

Dance is defined (as a phenomenon) in its uses and in our perception. *Dance* is a name we give to a wide range of activities and behaviors. Wittgenstein holds that naming is a preparation for description in the language game. We also define in language, when we look for common features that exist among known examples. We give further meaning to the word when we contextualize it in sentences and larger composites of language: "always ask yourself: How did we learn the meaning of the word ('good' for instance)? From what sort of examples? In what language-games? Then it will be easier for you to see that the word must have a family of meanings."[19]

As human activity, dance is movement evolved through creative processes, sometimes through ritual processes valued over time, endowing history and tradition. Dance is by no means bound by history and tradition, however. New dances may be ritualized in contemporary practices. Dances are done in play, for socializing, for entertainment, and for spiritual and therapeutic purposes. As qualitative movement intentionally given special forms, dances are aesthetically constructed. Dances are contextualized events; they are cultural, historical, and experiential. They require at the very least the dancer in motion, so their intrinsic values derive from human movement and the intentions embodied therein. Dances also derive their meaning from the dancing ground, as they are performed in various cultural settings: theaters, churches, village squares, streets, sports arenas, temples, palaces, forest clearings, dance halls, healing places, and underground in sacred chambers. Dances are aesthetic historico-cultural movement performances. They are created for various purposes; they have intrinsic values and attain significance in experience and interpretation.

An Objective Game Plan

Albert Opoku, who founded the Ghanaian Dance Ensemble in Africa and taught dance at State University of New York at Brockport for several years, used to ask me: "Don't you think it curious that Westerners call their own dance 'fine art' and relegate the rest of the world's dance to the position of 'ethnic'?" He said that he thought of the art and dance of Africa not as ethnic but as "living art." His comment helped me understand how we typically interpret the world from a learned and subjective vantage point.

Blind spots may also originate in a cultural substratum, including sex and gender. For instance: I once listened to a paper on hegemony. The speaker pointed out some cultural and social enclosures that isolate our understandings and enforce political boundaries but, unaware of his own position, he broached the subject of women by repeatedly saying "women are different"—although he was careful to espouse what he presumed to be a feminist point of view. I told him that "I am a woman, so for me women are not different: they are what I am."

Our biases stem from and reinforce our gender perceptions and concepts of normalcy, our inherited and learned culture, and the known territory of our experience. Our ingrained prejudices, as they grow from fears of the unknown, are dangerous because they limit our sight and insight. Our aesthetic preferences, our cultural biases and prejudices are often unexamined. We are indeed bound up in, and bound by, our culture. We transcend these boundaries through education, through familiarity with other cultures, and through research. Then the unknown becomes the known, mind is expanded. Good research is predicated on being "open-minded," but I suggest that mind is simply not always open to us. As researchers, questioners, and learners, we seek to move the mind toward the unfamiliar and conjure up family resemblance. As explained in our chapter on aesthetic inquiry, dance can be perceived in terms of quantitative measure or qualitative change. In the broad sense, quantitative research seeks to establish that which is predictable, the dependable boundaries of the dance phenomenon being investigated. We do not generally think of dance as a science, except in the very loose sense that it may be the subject of studies in the physics of motion. If dance is not a science, except in the sense of well-doing that crosses both science and art, we can nevertheless benefit from applications of scientific methods (of physical, behavioral, and social science) to dance problems. What goes into the performance of a successful pirouette, for instance, as measured and observed through scientifically designed processes with the aid of "kinematic" technology?[20]

Qualitative methods that examine and interpret dance from aesthetic, historical, and cultural points of view are consistent with the nature of dance, providing rich approaches for study. This text is concerned with both qualitative and quantitative modes of inquiry, but on balance it places much more emphasis on the qualitative, since dance crosses so many categories of qualitative value from the sociopolitical to the aesthetic/historic, including the spiritual, psychological, and therapeutic. Qualitative values are intrinsic to dance. They are the values we name when we identify something as dance, the various kinds of values that we experience when the dance fulfills its potential. Qualitative values issue from experience, or we could say that they are qualities of experience—as all intrinsic values are.[21]

Dance as human movement and human behavior also has observable properties that can be measured; thus dance is subject to quantitative research designs.

Qualitative and quantitative research designs serve different purposes, as this text explores.

We are familiar with the limits of scientific inquiry, but shouldn't questions also be raised concerning the limitations and pitfalls of qualitative and postpositivist research? *How does the researcher keep some measure of objectivity,* if objectivity is not the entire game plan, for instance? Without some level of objectivity and distance, the researcher might simply be guided by prejudice and bias, and conclusions could be drawn to suit any purpose. This can be particularly problematic when the research involves human subjects and situations close to the researcher. Self-reflexive questions are basic in all research. How do I understand my own position relative to the research design? Or, put more directly: why do I want to do this study (what are my motives)? And why am I using this particular approach? The researcher often wants to show or prove something; thus, motives should be examined. The very definition of the research problem and choice of procedures will begin to direct the outcome.

The approach of any qualitative research design is also its limitation. "Ideological critique," a recent approach in dance history research, admits its agenda to reduce the past to its ideological components, to read (reduce, reconstruct, or deconstruct) history in sociopolitical terms. This is bound to influence the author's interpretations. For instance, in Susan Manning's critique of Mary Wigman's career through an exposition of her "feminism" and "nationalism," it is not surprising that Manning found what she was looking for. Her highly interpretive ideological reconstructions of Wigman's dances are guided by the concept of the "male gaze" (as developed in modern feminist theory) and Benedict Anderson's definition of nationalism (as an "imagined community"). The latter leads Manning to a gauzy view of Wigman's solos as projecting "a mystical aura of Germanness." The use of loaded terms like "fascist alliance" and "collaboration" are not contextualized in terms of the pressures and prohibitions of the times. Manning sees Wigman's dances as "both fascist and resistive."[22] Can she have it both ways? When does "cooperation" with a fascist dictatorship (how and under what circumstances) equal "collaboration"? I think this is an interesting question. Nationalism (and patriotism) cover a lot of complex territory, just as dances and lives do not reduce to simple expositions of ideological terms.[23]

Like Manning, Isa Partsch-Bergson also questions romanticized versions of the rise of modern dance, but her writing emerges from an attempt to gain a contextualized perspective that neither condemns nor condones the path of individual artists as she tries to see them in the political context of their own times. Her account of Wigman's career and dances (from much of the same archival material) differs in many respects from that of Manning.[24]

As prototype for research, game plans are also explored (and pushed) in choreography, even as elements from folk and popular culture are bracketed in recent dance, and genres mix. Doug Elkins's irreverent work, *Where Was Yvonne Rainer when I Had Saturday Night Fever* (1996), is a good example. It draws hip-hop and capoeira (Brazilian martial art requiring extensive upper-body strength) into the orbit of funky-modern dance and "ballet-on-yer-butt" as Elkins calls it. Speed and detailed rhythm give the dancers unique challenges. In Elkins's lecture-demonstration, he wears a baseball cap. Explaining that postmoderns consider their dances to be "texts," Elkins sporadically draws large lettered "ism" words like "foundationalism" from his notebook. He displays them, then puzzles: "I don't know whether I'm deconstructing romanticism, or romanticizing post-modernism, or just involved in my own form of post-Hegelian therapy?" Elkins satirizes the historical-aesthetic process that researchers try to sort out. When boundaries are crossed, established forms are questioned, sometimes transformed, and maybe deconstructed (given that interpretation). New forms emerge in con-text of our understanding of what has gone before. Meanwhile, something con-tinues that we recognize as dance: a family of examples—old and new—results.

Isadora Duncan (with the aid of romantic waltzes) was also pushing history, as she introduced a new dance in the form of "the freedom of women" that would serve to critique what had gone before. An implicit feminism fueled Isadora's cri-tique[25] and has been a continuing theme in modern and postmodern dance. Feminist research, like feminist dance, has political aims that color objectivity. (But *dance* does not care so much about objectivity, while *theory* usually does.) Feminists could counter (with good reason) that so-called "objective" research has cloaked an entrenched patriarchy.

Nevertheless, the operations of anything called "research" implore fairness and objectivity, even as they admit interpretation and valuation. The issue of ob-jectivity in dance research is situated contextually. Objectivity may refer to process as in science, and it can also point toward removal of bias or prejudice in qualitative game plans. In both cases the researcher achieves observational and analytical tools that are in some measure objective if not governed by the scien-tific use of the term.

If I want to find out something—research it—I need to invoke my beginner's mind and, thus, the beginnings of an objective game plan. For it means that I do not yet know the thing I seek to understand, and that I am open to discovery. In this case, I remove myself or remain teachably detached (objective) in the learn-ing process.

NOTES

1. The concern for "family resemblance" in the matter of linguistic definition is explored in the philosophy of Ludwig Wittgenstein, *Philosophical Investigations*, 3d ed., trans. G. E. M. Anscombe (New York: Macmillan, 1958), 66–77.

2. Joann Keali'inohomoku, "An Anthropologist Looks at Ballet as a Form of Ethnic Dance," in *Impulse* (1969–1970) (San Francisco: Impulse Publications, Inc., 1970), 24–33.

3. For a further exploration of dance as "theater" see Roger Copeland, "Theatrical Dance: How Do We Know It When We See It If We Can't Define It?," paper presented at Dance Critics Association conference, 1985.

4. On *Yanvalou*, see Joan Hamby Burroughs, "Yanvalou: Movement, Myth and Ritual in Haitian Vodou" (paper presented at the Congress on Research in Dance, Miami, Florida, 1995). On the Inupiat, see Edith Turner, "Gentle Inviting—The Power Dance —Off-Beat Stop: The Style and Meaning of Inupiat Eskimo Dance," keynote panel presentation, Congress on Research in Dance, Miami, Florida, 1995.

5. Garth Fagan, *River Song: From Earth Eagle First Circle*, Rochester premiere, April 1995. This work grew out of an on-site exploration of *Garth Fagan Dance* with the dances of the Salish Kootenai Tribe of Montana and is given a further cultural context through the costumes of Linda King, member of the Confederation Salish and Kootenai Tribe, known throughout the Northwest for her beadwork, Indian dance outfits, dress, and fabric design.

6. This view of style as integral to a work involving the *what* as well as the *how* is consistent with Nelson Goodman's more technical explanations of style as a metaphorical signature by which we recognize works as belonging to a period, group, or person: Nelson Goodman, *Ways of Worldmaking* (Indianapolis: Hackett Publishing Co., Inc., 1978), 34–40.

For further explanations of this in terms of dance, see Sondra Horton Fraleigh, *Dance and the Lived Body: A Descriptive Aesthetics* (Pittsburgh: University of Pittsburgh Press, 1987), 90–91; also Mary Sirridge and Adina Armelagos, "The Ins and Outs of Dance: Expression as an Aspect of Style," *Journal of Aesthetics and Art Criticism* 36 (fall 1977): 13–24.

7. Susan W. Stinson, "Adolescent Perceptions of Dance Education" (paper presented at the Congress on Research in Dance, Miami, Florida, 1995). Jill Green, "Somatic Authority and the Myth of the Ideal Body in Dance Education" (paper presented at the Congress on Research in Dance, Miami, Florida, 1995).

8. For a discussion of somatic education and therapy in its relation to aesthetic values (of dance), see Sondra Fraleigh, "The Spiral Dance: Toward a Phenomenology of Somatics," *Somatics* 10, no. 4 (spring–summer 1996): 14–19.

9. For a thorough treatment of sense perception as the root of aesthetics, see Richard Griffith and Erwin Strauss, eds., *Aisthesis and Aesthetics* (Pittsburgh: Duquesne University Press, 1970).

10. Daniel N. Stern, "The Role of Feelings for an Interpersonal Self," in *The Perceived Self*, ed. Ulric Neisser (Cambridge: Cambridge University Press, 1993), 205–15.

11. Ulric Neisser, "Five Kinds of Self-Knowledge," *Philosophical Psychology* 1, no. 1 (1988): 35–59.

12. J. J. Gibson, *The Senses Considered as Perceptual Systems* (Boston: Houghton Mifflin, 1966); *The Ecological Approach to Visual Perception* (Boston: Houghton Mifflin, 1979); Elanor Gibson, "Ontogenesis of the Perceived Self," in *The Perceived Self*, ed. Ulric Neisser (Cambridge: Cambridge University Press, 1993), 25–42.

13. For dance as a source for self-knowledge, including perspectives from cognitive psychology and descriptive phenomenology, see Sondra Fraleigh, "Good Intentions and

Dancing Moments: Agency, Freedom and Self-Knowledge in Dance," in *The Perceived Self*, ed. Ulric Neisser (Cambridge: Cambridge University Press, 1993), 102–11.

14. Ellen Dissanayake, "Movement, Time, and Emotional Communication," keynote speech, in *Proceedings, 30th Annual Conference, Congress on Research in Dance*, ed. Nancy L. Stokes (Tucson: University of Arizona Press, 1997), 1–2.

15. Joann W. Keali'inohomoku, "Dance, Myth and Ritual in Time and Space," *Dance Research Journal* 29, no. 1 (spring 1997): 68.

16. Parul Shah, lecture-demonstration, State University of New York, College at Brockport, Nov. 12, 1997.

17. Keali'inohomoku, "Dance, Myth and Ritual in Time and Space," 69.

18. Fraleigh, *Dance and the Lived Body*, 88–93.

19. Wittgenstein, 43–49, 77.

20. Citlali Lopez-Ortiz, "Kinematic Trend of *Pirouette* Performances as a Function of Skill Level" (master of arts thesis, Department of Dance, State University of New York, College at Brockport, 1994).

21. See studies in value theory and aesthetics for fuller definitions of "qualitative value," and "intrinsic value," especially value theorist Paul W. Taylor, *Normative Discourse* (Englewood Cliffs, N.J.: Prentice Hall, 1961).

22. Susan Manning, *Ecstasy and the Demon: Feminism and Nationalism in the Dances of Mary Wigman* (Berkeley: University of California Press, 1993), 3, 4.

23. Much of Manning's desire to "rewrite the history of modern dance" (an ambitious enterprise) also rests on her ability to aptly intuit and describe the dances (and reconstruct their inherent ideologies). I would interrogate the objectivity of her book on this ground alone. Manning interprets the famous photograph of Isadora Duncan's *Ave Maria* as demonstrating the downward pull of gravity juxtaposed with an "upward struggle against gravity." This is a curious reading of Isadora's soft and given posture as her head falls easily backward, her knees bend slightly under her relaxed torso, and her arms lift without fully extending. To me there is pathos and a surrender to gravity in this picture. See the photograph in Manning, 36.

24. Isa Partsch-Bergsohn, *Modern Dance in Germany and the United States: Crosscurrents and Influences* (Australia: Harwood Academic Publishers, 1994).

25. Isadora Duncan's speech, "The Dance of the Future," by invitation of the Berlin Presse Verlin was published as a pamphlet in 1903. "It became the manifesto of Modern Dance and a feminist classic," as recounted in *Life Into Art: Isadora Duncan and Her World*, ed. Dorée Duncan, Carol Pratl, and Cynthia Platt, foreword by Agnes de Mille (New York: W. W. Norton and Company, 1993).

2 FROM IDEA TO RESEARCH PROPOSAL

Balancing the Systematic and Serendipitous

Penelope Hanstein

RESEARCH IS A CONFUSING TERM; it has so many meanings and applications that it is difficult to understand precisely what we mean when we speak about research in a scholarly sense. We all have done research of one sort or another—looked up the date of the first performance of a favored dance work, sought pedagogical information by asking several experienced teachers about the best way to present material in a choreography class, or consulted *Consumer Reports* to select the best VCR to purchase. All of these activities do indeed involve research, but are they research as scholarship?

What Is Scholarly Research?

Consider your last research project. This may have been a term paper for an undergraduate dance history course or the writing and oral presentation of a report about a contemporary dance company based on interviews with the artistic director. Ask yourself the following questions:

- Did I begin with a question in mind?
- Did I have a clearly stated research purpose and a set of research questions to guide the investigation?

- Did I approach my research with a plan and a design for gathering and analyzing the data?
- Did I carefully scrutinize my own and others' biases and assumptions?
- Did I assess the credibility of the information I uncovered?
- Did I interpret the data to discover the meaning and significance of the facts?
- Did I construct meaningful conclusions from my interpretations to answer my questions?

In answering these questions, you may have discovered that you, like many other students, gathered the facts and presented them in a well-documented paper or oral report. Fact-finding and the transference of information from existing sources to your paper may have been the extent of your research endeavor. However, as careful and thorough as your data gathering and presenting may have been, *research as scholarship* must go beyond collecting information and making that information available to others. The researcher as scholar is someone who is on the leading edge of the field. He or she is able to synthesize ideas in new ways and see unique possibilities by considering not only what is, but what might be.

Scholarly research is a process of creating new knowledge, and as such, it seeks to expand the realm of human knowing and understanding. It is a way of thinking and acting; a way of posing and responding to questions; a way of expressing and communicating ideas. It is the search for truth and meaning rooted in our capacity for astute observation, critical analysis, meaningful interpretation, rational understanding, insightful contextualization, and defensible judgment. The researcher as scholar engages in careful study, examination, and observation of facts, which often include what people say and do. Through a rigorous and systematic process using appropriate research methodologies and procedures, he or she gathers, scrutinizes, and assesses the credibility of information. The researcher analyzes the data by seeking relationships and making connections between often seemingly unrelated pieces of information. During this process of gathering and analyzing data, themes emerge, ideas take shape, and meaningful interpretations are discovered. The researcher considers these interpretations within the context of the existing body of knowledge, advances new theories, and considers the significance of her or his discoveries.

In this sense, research shares much in common with dance making. Just as choreography is far more than assembling steps, scholarly research is far more than collecting and assembling data. Like dance making, research is a purposeful, creative, interpretive, and intuitive process that is often circuitous and improvisational. The quintessential element of both choreography and research is discovery —we enter without knowing, in order to discover what we need to know to lead us to what there is to know. The skills that we know so well as choreographers are also the skills that we use as researchers. One of my students recently pointed out to me that something I had written about the choreographic process had as much to say about the research process as it did about dance making. She suggested substituting the word *research* for *choreography* in the following passage, thinking of the choreographic idea and medium as the research purpose and data:

> The process of [research] is not a matter of instantaneous creation, but rather a prolonged interaction between artistic conception [research purpose] and medium [data]. This problem-finding and solving, discovery-oriented process, is a working out of . . . relationships; the emerging work guiding the artistic thinking of the [researcher] and the evolving idea in turn impacting the shaping of the medium [data]—the [researcher] learning about the work as the process unfolds.[1]

Sue Stinson made this same connection between research and the artistic process in her National Dance Association Scholar's Lecture, "Research as Choreography." Speaking about her own work as a researcher, which focuses on sensing and understanding the experiences of children and dance educators in a variety of settings, she draws a parallel between data and movement themes as raw material. Her data is composed of the words of her participants gathered through open-ended interviews and her own observations, which she records in her journal.

> This gathering is actually the easiest part of my research, even though it may take quite a long time. Like the choreographer, I generate a lot more material than I will eventually use in a particular work. The more difficult tasks are selecting out what is worthwhile, meaning what has the possibility to generate insights; figuring out what it means; and then coming up with a way to construct a cohesive paper that can communicate my process and my insights to others.[2]

Qualitative researchers, like Sue Stinson, often enter the field without knowing what specific questions to ask or how to ask them. These researchers, as well as those who use other modes of inquiry ranging from interpretive to experimental, often describe themselves as "being in dialogue with the data" and talk of the data "speaking to them" and suggesting new avenues of inquiry. This idea of being engaged in a dialogue with the data is in many ways similar to the choreographer interacting with and responding to her or his dance as it emerges in the making process. Exploration, trial and error, improvisation, and such acts as defining, refining, elaborating, selecting, rejecting, shaping, and reshaping—all experiences that are familiar to us as dance makers—are the fundamental processes of the researcher.

Not only is scholarly research a process of discovery, it is also "part constructive . . . and in part constructively destructive."[3] The "constructive" aspect of our work as researchers is, as we discuss above, the adding of new knowledge to the field of dance, which ultimately results in reshaping our understandings of dance as an art form, cultural phenomenon, and discipline. The "constructively destructive" aspect of scholarly inquiry engages us in examining what is, questioning the status quo, and exposing and dispelling mistakes, misinterpretations, and misrepresentations. Dance, like all disciplines, changes and evolves over time. Established and emerging artists create new works that expand our ideas about what we call dance, and research contributes new ways of understanding and knowing dance. As tradition meets innovation, competing theories cause us to question the aesthetic, cultural, critical, historical, and pedagogical canons of the field. New ideas replace old ones and new language emerges when traditional discourse can no longer adequately express our ideas. When this occurs, the boundaries of dance knowledge give way and make possible the exploration of new territories. In this sense, the production of new knowledge is always *generative*—questions lead to answers and answers always beget more questions.

This notion of scholarly inquiry being both "constructive and constructively destructive" suggests that, in addition to being insightful, the researcher must also be a thoroughgoing skeptic. It is important for the scholar to maintain an objective posture in relation to her or his work and not become so enamored with the subject that comprehension and acuity of insight are clouded by personal attachment to the research process or preconceptions about the outcome. One of the hallmarks of good scholarship is the ability to assess the authenticity and credibility of factual information. In addition to critically evaluating information and sources of information, the good scholar must also question her or his own assumptions and biases. These fundamental ways of seeing the world inevitably influence how we engage in and make sense of every aspect of the research process. Much has been written about the contingency of truth and, in fact, scholars often debate the basic issue of what constitutes truth. These debates notwithstanding, it is important for the researcher to remember what Elliot Eisner emphasizes in *The Enlightened Eye:* the world can be known in multiple ways and knowledge is made, not simply discovered.[4] The role of the individual researcher in the construction and constructive destruction of knowledge is intrinsic to the scholarly process. All the more reason for us all to be reminded that adhering to the presumption of absolute and authoritarian truth is the greatest obstacle to personal inquiry and the scholarly pursuit of knowledge.

The Research Process

Research as a process means to *search* and re-*search*. It is a process characterized by critical and exhaustive investigation and, in some cases, experimentation. The goal is to uncover, discover, and recover data that will allow the researcher to arrive at a dependable solution to a problem. It is an ongoing process, much like the creative process, of looking, guessing, examining, and revising followed by more looking, guessing, examining, and revising.[5]

Even though the researcher may be (to use Donald Schon's analogy)[6] mired in the swampy lowlands of uncertainty rather than traversing the high ground of absolute clarity of vision, the research process should always be a *planned* and *systematic* enterprise. Planned and systematic does not necessarily mean linear, standardized, and objective. In fact, as you study the various approaches presented in this text you will come to realize that much of research is circuitous and improvisational, drawing heavily on our subjective experiences of dance.

The research process is a balance between the planned and the unplanned and between the predictable and the serendipitous. In dance, particularly, it should also be a process that merges objective and subjective ways of knowing and understanding reality. We must not forget that at the heart of everything we do in dance is dance and dancing. While we may be engaged in a more reflective mode than physical one when we are researching and writing, our point of reference must always be rooted in the experience of dancing. Research that loses its connection to what it means to experience dance as a participant or viewer loses its relevance and connection to the field.

All productive researchers have a plan and approach the gathering, analysis, and interpretation of their data in systematic ways. Researchers, like choreographers, are responsive to the process and the special way that the research tasks, activities, and events unfold. Just as no two dance-making endeavors are ever the same, no two research projects are exactly alike. Responding to new information, changes in perspective, and often roadblocks along the way, the researcher revises her or his plans in order to follow pathways that may or may not have been known or even present at the beginning. Although trial and error are typically part of the research process, trial and error should *not* be the defining features of the research methodology. "Shotgun" approaches to research almost always prove to be inefficient, ineffective, and in the end, unproductive.

The purpose of this chapter is to help you define a research agenda and develop a systematic approach to pursuing your research. The process for designing and implementing research presented here is intended to be general so that you may apply it to any of the modes of inquiry examined in this text or adapt it to the policies guiding research in your particular institution. I focus on the typical components of a research proposal, or prospectus, as it is called in many universities. These are the same elements that make up most grant applications, and therefore, what you learn here, and throughout this text, will be applicable to grant writing.

Questioning: Setting the Process in Motion

All research begins with questions. The questions you ask reflect what interests you about the field of dance and how you see the world of dance. If you are interested in dance history you are likely to ask questions about the past and how people and events contributed to the development and evolution of dance. If your interests are in the area of dance science and somatics your questions may focus on ways to improve performance, on how to promote and enhance the health and well-being of dancers, or on expanding our traditional notions of teaching dance technique. You may be intrigued by the idea of dance as a culturally situated experience, and this interest may give rise to questions about the significance of dance and movement as experienced and understood by racially and ethnically diverse peoples. These interests, and many others, may grow out of your course work, have their origin in something you read, or might be sparked by a dance performance attended or a conversation with a peer or faculty member. The more familiar you are with the breadth of the field and the body of knowledge that defines the field, the greater your foundation for questioning. As Elliot Eisner wrote, "the kinds of nets we know how to weave determine the kinds of nets we cast. These nets, in turn, determine the kinds of fish we catch."[7] The curious and inquisitive person will always have a wealth of questions, but not all questions are research questions.

Research questions are those questions that can be answered by research. They are not yes/no questions. They suggest the intellectual pursuit of something more by including elements that call for research. Researchable questions set in motion a process of discovery that pursues meaning, cause, relationship, interpretation, or significance. Rainbow and Froehlich point out that "a differentiation should be made between genuine questions and pseudo questions. A genuine question truly seeks an answer, whereas a pseudo question expects no answer, cannot be answered, or has an answer that is already known to the person asking the question."[8]

A question such as, "When will the public learn to appreciate dance?" is not a question that can be answered. This question does, however, suggest several important issues about public perception of dance, factors that influence the appreciation of dance, and action dance advocates might take to promote public awareness and participation in dance events. Each of these issues gives rise to several researchable questions. One line of questioning might be: What draws people who are not dancers to assume dance advocacy leadership roles in their communities? Are they influenced by previous education, opportunities for public visibility, or symbolic prestige, or is their involvement motivated by a genuine love of dance, and if so, how did they acquire this love?

Questions of clarification such as "What does 'aesthetic' mean?" and similar queries that can be answered by looking up information are not research questions. However, a philosophical concept analysis question such as "What characterizes aesthetic movement of the body?" can develop into a viable research project. Let us explore two more examples, which come from actual research projects.[9]

Pseudo-question: Is choreography problem-solving?

Research question: What is the nature of problem-solving in choreography and how is it manifested in the work of individual choreographers?[10]

Pseudo-question: Why does Mary move the way she does?

Research question: What is the relationship between who we are and the spatial and dynamic range reflected in our movement, and what defines and influences this relationship?[11]

In the first example the pseudo-question is a yes/no question about something that is generally considered to be axiomatic—problem-solving is part of creative activity. It also merely states the existence of the phenomenon by virtue of asking the question. The research question seeks to understand what it means to engage in problem-solving in choreography, what distinguishes this process, and whether it is idiosyncratic in character. The second pseudo-question, "Why does Mary move the way she does?" is actually a very interesting question and reflects the observation that initiated this research project, but in this form it contains no researchable elements. While the research question is still very general and the subject elusive, you can see the beginnings of the inquiry that eventually took form.

Initiating Research: Seeing What Is and What Might Be

Scholarly research is a visionary process and is guided by the researcher's ability to see and think about ideas in new ways. This creative and imaginative engagement with ideas is what initiates research and ultimately results in the researcher making a significant contribution of new knowledge to the field. Like dance making, initiating research is a cyclic and improvisational process that eventually spirals inward toward a specific research purpose, which is not unlike the artistic concept for a dance work. The process is one of moving forward and backward, gathering information, shaping ideas, and rejecting some possibilities and elaborating on others, with a view toward discovering what you will want to know and how you might find it out. Figure 2.1 is a model of this heuristic process and will help you visualize the forward-and-backward nature of initiating research as well as the goal of eventually discovering a specific research purpose.

Questioning at this beginning stage of the research process is very broad in scope. It is intended to help you discover your areas of interest and formulate re-

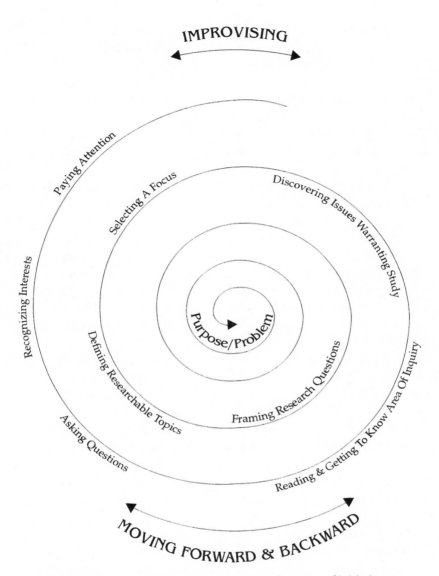

FIG. 2.1. The creative, imaginative, and improvisational process of initiating research: Seeing what is and what might be.

search topics. Each of your initial research questions, like the examples above, may suggest any number of specific research problems or projects. In order to ask researchable questions that will eventually develop into a focused research problem you must become familiar with your area of interest. The first step in doing this is reading. Reading in your area or areas of interest should be extensive. You will want to read books, journal articles, magazines, newspapers, monographs, conference proceedings, professional papers, theses, and dissertations, as well as peruse electronic media available on video, CD-ROM, and through the Internet. If you do not already know how to use your library and conduct a general search for resources related to your area of interest, consult your research librarian. Professional librarians are trained to assist researchers. Their knowledge of how to access information and their technological expertise are invaluable. It is a good idea to establish a working relationship with your research librarian early in the research process. In addition, you will find Mary Bopp's book, *Research in Dance: A Guide to Resources*,[12] a very useful guide to dance-related resources.

Reading in your area of interest, at this stage, is a *general* reading to help you become acquainted with the breadth and depth of the body of knowledge, the questions that other researchers have pursued, and the various dimensions of inquiry that might warrant further study. This reading is far more extensive in scope than the review of related literature that we discuss below. Think of your reading as an exploration—a journey toward understanding the field of inquiry that encompasses your research interests. If you are tempted to dig one hole deeply at this stage, remember that there will be ample opportunity to delve into specific areas when you have decided on a topic and formulated your research purpose and problem.

Through your reading you will discover a number of issues, concerns, ideas, controversies, or circumstances that you may think are worthy of further study. Select a specific focus, which at this point will still be rather broad, and based on your interests, identify several topics or areas of study. Refining your thinking further, frame more specific research questions. You are now ready to begin the process of designing your research project. The first step, and typically the most challenging, is writing the purpose and problem statements. Before we address how to develop research purpose and problem statements, it is important to consider what factors might influence your selection of a research project.

Choosing a Research Project

The choice to pursue one research idea over another may be based solely on your interest level or it may be determined by the expertise you already possess that will enable you to conduct a particular kind of research. Pragmatic concerns such as time constraints, financial resources, and faculty support are also factors that will influence the choices you make. In addition, many researchers take into consideration the state of the field; their perceptions of what areas have been studied, as well as existing gaps in information, may lead them to pursue certain research projects.

Research is an intensive and time-consuming endeavor. It is also, at times, frustrating, discouraging, overwhelming, and, oh yes, intimidating. Ask any researcher and she or he will probably tell you that, in spite of such intense emotional experiences, it is the love of the subject, like the love of dance making, that causes them to persevere through difficult moments. For this reason alone, it is very important that you select a research project that captures your interest, excites you, and draws you to it in a most compelling way. Many students select topics because they think they will be easy. No research that will amount to any significant results is ever easy, so do not use this as a criteria. All research is fraught with challenges; choose those you are able and willing to meet. In some graduate programs students are encouraged to pursue the research topics of their major professors, but this is not always the best course to take unless you share your professor's scholarly interests.

If you choose to pursue a research project in which you have little background in the area of inquiry or have limited expertise in the methodology, understand that it will be necessary for you to do considerable preparatory work before you can proceed. Many researchers do this, but with the full recognition that it will extend the research process. Preparing to do your research may require you to take additional courses, engage in an in-depth, directed reading project, or work for a period of time as a research or laboratory assistant to learn necessary research techniques.

If you have limited financial resources, you will not want to undertake, for example, a project requiring international travel unless you have identified sources of external support such as grants and fellowships for which you *will be competitive*. Financial commitments should always be taken into consideration when deciding to pursue any study that is likely to require an outlay of funds, such as conducting survey research, doing fieldwork, interviewing subjects not within your geographic area, or traveling to archival collections. Many universities, professional organizations, and private and public funding agencies have programs to support graduate research, particularly doctoral dissertations. The best advice is to plan ahead and make good use of the support services at your university. These may include your departmental or college office, the graduate school, and the office that facilitates the research efforts of faculty and students. On every campus there are experienced and knowledgeable faculty and staff who can help you identify services and funding sources to support your research.

Not all research requires the same amount of time. Some projects by nature have more defined parameters and relatively predictable time frames. Other studies, such as conducting fieldwork, require a significant amount of time in the research site and, due to the complexity of the data, demand a considerable investment of time for analysis and interpretation, followed by the writing of the narrative, which can be a challenging creative writing experience for some. Gathering detailed data from many different kinds of sources, as often occurs in historical research, can also be time-consuming. If you are proceeding on a specific schedule for the completion of your research, including the writing of the final paper or report, you will want to assess carefully the time required to pursue the research and not compromise your standards of excellence or the integrity of the project. It may be necessary for you to revise your schedule or modify the research study. Keep in mind that, as in producing a dance concert, things rarely happen the way we plan with research, and it is impossible to anticipate all of the roadblocks and the amount of time necessary to correct your course or rechannel your efforts. Furthermore, while you will want your work to be a significant contribution to the field, you should not paralyze your efforts by approaching it as if it is going to be the definitive work on the subject. Perhaps it might be, perhaps it might develop into this at a later time, but the important thing to remember is that, as a graduate student, your research, like your dance making, is only an interval in your ongoing journey as an artist, researcher, and scholar.

Finally, it is very important to have a scholarly mentor who shares your research interests and will be available to guide you through the research process. While this should not be the sole factor in choosing a research project, it is an important consideration. Those of us who have benefited from strong professional and scholarly mentoring relationships will testify to the value of having the opportunity to work with someone who will provide an honest and informed critical review of your work, as well as advice and direction that will help you achieve your research goals. You will want to learn which faculty, both in and out of your home department, are available and willing to be a part of your project. It is your responsibility to seek out a mentor and initiate this relationship that will develop over time.

Purpose and Problem Statements: The Heart of the Research

The purpose and problem represent the heart of your research. These are the core elements of the research design. You may encounter different uses of this terminology as well as the use of such terms as *problem/subproblem* and *the research question* to refer to the core elements. I prefer to use purpose and problem because this use allows for the differentiation between the focus of the research and the specific issues that the research will address.

The research *purpose statement* literally indicates the purpose of your research. It states in very explicit and succinct language what you expect to accomplish. The *problem statement*—sometimes called the subproblem when the purpose is called the research problem—states what you will do in order to fulfill the purpose of your research. It identifies the specific issues and questions embedded in the research purpose. It is very helpful to think of the problem statement as a series of questions that the study or investigation will seek to answer in order to achieve the goal (purpose) of the research. These questions have the same characteristics as the more global research questions that we discussed earlier; they differ only with respect to the fact that the research questions are now far more narrowly focused and are specifically related to the research purpose statement.

The *purpose statement* clearly articulates what will be studied and includes an indication of how the research will be more than just data gathering. The focus of analysis and interpretation, as well as the intended outcome of the research, should be stated in the purpose. Consider the following purpose statement:

> The purpose of this study is to organize the presently scattered information about Leonide Massine in order to provide an understanding of the man and his choreography and to investigate the importance of artistic collaboration in his life and work.[13]

In this particular case, the purpose of the study is threefold:

1. Organize information about Massine.
2. Understand the man and his choreography.
3. Examine the significance of collaboration in his work.

Had the purpose statement read: "The purpose of this study is to organize the presently scattered information about Leonide Massine" the research would have focused only on the assembling of data without an indication of why such an endeavor is important and what might be the intent of such a project. Organizing, collecting, and cataloguing information is an important task, especially to those who may have need of this information, but it is not considered scholarly research. In this example, it is parts two and three of the purpose statement that provide the essential aspects of the *research purpose* and indicate the analytical and interpretive focus of a study that would generate new knowledge about Massine, his life, and his work.

Let us look at another example.

> The purpose of this study is to describe the movement component of the Yaqui Deer Dance focusing on the relationship between the physical reality and the symbolic content of the dance. The performance space, accompanying dancers, and the poetry of the song comprise the physical reality.[14]

This research purpose identifies two objectives:

1. Describe the movement.

2. Examine the relationship between the physical reality and the symbolic content.

Again, had the purpose statement read only "to describe the movement component of the Yaqui Deer Dance" the project would have been limited to movement description (data gathering) without an analytical and interpretive frame of reference. The purpose of the research was to discover how all of the elements within the performance context worked together to create the symbolic meaning of the Yaqui Deer Dance experience—the description of the movement was only one aspect of this comprehensive study.

The *problem statement* is a direct outgrowth of the research purpose. The content, specificity, and language of the problem statement questions are influenced by the mode of inquiry. Empirical and experimental modes of inquiry lead to specific research questions that the researcher will seek to answer. Frequently, these questions reappear in the final report of the research and each question is given specific attention in the discussion section or chapter. When conducting qualitative inquiry, for example ethnographic research, the researcher enters the field without knowing what the specific focus will be and what questions will need to be asked. A characteristic feature of qualitative research is that the specific purpose and problem emerge from the data.[15] In this instance, the purpose and problem statements written at the planning stage of the research process reflect the researcher's initial thinking and serve to *guide* the study rather than *define* it.

When Joan Laage began her two years of fieldwork in Japan to study the contemporary dance form butoh, she had only a very general purpose and problem statement to guide her research. It was only after her fieldwork and several months of analyzing and interpreting vast amounts of data from observations, performances, interviews, newspaper reviews, and many other sources that the focus of her dissertation emerged:

> to gain an understanding of how the "body" as used in Butoh is a reflection of the body as it is manifested in everyday Japanese life and how the Butoh aesthetic is related to the traditional Japanese aesthetic. Through using the body as the focus of the study, a frame of reference from which to view Butoh was constructed. Inspired by and developed within the Japanese culture, the Butoh art culture may be viewed as a microcosm of the greater cultural world which encompasses it.[16]

The *problem statement* hones in on the specific aspects of the research purpose that will be subjected to in-depth study. The problem statement delineates the logical subdivisions or component parts of the whole of the research purpose. It accounts for all aspects of the research that are known at this stage. Data interpretation and the significance of the research should be apparent in the problem statement.

In the following examples note the relationship between the purpose statement and the research questions. Consider whether the problem statement serves to define the parameters of the study or guide the research.

Example One: Empirical Inquiry— Prospectus for a Doctoral Dissertation[17]

The purpose of the study is to contribute to dance pedagogical theory by 1) determining dance graduate students' personality types as measured by the Myers-Briggs Type Indicator, 2) determining selected instructional preferences of dance graduate students as indicated by the Instructional Preference Checklist, and 3) suggesting general teaching strategies that are informed by the relationship of personality preferences to instructional preferences.

To fulfill the above-stated purpose, the following research questions will be addressed:

1. What is the distribution of personality types of dance graduate students as determined by the Myers-Briggs Type Indicator?

2. How does personality type distribution among dance graduate students compare with personality type distribution among other college graduates?

3. How do personality preferences of dance graduate students differ between males and females?

4. How do personality preferences of dance graduate students differ among the genre specializations of ballet, modern dance, jazz/tap, and cultural dance forms?

5. How do personality preferences of dance graduate students differ among the career specializations of performer, choreographer, educator, and theorist?

6. What is the distribution of instructional preferences of dance graduate students as determined by the Instructional Preferences Checklist?

7. How do instructional preferences of dance graduate students differ among the genre specializations of ballet, modern dance, jazz/tap, and cultural dance forms?

8. How do instructional preferences of dance graduate students differ among the career specializations of performer, choreographer, educator, and theorist?

9. What is the relationship between personality type and instructional preferences among dance graduate students?

10. What are the implications of this relationship for the development of pedagogical theory in dance?

Example Two: Ethnographic Inquiry—
Prospectus for a Doctoral Dissertation [18]

The purpose of this study is to identify the cultural elements manifested, or *voiced,* in the dance-making of the contemporary dance companies of Vitória, Brazil, and understand how these elements are characteristically expressive of Brazilian culture.

The following questions will guide this investigation: What is the origin of the thematic and movement ideas in the dance-making of the contemporary dance companies of Vitória, Brazil? How are contemporary choreographers of Vitória developing their themes and movement patterns? How do the use of the body and the qualitative characteristics of the movements form an overall impression about the contemporary dance of Vitória? What cultural elements (aspects of daily life) are present in the dance-making of the contemporary dance companies of Vitória, and in what ways are these elements manifested, or *voiced?* What is the relationship between the dance-making of the contemporary dance companies of Vitória and the main cultural voices of Brazil, i.e., popular festivals, music, sport, and religious rites?

Example Three: Philosophical Inquiry—Prospectus
for a Master of Fine Arts Professional Paper [19]

This study, in order to provide a better understanding of the idea processing and shaping methods of the choreographer, proposes to elucidate the relationship between idea and movement. This will be accomplished by describing and analyzing the transformation process (when idea evolves into movement). A phenomenological inquiry focused on the transformation process will be guided by the following questions:

1. How do we as choreographers interact with the world around us when developing a movement idea?

2. What is the nature of a movement idea with reference to mind activity (creation of idea) and body activity (kinesthetic shaping of idea)?

3. How do idea and movement interact and how does this interaction lead to change in the idea, the movement form and/or the making process?

4. What is the significance of the transformation process with reference to the shared meaning of a dance work?

Typically, the problem statement is composed of four to six research questions; however, experimental and empirical problem statements may include more due to the required specificity of the research questions. If you are having difficulty narrowing your problem statement and delineating the research issues, ask yourself the following questions:

- Am I dissecting the research purpose into too many small units and therefore do not understand the core issues?
- Is my research purpose still too broad, suggesting too many questions, and should it, therefore, be narrowed?

If you are having difficulty formulating research questions, ask yourself these questions:

- Do I have a research purpose that includes more than gathering and assembling data?
- Is my purpose so narrow that it lacks sufficient substance to suggest a research problem, and should it, therefore, be developed further?
- Do I know enough about this area of inquiry to see the various research possibilities or should I continue reading?

Reviewing the Literature

The review of literature is a very important part of your research process. It involves finding, studying, and evaluating research that is related to your area of study. Reviewing the literature is a process of *viewing* and *reviewing* materials related to your research purpose. The purpose is to understand fully the breadth and depth of the ideas that define or characterize your area of inquiry and gain insight into previous research in this area.

Reviewing the literature that is *related* to your research purpose will contribute not only to researching your topic, but also to designing your study. As you formulate a systematic approach to your literature review it will help you to remember that the review is useful because it will:

- Reveal other investigations that are germane to your area of inquiry.
- Suggest new methodologies, procedures, and interpretive frameworks that might be appropriate for your study.
- Reveal new sources of data that you may not have thought of or that you may not be aware exist.
- Acquaint you with scholars whose work is related to yours.
- Help place your study in a historical or contextual frame of reference.
- Inform you if the research you intend to perform has already been conducted.
- Provide you with new ideas and diverse perspectives on your subject.
- Assist in helping you critique your own research design.
- Help narrow or broaden your research agenda, if necessary.

Scope of the Review

How extensive should the review be? How many sources and what kind of sources should I include? How do I determine which areas are important and which are tangential? These are typical questions that students, and many experienced researchers, face when planning and implementing the literature review. Unfortunately, there are no answers that will work for all instances. However, there are some useful strategies and guidelines to help you determine the scope of your review.

First, write out your purpose and problem statements and keep them in front of you. When considering whether to review a source ask yourself if it *relates* to your study and if so, how. *Relatedness,* like many other aspects of research, is relative and it will be your task to decide what areas are related to your research. If you are doing a study on how teachers of dance technique develop their personal pedagogies, and your research will be based on interviews and in-depth case studies, then reviewing studies using these methodologies, whether they are in the area of dance or not, may be very useful. The philosophical orientation of feminist pedagogy is very similar to the concept of personal pedagogy; therefore, reviewing literature in this area might be invaluable in helping you discover new ways of thinking about your research. If we consider personal pedagogy as being intimately connected to our artistic work, then reading what teaching artists have to say about their own art making and its relation to their teaching might be very insightful. Expanding the field of inquiry from *dance* to the *arts,* or relating your subject to another discipline such as women's studies, sociology, or contemporary educational theory, will open your review to many new areas and might bring you to reconceptualize your research in ways that may not have been possible had you restricted your reading to only dance literature. As you begin to make connections or expand the territory of your review, always evaluate these decisions by explicitly stating *how they are related* to your research purpose and problem.

The extent of previous inquiry in your area of study will serve as a guide to helping you determine the breadth and depth of your review. If your area has been thoroughly explored, there will be many studies to review and, therefore, you have the opportunity for a review of considerable depth. However, if you are working in a new area of inquiry in which little research has been conducted or sources are as yet not available, then less depth is possible and it will be necessary for you to connect your ideas to other ideas in order to discover potentially insightful and useful literature to review. Figure 2.2 will help you design your review.

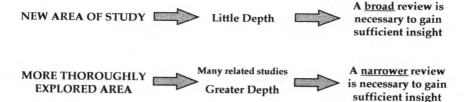

FIG. 2.2.

Types of Sources

The quality of scholarship is often judged on the kinds of sources a researcher has used to develop and support her or his conclusions. There are three types of sources: primary, secondary, and tertiary. A *primary* source is the first explanation of something, the expression of an idea by the person who originated it, or the direct description of an event by the person who actually experienced it. A *secondary* source is a document that refers to the original explanation, expression, or description. A *tertiary* source is one that uses secondary sources, that is, a description (source number 3) of an event based on a description (source 2) derived from the original observation (source 1).

For example, Susanne Langer's discussion of virtual space in her book *Feeling and Form*[20] is the primary source or original expression of this idea. Valerie Preston-Dunlop's discussion of this idea in her dissertation[21] is a secondary source. An article with a discussion of Langer's idea of virtual space based on Preston-Dunlop's discussion would, in turn, be a tertiary source. Professional papers and theses and dissertations advancing new ideas are considered primary sources, as are the articles resulting from these documents. However, when using articles published from theses and dissertations it is a good idea to review the original document to give you a full understanding of the scope and context of the original research. Dance history survey textbooks are typically tertiary sources. While they serve a very important function in dance education, they are not credible sources for scholarly research.

The disadvantage of using secondary sources, and especially tertiary sources, is that one never knows what transmutations have occurred as authors have translated original ideas and applied them to their own work. Often the original intent and authenticity of an idea, description, or explanation is mitigated or misrepresented, placing the credibility and validity of the source in question. For this reason, one of the hallmarks of good scholarship is the principal use of primary sources. However, in some instances, the use of secondary sources is appropriate; for example, the use of existing histories to establish the historical background for an ethnographic study. In this case, the purpose of the research is to study the presence and significance of a particular dance form in its natural setting and not to write a history of the community or the surrounding area. Once again, your purpose and problem statements serve as your best guide for making decisions about which sources are most appropriate for your study.

Conducting the Review

All experienced researchers will have advice for conducting the review of literature and working with literary data. Most of us have developed our own methods for successfully finding and accessing sources and for keeping track of information. With an idea in mind of *what you want to accomplish* with your review of literature, ask others for suggestions about what sources might be useful and for any techniques they have found to be particularly productive.

As you review each source avoid the tendency to reproduce the article in your notes. Study the article, and if you consider it appropriate to your review, evaluate the content and write down only the key ideas and note how they are related to your research. If you have a good understanding of your research purpose and problem you should be able to separate important information from that which is not important to your study. Copy *only the most significant* quotes and double-check to be sure that you have been accurate. Take time to record all bibliographic information, including the author's full name and page numbers.

As you are reviewing and making notes on particular articles you will no doubt have your own ideas and it is important to write them down in your notes. If you do this adjacent to your notes on the article, devise a system to distinguish your ideas from those of other authors. When you return to your notes some weeks later you may not be able to recall whether that important insight was yours or someone else's. Being careful and thorough throughout the literature review process will save you valuable time later on.

The following steps will help you get started on your review. Use them as a guide and feel free to adapt them to your needs and to accommodate the suggestions of others. While you will probably move forward and then need to retrace your steps as your ideas become clearer, your review should proceed in the logical sequence that follows. Remember to be *focused, organized, systematic, and critical.*

- Define the purpose and problem of your study and keep them in front of you.
- Make a list of key words—descriptors. Concept maps are helpful.[22]
- Organize your computer search—use your research librarian as a resource.
- Conduct the computer search.

- Conduct a search of indices related to your area of inquiry that are not on-line.
- Review printouts and listings gathered from indices.
- Locate materials—begin with the most recent.
- Review and select appropriate and related materials.
- Read critically and determine the relatedness of the source, beginning with the most recent.
- Take notes and record all bibliographic information accurately.
- Record source and page number for all quotes.
- Design a coding system that will help you keep track of the sources you have reviewed. Particularly useful is identifying (1) the usefulness of the source and (2) the topic or subject of the article.

There are many pitfalls in conducting the review of literature, which you will no doubt discover on your own; but to help you anticipate and avoid some of these, Walter R. Borg and Meredith Gall offer a list of mistakes to avoid.[23] These serve as good reminders, and you should make every effort as you review the literature to avoid the following mistakes:

- A hurried review
- A review that relies too heavily on secondary sources
- A search that is not organized and systematic
- Poor record keeping
- Concentrating only on the findings of a study, which often results in missing how the researcher approached the study and the research methods
- Overlooking important sources
- Searching too narrowly or too broadly
- Making incomplete or incorrect bibliographic entries
- Copying too much information
- Getting off track
- Assuming that every article is worth your time

A Way of Proceeding: Modes of Inquiry, Methodologies, Procedures

The mode of inquiry, research methodology, and procedures represent the *how* of research and are inextricably linked to the purpose and problem of your research. Your design of a coherent, systematic, and productive inquiry will result from developing an understanding of how your vantage point, the research strategies that are consistent with this perspective, and *your* plan for conducting research are interrelated.

Evolving Modes of Inquiry

A mode of inquiry is a research paradigm that reflects a way of seeing and making sense of the world, and this point of view, in turn, influences how we ask questions and how we proceed with discovering the answers. The modes of inquiry to which we are drawn and, thus, use to frame our understanding of reality are the paradigms or points of view that influence the ways we construct meaning. In chapter 1, Sondra Fraleigh writes of the many manifestations of dance, its meanings and contexts, and how our knowledge and interpretation of dance are shaped by how we experience it. She connects these ideas to qualitative and quantitative approaches—the broadest mode of inquiry distinction—and then looks more closely at the contexts of systematic inquiry in dance and the various ways of approaching the study of dance.

Your background in dance, how you have chosen to be involved in the field, your interests, and your personally constructed system of beliefs and values all contribute to determining how you know the world of dance and thus the kind of research that will interest you. For example, if you have an overriding interest in the origin and development of the aesthetic ideas that shape the nature of dance as an art form and cultural phenomenon, you are likely to be interested in pursuing philosophy as a mode of inquiry. This way of thinking about the discipline and the larger world in which dance resides leads us to questions that examine the authentic experiences of dance and dancing, how we construct meaning in dance, and how we understand concepts such as "meaning-making in dance," "movement as expressive medium," or "feminist performance." Philosophy as a mode of inquiry also delves into problems of language clarification, such as "What do we mean when we call dance a space/time/motion art form?" Philosophical inquiry also concerns itself with identifying and probing problems and issues that concern the field of dance. These may be in the area of public policy, curriculum development, artistic integrity, ethical behavior, the roles and responsibilities of professionals in the field, or any number of other areas that raise your concern and interest. Working with ideas, logical reasoning, and developing lines of argumentation are the hallmarks of philosophy as a mode of inquiry.

Historiography as a mode of inquiry reflects a way of thinking about dance that draws one to understand and explain the past. The historian asks questions about the events, art works, and personalities that shaped dance in the past. Historical inquiry seeks to create a meaningful interpretation of what happened, and in some cases, why it happened and how it relates to who and what we are today. Shelley Berg points out in chapter 8 that historians "have described motion, movement and formal choreography, grappling with the problems of linguistic representation of a symbolic form." This description of the issues that interest historians sounds distinctly similar to those concerns of philosophical inquiry, and indeed it is. However, while there is always an element of philosophical discourse in historical inquiry and a consideration of the past to understand context on the part of the philosopher, the fundamental vantage of each of these modes of inquiry is different. The historian is not so much concerned with the analysis of aesthetic ideas as she or he is with making sense of the past.

Each of the modes of inquiry presented in this text is shaped by an intellectual tradition that forms a particular way of considering dance in its many forms, manifestations, and contexts. It is important to keep in mind that when we speak of quantitative and qualitative, we are not referring to two discrete concepts. The ways we see the world and how we choose to identify, organize, and interpret phenomena actually exist on a continuum ranging from predictable, measurable, and absolute to contextual, experiential, and relative. On one end of the continuum we have experimental research and on the other, postpositivist or interpretive research. Depending on the researcher's perspective, subject, and approach to the study, historical, philosophical, feminist-analytic, hermeneutic, and ethnographic research fall somewhere along the quantitative/qualitative continuum.

Differentiating the various modes of inquiry as we have done in this text is useful for understanding the different ways researchers approach the study of dance. However, in actual practice research is often shaped by overlapping or integrating modes of inquiry. Eluza Santos's study of the expression of cultural identity in the contemporary dance of her native Brazil is primarily an ethnographic study; however, as a member of this culture and dance community, a portion of her data comes from her phenomenological descriptions of her own experiences as a dancer and choreographer.[24] Kim Grover-Haskin's study of the artistic processes and dance works of three contemporary women choreographers as feminist world-making endeavors uses a mode of inquiry that is fundamentally interpretive. Yet the nature and conceptualization of the study integrates ethnographic, philosophical, and feminist analysis modes of inquiry.[25] While we may be able to distinguish the modes of inquiry by definition, in actuality, there are similarities of perspective between those that are more qualitatively oriented and those that have a predominant quantitative orientation.

Each mode of inquiry allows the researcher to pursue a particular area of research interest from a different vantage point. Consider, for example, a study focusing on student learning in a dance technique class. One may frame the question and design the study using either an experimental or empirical mode of inquiry in which variables will be studied under controlled conditions, and observations (the data) will be expressed in numerical value and analyzed statistically. The distinguishing feature of experimental inquiry is the use of an experimental group that receives the treatment *and* a control group that does not; in other words, this method uses the control of some kind of intervention. One way to study student learning in technique class from this perspective might be to test and measure the effectiveness of specific instructional strategies using pre- and post-tests and evaluators trained to assess certain variables. Another researcher may choose to study student learning in the naturalistic setting of the actual technique class using ethnography as the mode of inquiry. In this instance, the studio would be considered the ethnographic setting and the researcher would seek to develop a meaningful interpretation of what happened over the course of the semester based on data from such sources as observations of actual teaching and interviews with the teacher and the students. The historian would approach the question of student learning from an entirely different perspective. This researcher, using historical research as the mode of inquiry, might be interested in learning about the development and evolution of particular approaches to teaching technique, the key historical figures who shaped and refined these philosophies, and how they have influenced student learning over time. Philosophy as a mode of inquiry would be an appropriate way to examine how a teacher's personal pedagogy becomes a theory of teaching/learning in the technique class and how this theory accounts for the phenomenon of student learning.

Each of these four hypothetical studies are framed by different ways of seeing and understanding dance technique and student learning. The questions posed are different, each will require a different research methodology, and in the end, each will contribute very different knowledge to our understanding of student learning in a dance technique class. One of the most intriguing and valuable aspects of our field is its inherent diversity, and this is reflected in the pluralistic worldviews that researchers bring to the study of dance. Our understandings are enriched by the wealth of new knowledge that emerges when individuals choose to see and pursue the study of dance using distinctly different yet equally valued modes of inquiry.

As the boundaries of what defines dance change and as disciplines related to ours contribute to our thinking, the study of dance will require new modes of inquiry. Some years ago the principal modes of inquiry influencing graduate dance research were the rather limited categories of descriptive, historical, and experimental. Over the years as the body of dance knowledge has expanded we have redefined traditional research paradigms, shaped new ones for our field based on ideas from other disciplines, and created ways to study dance out of our own experiences as dance makers. This trend will continue and it is this recognition of the ever-changing nature of dance and the study of it that inspired our title of this section: *Evolving Modes of Inquiry.*

Methodology

As we discuss above, each mode of inquiry is shaped by an intellectual tradition that typifies a particular research paradigm or philosophical perspective. This perspective, in turn, determines the method for approaching problems and seeking answers. The research method prescribes how a study will be designed and how data will be gathered, analyzed, and interpreted. Not only should there be consistency between the mode of inquiry and methodology, but also the form of the research paper or report should reflect the same philosophical orientation. For instance, a written narrative using expressive language telling the story of those studied and the significance of their lived experiences is an appropriate form for phenomenological, interpretive, or biographical research, but it is not consistent with, for example, the tenets of an empirical study based on survey research methodology.

The primary purpose of this text is to provide you with an introduction to the modes of inquiry and methodologies appropriate for pursuing the diversity of questions in dance research. Each chapter presents an overview of the foundational ideas that characterize the mode of inquiry and an in-depth discussion of the research methods appropriate to that particular paradigm or worldview. It is important to remember that the mode of inquiry and the research method are inextricably linked. The *mode of inquiry* is a way of thinking about dance and asking questions; the *methodology* is a way of seeking answers to these questions.

If you are asking questions about dance from an experimental perspective, then control, measurement, and objectivity should be essential features of your research methodology. In this instance, gathering data from open-ended interviews and phenomenological narratives contained in the journals of those studied would not provide the kind of data that can be measured and subjected to statistical analysis. Furthermore, such a qualitative approach does not allow for the control of variables in the research design so that the research can be replicated and evaluated using the criteria of reliability and validity.[26] However, these methods would be appropriate for ethnographic research that is field-based and seeks to study the phenomenon in its naturalistic setting. In this case, the methodology takes into account the ambiguities of the situation, the wide variations in human behavior, and the role of the researcher as an interpreter of what is seen, heard, and felt. The goal is to describe multiple realities, develop understanding, and generate theory rather than test theory or predict behaviors or outcomes.

Procedures

Procedures are the specific research methods that you will use to conduct your research and these follow directly from your mode of inquiry and methodology. Kelley Pierce-Byrd's historical study of the eighteenth-century choreographer–director–ballet master John D'Auban's artistic contributions required procedures that would allow her to access and discover information about dance and theater in the Victorian era. These procedures included, among others, the following:

- Examining newspaper and journal accounts of the period to gather pre-production information and specific performance information;
- Examining playbills, and management, business, and artistic artifacts; scripts, scores, and stage notes; and schedules and contracts contained in the theater archives of the Pierpont Morgan Library, Theatre Museum of London, as well as the holdings of the Drury Lane and Savoy theaters;
- Examining the critical writings of the period as a way of assessing the artistic standing of D'Auban's work against that of his contemporaries.[27]

Jaime Baures's study of the working processes of four dance notators employed a multiple-case, case-study methodology. From the methodology and procedure section of her proposal, Baures describes her specific research approach:

> The procedures for conducting this case study will be to collect data through personal interviews of four professional Labanotation dance notators. This data will be analyzed and interpreted to present a descriptive narrative of the cognitive processes underlying the notating of dance in Labanotation for these individuals. Interviews ... will be of an open-ended nature. ... The respondents [will be] allowed, even encouraged, to raise and pursue issues and ideas they feel are relevant.[28]

Baures follows this with specifications for conducting the interviews and a set of questions designed to guide rather than control the interview process.

In an experimental or empirical study procedures specifically address the selection of subjects, the physical conditions of the experimental setting, use of equipment, procedures for gathering data (for example, surveys, types of tests, observation protocols), procedures for analyzing data (statistical tests, procedures for recording and scoring data, computer processing of data, and so on), and the approach that will be used to interpret and present the results of the research.

To summarize, the *mode of inquiry* is the research paradigm and this determines the *methodology* or characteristic ways of conducting research. These guide the researcher in designing the study and selecting the specific *procedures* for gathering, analyzing, and interpreting data and communicating the results of the research.

The Research Proposal

The most important phase of the research process is the writing of the research proposal or prospectus. It is at this initial stage that the focus of the research is clarified and narrowed to workable proportions; the parameters of the study are defined and the research design is conceived. It is also at this stage that the researcher develops an understanding of how her or his research is part of a larger field of inquiry and how it is situated in the world of intellect that defines the discipline of dance.

It may take you several, if not many, drafts to formulate clear, coherent, manageable, and significant research purpose and problem statements as well as a research design that will lead you to the answers you seek. Many novice researchers make the mistake of selecting a research method first and then try to find a question that fits the method. Unfortunately, such an approach fails to provide the researcher with a larger understanding of the kinds of questions she or he might ask about a given area of study as well as making it very difficult to develop a proposal and research agenda that have internal consistency. Begin with your initial questioning and develop your purpose and problem statements to reflect your interests. Clear and carefully formulated purpose and problem statements will inherently suggest a mode of inquiry and will lead you to appropriate research methodologies.

It is critically important that this developmental stage of the research process and the necessary exploratory thinking and decision making not be glossed over or bypassed in favor of working out details during the research process. If your proposal is vague and without clearly defined parameters, you will find yourself floundering at best. At worst, you will have spent many hours, and possibly a good deal of money, only to discover that the data you thought you should have gathered does not lead you anywhere. It is not unusual for researchers to spend almost as much time developing a research proposal as they do gathering and analyzing the data. A poorly conceived proposal will almost without exception result in a confusing, lengthy, and frustrating research experience.

The nature of the research and the mode of inquiry impact the specificity contained in the research proposal. Proposals for experimental and empirical research projects are extensive, providing detailed and specific descriptions of focus and procedures. A hypothesis is usually stated and the proposal contains a thorough review of related literature. Since the specific focus of a qualitative research project may not emerge until well into the research process, proposals are by necessity brief and speculative, suggesting areas of study that might be relevant to the research purpose. The proposal presents a general statement of approach and intended procedures while the researcher knows full well that these may need to be modified as the research progresses. There is no hypothesis to be stated and the review of related literature is not extensive, attending particularly to articulating a context for the study and identifying appropriate points of entry. This does not suggest, however, that proposals for qualitative research can present a kind of "anything goes" agenda. On the contrary, qualitative research proposals should present a very clearly defined orientation to the study and a relevant framework for initiating and guiding the research process. As Elliot Eisner points out:

> The function of [qualitative] proposals is not to provide a watertight blueprint or formula the researcher is to follow, but to develop a cogent case that makes it plain to a knowledgeable reader that the writer has the necessary background to do the study and has thought clearly about the resources that are likely to be used in doing the study, and that the topic, problem, or issue being addressed is . . . significant.[29]

Elements of a Research Proposal

Whether you are developing a proposal for graduate research or writing a grant for funding to support your research or dance-making endeavors, the contents of proposals are similar. The elements may differ by name or the order of presentation may vary but, typically, grant applications and research proposals require similar information. The primary distinguishing factor between proposals for graduate research and grant applications is the inclusion of a budget in grant applications. Read guidelines *very carefully* and consult a knowledgeable faculty member or colleague if you are unsure what is being asked. If you are writing a proposal for your graduate research project be sure to ask if there are specific departmental or graduate school guidelines that you are expected to follow.

Research proposals, depending on the type of the research, include some or all of the following elements:

- Introduction
    Orientation of the study or context for the study (Background)
    Setting of the problem (who and what)
    Rationale for the study (why)
    Significance of the study (contribution of new knowledge)
- Statement of the purpose
- Statement of the problem
- Assumptions
- Hypothesis
- Delimitations

- Limitations
- Definition of terms
- Mode of inquiry, methodology, and procedures
- Review of related literature

Introduction

Your purpose and problem statements should determine the form and content of your proposal. Some universities require that students use a standardized format and set of subheadings; others allow considerably more latitude. Regardless, all proposals should present a clear indication of the context of the study and why the research is important or worth doing. Indicating that the research has never been done before is not a credible rationale for the study. Indeed, there may be good reasons why no one has bothered to study the question. In your introduction you will want to provide a background for your research project. You may do this by discussing the ideas that inspired your interest in the topic or the current issues that make the research warranted. Put your purpose and problem statements in front of you and consider these questions as you begin to outline your introduction:

- What are the ideas that form the context for the study? Are they ideas related to, for example, enhancing the quality of teaching/learning settings for dance in secondary schools, developing an understanding of the contributions of dance artists of color who have been underrepresented in historical discourse, making sense of how we engage with and experience the work of a particular choreographer, or examining the presence of gender as a social and political construct influencing the creating of contemporary dance works?
- What is the specific setting of the study? For example, what issues, group of people, dance works, or specific dance science or somatic concerns will the study address?
- How will the research advance our knowledge and understanding of dance? Why is the research important and what will it contribute to the field at large?

Your introduction should lead directly to your *statement of the purpose* and *statement of the problem*—the heart of your research. I tell my students that the introduction should be so clear and logical in its development that I should be able to determine the focus of the research project at the end of the introduction, before reading the purpose and problem statements. These follow logically from the introduction and are both contextualized and supported by the ideas contained in the introduction. Below is an example of a rationale, a purpose statement, and research questions taken from Frances Bruce's proposal for her master's thesis.[30]

Dance scholars agree that to understand the dance as it exists in any temporal or spatial location is to understand the sociocultural context of its genesis. In complex polycultural societies, however, contextual dimensions and parameters are not easily defined. How can we know we are not arbitrarily plucking from social and historical contexts these facts, which from our perspective, seem best to explain a specific dance phenomenon?

The problem is compounded in industrial western cultures, where dance as a performing art is separated "from the generality of other human activity" (Brinson, 1985, p. 210). Writer and lecturer on dance, Peter Brinson (1986) perceives dance as marginally situated in relation to modern society as a whole.

A paradox dwells within this perception. In the United States, with no tradition of royal patronage for the dance, each dance company emerges *de novo*, dependent on the support of the surrounding society. This is particularly true of major ballet companies associated with urban areas or cities, from which the company often takes its name; the New York City Ballet, the San Francisco Ballet, etc. The city ballet company occupies a position among the other cultural institutions of the city, such as the symphony, opera, and art museums.

From this perspective, the dance, or specifically the ballet, is in one respect centrally situated to the extent it is part of the city's cultural framework. The tension that exists between this centrality and the perceived marginality of dance in general must be explored if we are to untangle the complexities of the sociocultural context of dance in urban society.

This study proposes to analyze the sociocultural context of a ballet company, and the situation of the ballet company within that sociocultural context. The focus of the study is Dallas, Texas, and the relationship between the Kosloff Ballet Company and the city of Dallas, from 1929–1934.

Therefore, a conceptual framework for the analysis of the sociocultural context of the Kosloff Ballet must answer the following questions:

1. What was the identity of the city of Dallas in terms of both its empirical and symbolic structures?

2. With reference to this identity, what did the Kosloff Ballet signify to those who supported it?

3. To what extent did the Kosloff Ballet's significance depend on the charismatic qualities inherent in or attributed to Kosloff himself; the compatibility of the symbolic function of the Kosloff Ballet with the symbolic identity of the city; and the symbolic function of ballet, as a performing art and producer of culture?

Assumptions

Depending on the kind of research you are proposing it may or may not be necessary to specifically state the *assumptions* upon which the research is based. Assumptions undergirding the research not commonly accepted in the field are presented in the introduction. For example, a study proposing to examine the effectiveness of varying approaches to teaching choreography is based on an inherent or implicit assumption that choreography is both teachable and learnable. While, granted, there are those who believe that choreographic ability is an innate talent and no amount of teaching will enhance what is not there to begin with, it is not necessary to argue the teachability of dance making unless a specific issue is germane to the study. A more tenuous assumption in such a study is whether we can determine "effectiveness" and if so, how. In another instance, a study that seeks to examine the relationship of teacher behaviors in ballet class and the incidence of eating disorders presumes a connection between what teachers do and the behaviors of their students. This assumption is fundamental to the intent of the research and must be supported by existing research or logical lines of argumentation. However, do not confuse stating and arguing one's assumptions with determining cause and effect or the lack of correlation—the latter is the purpose of the research. Assumptions provide a theoretical framework for the study and are based firmly on existing theories and principles, such as previous studies that have demonstrated a relationship between teacher behavior and student behavior. These assumptions can be, and often are, based on research in areas outside of dance. To do this you must argue the applicability and appropriateness of this research to dance and your study.

Hypothesis

A *hypothesis* is an educated guess, and while most research is inspired by educated guesses, speculation, and the desire to know more, not all research proposals present a formal hypothesis. The inclusion of a testable hypothesis in a research proposal is a characteristic feature of experimental and empirical research. The hypothesis is a very brief statement that clearly states a relationship between two or more variables that can be tested. The hypothesis is a statement of what the research will prove, disprove, or find null. In experimental and empirical investigations the hypothesis is an educated guess about each of the research questions in the problem statement and "takes on the characteristic of an assertion subject to corroboration. The research seeks to confirm or refute the accuracy of that assertion by the evidence gathered."[31]

Since in qualitative research the point is not to prove or disprove but rather to construct meaningful interpretation, hypotheses are not determined a priori and, therefore, a hypothesis statement is not typically stated in the proposal. During the research process, the researcher remains flexible and receptive to emerging themes, formulating hunches, and working hypotheses along the way. In the case of participant observers in the field, "after they develop some working hypotheses, observers round out their knowledge by asking informants to elaborate on subjects they mentioned previously and following up on things mentioned by . . . others."[32] In this way, working hypotheses or hunches are an important part of qualitative research, but they do not function in the same way as testable hypotheses in quantitative research.

Delimitations and Limitations

All studies must be *delimited* or narrowed in some fashion appropriate to the research purpose. Delimitations establish the boundaries of the study and may be part of the purpose statement or stand alone as a separate section in the proposal. Narrowing a biographical study to a particular twenty-year period or focusing the research on the role of one particular ritual in a tribal community are examples of delimitations.

Limitations are those conditions or circumstances that may affect the study and for which the researcher cannot control. A study may be limited by the fact that key members of a community may not be willing to speak to the researcher or that all relatives and close friends of a biographical subject are no longer living, thus limiting access to particular kinds of information. Experimental and empirical studies testing treatment protocols are always limited by the participant's commitment to following through on the prescribed course of action. Survey research, particularly when the focus is on opinions and attitudes, is always limited by the truthfulness of the respondents. *Delimitations* are those boundaries or restrictions deliberately placed on the study by the researcher; *limitations* are those aspects of the study that, by nature of the research design and situation, may limit or impact the results of the study.

Definition of Terms

The *definition of terms* is an important part of clarifying the problem of the study and presenting the context for the research. Terms that should be explained are those that have a specific function in the study, are open to various interpretations, or are technical in nature. *Conceptually based choreography* may have a specific meaning and function within the context of a study examining the ways that choreographers initiate their dance making and develop their ideas. A term such as *formalist literary theory,* used across disciplines, should be defined in relation to both literary criticism and its application to dance discourse. *Technique class,* a term that is well-known to all dancers, may indeed be open to many interpretations and needs defining as it might refer to a ballet or modern dance class, a particular style such as Cunningham or Graham, or different understandings of the nature of the content of a technique class.

It is essential that terms be clearly and precisely defined and that these terms *as defined* be used consistently throughout the proposal and the research. In the proposal, terms may be defined in the introduction and at appropriate places in the body of the text as the terms are used in the context of discussing particular aspects of the research. It is not necessary, although in some cases it is more appropriate, to have a section with a subheading for the definition of terms. Whether the terms are defined in the body of the text or in a separate section depends on the number of terms that require definition, the relative complexity of the terminology, and the appropriate proposal format for the type of research being proposed. Typically, proposals for empirical and experimental research have a separate section for the definition of terms, while for most other types of proposals it is more effective to define the terms in the context of their use within the body of the proposal.

Methodology and Procedures

Almost as important as the purpose and problem statements is the *methodology* section. This section outlines how the research will be carried out. First, an argument is presented for the methodological perspective of the research by relating the mode of inquiry and methodology to the purpose of the research: Why is historical inquiry an appropriate approach for the study? Why will the research questions best be answered by an experimental design as opposed to, for example, survey research or multiple single-case studies? What are the innate characteristics of the purpose and problem of the study that suggest that phenomenological inquiry will be the most appropriate avenue to understanding the experience being studied? These are the kinds of questions that the methodology section should address in order for the proposal to provide a sound methodological grounding for the study.

Next, this section, in a very organized fashion, outlines the specific *procedures* for the study. This is an accounting of *what you intend to do*. The degree of specificity and detail of the procedures presented in the proposal depends, again, on the kind of research being proposed. Proposals for experimental and empirical studies present procedures in considerable detail, while ethnographic research proposals provide a more general overview of how the research will be conducted. This overview typically includes a discussion of the research site, how access will be gained, the strategies that will be used to gather data (such as interview, observation, participant-observation, or videotape analysis), and an indication of how the data will be analyzed, for example, domain, taxonomic, componential, or theme analysis.[33] If the study involves in-depth interviews, interview questions should be included in the proposal. The procedures for a philosophical study include outlining the argument and providing an indication of how literary data will be used to support this argument.

Review of Related Literature

The primary purpose of the *review of related literature* section in the proposal is to provide a context for your research. To do this you must determine the proper perspective or orientation for the review. For example, are you using the review of literature to:

- Define a theoretical or philosophical base for the study?
- Relate your proposed research study to a larger area of inquiry?
- Support an interdisciplinary approach to designing and conducting the research?
- Enhance understanding of methodological issues?
- Bridge the gap between theory and practice and demonstrate how the proposed research will inform practice?

The review of related literature section in the proposal typically focuses on five to eight sources and addresses how these *relate* to your study. Keep in mind that you are *reviewing* the literature, *not* reproducing it, writing a synopsis, or outlining the contents of a book or article. Identify the key issues or ideas in each of the sources and discuss how they relate to the purpose and problem of your research. These relevant issues and ideas form the substance of the review of literature section. In addition to studying good examples of literature reviews contained in proposals, you may find the following suggestions for writing the review of literature useful:

- Get the proper orientation—know what you are attempting to accomplish with the review of literature section.
- Remember, the review of literature is a *discussion.*
- Have a plan—an organizational structure that is suggested by the purpose and problem statements.
- Outline the discussion—the best guide is the purpose/problem. It should suggest relevant areas for discussion.

- Begin with a comprehensive perspective and narrow to more specific studies that focus more and more closely on your specific problem.
- Emphasize relatedness—*do not summarize the sources.* Account for why you are using the study by asking, "Why is it related?"
- *Review the literature—do not reproduce it.*
- Present your own discussion.
- Paraphrase.
- Use short direct quotes, if necessary. Use long direct quotes only as a last resort and for a very good reason.[34]

Human Subjects Review

It is imperative any time human subjects are used in research that appropriate measures are taken to protect their rights and welfare. Federal law requires all institutions to have an Institutional Review Board (IRB) to review all research that involves human subjects. This includes not only those studies involving experimental treatments but also all studies in which subjects will be interviewed, observed, and surveyed. There are always potential risks to subjects when they are involved in research and it is the ethical responsibility of the researcher to ensure that the rights of these individuals are protected; the IRB is responsible for overseeing compliance with federal law.

The risks to subjects as a consequence of participating in a research study may be physical, psychological, or social. In many cases the potential risks are minimal; however, the researcher has an ethical responsibility to provide subjects with a true and accurate statement of the purpose of the research, the conditions under which data will be collected, and how the results of the research will be made public. The researcher must obtain informed consent from all subjects, and if anonymity cannot be protected due to the nature of the research, subjects must know this before they consent to participate. Subjects also have a right to know what the *real* purpose of the research is; what measures will be taken to protect their rights, including confidentiality; any benefits they may receive from participation; and who to contact if they have pertinent questions.

As soon as you know that you are likely to be using human subjects in your research, contact a member of your IRB and secure the necessary forms for requesting approval of research using human subjects. The packet of information will include specific guidelines that you must read very carefully and follow to the letter. If you are planning to use minors, such as working with elementary school children in a creative dance class, allow additional time for approval as all research using minors is subjected to more extensive review by IRBs. Your research advisor or a member of your IRB will be able to guide you through the human subjects review process; it is your responsibility to seek the information and contact someone to assist you with this process.

Conclusion

The research process is at once systematic and creative. While these adjectives may seem to suggest contrasting characteristics, it is very important to remember that systematic does not necessarily mean proceeding in a linear, predetermined, or rigid fashion. Systematic, in the sense I have used it throughout this chapter, has more to do with having a *plan* and being *thorough* than it does with following a prescribed set of steps. I have offered here ways of proceeding and described logical phases of the research process as a means of helping you enter into the research enterprise and discover your own process. Individuality and flexibility, remaining open to the unexpected, should be balanced with your continued efforts to define and redefine the focus of your research. It is your creativity and imagination that will open the space for new ideas and new ways of proceeding; it is your critical and systematic pursuit of knowledge that will bring your research ideas to fruition and lead you to discovery.

Research Process Learning Projects

Project 1: Identifying and Analyzing Scholarly Research

Review two to three *scholarly* articles from dance journals, conference proceedings, or scholarly journals containing dance articles.

- Why in your view is this a scholarly article?
- Identify the central research problem or question.
- Are there any subproblems? These are more narrowly defined aspects of the research that grow out of the central research question.
- Identify the type of research, such as historical, philosophical, qualitative (interpretive or ethnographic), or quantitative (empirical or experimental).
- What hypothesis or hypotheses, if any, were stated? Note: Qualitative research does not set forth a hypothesis to be tested.
- Briefly outline the research methodology. How was the study carried out? What steps did the researcher follow to gather, analyze, and interpret data?
- Briefly describe what references to, or discussion of, related literature or studies by other researchers were contained in the article.

- How was the content of the article organized and how did this relate to the content and context of the research topic? Here are some suggestions, but look for other organizational structures as well: Did the author set forth her or his theory at the beginning and then proceed to support it? Did the ideas develop from general to specific or specific to general? Was the organization chronological? Was the presentation organized around themes emerging from the analysis and interpretation of the data?

Project 2: Planning the Research

This project focuses on the planning stage of research. It follows the orientation stage in which, through extensive reading, the researcher formulates a research purpose by progressing from a general area of research interest to topics, ideas, questions, a research purpose and, finally, to a particular research problem.

The planning stage entails (1) determining the reason for and purpose of the investigation, and (2) the data to be gathered in order to accomplish the purpose of the study. During the planning stage the researcher uses her or his personal observations and critical reading skills to:

- Develop a rationale for the study (why)
- Develop a research purpose (what)
- Specify research problems (questions) that will be subjected to an in-depth investigation in order to carry out the purpose of the study (how)
- Delimit the scope of the study (frame, territory, boundaries)
- Determine specific procedures associated with the mode of inquiry by which the problems, events, or questions are to be investigated (method)

Select an area of research interest and develop the following:

- Rationale for the study (1–3 double-spaced pages)
- Statement of the purpose
- Statement of the problem (usually 3–6 questions)
- Delimitations
- If appropriate, limitations and definitions of terms

Project 3: Designing the Study

- Describe the mode of inquiry most appropriate for the study you have planned and in one to two pages discuss the nature of this mode of inquiry and why it is particularly relevant to your study. For example: Why is an integration of historical inquiry and feminist analysis appropriate for your study?

• After you have studied the various modes of inquiry presented in the following chapters, return to this project and prepare a discussion of the methods you might use for gathering, analyzing, and interpreting data for your research problem. Remember, methods are *general* strategies such as conducting in-depth interviews, administering a questionnaire, or analyzing choreographic works. Procedures are described with *specific* statements of what you will do, such as conduct in-depth interviews with three women choreographers of modern dance, use Susanne Langer's theory of virtual form to examine how movement creates space, or teach a prescribed conditioning program to advanced-level dancers over a six-week period.

NOTES

1. Penelope Hanstein, "The Choreographer at Work: Illuminating a Heuristic Process" (paper presented at the annual meeting of the Congress on Research in Dance, New York City, October 1987).

2. Susan Stinson, *NDA Scholar's Lecture: Research as Choreography* (Reston, Va.: American Alliance for Health, Physical Education, Recreation and Dance Publications, 1994), 8.

3. Richard Altick, *The Art of Literary Research* (New York: W. W. Norton, 1981), 22.

4. Elliot Eisner, *The Enlightened Eye: Qualitative Inquiry and the Enhancement of Educational Practice* (New York: Macmillan, 1991), 7. For an insightful discussion of the contingency of truth relative to both art making and research, see Nelson Goodman, *Ways of Worldmaking* (Indianapolis: Hackett Publishing Company, Inc., 1978).

5. Edward F. Rainbow and Hildegard C. Froehlich, *Research in Music Education: An Introduction to Systematic Inquiry* (New York: Schirmer Books, 1987).

6. Donald Schon, *The Reflective Practitioner: How Professionals Think in Action* (San Francisco: Jossey Bass Publishers, 1983), 42.

7. Elliot Eisner, *Cognition and Curriculum: A Basis for Deciding What to Teach* (New York: Longman Inc., 1982), 49.

8. Rainbow and Froehlich, 59.

9. This chapter contains many examples to illustrate the various aspects of the research process and elements of the research proposal. Some of these examples are hypothetical; however, most are taken from actual graduate research proposals, professional papers, theses, and dissertations completed by students at Texas Woman's University. At TWU, master of fine arts students are required to write a professional paper, which is defined as a twenty- to twenty-five–page scholarly paper based on original research. The master of arts thesis is an extensive research project resulting in a document composed of typically four to five chapters and also must be based on original research. The dissertations completed by students in the Ph.D. program in dance are expected to represent contributions of new knowledge to the field of dance, have a significant theoretical orientation, and be presented in a format and style that is consistent with the nature of the research. The graduate school at TWU expects proposals for professional papers, theses, and dissertations to be very focused and concise. The preferred length is approximately ten pages, excluding references.

10. Penelope Hanstein, "On the Nature of Art Making in Dance: An Artistic Process

Skills Model for the Teaching of Choreography" (Ph.D. dissertation, Ohio State University, 1986).

11. Leslie Siegle, "Movement as Identity" (master of fine arts professional paper, Texas Woman's University, 1996).

12. Mary Strow Bopp, *Research in Dance: A Guide to Resources* (New York: G. K. Hall, 1994).

13. Lisa Fusillo, "Leonide Massine: Choreographic Genius With a Collaborative Spirit" (Ph.D. dissertation, Texas Woman's University, 1982).

14. Susan Burton, "Malichi, The Flower Fawn: Symbolism of the Yaqui Deer Dance" (master of arts thesis, Texas Woman's University, 1990).

15. James Spradley writes that "instead of coming to the field with specific questions the ethnographer analyzes data . . . to discover questions." Spradley describes enthnographic research as a cyclic process of questioning, collecting data, analyzing, and more questioning. In this sense the ethnographer analyzes data to discover questions in order to learn what to look for during the next period of observation. (James P. Spradley, *Participant Observation* [New York: Harcourt Brace Jovanovich, 1980], 33.)

16. Joan Laage, "Embodying the Spirit: The Significance of the Body in the Contemporary Japanese Dance Movement of Butoh" (Ph.D. dissertation, Texas Woman's University, 1993), 9–10.

17. Elaine Gelbard, "Dance Graduate Students: Their Personality Types and Instructional Preferences" (Ph.D. dissertation, Texas Woman's University, 1991), 3–4.

18. Eluza Santos, "The Dancing Voice of Culture: An Ethnography of Contemporary Dance in Vitória, Brazil" (prospectus for a dissertation, Texas Woman's University, 1995), 2.

19. Ann Marie Panalsek, "The Idea and Movement Relationship: A Phenomenological Inquiry Into the Transformation Process" (prospectus for a master of fine arts professional paper, Texas Woman's University, 1992).

20. Susanne K. Langer, *Feeling and Form* (New York: Charles Scribner's Sons, 1953).

21. Valerie Preston-Dunlop, "The Nature of the Embodiment of Choreutic Units in Contemporary Choreography" (Ph.D. dissertation, University of London, Goldsmith's College, 1981).

22. The process of concept mapping or idea mapping encourages divergent thinking and the generation of new ideas. It will help you discover new insights into your initial research questions as well as various avenues that should be explored in your research. Concept mapping is also a strategy for organizing your ideas, seeing connections between seemingly unrelated ideas, and identifying relationships that will provide the basis for developing logical lines of argumentation in your writing. David Hyerle's book *Visual Tools for Constructing Knowledge* (Alexandria, Va.: Association for Supervision and Curriculum Development, 1996) is a very useful source for understanding how visual models can be effective ways for discovering, organizing, analyzing, and critically evaluating complex sets of ideas.

23. Walter R. Borg and Meredith Gall, *Educational Research: An Introduction* (New York: Longman, 1983).

24. Eluza Santos, "The Dancing Voice of Culture: An Ethnography of Contemporary Dance in Vitória, Brazil."

25. Kim Grover-Haskin, "Put Your Mother on the Ceiling: Feminist Performance in Modern Dance as a Worldmaking Process of Three Women Choreographers" (prospectus for a dissertation, Texas Woman's University, 1995).

26. The criterion of *validity* asks whether or not the research actually studied what it

purported to and is concerned with the *accuracy* of scientific findings. The criterion of *reliability* refers to the degree to which an independent researcher will discover the same results as the original researcher and is concerned with the *replicability* of scientific findings. In other words, did the research "hit the right target" (validity) and can the research "hit the *same* target" again? The canons of reliability and validity as criteria for evaluating the credibility of research present factors that are inapplicable to some modes of inquiry and are often defined in special ways relative to qualitative and quantitative research designs.

27. Kelley Pierce-Byrd, "John D'Auban: Eighteenth Century Choreographer/Dance Director/Ballet Master" (prospectus for a dissertation, Texas Woman's University, 1996).

28. Jaime Baures, "Exploring the Cognitive Processes of Four Labanotators" (prospectus for a master of arts thesis, Texas Woman's University, 1996), 5–6.

29. Elliot Eisner, *The Enlightened Eye,* 241.

30. Frances Bruce, "An Analysis of the Sociocultural Context of a Ballet Company: The Kosloff Ballet in Dallas, Texas, 1929–1934" (prospectus for a master's thesis, Texas Woman's University, 1990).

31. Rainbow and Froehlich, 171.

32. Steven J. Taylor and Robert Bogdan, *Introduction to Qualitative Research Methods: The Search for Meanings* (New York: John Wiley and Sons), 49.

33. Spradley, *Participant Observation.*

34. These suggestions are derived from Borg and Gall, *Educational Research: An Introduction.*

REFERENCES

Altick, Richard. *The Art of Literary Research.* New York: W. W. Norton, 1981.

Baures, Jaime. "Exploring the Cognitive Processes of Four Labanotators." Prospectus for a master of arts thesis, Texas Woman's University, 1996.

Bopp, Mary Strow. *Research in Dance: A Guide to Resources.* New York: G. K. Hall, 1994.

Borg, Walter R., and Merideth Gall. *Educational Research: An Introduction.* New York: Longman, 1983.

Bruce, Frances. "An Analysis of the Sociocultural Context of a Ballet Company: The Kosloff Ballet in Dallas, Texas, 1929–1934." Prospectus for a master's thesis, Texas Woman's University, 1990.

Burton, Susan. "Malichi, The Flower Fawn: Symbolism of the Yaqui Deer Dance." Master of arts thesis, Texas Woman's University, 1990.

Eisner, Elliot. *Cognition and Curriculum: A Basis for Deciding What to Teach.* New York: Longman Inc., 1982.

———. *The Enlightened Eye: Qualitative Inquiry and the Enhancement of Educational Practice.* New York: Macmillan, 1991.

Fusillo, Lisa. "Leonide Massine: Choreographic Genius With a Collaborative Spirit." Ph.D. dissertation, Texas Woman's University, 1982.

Gelbard, Elaine. "Dance Graduate Students: Their Personality Types and Instructional Preferences." Ph.D. dissertation, Texas Woman's University, 1991.

Goodman, Nelson. *Ways of Worldmaking.* Indianapolis: Hackett Publishing Company, Inc., 1978.

Grover-Haskin, Kim. "Put Your Mother on the Ceiling: Feminist Performance in Modern Dance as a Worldmaking Process of Three Women Choreographers." Prospectus for a dissertation, Texas Woman's University, 1995.

Hanstein, Penelope. "On the Nature of Art Making in Dance: An Artistic Process Skills Model for the Teaching of Choreography." Ph.D. dissertation, Ohio State University, 1986.

————. "The Choreographer at Work: Illuminating a Heuristic Process." Paper presented at the annual meeting of the Congress on Research in Dance, New York City, October 1987.

Hyerle, David. *Visual Tools for Constructing Knowledge.* Alexandria, Va.: Association for Supervision and Curriculum Development, 1996.

Laage, Joan. "Embodying the Spirit: The Significance of the Body in the Contemporary Japanese Dance Movement of Butoh." Ph.D. dissertation, Texas Woman's University, 1993.

Langer, Susanne K. *Feeling and Form.* New York: Charles Scribner's Sons, 1953.

Panalsek, Ann Marie. "The Idea and Movement Relationship: A Phenomenological Inquiry Into the Transformation Process." Prospectus for a master of fine arts professional paper, Texas Woman's University, 1992.

Pierce-Byrd, Kelley. "John D'Auban: Eighteenth Century Choreographer/Dance Director/ Ballet Master." Prospectus for a dissertation, Texas Woman's University, 1996.

Preston-Dunlop, Valerie. "The Nature of the Embodiment of Choreutic Units in Contemporary Choreography." Doctoral dissertation, University of London, Goldsmith's College, 1981.

Rainbow, Edward F., and Hildegard C. Froehlich. *Research in Music Education: An Introduction to Systematic Inquiry.* New York: Schirmer Books, 1987.

Santos, Eluza. "The Dancing Voice of Culture: An Ethnography of Contemporary Dance in Vitória, Brazil." Prospectus for a dissertation, Texas Woman's University, 1995.

Schon, Donald. *The Reflective Practitioner: How Professionals Think in Action.* San Francisco: Jossey Bass Publishers, 1983.

Siegle, Leslie. "Movement as Identity." Master of fine arts professional paper, Texas Woman's University, 1996.

Spradley, James P. *Participant Observation.* New York: Harcourt Brace Jovanovich, 1980.

Stinson, Susan. *NDA Scholar's Lecture: Research as Choreography.* Reston, Va.: American Alliance for Health, Physical Education, Recreation and Dance Publications, 1994.

Taylor, Steven J., and Robert Bogdan. *Introduction to Qualitative Research Methods: The Search for Meanings.* New York: John Wiley and Sons.

3 MODELS AND METAPHORS

Theory Making and the Creation of New Knowledge

Penelope Hanstein

The Role of Theory in Research

NEW KNOWLEDGE MAY TAKE many forms, ranging from art works to personal narratives to mathematical theorems to scientific findings. Such knowledge emerging from the research process is most often in the form of theory. Theory, like research, has many definitions and applications. Some of these are narrow and restrictive, requiring a theory to be derived from quantifiable data and capable of being tested. Other definitions are more inclusive and consider a theory to be a systematically organized set of statements that analyze and explain the nature and behavior of a specified set of phenomena. This understanding includes those theories resulting from empirical and experimental methods of inquiry as well as those that are based in subjective modes of inquiry such as phenomenology, ethnography, and hermeneutics.

In the broadest sense a theory serves to account for or characterize phenomena in a particular area of inquiry. For example, Cynthia Novack's[1] theory of movement and culture presents an analysis of structural movement systems as embodying social meanings, reflecting cultural reality and changing over time in response to the social and cultural environments. Her theory accounts for and characterizes aspects of movement in relation to social and cultural experiences and advances the notion that movement functions as a social-cultural metaphor. Novack's theory has explanatory power because it explains and provides insight into the phenomenon of movement as culturally situated and intimately connected to personal identity and social interactions.

A theory also has descriptive power by virtue of its capacity to describe and classify phenomena. Among the most well-known descriptive theories in our field is Rudolf Laban's effort theory describing, in the form of a taxonomy, the phenomena that constitute dynamic energy in movement. Laban's theory describes movement as an outward expression of an inner drive and analyzes various manifestations of energy investment. The theory is represented in a theoretical construct comprising four motion factors, effort elements accounting for the polarities of energy in each of the motion factors, and two- and three-effort combinations identified as states and drives. Laban's theory provides one way of analyzing and describing the phenomenon of movement dynamics.

A theory may have predictive power as well and be invaluable in indicating how phenomena are likely to react in given situations. Often predictive theories result from studies using empirical and experimental methodologies such as those described by Steven Chatfield in chapter 5. A study conducted by Tom Welsh, Sally Fitt, and Wendy Thompson, which sought to examine the effect of a particular teaching strategy known as "chaining" on dancers' abilities to learn and perform complex movement sequences in technique classes, resulted in a predictive pedagogical theory.[2] The study compared forward and backward chaining and found "that trainees made fewer errors when taught with a forward chaining progression."[3] Research studies such as this one provide useful information to dance teachers by offering predictions about what teaching strategies are likely to be most effective with a given population in a given setting. The results of these studies may or may not be generalizable to other settings, groups, or activities. This notwithstanding, they do provide valuable pedagogical information when there is a translation from theory to practice.

The Functions of Theory

Theories, as products of research and contributions of new knowledge, serve to describe, explain, and predict phenomena. These functions of theory can be further defined by considering how they might address the field of dance and how they relate to varying approaches to research.[4]

Descriptive theories address the question, "What is this?" Research resulting in descriptive theories is often undertaken when nothing or little is known about an area of inquiry. The task of the researcher is to describe, analyze, classify, and name phenomena in an attempt to understand what something is.

Christine Loken-Kim and Juliette T. Crump's study, "Qualitative Change in Performances of Two Generations of Korean Dancers," is an example of a study leading to a descriptive theory.[5] Loken-Kim and Crump explain that "older specialists in Korean culture and arts have noted that recent performances involve changes in the movement qualities and moods created by dancers" and that "'something' is being lost."[6] This observation led these two researchers to ask the questions: What are these changes, what is being lost, and how do these relate to the current modes of training in Korean dance? With this question in mind they pursued a study that used Laban Movement Analysis to analyze and describe performances of Korean dancers from two different types of training. The descriptive theory resulting from this study describes the nature of the changes they observed:

> the loss of some of the desired formal and affective qualities of Korean dance is due to the fact that although dancers continue to use similar movement patterns, they are not using the same efforts to do them. By bringing the Space Effort to the fore, the modern performers in this study eliminate the inner, absorbed feeling in their performances and there is a corresponding loss of engagement in the dance.[7]

Explanatory theories address the question, "What is happening here?" and build on the information provided by descriptive theories. Research questions focus on relationships and on how phenomena interact in distinctive ways to characterize the particularity of an individual or group of people and their dance, as well as dance events and activities. The explanatory theory provides insight into the complexity of such phenomena in our field as the choreographic process, dance discourse, teaching practices, the development and evolution of dance forms, current trends in dance education, performance experience, audience appreciation of dance, and many, many others.

Marc Strauss's dissertation examining the work of *New Yorker* dance critic Arlene Croce is an example of the development of explanatory theory. In an effort to uncover Croce's aesthetic framework, Strauss used a literary-interpretive analysis approach to study 207 of her essays.[8] Strauss's theory articulated a portrait of Croce as a "classical rhetorician who bases her critical interpretations and evaluations in a rigorous formalistic aesthetic."[9] His theory explained Croce's critical methodology as being distinguished by "three distinct yet interrelated pillars of artistic excellence [with] which [she] appraises dance: sympathetic musicality; apollonian craftsmanship; and enlivening tradition."[10]

The categories of descriptive and explanatory theories are presented here as a way to understand the diversity and scope of theory; however, it is important to remember that theory-generating research may indeed encompass both description and explanation. A good example of this is Jessica Wood's study of the Apache girl's puberty ceremony.[11] Her research presents a detailed narrative description of the four-day ceremony (What is this?) and explains the significance of the ceremony to the tribal people and their commitment to the preservation of the Apache lifeway (What is happening here?). Similarly, Joan Laage's study of butoh developed a descriptive theory of the presence of the body in the Japanese contemporary dance form and advanced an explanatory theory of the butoh aesthetic as being grounded in these various manifestations of the body.[12]

Predictive theories address the question, "What will happen if . . . ?" Research resulting in a theory that predicts phenomena concerns itself with cause and effect. For example, a researcher may seek to learn the effect of a particular training regime on dancers' cardiovascular endurance. Typically, predictive theories emerge from experimental research characterized by having an experimental group and a control group. Such an example is Karen Bond's study, "Personal Style as a Mediator of Engagement in Dance: Watching Terpsichore Rise."[13] This study, which had an experimental component as well as qualitative components, sought to analyze "the influence of an intensive dance program on social and task engagement" on a group of nonverbal children.[14] In her experimental portion of the study, a dance program was compared with a program based on play in order to answer the question, What would happen if dance was used as an avenue to engage nonverbal children in expressing, communicating, and learning? The study found that for all children in the study, "accommodation of personal style fostered self-transaction, evidenced in heightened affect, whole body engagement, creation of new forms, cumulative learning, and conscious self-presentation."[15] Other aspects of Bond's predictive theory emerging from her research included the affirmation of stylistic similarities and differences among the children and the significance of a group process she identified as "aesthetic community."

The Function of Research

The function of scholarly research is to generate theory and to test theory. Theory-generating research identifies phenomena, discovers characteristics, and specifies relationships. Theory-testing research tests the adequacy of existing theory by developing evidence to test the hypothesis set forth by a particular theory.

The majority of research in dance, in fact almost all of the research, is theory-generating. This is in large measure due to the fact that there are relatively few theories in dance that are appropriate for testing. The qualitative nature of dance as an art form and cultural experience predisposes the field to more qualitative modes of inquiry. Historical, ethnographic, philosophical, interpretive, and hermeneutic research efforts do not result in theories that can be tested in the same way that theories developed by empirical and experimental methods can be. Furthermore, at this stage of dance research, researchers appear to have an overwhelming interest in generating theory rather than testing existing theories. This is true of all kinds of researchers; the qualitative researcher as well as those using empirical and experimental modes of inquiry.

Theory as Process

We have been speaking of theory as a product, but for the researcher, theory is as much a process as it is a product. As a novice researcher, one can be easily intimidated by the idea of generating theory; but generating theory can be no more intimidating than creating a new piece of choreography, if the focus remains on the process.

Theory generating, theory building, and theory constructing are used here interchangeably. Theory building, as the avenue to creating new knowledge, involves identifying and defining concepts, integrating and juxtaposing concepts to form statements, and relating statements to other statements with a view to presenting a unified, coherent, and logical expression of a new idea or insight about some dance phenomenon. The theory constructing process involves defining, integrating, juxtaposing, relating, and ordering. The elements of the process or the theoretical building blocks are: concepts, definitions, statements (propositions), and the line of argument or the ordering or hierarchy of the statements.

Concepts are the basic building blocks of theory. "A concept is a mental image of a phenomenon; an idea or a construct in the mind about a thing or action. It is not the thing or action, only the image of it."[16] The foundation blocks of a theory are the concepts the researcher chooses to use to represent her or his ideas. To examine the process of developing theory let us use as an exemplar Cynthia Novack's article, "Looking at Dance as Culture: Contact Improvisation to Disco."[17] A foundational concept of her theory is "structured movement systems," a concept Novack explains she borrowed from Adrienne Kaeppler. Other key concepts of the theory include "movement," "movement as a cultural component," "dancing," and "change."

Definitions articulate how a concept will be used within the theory. The clarity, coherence, and internal consistency of a theory depend on how concepts are defined and used throughout the theory-generating process. Some concepts in our field may be taken as understood but most require defining since they are often used in very specific ways within a theory. While "movement" and "dancing" are concepts familiar to all of us, each of us, including Novack, contextualizes, interprets, and applies them in different ways. The theory builder uses concepts with specificity, and often the debate over the viability and credibility of a theory revolves around how she or he defined her or his concepts in the context of the research and the emergent theory.

Movement as a concept may be defined in any number of ways; Novack has defined *movement,* in the context of her theory, to be "the primary basis for personal identity and social interaction . . . it is kinesthetic and visual . . . less specific than language. . . . It has observable patterns and qualities which can be identified with cultures and historical periods."[18] *Dancing* is defined as "a multi-vocal and flexible sphere of social activity."[19]

Statements or propositions present the theory builder's claims about concepts. Statements express the ideas that support and make up the theory. Statements are declarations about concepts and the most important idea to remember here is that these claims *must be supported by data.*

Data are the evidence that the researcher gathers and they may come from a variety of sources such as observations, interviews, literature reviews, surveys, journals, artifacts, and documents. In addition to coming from a variety of sources, data may also take many forms; for instance, historical facts, measurements, statistics, phenomenological narratives, personal accounts and reflections, notation scores, descriptions of performances, and observations of dance and dancing, as well as the behaviors of individuals and groups. In addition to supporting claims with data, the researcher can make a case for her or his points of view by developing logical lines of argument as used in philosophical inquiry. In this case, the data are the ideas and the credibility of the support resides in how persuasively the researcher can argue her or his position or claim. Claims may also be supported by previous research cited in the literature. Novack's use of Adrienne Kaeppler's ideas about movement systems to support her own claims is an example of using existing literature to support statements about phenomenon. The credibility or "rightness"[20] of the research and the quality of the scholarship is judged by how effectively the theory builder is able to make and support her or his statements using the data.

Theory construction uses two forms of statements: nonrelational and relational. Nonrelational statements state the existence of a phenomenon as well as describe the characteristics of the phenomenon.[21] As the conclusion to a line of argument Novack makes the statement, "Thus, the movement system needs to be viewed as part of the cultural reality"[22] and in so doing states the cultural existence of movement systems. Another example, "Disco dancing becomes a metaphor for life,"[23] states the metaphorical characteristic of disco dancing.

A relational statement "declares a relationship of some kind between two or more concepts."[24] Here are two examples of relational statements from Novack's theory: "Evoking the way a group of people move can call up cultural time and place."[25] This statement draws a relationship between the way people move and the cultural milieu in which the movement is situated. The statement, "The movement in contact improvisation and the social structure of its practice and performance were mutually reinforcing,"[26] identifies a reciprocal relationship between movement and social structure. Careful study of Novack's article reveals how she supported these and many other statements with data from her observations of contact improvisation, disco dancing, and wrestling, as well as the words of the participants in these various activities. In other instances one sees Novack's use of skillful argument to set forth her assumptions and support her claims.

Ordering statements are a very important aspect of the theory-building process. How the theory builder presents her or his ideas shapes the logical consistency and persuasiveness of the theory. This can often be the most difficult part of the theory development process since the way the research was conducted may not be the most effective way to tell the story. Is it best to begin with a general or global view leading to the specificity of the theory using a deductive reasoning approach? Or, might it be more effective to begin with a specific or particular discussion and build toward more universal themes using an inductive reasoning approach? While some might disagree, it is also possible to begin with a global discussion shaping a line of argument that leads to a specific premise and then expanding the argument to conclusions that are more generally or universally applicable.

The type of research may be a useful guide in helping to determine the most appropriate way to express the ideas and communicate the theory. If research is inductive in nature, proceeding from specific observations to general conclusions or from the personal to the universal, as in the case of phenomenological study, grounded theory, interpretive research, and most varieties of qualitative inquiry, then an inductive ordering of ideas is likely to be more consistent with the character of the study. However, such open-ended argument is not necessarily appropriate for or consistent with the nature of empirical and experimental methodologies. These modes of inquiry are rooted in a deductive process for analyzing and interpreting data in order to form a conclusion. The theory, in this case, may be more effectively expressed by beginning with general statements leading to the specific conclusion.

Inductive and deductive research proclivities notwithstanding, the logical line of argument should emerge from the ideas that will support and make up the theory. The following are the kinds of questions to ask when beginning to develop a structure for the presentation of the theory resulting or emerging from research.

- What foundational ideas should be argued first, and how do these develop and lead to other sets of ideas?
- Is development over time an important aspect of the theory and, therefore, should the argument have an inherent chronological element?
- If the theory emerged from a thematic analysis, how do these themes interconnect and should the argument be shaped by these pervasive themes?

Each theory, like each dance work, has its own internal logic, and it is the task of the researcher, like that of the choreographer, to discover that logical structure.

Understanding and Analyzing Theories

Studying the work of other choreographers can be an enlightening way to refine and enhance our own art-making processes, and the same is true for developing abilities to express and communicate ideas in written form. We are all accustomed to looking at dance and asking such questions as: What is going on in this dance? What choices did the choreographer make? How are the elements in the dance woven together to create a meaningful whole? What is the world created here into which I enter? Applying this same critical (and aesthetic) analysis process to the scholarly writings of other researchers is an excellent way to develop an understanding of how different researchers approach their work. It helps the student identify styles of writing, modes of communication, and research agendas with which she or he may have a particular affinity. It also provides the student with comparisons for assessing the effectiveness of his or her own work and helps in developing the confidence to make critical and defensible judgments about the literature related to the research.

Jacqueline Fawcett and Florence Downs, in their book *The Relationship of Theory and Research,* upon which several of the ideas in this chapter are based, present a five-step theory analysis or theory substruction process that is helpful in understanding how theories are constructed.[27] Below is a summary of this framework and key questions to ask at each step of the analysis:

Step 1. *Identify the concepts used in the theory.*
Are all concepts given equal emphasis or is there a hierarchy of importance?

Step 2. *Determine how the author defined the concepts within the context of the theory.*

Are definitions used consistently throughout the development of the theory?

Step 3. *Identify the statements that lead to the development of the theory.*
Is there adequate support for these statements and how was data used to support the claims?

Step 4. *Analyze the line of argumentation or progression of ideas leading to the theory.*
Was the research inductive or deductive?
Did the author develop the ideas in the article using inductive, deductive reasoning, or did you discern another form of reasoning?

Step 5. *Diagram the theory.*
Are you able to discern how the parts of the theory work together?
What does the theory say and what does it not say?
Are there gaps or overlapping ideas in the theory?

Writing for the discipline of nursing, their work has a decidedly empiricist perspective; however, the analytical framework is applicable to all types of theory analysis, including philosophical discourse. Few, if any, theory articles fit neatly into the categories of Fawcett and Downs's theory analysis framework; however, with careful critical reading one can uncover the concepts, definitions, and propositions that make up a theory, as well as hone in on the essential relationships that make up the substructure of the theory.

Joann McNamara in her dissertation, "From Dance to Text and Back to Dance: A Hermeneutics of Dance Interpretive Discourse," provides another useful strategy for analyzing dance writing.[28] Her focus is not on the analysis of theory, but rather on how dance writers negotiate meaning in their written discourse about dance. McNamara applies her framework not only to the study of the texts of seven well-known dance writers but also to what these authors say about their writing process and their perceptions of dance. A description of hermeneutic inquiry, the research methodology used in this metacritical study of dance writing, is presented in chapter 6 of this volume. Of particular interest here, however, is the framework of analysis that McNamara designed. It provides another way of coming to know and understand the writings of others and how a writer's personal perspective influences and undergirds the theory she or he develops. McNamara's text analysis framework suggests the following questions:

- What approach to the analysis of dance does the writer use?
- What questions are raised by this approach?
- How is this approach manifested in the text?
- How does the writer make sense of the performing body/movement, space, and dynamics?

• How does the writer function as an interpreter of the dance about which she or he is writing?

Models as an Aid to Theory Building

The process of analyzing and interpreting data with a view to building theory requires the researcher to work with a vast amount of often complex and multidimensional ideas. One of the fundamental tasks involved in the construction of theory is determining how these ideas might be connected, related, integrated, or overlapping, as well as how they might represent discrete phenomena. Models can be an effective way to help researchers see relationships as well as discover new ways to think about the themes, ideas, and conclusions resulting from the research process. As Sue Stinson points out:

> A theoretical framework is about relationships—what is the relationship between ideas and concepts, between the parts of a whole? If this sounds like choreography, concerned with the relationship between movements and dancers, that is the way I think about it. In fact, theory is not about words. Einstein (cited in North, 1973) said that, for him, visual and kinesthetic images came first; the words of a theory came later. I often tell my students, in relation to theory, "If you can't draw it or make a three-dimensional model of it or dance it, you probably don't understand it."[29]

A model is a structure, usually visual but sometimes literary or mathematical, that represents ideas. The model as a visualization of our analytical and creative thought processes can serve several purposes for the researcher. The model organizes phenomena. It may take the form of categories, hierarchies, inventories, or flowcharts representing how concepts are grouped together, ordered by importance, or interconnected. A model might also be designed as a schemata to show how activities or events occur over time, either sequentially or simultaneously.

Models also function to analyze and synthesize data or ideas. Often it is necessary to dissect the whole in order to understand how each part contributes to creating the unity of the theory. The pitfall most of us encounter when using this analytic strategy is creating the impression that the parts function independently of the whole, or that the concepts represent discrete phenomena functioning with little or no overlap, integration, or fluidity among the ideas. By means of designing an organizational structure that is a visual whole, it is possible for the researcher to delineate and examine the concomitant parts of an emerging theory while maintaining a sense of how these parts are synthesized to form a unified conception.

Modeling as a process is also a useful tool for the researcher attempting to understand the inner workings of a theory that she or he may want to use as a theoretical base for his or her study. This is Step 5 of the Fawcett and Downs theory analysis process. Figure 3.1 presents Joann McNamara's model synthesizing the theoretical concepts of Gadamer and Heidegger related to how preunderstandings and prejudices influence interpretation. This analytical model enabled McNamara to understand how Gadamer's and Heidegger's theories were related and how each contributed to an understanding of the hermeneutic circle as a theoretical construct. These theories were integral to the development of the premise of McNamara's study, which argued the presence of the dance writer as interpreter. Her methodological approach to examining the role of interpretation in dance discourse, in turn, emerged from this hermeneutic phenomenological premise. The model assists both McNamara's and the reader's understanding of these complex ideas.[30]

Creating visual models of theories facilitates students' ability to critically analyze the literature that is integral to their research. The process of modeling the theory helps identify aspects of the theory that exceed the data, areas that seem to lack significance related to one's understanding of dance, and areas where the

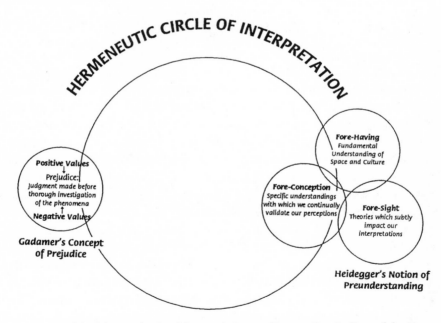

FIG. 3.1. Model of the synthesis of the preunderstandings and prejudices of the interpreter. From Joann McNamara, "From Dance to Text and Back to Dance: A Hermeneutics of Dance Interpretive Discourse" (Ph.D. diss., Texas Woman's University, 1994). Courtesy of Joann McNamara.

theory falls short with respect to clarity, internal consistency, and coherence. This information allows a researcher to decide whether or not, in his assessment, the theory has sufficient scholarly credibility or relevance to be used in the course of his research, as well as how it might be most effectively used to further the research purpose.

Inevitably researchers are faced with a plethora of data that they must, in some way, make sense of. Often the data analysis and interpretation stages of research can be overwhelming when one encounters enormous amounts of information, observations, and facts. Each mode of inquiry presented in this book suggests ways of handling data. While the historiographer may approach her or his theory development process differently than the ethnographer, all researchers share the same experience of having to order and shape the data as the avenue to discovering meaning and formulating a credible theory. Creating models during the research process as a means of identifying pervasive themes or categorizing observations helps to create some kind of order and organization. Some researchers use existing theoretical frameworks to analyze data. For example, Howard Gardner's theoretical model of multiple intelligences[31] might be used to analyze data in a pedagogical study. However, a cautionary note is warranted here. If one uses an a priori framework to analyze and interpret data, this framework must be an integral part of the purpose and problem of one's research and not an afterthought.

Other researchers allow the themes to emerge from the data and create models along the way. Eluza Santos developed a matrix (see figure 3.2) consisting of the recurring ideas and the voices of her participants in order to begin to make sense out of hours of interviews and weeks of observations. From this matrix she was able to see the patterns and relationships that eventually crystallized into pervasive themes. These themes became the core of her explanatory theory of how cultural voice is expressed and embodied in the contemporary dance of her native area of Vitória, Brazil.

Whether you choose to work with an a priori framework or develop your own, creating a visual model requires you to hone in on the salient features and key ideas contained in the data, and at the same time, makes it possible to develop and maintain a sense of how all of the elements contribute to the whole of the area you are studying. It can be both interesting and instructive for you to create several different models of analysis and interpretation as a way of bringing multiple perspectives to the theory-building process. This strategy typically helps researchers go beyond the preconceptions and assumptions that set up the disposition to see things in a certain way, preventing them from discovering new and imaginative answers to their questions. The key to successful modeling of data analysis and interpretation is to maintain the balance between letting it happen and mak-

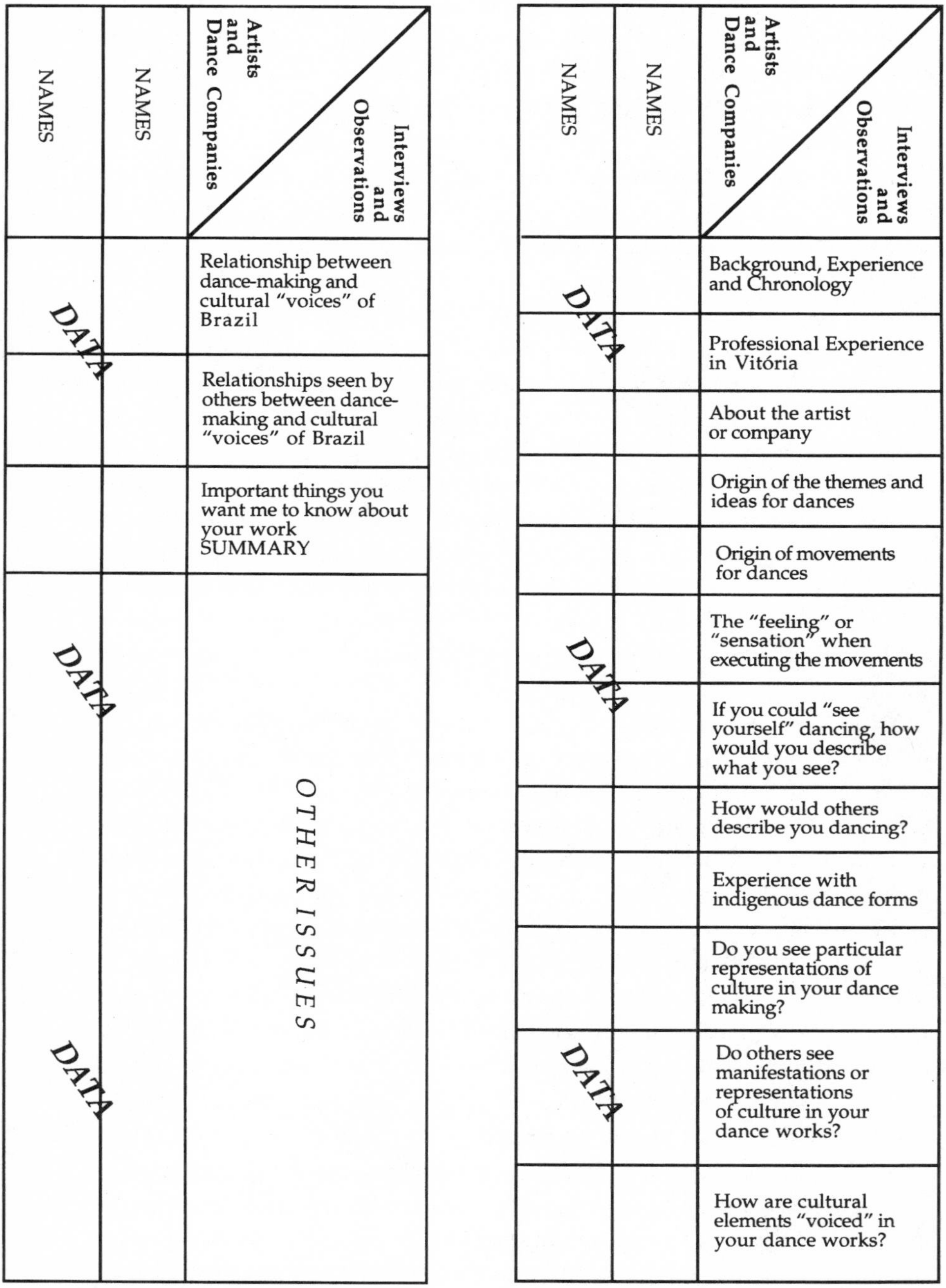

NAMES	NAMES	Artists and Dance Companies / Interviews and Observations
DATA		Relationship between dance-making and cultural "voices" of Brazil
		Relationships seen by others between dance-making and cultural "voices" of Brazil
		Important things you want me to know about your work SUMMARY
DATA		OTHER ISSUES
DATA		

NAMES	NAMES	Artists and Dance Companies / Interviews and Observations
DATA		Background, Experience and Chronology
		Professional Experience in Vitória
		About the artist or company
		Origin of the themes and ideas for dances
		Origin of movements for dances
DATA		The "feeling" or "sensation" when executing the movements
		If you could "see yourself" dancing, how would you describe what you see?
		How would others describe you dancing?
		Experience with indigenous dance forms
		Do you see particular representations of culture in your dance making?
DATA		Do others see manifestations or representations of culture in your dance works?
		How are cultural elements "voiced" in your dance works?

FIG. 3.2. Data analysis matrix. Courtesy of Eluza Santos.

ing it happen—knowing when it is appropriate to impose an order and structure on the data and when you should continue allowing the structure to evolve. As you study the several chapters focusing on the different approaches to research, consider how you might use modeling relative to the particular perspective inherent in each of the modes of inquiry presented in this text.

Models as Metaphors

Models can also function as visual or literary metaphors by providing an implicit comparison or analogy between two or more seemingly unrelated ideas or areas. By transferring meaning from a familiar concept or area of inquiry to one of less familiarity the metaphor can result in a relationship of new understanding. Metaphors and theories have in common the task of organizing our thinking by drawing comparisons between what we might understand in one area and a construct that we are attempting to explain in another.[32] For example, the "rope of dance knowledge" embodies an understanding of concepts being braided together rather than existing as separate strands of knowing; a "web of ideas" suggests a mental image of connectedness; and "convergent streams of life experiences"[33] creates an image of past and present coming together.

Although some writers sharpen the distinction between a model and a theory, Kliebard, within the context of developing curriculum theory, views theory and model as more or less interchangeable concepts. "Metaphors that evolve into models and theories serve not only to direct research by creating a symbolic language that provides the framework for the collection and interpretation of data, but as a way of isolating a dimension of the question to be explained that is not visible without the aid of the metaphor."[34]

One application of this model-as-metaphor strategy is to use an existing theoretical model as an organizational visual analogy to express how ideas should be understood. (See figure 3.3.) Such an approach was useful to Christina Hong-Joe in representing her theory of how knowing (content concepts) and doing (modes of inquiry) should be inextricably linked in the dance curriculum.[35]

Dance processes and life processes are closely analogous and can be mutually supportive. Metaphorically, just as movement . . . is a common denominator in life so deoxyribonucleic acid (DNA), on the microcosmic and cellular level is the genetic material common to all living organisms. . . . The content concepts and modes of inquiry . . . are therefore analogous to the representative structure of the DNA molecule with its twin strands organized in the form of a double helix. In the models the twin strands, representative of the modes of inquiry and the content concepts, spiral infinitely within the context of the dance which remains

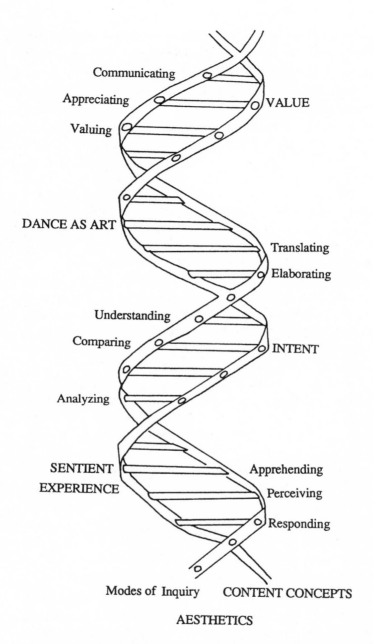

Communicating

Appreciating

Valuing

VALUE

DANCE AS ART

Translating

Elaborating

Understanding

Comparing

INTENT

Analyzing

SENTIENT
EXPERIENCE

Apprehending

Perceiving

Responding

Modes of Inquiry   CONTENT CONCEPTS

AESTHETICS

FIG. 3.3. DNA metaphor curriculum model of the interweaving of knowing and doing in the area of dance aesthetics. From Christina Hong-Joe, "Discipline-Based Dance Education: A Translation and Interpretation of Discipline-Based Art Education for the Discipline of Dance" (master's thesis, Texas Woman's University, 1991). Courtesy of Christina Hong-Joe.

central to the experience. Each strand reinforces and informs the other, which in turn strengthens and informs the total discipline.[36]

Another application of the model-as-metaphor approach is to use theories and models from an area in which there is an extensive body of literature to formulate research questions or hypotheses about an area of inquiry about which little is known. For example, the philosophical study of what constitutes and influences style in dance is an area receiving limited scholarly investigation. However, this is not the case in music and the visual arts where the subject of style has been extensively pursued from a variety of perspectives. A careful examination of the literature on the subject of style in music and visual art has the potential to yield theoretical models that define, analyze, and identify factors that influence how others determine and name style. These models, although related to art forms with characteristics different from dance, may serve to inform a parallel study of style in our field.

It is important to point out here that the transference of knowledge via the model-as-metaphor approach can be tenuous. The metaphor (such as in the case of Hong's DNA-inspired model) and the parallels between two areas of study (such as style in visual art and dance) must be very carefully and thoughtfully examined for logical consistency. It is the responsibility of the researcher to convincingly argue these relationships or connections so that the reader understands the origin, translation, and transformation of the ideas. Without such careful analysis it is likely that the research will be fraught with misrepresentations and misinterpretations.

If you choose to use this strategy, your analysis should include placing the theory from the better-known area into a direct correspondence with your area of study in order to demonstrate that both share sufficient commonalities and adequate or compatible structures to warrant the transference of knowledge from one area to the other. At the same time, you should take care not to ignore the differences but rather, account for these deviations. Frequently, the differences between areas of study can be more instructive than the apparent commonalities. These differences can heighten our understanding of what distinguishes the area we are investigating. For instance, accounting for the fact that dance is a mediated art form unfolding over time and visual art primarily a nonmediated art form captured in time brings into sharp relief issues of temporality, the performance process, the role of the performer, and the ephemeral or impermanent nature of dance. Furthermore, any choices that you make about the use of theoretical models should be guided by the nature of the data and your interpretation of it. Imposing an incompatible framework is likely to result in a theory that cannot absorb or explain fully all that is uncovered. Forcing the data into an artificial theoretical scheme, in the end, will create an artificial theory.

The bridging of areas of inquiry using theoretical models to develop new theories is often the culmination of the research investigation. However, a researcher can use the model-as-metaphor strategy to develop what might be called a model-in-progress. In this sense, the model serves as a way to identify, organize, and define phenomena that should be studied in the investigation. The concepts or elements that make up this model-in-progress function as analytical and logical building blocks to form a framework for further theorizing. This is an approach to research developed by Elizabeth Steiner known as the "theory models approach."[37]

Theory Models Approach

Many of my students have found the theory models approach, sometimes referred to as theory derivation,[38] useful in helping them shape frameworks for the study of their particular areas of interest. Frequently these students are working in areas where there has been little, in any, previous inquiry, and they find themselves faced with the challenge of not only designing a way to study the area but determining what constitutes the area as well as discovering what should be studied. Developing theory models is a way of looking at a research question from a particular vantage point. This vantage point reflects the researcher's personal perspective on dance and related areas, her or his scholarly interests, and how she or he chooses to make sense of and understand the area of inquiry.

The usual method of formulating theory, Steiner argues, follows the logical inferential thinking process of inductive and deductive reasoning. Steiner suggests a third form of reasoning for the theory models approach that she identifies as "retroductive" inference. If we recall that *deduction* is an inference by reasoning from the general to the specific and *induction* from the particular to the general, then retroduction—related to retrospective—is inferential reasoning, not necessarily from things past, but from things already in existence. In other words, retroduction is the originating of ideas, concepts, hypotheses, and theories from *other* concepts and theories. Derivation is the avenue to originating ideas. Retroduction derives theoretical frameworks from other theories and uses existing theories "to support lines of thought worthy of explanation and testing."[39]

In her article on mentoring, Kelley Pierce-Byrd argued that the all too prevalent noninterference in the careers of emerging professionals, often identified as "benign neglect"—doing no harm but also doing no good—is far from benign.[40] She adapted a systems model from the health professions to examine the lack of mentoring as promoting malignancy and mitigating against the "well-being" of junior faculty (see figure 3.4).

In a malignant condition a unit becomes dysfunctional due to the disease process, and due to the interrelatedness of all of the systems, the disease affects all other units. . . . The end result is a sickness of the whole organism. . . . It therefore becomes clear that to ignore a young faculty member's deficiencies and inexperience (benign neglect), to deny him/her mentoring, is to place him/her in danger of failure.[41]

The use of the health systems model helped Byrd formulate an understanding of mentoring junior dance faculty as an investment in promoting the whole well-being of the faculty member within her or his institution. This use of the theory models approach allowed Byrd to clarify her perspective on mentoring and led her to identify the aspects that she wanted to examine further, that is, understanding the academic setting, developing social and interpersonal interactions, managing outside stressors, and achieving self-actualization. In her research process she moved from her initial one-dimensional understanding of mentoring to a conceptualization of mentoring as an interactive and dynamic process focused on facilitating professional "well-being."

J. A. Lazarus's dissertation, "Contemporary Dance and a Feminist Aesthetic," is an excellent example of the theory models approach on a much larger and more complex scale.[42] She aligns, integrates, and overlaps theoretical models from feminist theory, dance anthropology, creative process, and new age physics to form a framework integrating futuristic analogs and the concepts of diversity inherent in feminist pedagogy. The several theory models developed in the study provide the analytical structure for Lazarus to create her own theory of a feminist aesthetic for contemporary dance. Throughout her dissertation Lazarus uses visual models to organize and interrelate complex ideas derived from these several areas of study. These models provide the reader with meaningful frameworks to follow Lazarus's intricate and imaginative argument that leads to and supports her theory.

Lazarus's research, and others using the theory models approach, are predicated on the assumption that if things are alike in some respects, they will be alike in others. This analogical thinking can be fruitful in constructing models to facilitate the generation of theory. Unlike the theory that eventually emerges from the research (Lazarus's theory of a feminist aesthetic for contemporary dance), the theory model is a theory *for*, rather than a theory *of*. This distinction is an important one if you intend to use this approach for your research. Steiner emphasizes that a theory *of* explains and describes phenomena whereas a theory *for* is a framework of ideas to be included in a theory explaining or describing phenomena. In other words, the theory model is a framework for the study of a particular area. Figure 3.5 presents the framework I used for the study of the choreographic process, which facilitated the development of my explanatory theory of dance

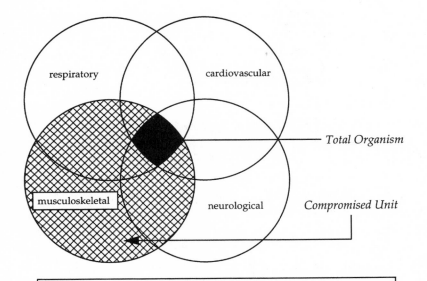

respiratory

cardiovascular

Total Organism

musculoskeletal

neurological

Compromised Unit

If the systems model is applied to the career of a young professional in higher education it might appear as follows:

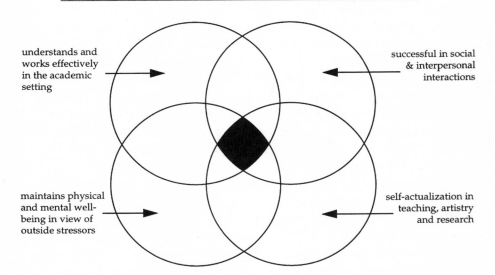

understands and works effectively in the academic setting

successful in social & interpersonal interactions

maintains physical and mental well-being in view of outside stressors

self-actualization in teaching, artistry and research

FIG. 3.4. Use of a systems model of the factors affecting an individual's state of health to understand aspects of the well-being of junior dance faculty. From Kelley Pierce-Byrd, "Benign Neglect: Issues in Mentoring," in *Dance in Higher Education,* ed. Wendy Oliver (Reston, Va.: American Alliance for Health, Physical Education, Recreation and Dance Publications, 1992). Courtesy of Kelley Pierce-Byrd.

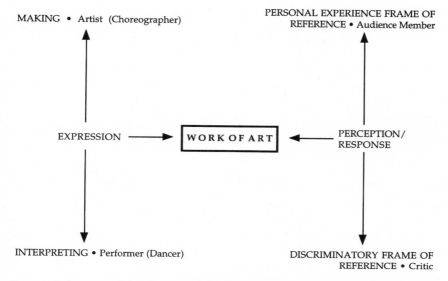

MAKING • Artist (Choreographer)

PERSONAL EXPERIENCE FRAME OF REFERENCE • Audience Member

EXPRESSION ⟶ **WORK OF ART** ⟵ PERCEPTION/RESPONSE

INTERPRETING • Performer (Dancer)

DISCRIMINATORY FRAME OF REFERENCE • Critic

FIG. 3.5. A theory model of framework for the study of the choreographic process. From Penelope Hanstein, "On the Nature of Art Making in Dance: An Artistic Process Skills Model for the Teaching of Choreography" (Ph.D. dissertation, Ohio State University, 1986).

making. This theory model or framework that guided my study resulted from an interdisciplinary research endeavor that led me to source theories that addressed the arts and art education in holistic, interactive, and dynamic ways.[43]

Returning to our discussion above about the importance of carefully examining commonalities and differences among areas when attempting to transfer concepts, the issue of consistency is particularly relevant to the theory models approach. In addition to identifying what characteristics are similar and dissimilar, it is important, according to Steiner, to also consider the qualitative compatibility of a source theory with regard to how the ideas that make up the theory are inherently structured. For instance, if the focus of the research is on understanding phenomena that are by nature linear and sequential and the parts seem to be of greater importance than the unified whole, the source theory or theories and the theory model should possess a similar qualitative character. Such a mechanistic view, not particularly prevalent in the study of dance, suggests the need for a model that is machinelike in character, one in which the parts "act in predetermined ways to bring about certain effects."[44]

Much more common in our attempts to understand dance is a perspective that recognizes the complex, nonlinear, multidimensional, and interactive nature of many of the areas of inquiry pursued by researchers in the field. Research

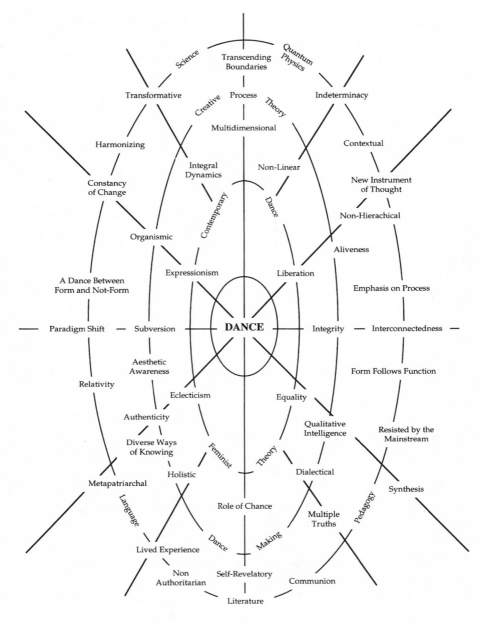

FIG. 3.6. Organismic model of a feminist aesthetic for contemporary dance. From J. A. Abbiechild Lazarus, "Contemporary Dance and a Feminist Aesthetic" (Ph.D. diss., Texas Woman's University, 1987). Courtesy of J. A. Lazarus.

problems emerging from this holistic view, according to Steiner, require models that are capable of representing the organismic nature of ideas. The selection of source theories and the design of theory models are guided by the understanding that "an organism is a structural whole, i.e., one in which the content and the form of its parts are determined by its function."[45] Organismic models allow for the representation of organized complexity by accounting for the understanding that the parts do not have fixed and separate actions but rather, "act interdependently to maintain function, and thereby wholeness. The parts do not simply combine and then determine what the whole is to be. The content and form of the parts change relative to the whole. Therefore, in an organismic state of affairs the emphasis is on the whole . . . taken as determining its parts."[46]

Throughout her dissertation, Lazarus uses the metaphor of the web to express the organismic nature of her study and its underlying assumptions of wholeness, interrelatedness, transcendence of dichotomies, and attention to process. Her explanatory theory of a feminist aesthetic for contemporary dance (figure 3.6) "conveys a web of ideological connections derived through an anthropological, historical, philosophical and theoretical analysis of the creative process of contemporary dance making and feminist theory."[47]

Conclusion

Although Steiner is referring specifically to the selection of source theories and the development of theory models, these ideas about the qualitative nature of areas of study are relevant to the theory-building process in general. It is easy to become so mired in the minutiae of data, the specificity of research methodologies and procedures, and the intricacies of theory building that we lose sight of the aesthetics of the research enterprise. On the one hand our research endeavors should be guided by a commitment to the tenets of systematic inquiry and intellectual rigor, which include careful attention to detail and organization. Yet on the other hand, our quest for new knowledge must be shaped by how we come to know, understand, and appreciate the unique features of our areas of inquiry. The discovery and creation of new knowledge is the pursuit of truth and meaning and this pursuit is fundamentally guided by how we experience and interpret the world.

Theory Analysis Study Projects

ANALYZING CONCEPTS

Select an article of interest and read the article carefully. Develop a list of concepts used by the author and note how each is defined and used within the text.

- Are these concepts and definitions common to the discipline of dance?
- Are they concepts derived from other disciplines?
- Are the definitions ones that might be generally understood or are they defined in very specific ways relative to the context of this particular research?
- Is there consistency in the way these concepts and their definitions are used throughout the article?

IDENTIFYING CONCEPTUAL BUILDING BLOCKS

Using the same or a different article, analyze how the author builds her or his theory.

- What are the conceptual building blocks that make up the theory?
- How has the author chosen to relate these conceptual building blocks to create a theory that is cohesive and unified? How do the parts make up the whole?
- How does the author support her or his claims? What data is used to substantiate the theoretical building blocks, the relationship of these concepts, and the theory itself? Is the theory consistent with the available evidence or does it exceed the evidence?

ANALYZING THEORY GENERATION

Select and carefully read a scholarly research article that uses a mode of inquiry consistent with your research interests. Using Fawcett and Downs's *Five Step Process for Theory Analysis*, analyze the article. After you have completed the analysis make a list of what you have learned about theory-generating research and how these insights (both positive and negative) might inform your own research and writing.

DESIGNING A THEORY MODEL

Design a theory "for" the study of a particular area of inquiry. Be sure that you have done sufficient reading to have a breadth of understanding of the field and the related fields relative to this area of research interest. If you have developed purpose and problem statements and conducted an extensive review of the literature you should have adequate background to proceed with developing a theory model. Use a diagrammatic representation to present the clusters of ideas and the relationships that make up your area of inquiry.

EVALUATING YOUR THEORY MODEL

- Does your theory model possess adequate complexity to account for the multidimensional aspects of your area of inquiry?

- Is the model cohesive and does it possess an internal logic that allows it to function as a whole?
- Is the fundamental premise of the model consistent with the nature of your inquiry? If you are using ideas from other disciplines, what is the justification for their relevancy to dance, in general, and your area of inquiry specifically? Simply, does the theory model make sense?
- What biases and assumptions are inherent in your theory model and what value and knowledge claims does it make?

NOTES

1. Cynthia Novack, "Looking at Movement as Culture: Contact Improvisation to Disco," *Theatre Drama Review* 32, no. 4 (1988): 102–19.

2. Tom Welsh, Sally Fitt, and Wendy Thompson, "A Comparison of Forward and Backward Chaining Strategies for Teaching Dance Movement Sequences," *Impulse: Journal of Dance Medicine, Science and Education* 2, no. 4 (1994): 262–74.

3. Ibid., 270.

4. This discussion of the role and function of theory in dance research is based on the work of Jacqueline Fawcett and Florence Downs, which provides an informative and detailed explication of the development, analysis, and evaluation of theory in nursing. Jacqueline Fawcett and Florence Downs, *The Relationship of Theory and Research* (Philadelphia: F. A. Davis Company, 1992).

5. Christine Loken-Kim and Juliette T. Crump, "Qualitative Change in Performances of Two Generations of Korean Dancers," *Dance Research Journal* 25, no. 2 (1993): 13–20.

6. Ibid., 13.

7. Ibid., 19.

8. Marc Strauss, "Assimilating Afterimages: Towards an Aesthetic Framework for Dance Based on Arlene Croce's *New Yorker* Essays (1973–1987)" (Ph.D. dissertation, Texas Woman's University, 1996).

9. Ibid., vii.

10. Ibid., 153.

11. Jessica Wood, "Dancing for Life: The Sunrise Dance of the White Mountain Apache" (Ph.D. dissertation, Texas Woman's University, 1996).

12. Joan Laage, "Embodying the Spirit: The Significance of the Body in the Contemporary Japanese Dance Movement of Butoh" (Ph.D. dissertation, Texas Woman's University, 1993).

13. Karen Bond, "Personal Style as a Mediator of Engagement in Dance: Watching Terpsichore Rise," *Dance Research Journal* 26, no. 1 (1994): 15–26.

14. Ibid., 15.

15. Ibid.

16. Lorraine Olszewski Walker and Kay Coalson Avant, *Strategies for Theory Construction in Nursing* (Norwalk: Appleton-Century-Crofts, 1988), 20.

17. Novack, 102–19.

18. Ibid., 103.

19. Ibid., 107.

20. Elliot Eisner uses Nelson Goodman's concept of "rightness" (*Ways of Worldmaking* [Indianapolis: Hackett Publishing Company, Inc., 1978]) as a criterion for assessing the

credibility of transactive accounts—the believability of what we see, understand, and present in a qualitative narrative. "Rightness" related to qualitative research is concerned with whether the depiction or exemplification (statements made by the researcher) represents credible conclusions and interpretations within the framework the researcher chooses to use. For a useful discussion of the features of believability (coherence, consensus, and instrumental utility) relative to qualitative narratives, see Elliot Eisner, *The Enlightened Eye: Qualitative Inquiry and the Enhancement of Educational Practice* (New York: Macmillan, 1991), chapter 3.

21. Fawcett and Downs, 24–25.

22. Novack, 104.

23. Ibid., 111.

24. Walker and Avant, 5.

25. Novack, 106.

26. Ibid., 109.

27. Fawcett and Downs.

28. Joann McNamara, "From Dance to Text and Back to Dance: A Hermeneutics of Dance Interpretive Discourse" (Ph.D. dissertation, Texas Woman's University, 1994).

29. Susan Stinson, *NDA Scholar's Lecture: Research as Choreography* (Reston, Va.: American Alliance for Health, Physical Education, Recreation, and Dance Publications, 1994), 12.

30. McNamara.

31. Howard Gardner, *Frames of Mind: The Theory of Multiple Intelligences* (New York: Basic Books, 1983).

32. H. M. Kliebard, "Curriculum Theory as Metaphor," *Theory Into Practice* 21, no. 1 (1982): 11–17.

33. Margery B. Franklin, "A Convergence of Streams: Dramatic Change in the Artistic Work of Melissa Zink," in *Creative People at Work: Twelve Cognitive Studies,* ed. Doris B. Wallace and Howard E. Gruber (New York: Oxford University Press, 1989), 255–77.

34. Kliebard, 17.

35. Christina Hong-Joe, "Discipline-Based Dance Education: A Translation and Interpretation of Discipline-Based Art Education for the Discipline of Dance" (master's thesis, Texas Woman's University, 1991).

36. Ibid., 27.

37. Elizabeth Steiner, *Logical and Conceptual Analytic Techniques for Educational Researchers* (Washington, D.C.: University Press of America, 1978).

38. Walker and Avant.

39. Steiner, 9.

40. Kelley Pierce-Byrd, "Benign Neglect: Issues in Mentoring," in *Dance in Higher Education,* ed. Wendy Oliver (Reston, Va.: American Alliance for Health, Physical Education, Recreation and Dance Publications, 1992), 118–23.

41. Ibid., 120.

42. J. A. Abbiechild Lazarus, "Contemporary Dance and a Feminist Aesthetic" (Ph.D. dissertation, Texas Woman's University, 1987).

43. Penelope Hanstein, "On the Nature of Art Making in Dance: An Artistic Process Skills Model for the Teaching of Choreography" (Ph.D. dissertation, Ohio State University, 1986).

44. Steiner, 22.

45. Ibid., 23.

46. Ibid.

47. Lazarus, 165.

REFERENCES

Bond, Karen. "Personal Style as a Mediator of Engagement in Dance: Watching Terpsichore Rise." *Dance Research Journal* 26, no. 1 (1994): 15–26.

Eisner, Elliot. *The Enlightened Eye: Qualitative Inquiry and the Enhancement of Educational Practice.* New York: Macmillan, 1991.

Fawcett, Jacqueline, and Florence Downs. *The Relationship of Theory and Research.* Philadelphia: F. A. Davis Company, 1992.

Franklin, Margery B. "A Convergence of Streams: Dramatic Change in the Artistic Work of Melissa Zink." *In Creative People at Work: Twelve Cognitive Studies,* ed. Doris B. Wallace and Howard E. Gruber, 255–77. New York: Oxford University Press, 1989.

Gardner, Howard. *Frames of Mind: The Theory of Multiple Intelligences.* New York: Basic Books, 1983.

Goodman, Nelson. *Ways of Worldmaking.* Indianapolis: Hackett Publishing Company, Inc., 1978.

Hanstein, Penelope. "On the Nature of Art Making in Dance: An Artistic Process Skills Model for the Teaching of Choreography." Ph.D. dissertation, Ohio State University, 1986.

Hong-Joe, Christina. "Discipline-Based Dance Education: A Translation and Interpretation of Discipline-Based Art Education for the Discipline of Dance." Master's thesis, Texas Woman's University, 1991.

Hyerle, David. *Visual Tools for Constructing Knowledge.* Alexandria: Association for Supervision and Curriculum Development, 1996.

Kliebard, H. M. "Curriculum Theory as Metaphor." *Theory Into Practice* 21, no. 1 (1982): 11–17.

Laage, Joan. "Embodying the Spirit: The Significance of the Body in the Contemporary Japanese Dance Movement of Butoh." Ph.D. dissertation, Texas Woman's University, 1993.

Lazarus, J. A. Abbiechild. "Contemporary Dance and a Feminist Aesthetic." Ph.D. dissertation, Texas Woman's University, 1987.

Loken-Kim, Christine, and Juliette T. Crump. "Qualitative Change in Performances of Two Generations of Korean Dancers." *Dance Research Journal* 25, no. 2 (1993), 13–20.

McNamara, Joann. "From Dance to Text and Back to Dance: A Hermeneutics of Dance Interpretive Discourse." Ph.D. dissertation, Texas Woman's University, 1994.

Novack, Cynthia. "Looking at Movement as Culture: Contact Improvisation to Disco." *Theatre Drama Review* 32, no. 4 (1988): 102–19.

Pierce-Byrd, Kelley. "Benign Neglect: Issues in Mentoring." In *Dance in Higher Education,* ed. Wendy Oliver, 118–23. Reston, Va.: American Alliance for Health, Physical Education, Recreation and Dance Publications, 1992.

Steiner, Elizabeth. *Logical and Conceptual Analytic Techniques for Educational Researchers.* Washington, D.C.: University Press of America, Inc., 1978.

Stinson, Susan. *NDA Scholar's Lecture: Research as Choreography.* Reston, Va.: American Alliance for Health, Physical Education, Recreation and Dance Publications, 1994.

Strauss, Marc. "Assimilating Afterimages: Towards an Aesthetic Framework for Dance Based on Arlene Croce's *New Yorker* Essays (1973–1987)." Ph.D. dissertation, Texas Woman's University, 1996.

Walker, Lorraine Olszewski, and Kay Coalson Avant. *Strategies for Theory Construction in Nursing.* Norwalk, Conn.: Appleton-Century-Crofts, 1988.

Welsh, Tom, Sally Fitt, and Wendy Thompson. "A Comparison of Forward and Backward Chaining Strategies for Teaching Dance Movement Sequences." *Impulse: Journal of Dance Medicine, Science and Education* 2, no. 4 (1994): 262–74.

Wood, Jessica. "Dancing for Life: The Sunrise Dance of the White Mountain Apache." Ph.D. dissertation, Texas Woman's University, 1996.

PART TWO

MODES OF INQUIRY AND
DANCE RESEARCH METHODS

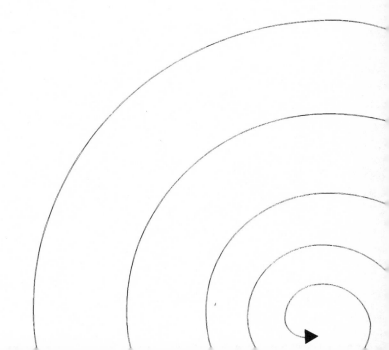

4 POSTPOSITIVIST RESEARCH IN DANCE

Jill Green and Susan W. Stinson

OFTEN, WHEN PEOPLE THINK of research, they think of the tradition of the natural sciences that began during the Enlightenment: an attempt to go beyond the word of God, tradition, folklore, and other nonempirical sources of knowledge. Scientific research is based on an assumption that the world is a predictable place, if only we can determine the laws by which it operates. Most of us were introduced to the guidelines of such research in secondary school, and they were elaborated in each science course from then on, as well as in most graduate research courses. We learned that good science is objective, value-free, and subject to verification by others. We learned how to operationally define terms so we could quantify that which we wanted to study, how to develop and test a hypothesis, how to select a sample and generalize our findings to the population from which it was drawn, and how to avoid as much error and bias as possible. Such research is used to answer some important questions, particularly related to physiological aspects of dance training; for example, questions like what traditional dance practices are highly correlated with dance injuries.[1]

The social sciences arrived later on the scene of modern research and, seeking legitimacy, adopted the orientation of hard science; the extension of scientific methods to the study of human beings is referred to as *positivism*.[2] Education, with even greater need for legitimacy considering its status as *applied* social science, fervently followed the guidelines of positivist research for a number of years. Dance education researchers, too, have sought status by following the paradigms of those researchers with the most prestige in academe; Bresler[3] reports that the same was true in early decades of music education research.

More recently, however, researchers in education as well as other social sciences have been using additional methodological approaches. They have identified a number of limits to traditional scientific research when applied to studying persons and have drawn from the arts and humanities as well as science in developing new forms of research with different assumptions about reality and knowledge.[4] Among these approaches to inquiry we find such labels as phenomenological, hermeneutic, interpretive, feminist, qualitative, naturalistic, autobiographical, narrative, ethnographic, postmodern, and others. As is the case with most language that is attempting to describe that which is still emerging, these words often have different meaning to different individuals.

We appreciate Locke's description of what he termed qualitative research, as being in a state of "zesty disarray."[5] This description reflects the absence of clear boundaries between the different types of methodologies that are being constructed, and the absence of hard and fast rules like those that have guided traditional scientific researchers. We use the term *postpositivist* as an umbrella term to describe the variety of approaches to research that have arisen in response to a recognition of the limitations of the positivist tradition in research.[6]

Postpositivist Inquiry

The multiplicity of terms and meanings that characterize the postpositivist approach makes it difficult to discuss and describe. However, some scholars strive to conceptualize various aspects of this general research approach and identify how it moves beyond traditional positivist science.

For example, Patti Lather, an educational theorist, discusses postpositivist research in her book, *Getting Smart: Feminist Research and Pedagogy With/in the Postmodern*.[7] Lather agrees with John Caputo that we are approaching a "postparadigmatic diaspora,"[8] a time when specific and rigid paradigms are problematic. She problematizes the term *paradigm* as a rigid conceptualization but uses it as a transition toward a more human science that does not neatly segregate paradigms or pose one against another.[9]

With this in mind, Lather presents a flexibly conceived framework for postpositivist inquiry (see table 4.1). This framework encompasses four categories

TABLE 4.1. Postpositivist Inquiry

Predict	Understand	Emancipate	Deconstruct
positivism	interpretive	critical	poststructural
	naturalistic	neo-Marxist	postmodern
	constructivist	feminist	post-paradigmatic
	phenomenological	praxis-oriented	diaspora
	hermeneutic	educative	
		Freirian	
		participatory	
		action research	

Source: Patti Lather, *Getting Smart: Feminist Research and Pedagogy With/in the Postmodern* (New York: Routledge, 1991), 7. Copyright © 1991. Reproduced by permission of the publisher.

according to their purposes: prediction, understanding, emancipation, and de-construction. Positivism is included in this framework. Although it differs from the other three postpositivist categories, it exists along with them.

Positivism and Postpositivism: Ontology and Epistemology

Inquiry focusing on understanding, emancipation, and deconstruction is significantly different from positivism in a number of ways, even though there are also differences among the postpositivist approaches. Most of the differences between positivist and postpositivist research have to do with two main concepts: ontology, or how we look at reality, and epistemology, or how we know.

Generally, positivists tend to claim that reality is found—that there is a real truth or big truth that we can know. Postpositivists, on the other hand, tend to believe that reality is socially constructed—that we construct reality according to how we are positioned in the world, and that how we see reality and truth is related to the perspective from which we are looking.[10]

Epistemologically, positivists tend to assert that we can *know* a "true" reality and by using "objective" research methods, we can uncover the "truth." In contrast, many postpositivist researchers[11] reject the claim that research can be value-free or that one sole truth can be found through objective research methods. Furthermore, some postpositivists[12] believe that subjectivity is not only unavoidable but may even be helpful in giving researchers and participants a more meaningful understanding of people and research themes. In accepting a socially constructed reality, we realize that our belief systems, or the stories we tell of who we are, may not be consistent and reliable in the positivist sense, because they vary each time we tell them. Consequently, reliability, while a basic tenet of empirical scientific research, is regarded by qualitative researchers as a concept equally as impossible as objectivity.

Rather than uncovering reliable facts or finding true measurable data, the postpositivist researcher self-consciously selects among a reservoir of possible data and seeks to determine what seems important or significant in relation to the research context. The postpositivist theorist is seeking coherence of a statement more than correspondence to an external reality. Coherence refers to "the unity, consistency and internal logic of a statement."[13] In other words, the researcher's selections are based at least in part on what seems to "fit" in this particular piece of work; this means that the choices are, at least in part, aesthetic ones. This is one reason why many researchers who do this kind of work experience it as a kind of art making.[14]

Positivism and Postpositivism: Methodological Differences

These differences in perspective and approach are also reflected in methodology. Positivist research attempts to prove or disprove a hypothesis, while postpositivist research attempts to interpret or understand a particular research context. Some postpositivist approaches (emancipatory and deconstructionist) actually strive to challenge a dominant social reality or create social change through the research process. While positivist methods strive to predict outcomes and determine measurable truths that can be generalized universally to every comparable context, postpositivist methods usually seek multiple perspectives and meanings.

Rather than starting with a hypothesis, postpositivist researchers tend to first ask broader questions such as "What is going on here, from the perspective of the persons having this experience? What does it mean to them? How does it come to have that meaning? What do their experiences, their meanings, mean to me as researcher? How do they come to have this meaning?" Sometimes research questions may be more specific, such as "How do students learn in a dance class?" They pursue such questions through a variety of methods, including but not limited to observation, participant observation, document analysis, and interviewing. Because the interpretations the researcher is seeking are constantly being constructed and reconstructed, short-answer questionnaires and surveys are not usually very useful. For this type of work, extended, open-ended interviews are often more helpful. This allows the subject to put his or her own frame around the experience, and the researcher can pursue each individual's emerging thought as it unfolds. The time required for this process, and the quantity of material generated, tends to limit the number of subjects that can be included. This is not considered problematic since the findings will not be generalized to a larger population.

In comparison with positivist researchers, there is less of a tendency to enter the research project with a particular theory, even though some postpositivist researchers may begin the study with clear theoretical leanings. Sometimes, having such an a priori theory may lead to inquiry.[15] Whether or not the researcher begins with an a priori theoretical stance, there is usually an attempt at theory building.[16]

Another characteristic of much postpositivist research is the emergent nature of the research design. Since many postpositivists charge that we construct reality according to our social and cultural experiences, the researcher cannot know what constructions will be introduced during the investigation and cannot predict beforehand what claims, concerns, and issues will arise. Lincoln and Guba, two main proponents of what they initially termed "naturalistic inquiry" and what they later referred to as "fourth generation evaluation," claim that

> designs must be emergent because the existence of multiple realities constrains the development of a design based only on one (the investigator's) construction; because what will be learned at a site is always dependent on the interaction between the investigator and context, and the interaction is also not fully predictable; and because the nature of mutual shapings cannot be known until witnessed.[17]

Thus, while general procedures for data collection and analysis may provide parameters and a general guide for the study, many of the "rules" must be created as the researcher goes along, in the context of this *particular* piece of research. In this sense, the researcher shares much in common with the choreographer, remaining open to emerging patterns and meanings and to forms that are appropriate for them.

The Research Report

Just as in the case of the choreographer, the postpositivist researcher allows the form of the final product to arise from the process. Consequently, the data collected and the report that ultimately results from postpositivist inquiry look quite different from traditional scientific data and reports.

Many postpositivists[18] argue that the act of writing up data for *any* kind of research necessarily involves the process of interpretation, based on social constructions and the writer's preconceived assumptions about what it means to do research. Richardson[19] claims that all writing is inscribed by our values and reflects metaphors that we use to communicate how we see the world. Even "science writing" is not excluded; it uses certain conventions that express knowledge as being problem centered and linear, even though it is displayed through a narrative form. Since writing is inscribed by our experiences and constructions, no data can be neutral. Therefore, according to this perspective, it is effective to make one's subjectivity visible and display how one's voice as researcher enters the text.

It is helpful to think about all research reports as a kind of storytelling. Even though most scholarly texts rely heavily on quantifiable data, they are telling what John Van Maanen[20] has named "realist tales." Realist tales employ the convention of the third person, taking the "I" out of the report in order to establish authority. According to Richardson,[21] when the researcher's presence is not visible, the myth of objectivity is maintained.

Although most conventional research accounts tell realist tales, there is a broad body of postpositivist literature[22] that attempts to recognize the researcher's presence and bring a sense of reflexivity to the process of writing up data. These accounts allow writers to reflect on their own perspectives and thus recognize how they are subjectively inscribed by their experiences and cultures. They attempt to include "multiple voices" in order to display the various positions and perspectives of the researcher and participants. Often experimental narrative forms are used as a vehicle to provide a voice to those participants who may ordinarily be unheard.[23]

The kinds of forms that may result from this process include storytelling, autobiographical accounts, split-page formats,[24] and narratives that reflect particular postpositivist leanings.[25] Furthermore, the presence of multiple voices may be projected through the juxtapositions of artwork, poems, journal entries, and other written expressions. Artistic expressions may help to display participant voices and give shape to the lived experiences of the participants.[26] In this way, the research becomes a kind of expressive art form, one which can be quite compatible with many research questions in dance.

Validity

One final difference between positivist and postpositivist research has to do with the concept of validity. Kvale[27] claims that validity concerns how we justify our claims to knowledge. Therefore, criteria for validity must adequately reflect the ontological and epistemological perspectives of the researcher.

Because postpositivist researchers and theorists do not attempt to generalize data, they have searched for a broader concept of validity that does not attempt to determine whether a knowledge statement corresponds to the objective world. There is a greater emphasis on finding consensus within a particular setting than on generalizing data to all situations. For this reason, while positivist methodology requires a random sample as a validity measure and a large sample to ensure generalization, postpositivist methodology requires neither. The researcher is interested in investigating a specific context and may use particular small group samples. Different validity measures emerge that reflect postpositivist tenets. The following discussion relates to several criteria for validity proposed by Kvale.[28]

Kvale notes that validation is about investigation, rather than measurement or generalization. As a method of investigation, validation becomes a way of checking. Kvale suggests Miles and Huberman's[29] twelve tactics for testing and confirming postpositivist research findings as a way of checking sources of potential bias that may invalidate qualitative observations and interpretations.[30]

To validate is also to question, to continually ask what is being investigated and why. Although a statement may not be factually true, the researcher may be interested in the participant's perception of that truth. In this context, the participant's statement would be valid.

Theorizing, as an outcome of postpositivist investigation, is also connected to validity. For Kvale, validation "leads to theoretical and philosophical questioning of the nature of the phenomena investigated."[31] He claims,

> The complexities of validating qualitative research need not be due to a weakness of qualitative methods, but, on the contrary, may rest upon their extraordinary power to reflect and conceptualize the nature of the phenomenon investigated, to capture the complexity of the social reality. The validation of qualitative research becomes intrinsically linked to the development of a theory of social reality.[32]

Validity in postpositivist research, therefore, is theory-related; investigating the truth of an interpretation depends upon how the researcher perceives the phenomenon studied.

Postpositivist research also regards evidence of self-reflexivity as a validity criterion. Self-reflexivity may be facilitated through a reflexive journal, which helps to sort out personal reflections and methodological choices,[33] as well as other reflective instruments. Kvale also calls for the testing of the validity of knowledge claims in dialogue, through what he calls "a community of scholars"; Lincoln and Guba refer to this as "peer debriefing."[34] The sharing of data and findings with colleagues who are familiar with the content of one's work as well as postpositivist methodology may bring authority to the research. Outsiders may also provide feedback about methods, practices, and findings.

Finally, there is "pragmatic validity," or how the investigation produces action for change or can be "used to improve the conditions studied."[35] Lather refers to this as "catalytic validity"; it requires that an investigation take action to produce desired results.[36] Although this might not be an appropriate criterion for interpretive approaches, it is particularly significant for emancipatory approaches that seek to make societal changes. Another way to think about pragmatic validity is whether or not the research is useful to readers—does it help them recognize more or understand differently than they did prior to reading the work?

Thus, postpositivist methodology and validity criteria are different because they are based on different perspectives of reality and knowledge. In this context, positivism is not truer, more correct, or more valid than postpositivism, but rather *different*. Neither is necessarily more valid or more correct.

Limitations of Postpositivist Inquiry

The differences between positivist and postpositivist inquiry surface through Lather's framework. Of course there are limitations to any classification system, including postpositivist models. While Lather's framework is flexibly conceived, the naming of categories may limit the movement between them. In our postmodern world, there is much movement between the categories and overlap of ideas and theories between the categories. Therefore it is ineffective to view these classifications as rigidly constructed and simplistic. For example, much feminist research crosses the categories of "understand," "emancipate," and "deconstruct."

Another limitation is raised by Robert Donmoyer, a curriculum theorist and art educator, who points out that raising differences in ontology and epistemology make it more difficult for the kinds of research we are discussing to be accepted in a positivist academic world. He suggests that we define our methodology not by ontology and epistemology, but by the kinds of questions we are asking. He describes two different methodological approaches, which he names science-based and humanities-based. While scientific research is trying to answer questions of truth, humanities-based research is concerned with questions of meaning. The goal of the latter is not to accept or reject a hypothesis, but to develop a language that can reveal some dimensions of the subject under study. Languages are neither true nor false, but each has the capacity to be useful to us because different languages allow us to "both see different things and see things differently."[37]

Still other researchers who reject traditional ways of studying people's experiences and the meanings they make from them have different ways of conceptualizing those differences; we note again the "zesty disarray" that characterizes what we are referring to as postpositivist research. Nevertheless, for purposes of clarity we now return to Lather's framework, to explore differences among the postpositivist paradigmatic conceptualizations she defines. We discuss these in the order in which they have arisen; one should not assume that this order reflects ascending or descending value.

Applications to Dance Research: A Scenario

In this section we discuss three different approaches to postpositivist research, following Lather's conceptualization: research directed toward *understanding,* research directed toward *emancipation,* and research directed toward *deconstruction.* Within each of these categories, we discuss major guidelines, strengths, and weaknesses. We also present a scenario for research that might be attempted by researchers from each of the three traditions. The setting for the research is a university-level modern dance technique class.

By way of comparison, it might be helpful to first speculate how a researcher from the positivist tradition might approach this situation. As with the other scenarios we present, this represents only one possibility for a researcher from this tradition. We have chosen to describe a classical scientific methodology for the positivist example. This positivist researcher, like the other three researchers we introduce, would spend time observing classes in the studio. One major difference from the other research approaches we discuss is that this positivist researcher uses a hypothesis to guide observation and data collection. For example, the researcher might be interested in what factors are responsible for student improvement in technique classes. S/he[38] would develop a hypothesis focusing on each factor suspected to be responsible for student improvement, and then test the hypothesis by gathering data to see if the hypothesis can be supported. One hypothesis might be, "Students who receive more corrections from an instructor will improve more than students who receive fewer corrections." The researcher would operationally define key terms, such as *correction* (which might be defined as a verbal comment regarding the correct performance of movement directed to one or more individuals and that may or may not be accompanied by a touch or a demonstration) and *improve* (which might be defined by a grade change in a positive direction given by the regular instructor or, alternatively, might be determined by a trained panel of judges scoring videotaped class performances). The researcher would collect data from a relatively large number of different technique classes, of different levels and at different institutions, and would randomly select students within each class to observe. The larger the number of observations, and the more the students in the sample resembled the total population of university dance students, the more generalizable would be the findings. A study based on only one technique class at one university would probably be considered a pilot study, done to develop the research procedures for a more extensive study.

The researcher would examine the data to see if there was any correlation between the number of corrections given to individuals and the improvement they demonstrated and would determine whether to accept the hypothesis (as true) or reject it (as false). The findings could be neatly summarized in a table.

In the next three sections of this chapter, we look at how three other researchers with very different goals might conduct and present their research.

The Interpretive Researcher

Interpretive researchers studying educational settings often think of themselves as ethnographers,[39] using a variety of methods to collect material that might be used in the interpretative analysis.[40] These include observation, interviews, and the collection of any other materials that might be made available; a study may include some quantitative data (how many students, their ages, gender, race, etc.), but qualitative material is generally the most productive for interpretation. Ordinarily the study will last for some period of time, involving weekly or even daily visits to the class for the length of the course.

One of the most challenging issues facing the interpretive researcher is the role s/he will play in the class. Some interpretive researchers choose to keep their research role hidden, such as when an individual who is a student in the class also becomes a researcher without letting other participants in the class know.[41] Such secrecy may raise ethical issues if individuals share confidential thoughts without being aware of how they might be used. While we consider ethical issues to be a significant objection to secrecy, we also note that there are many situations in which it is not possible to conceal one's identity as a researcher (for example, when a fifty-year-old researcher is interested in studying a technique class of twenty-year-olds).

Assuming her/his identity is known, the interpretive researcher must choose whether to participate in the class,[42] to sit and watch,[43] or to combine these.[44] There are advantages and disadvantages to each of these choices. Participant observation allows the researcher to fully experience the movement being taught, to have more intimate interaction with other students, and to be less obvious as an outsider, creating a greater degree of comfort for the participants. For example, the researcher in the dressing room seems less like an outsider if s/he is also changing clothes, rather than just observing the students and overhearing conversations. Further, the researcher who observes or overhears student conversations about breaking rules (such as "no eating in the dressing room") can cultivate a great deal of trust among students by not revealing this privileged information to those in charge.

Another issue that can arise during participant observation in a technique class has to do with the technical skill level of the researcher in comparison to that of students in the class. For example, a researcher who is less skilled technically than the students may not earn their respect; a researcher who displays considerably more skill may be viewed as "showing off," and may be shunned as much as a student in a similar position. There is also the issue of how the instructor will respond to the researcher's presence in class—whether or not corrections will be given as they are to other students, whether or not the researcher will be used to demonstrate, and so on. Each of these choices affects the relationships between participants and researcher.

Occasionally an interpretive researcher will decide to conduct a study within a class he or she is teaching. Again, there are advantages and disadvantages. The researcher who is already a part of the educational structure will not have to struggle to gain access to students and times to observe. Some students may be more open to the instructor than to an outside researcher and thus willing to share, for example, very personal material from a journal kept for the class. Other students may be more guarded; for example, they may not be willing to share negative impressions about the class with a teacher who is also assigning grades.

During the time of observation or participation-observation, the researcher will keep copious field notes, recording what the instructor says/does and what the students say/do, as well as other details such as a description of the setting, even the temperature and lighting—anything that seems important. Certainly selectivity is involved in this, and the researcher will not remember every detail when recording the notes. Some researchers[45] may use video recordings of classes so that more extensive analysis, including Labanalysis, may be done.

Extensive autobiographical reflection may be a major part of interpretive research.[46] Even without explicit autobiographical work, the researcher's personal responses become part of the field notes; interpretation does not wait until all the material has been collected but begins right away. At the same time, the researcher tries to avoid premature conclusions that might get in the way of emerging issues; for example, the researcher who immediately concludes that males in the class are treated as privileged might not recognize that the same kind of attention goes to female students who are aggressive in seeking the teacher's attention. Nevertheless, the interpretations that the researcher makes during the project do guide the development of the design. For example, identification of questions or issues might determine whether or when the researcher interviews the participants, what questions to ask, and whether the interviews should be done with individuals or groups.

Interviewing is very common in interpretive research, and sometimes it is the only source for collecting material. However, it does not typically follow the model of the detached interviewer asking the same questions in the same order for each individual.[47] Some researchers[48] even interview participants as a group. Even when interviews are conducted individually, questions are not necessarily asked in the same way of each participant; often the questions themselves vary.

After asking for some basic identifying information (how long the individual has been studying dance, styles of dance studied, and so on), the researcher usually begins with open-ended questions that will allow individuals to place their own frames around the experience. (For example, "Talk to me about why you dance," rather than "Do you prefer modern dance or ballet?") This means that the participant has a chance to define what is meaningful or important about the dance experience, rather than simply responding to what the researcher feels is important. The researcher might ask the instructor to describe ways the class is like and different from other dance classes or other similar experiences; s/he might ask students how the instructor is like and different from others. Students might also be asked how they would describe the class to someone not in it, or to select and describe one or more key incidents in the class. Some participants might bring up issues that others will be asked about in their interviews. In future interviews, the researcher might then check out whether the issues s/he perceived in the class are issues for the other participants. For example, a researcher might not have observed any racial tension in a class, but if one or two students bring it up, the researcher might ask other students about it as well.

Listening is one of the most important skills for the interpretive researcher. Many people in an interview setting give only brief mention of an issue until they know that the interviewer is interested. Thus the researcher will often end up responding, "Tell me more about what it's like when you perform," or "Can you tell me more about what it's like to be on the front row?"

Interviews are tape-recorded, and sometimes recorded on video.[49] The interviews are transcribed before analysis. Often, researchers return transcripts to the participants prior to analysis, giving an opportunity to clarify, change, or delete material.

Other materials may also be gathered for analysis. For example, the instructor may be willing to share the course outline or syllabus, assignments, and other handouts. Occasionally it is possible to have access to student journals or other forms of written work.

In positivist research, relationships with participants are thought to generate "bias"; in interpretive research, they are viewed as essential, despite their limitations.[50] To begin with, relationships are a pragmatic necessity. The instructor is the gatekeeper of the class and the researcher is dependent upon the instructor for access. Similarly, students will not share their thoughts with a researcher unless they feel safe. For example, if students perceive the researcher is closely allied with the instructor, they may hesitate to make comments they perceive as critical of the instructor. However, once the researcher has a relationship with students and instructor, it can get in the way of taking a critical perspective in the analysis. The researcher may find that the participants in the class feel more like friends after dancing with them and listening to them, and she may avoid interpretations that seem to cast them in a negative light. Further, relationships may pose dilemmas, if the researcher discovers illegal or unethical activities. For example, a researcher might discover that an instructor gives higher grades to students who provide personal services like baby-sitting; the researcher must decide whether to mention this in an article that will be read by the administration.

Once all material has been gathered, more formal analysis begins. This task sometimes feels overwhelming, simply because there is so much material, and it requires multiple readings, multiple viewings.[51] Eventually the researcher begins to identify patterns, themes, or metaphors within the material. For example, the researcher might conclude that the university technique class is serving to determine the "survival of the fittest," a way to justify "weeding out" those students who do not fit the department's conception of the ideal dancer, despite promotional language that proclaims "anyone can dance." Another study (or another interpreter) might observe that a primary theme of student experience is transcendence of everyday reality. Sometimes a researcher might identify themes that seem conflicting or paradoxical. For example, a researcher might identify a theme of intense concern with physical appearance along with a theme of kinesthetic awareness. In each case, the final research report must document a convincing basis for the researcher's interpretation—not that it is the *only* possible interpretation, but that it is a reasonable one.

While the analysis is the most challenging part of the research process, it is also the most creative. The researcher is essentially making a construction from the raw materials present, much like a choreographer creates a dance from movement material.

Throughout this process, the researcher is engaged in theorizing, in making relationships between what is perceived to be going on within the technique class and issues within the social-cultural world of which the dance class is a part. For example, the researcher may identify social issues such as gender, race, or social class; questions about different pedagogical approaches; or conflicts between different visions of what is considered beautiful or even correct. For example, after determining that the technique class is serving to eliminate students who do not fit the department's aesthetic, the researcher might discuss who decides what a dancer should look like, and how the image of the ideal dancer changes across cultures as well as historically within the same culture. In the final research document, these points will be reinforced by connections to relevant literature in or outside of dance.

It should be emphasized, however, that not all interpretive research includes this kind of analysis.[52] Some interpretive researchers attempt to limit their work to description, with as little interpretation as possible. Interpretive work with a great deal of critical interpretation and social analysis moves closer to the next category, emancipatory research.

Interpretive research is most helpful in allowing us to understand how participants in dance are making sense of their experiences, whether in taking class, teaching, performing, rehearsing, choreographing, attending a concert, or any other involvement in dance. It can give a voice to the otherwise silent participants in dance and allow those in decision-making positions to understand more about what is happening for their students, dancers, and colleagues, and thus help them make more sensitive decisions. The researcher must constantly keep in mind that the voices of the other participants are heard only through that of the researcher, who makes selections from among all of the material gathered and determines what will be used.

Interpretive research can also become problematic if the researcher or the readers of the research forget that this interpretation is only one out of an indefinite number that are possible. The interpretation offered by the researcher can give readers an opportunity to reflect, to pay attention to what they might otherwise miss in their own teaching settings, but it cannot be used to predict what issues might be identified in other classes or by other researchers.

In interpretive research, all interpretations that can be supported are valued. Because, as previously discussed, relationships with participants can make it difficult to draw conclusions that may be viewed as criticism, interpretive research may be less likely to result in a critical perspective. Without such a perspective of what may be problematic about dance, there is a danger of only reinforcing the status quo. The next research approach we discuss emphasizes the critical perspective.

The Emancipatory Researcher

An emancipatory researcher, like other researchers, would spend time observing classes in the studio. One major difference from the other research approaches is that the emancipatory researcher purposely becomes aware of social and political power issues that emerge from the research. The emancipatory researcher brings a critical perspective to the research, including issues such as race, gender, or class. Often, the investigation is part of a social advocacy project; there is an attempt to change participants and society.

Most emancipatory research reflects critical social theory. Critical theory generally calls for individual freedom and social and economic justice. It rejects inequality, the oppression of disenfranchised groups, the silencing of marginalized voices, and authoritarian social structures. Lather points out that emancipatory researchers and their texts "assume underlying determining structures for how power shapes the social world. Such structures are posited as largely invisible to common sense ways of meaning but visible to those who probe below hegemonic meaning systems to produce counter-hegemonic knowledge, knowledge intended to challenge dominant meaning systems."[53]

An emancipatory researcher would bring this perspective into the study. For example, while observing a university dance technique class, the researcher might look at how power is played out in the dance class or how specific groups are marginalized (that is, where gender bias, racism, sizism, elitism, etc., exist). The researcher might first notice that, for example, in a hypothetical class of all women students with a male instructor, larger women are continually scolded by the teacher for moving sloppily. The researcher might observe that these students are also told that they must go on diets or their grades will suffer. Emerging research questions might begin to address such issues as power in the technique class, body ideals, abuse, and trained bodily behaviors.

Through an emergent research design, after these observations are made, the researcher might decide to interview the students. Since standardization is not a requirement in postpositivist research, the researcher might ask different questions of each of the marginalized students, such as how they feel about being asked to go on a diet and whether or not they feel this is appropriate to their goals of dance. Questions might be asked in relationship to feelings about ideal weight and appearance in dance class and how this reflects attitudes of society in general. The goal is not just to understand students' ideas, but to help them reflect and ultimately change.[54]

The researcher might also conduct a group interview with the intention of informing students about ways women can be marginalized through objectification of their bodies in society as a whole, and a discussion might ensue. This is another way that the researcher or teacher in a class situation might attempt to create awareness and change through the research process.

Next, the researcher might ask the students to write journal entries or even possibly create a dance in order to express their feelings and the changes that have taken place regarding their ideas before they entered the project and at the end of the project. The researcher would record the changes and attempt to interpret the data by identifying and analyzing themes.

The researcher might also decide to interview the teacher to find out more about the teacher's attitudes toward the student dancers and might, for example, explore his own dance training and education as an effect of a patriarchal system of education that strives to create ideal bodies and ways of bodily being through an external mechanized perception of dance.

The final write-up would reflect this critical perspective. Written from a viewpoint of political change, the researcher might trace whether the participants were transformed through the research process and, if so, how. The narrative would reflect the researcher as social advocate in this process of change. It would also reflect how the participants moved from maintaining false consciousness[55] to an awareness of their oppression, through, for example, the adherence to an ideal body type and bodily presentation (a rigid upper body posture). In other words, false consciousness is the state whereby marginalized groups (according to economics, gender, race, etc.) learn to believe the messages taught to them in order to maintain a status quo. The critical pedagogue's job is to uncover hidden dominant meaning systems and teach marginalized groups to be conscious of their own disempowerment. However, it is significant that Lather also notes that framing a false consciousness also assumes a true consciousness on behalf of the researcher or teacher. In other words, critical theorists may tend to believe they know the "true reality" where other perspectives are "false." The researcher might also use participant responses and expressions to emphasize this change.

This scenario basically illustrates a typical critical research project. It is important to understand, however, that many critical research projects inherently are also pedagogical projects; the researcher is often also the teacher during the same project. In this case, the researcher might actually be the teacher and the resulting technique class would look much different since social change would be a particular goal of the class. However, in order to keep this scenario consistent with the other research scenarios, we assume that researcher and teacher are separate.

This scenario also reflects some strengths and weaknesses of this approach. Strengths, *depending on the reader's own perspective,* may include a commitment to social activism and the capability to critique and change social reality; "empowerment"[56] of marginalized groups; a more nuanced understanding of a sociopolitical research context;[57] and a more flexible research design.

Emancipatory research limitations are also related to a social advocacy agenda. Elizabeth Ellsworth problematizes the term *empowerment* and suggests that a demand for speaking may be as oppressive as a demand for silence.[58] Orner points out that we cannot simply label gender silences as resistance or false consciousness.[59] Lather argues, "We must be willing to learn from those who don't speak up in words. What are their silences telling us?"[60]

Consequently, emancipatory studies may be limited because they assume that any subjects are capable of "full consciousness,"[61] since all are shaped by culture. Lather points out that critical pedagogues have been criticized for assuming they have privileged knowledge free of false beliefs and for attempting to speak for others. In other words, critical theory and critical tales may profess foundational claims to help dominated groups understand the "true" nature of social reality. In this way, critical research is different than other postpositivist approaches. Where deconstructivist research, for example, professes the display of multiple voices or perspectives, critical research tends to subscribe to a "truer" or more "correct" nature of social reality. Thus, there is a significant moral dimension reflected in the goals of the project, research process, methods, and written report.

Furthermore, critical narrative may fall into the pitfall of creating a "binary logic" that "demonizes the 'Other' and positions itself as innocent."[62] It does not often address how the researcher can be oppressive or attempt to speak for the participants, nor does it address what the researcher may have overlooked.[63]

Moreover, like the realist tale of postpositivist research, critical narratives usually speak in an argumentative style and assume a rationalistic logic. While, on the one hand, they do provide an argument that is critical of dominant meaning systems, on the other hand, they do not challenge traditional forms or "the powers of the reasoning mind."[64] Thus, another limitation may be that emancipatory narratives, like realist tales, support a dualistic rationale and a privileging of mind over body and the rational over the emotional, intuitive, and expressive. While attempting to change dominant power structures, ironically they use a dominant form, particularly one that has been problematized by feminists and artists: rational thought.

Regardless of these potential dangers, emancipatory research may be used as a powerful approach; it is capable of changing people's lives and society. With a dimension of self-reflexivity to keep biases and agendas in check, it may help researchers to create pedagogical and sociopolitical change.

Dance theorists, researchers, and teachers tend to think of traditional dance classes as expressive and empowering. A critical approach may provide, for dance researchers, a system of inquiry that seeks to explore how we can change dance pedagogy rather than accept it blindly.

We have been unable to locate any published examples of pure emancipatory research in dance education, although there are some examples that include emancipatory dimensions. A dissertation by Suzanne Oliver[65] briefly describes research in which dance students participating in Alexander technique classes and dialoguing with the researcher developed a critical perspective about their dance training. In addition, there is some research and scholarly writing that focuses on emancipatory research in areas outside of dance or related to dance, while other studies that focus on dance have some dimensions of an emancipatory approach. For example, Sherry Taylor[66] uses an emancipatory research design with content focused on general pedagogy. Her later work (Shapiro)[67] describes her approach to choreography as critical praxis and emancipatory research. Jill Green[68] brings in sociopolitical and feminist elements and uses dimensions of emancipatory research and deconstructivist research designs with content focused on somatics and arts education. Donald Blumenfeld-Jones[69] also brings in sociopolitical and feminist elements to an analysis of significant texts on dance education grounded in critical theory. Susan Stinson[70] brings critical issues into an interpretive methodological research framework. Helen Thomas[71] uses an interpretive framework in the tradition of sociology with an analysis grounded in critical theory and feminist concerns. Isabel Marquez, having been involved in a historical moment in the application of emancipatory pedagogy in Brazilian schools, uses Freirian theory to look critically at dance education.[72]

Other examples of research with emancipatory dimensions may be found in dance ethnology, aesthetics, criticism, and historical studies. Gotfrit[73] and Roman[74] have conducted ethnographic research on women dancing in popular culture, with analysis grounded in critical theory. Cowan's ethnographic research[75] on dance events in northern Greece focuses the interpretation on the social construction of gender. Carol Martin[76] does cross-cultural analysis from a critical feminist perspective. Christy Adair's research[77] on women in dance brings together feminism, critical theory, issues of the body, and historical analysis from the point of view of gender. Susan Manning's research[78] analyzes Mary Wigman's work from feminist, critical, and historical perspectives. Cynthia Novack's[79] study of contact improvisation, while an anthropological analysis that would place it in the interpretive category, also brings sociopolitical issues into the analysis. Ann Daly's feminist research uses a critical writing style but with clear deconstructivist leanings.[80]

These are just some of the critical-related research projects relevant to this particular category. Once again, it is difficult to define rigidly because so many of these studies cross over into other related categories.

The Deconstructivist Researcher

Deconstructivist research is not really a method but more of a way of thinking,[81] often embodied through a literary form, that reflects postmodern thought. Postmodernism may be thought of in a number of ways. Some scholars refer to a postfoundational postmodern perspective that challenges theories that are reliant on the concept of universal truths; others speak more generally of living in a postmodern world of conflicting and competing ideas and worldviews. In other words, postmodernism may be thought of as a state of the world in which diverse ideas bump up against each other, or as a theoretical perspective itself. Lather's framework, as a whole, projects a sense of postmodern multiplicity, while the deconstructivist category specifically reflects postmodern thought.

In her review of postmodernism, Jane L. Parpart summarizes the main themes of postmodern thought through a discussion of such postmodernists as Lyotard, Foucault, and Derrida. Basically, she claims that postmodern thinkers have questioned assumptions of the modern age such as the belief that reason and scientific inquiry can provide an objective and universal foundation for knowledge. According to Parpart,

> The postmodernists challenge the notion that concepts such as knowledge, justice and beauty can be evaluated and established as universally correct. They argue that the hegemonic metanarratives [grand theory] of both Enlightenment and Marxist thought, rather than reflecting a universal reality, are embedded in the specific historical time and place in which they were created and are associated with certain political baggage. Rather than explain all reality, these metanarratives are privileged discourses that deny and silence competing discourses.[82]

While postmodernism professes a view that challenges assumptions of universality and dominant meaning systems, deconstructivist and poststructural research primarily demonstrate a discursive practice that displays privileged discourses and multiple realities through narrative literary forms. Often the silenced voices of marginalized and disenfranchised groups are juxtaposed against the researcher's authoritative voice.[83] All realities, including the author's written account, are admittedly partial and problematic. According to Lather, the goal of deconstruction

> is neither unitary wholeness nor dialectical resolution. The goal of deconstruction is to keep things in process, to disrupt, to keep the system in play, to set up procedures to continuously demystify the realities we create, and to fight the tendency for our categories to congeal.[84]

In other words, the deconstructivist researcher seeks ways to display multiple realities; as Lather notes, this is done "in order to juxtapose alternative representations and foreground the very constructed nature of our knowing."[85] Even the concept of lived experience, so prominent in interpretive research, is viewed as a construction dependent on who is doing the experiencing. Although some interpretive and emancipatory research may ultimately deconstruct dominant meaning systems, this is not usually the primary intent. However, such examples point out the problematic nature of categories.

Entering the dance research setting, the deconstructivist researcher looks for ways to break down the dominant meaning systems that have been absorbed in traditional dance classes and reflected in assumed ways of thinking about dance and dance education. In the aforementioned scenario with a male teacher and female students, the researcher might highlight, for example, how the teacher's training and teaching style reflect attitudes that have been constructed through the history of dance and dance pedagogy. The researcher might observe how the teacher perceives his role as authority figure, perhaps by demanding silence and attention to his own voice and prohibiting questions in class. The researcher might examine how the teacher's attitude, although rationalized through a desire to maintain classroom decorum and respect for the teacher as expert artist, affects the progress of dance students. The researcher might then look at the teacher's dance history and the influence of traditional dance training on his own style. Finally, the researcher might provide a historical deconstruction or historical analysis of power in dance training in the form of a series of case studies of dance teachers.

Like the classical critical researcher, postmodern researchers often enter the setting with a particular agenda. However, many deconstructivist and poststructural researchers believe that all types of research, even critical research, may be oppressive[86] and that researchers should strive to be reflective and deconstruct even their own agendas. All constructed realities are subject to deconstruction and no constructed realities are accepted as universally true. Furthermore, rather than advocate a particular type of social change, many deconstructivist researchers are more concerned with displaying a particular reality from a historical perspective, although many critical theorists are also moving toward this approach. However, due to the adherence to multiple perspectives, many deconstructionists do not advocate a particular moral agenda but use discourse as a tool to display power relations. Thus, where critical researchers often enter the setting with a strong moral agenda and an idea of "right" or "true," many more classic postmodernists see all realities as constructed and seek to disrupt a particular dominant reality by deconstructing it or displaying it in a historical context in order to turn it upside down.

This more classic literary deconstructivist researcher might not enter the technique class at all. S/he might be likely to use and deconstruct written sources from which specific attitudes about dance and dance education are based. Sources such as dance instructional texts, dance history books, dance teacher journals, and other texts and documents that exhibit particular attitudes about dance, dance etiquette, dance class rituals, and hidden rules regarding teacher-student behavior may be used to illustrate how teachers have traditionally been viewed in relationship to power and in power relationships with students. In order to describe traditional constructions of dance, the researcher might highlight how, for example, dance education may be viewed as an elitist system whereby groups of students (such as women and African Americans) are marginalized through the social construction of an ideal body model, a solely technical approach rather than a creative and expressive approach to dance pedagogy, and the concept of the dance teacher as an "all-knowing expert."

Some researchers who ride the line between critical and postmodern thought, including many feminists who consider themselves emancipatory theorists but move toward a postmodern realm, may actually enter the research setting as observer and participant.[87] In fact many "praxis"[88] oriented feminist researchers are finding themselves in the dual roles of teacher and researcher or collaborating with teachers as part of the research process. These researchers would also go into the classroom and, like interpretive and critical researchers, use such data-gathering methods as observation, interviews, and document analysis. However, the postmodern intent here is still to present the multiple perspectives of participants, to deconstruct accepted dance class norms, and to display dominant and silenced voices through a literary or artistic form. Moving beyond interpretive and critical research, they attempt to deconstruct a dominant social reality while they also focus on "the ways an intendedly liberatory pedagogy might function as part of the technology of surveillance and normalization."[89]

The written report is of particular significance to deconstructivist researchers. Some of these researchers are experimenting with new deconstructivist forms and literary styles that attempt to display multiple voices and look at what has been overlooked and absent in the production of meaning. They attempt to present multiple readings and meanings in order to fragment univocal authority, decenter[90] the writer, and interrupt totalizing claims to "know" reality.

In this scenario, the researcher-writer who does include interviews and journal entries might present a split-page format, whereby the page is divided into vertical thirds. Student voices (comments) might be displayed in the left-most column, the teacher voice in the middle column, and the research comments in the right-most column. In this way the writer would strive to present all viewpoints and not necessarily bring total authority to the researcher voice. This would purposely separate voices and interrupt the flow of the text so that the reader is not led to assume one reality. By highlighting the multiple perspectives of the participants through a physical and spatial split, the writer purposely does not make the narrative style neat and easy. By creating a juxtaposition of voices, the form functions to interrupt the authorial voice as well as the authoritarian voice. Other deconstructivist stylistic approaches may include telling multiple tales to reflect the interpretations of the participants; juxtaposing journal entries, poetry, artwork, or videotaped dances that provide expressions of the participants in artistic forms; or superimposing images and comments in a number of other creative ways. The infinite possibilities of writing text may in fact draw the researcher into a creative research process that reflects the creative processes of dance itself. For this reason, dance researchers may particularly be drawn to this approach.

There are some limitations to a deconstructivist research approach. One is that it may be difficult to capture the many perspectives of the participants, including their own multiple perspectives. Another criticism that has been levied against this approach is that it may collapse into relativism. In other words, if all reality is constructed, no reality can be "right" or "true" and it may make no difference what one thinks or feels. Values might be considered irrelevant. However, although critiquing postmodernism and its potential for relativism are currently popular among scholars in a variety of fields, many postmodern thinkers do not profess or stress radical relativism. There is often an attempt to be reflexive and acknowledge that postmodernism itself may be constructed. Further, there are postmodern thinkers who attempt to be responsible for social action while simultaneously maintaining a focus on the "uncertainty of a particular position." Many emancipatory researchers, for example, choose to struggle within a postmodern world of paradigmatic tension and multiple meanings, while still striving to make a difference.

It is difficult to find a purely deconstructivist research design in dance; this is not surprising since the number of dance researchers is relatively small and deconstructive research is a fairly new development. However, some dance researchers have used dimensions of the deconstructivist approach. Green[91] uses a deconstructivist approach in part of the write-up of data by including multiple voices and a split-page format. Marianne Goldberg deconstructs perceptions of the body in both Graham technique and ballet;[92] in the latter, she stylistically juxtaposes diverse types of writing in nonlinear forms. Jude Walton[93] discusses postmodern thought while using postmodern forms such as pastiche and poetic display. Sally Ann Ness's work in ethnography and cultural anthropology[94] has a reflexive and postmodern sensibility. Clyde Smith's research also brings a postmodern sensibility to critical and feminist analysis.[95] Cynthia Novack deconstructs ballet, in a sense, through personal memories about her life as a dancer and through an analysis of texts that focus on gender in the ballet world.[96] Donald Blumenfeld-Jones treats dance as a scholarly text. The performance is the postmodern interpretation of the study.[97]

Again, these are a few examples of the ways deconstructivist writings and themes emerge in dance and dance-related research. Much research in these areas crosses over categories and frameworks for research design, methodology, and theory.

Conclusions

It is apparent, then, that postpositivist research is not a monolith. Postpositivist researchers have disagreements with each other that can be at least as hearty as those they have with positivists. Further, as we have previously emphasized, the categories of postpositivist research are not fixed; new forms are continually evolving.[98] To a certain extent, each study is an original form, and each researcher creates the form to suit the content. Again, this makes categorizing methodologies particularly problematic.

Ultimately, the choice of methodology is based not only on philosophical beliefs about reality and knowledge, but also on personal preferences and on the aims and purposes of the research. Personal preferences are important because postpositivist research is a literary form, and the researcher who will engage in it must enjoy working with words; those who prefer numbers will ordinarily be happier in positivist research. Because words cannot be summarized or displayed as readily as numbers, research reports may be lengthy and difficult to summarize in the fifteen-to-twenty–minute time periods that limit most conference presentations.

Postpositivist research is also quite labor-intensive. While there are computer programs that can be used in interpretive research, we have found no substitute for multiple readings or viewings of lengthy material. If data need to be gathered quickly so that a project can be finished in a few months, postpositivist methods may not be appropriate.

In addition to philosophy and personal preferences, the purposes of the research provide an important guide in selecting methodology. If the researcher is interested in determining the most *effective* and *efficient* way to do anything in dance, such as teach, select dancers, or market a performance, and he or she wants to generate information that can be used to predict or affect outcomes, then the positivist approach is called for. If the primary purpose is to understand an aspect of the dance experience from the participants' points of view, and to reflect on the meanings that are expressed, then an interpretive approach will be most helpful. If the researcher wants not just to understand but also to change the participants' understanding, and to change the institutional or other structures in which the experience exists, then an emancipatory approach is needed. If the intent is to create multiple interpretations of some dimension of the dance experience or critique universal or grandiose meanings based on a dominant dance model, the researcher will be most likely to take a deconstructionist approach.

Finally, we must note that methodological decisions made ahead of time are not always followed as anticipated. Because postpositivist designs are emergent, what starts as one kind of study may transform into another. Certainly some institutional settings may limit some possibilities—for example, not all dance instructors would allow in their classes the kinds of studies discussed here. However, within such externally imposed limits, postpositivist researchers can claim their creative right to practice the art of research.

Study Questions

1. Review the strengths and limitations of each of the four approaches discussed in the chapter.

2. Select a scenario for research other than the one presented in this chapter. Discuss how a researcher from each of the four perspectives might go about doing research in this scenario.

3. Select a research approach discussed in the chapter. Provide a rationale for using this approach during a particular research scenario.

NOTES

Small portions of this chapter were previously published in *Impulse: The International Journal of Dance Science, Medicine and Education* 1, no. 1 (July 1993): 52–64, and in *Journal of Interdisciplinary Research in Physical Education* 1, no. 1 (1996): 43–54.

1. Because the assumptions underlying this research are quite different from those in traditional scientific research, we spend quite a bit of time discussing the theory underlying postpositivist research before we discuss its application to research in dance.

2. This term, coined by August Comte during the Enlightenment, originally referred to a philosophy that advocated that the logical, systematic study of science be applied to human affairs in order to better human lives (see Anthony Giddings, ed., *Positivism and Sociology* [London: Heinemann, 1974]). We acknowledge that the term *positivism* today has political connotations, if not derogatory ones. As philosopher of science Sandra Harding notes, "Opinions are divided about whether one should discuss the remnants of positivism under that name. Some natural scientists, many social scientists, but almost no philosophers of science will happily describe their own philosophy of science as positivist. Other observers are quite sure that no one at all is really a positivist any more, so to criticize positivism (or 'excessive empiricism,' as some of us have called it) is only to criticize straw figures" (Sandra Harding, *Whose Science? Whose Knowledge?* [Ithaca: Cornell University Press, 1991], 57–58). Despite the shortcomings of the term, we join many contemporary researchers in using it to discuss the limitations of traditional scientific research in the study of human beings because no other term has yet emerged.

3. Liora Bresler, "Qualitative Paradigms in Music Education Research," *The Quarterly Journal of Music Teaching and Learning* 3, no. 1 (spring 1992): 64–79.

4. Some researchers in the natural sciences too have been questioning these assumptions. See, for example, Sandra Harding, ed., *Sex and Scientific Inquiry* (Chicago: University of Chicago Press, 1987).

5. Lawrence F. Locke, "Qualitative Research as a Form of Scientific Inquiry in Sport and Physical Education," *Research Quarterly* 60 (March 1989): 1–20.

6. We recognize that the prefix *post* ordinarily is assumed to mean "after." Certainly the forms we discuss arose after positivism, but we do not wish to imply that positivism may be viewed in the past tense. To the contrary, it remains the dominant worldview for research. Many postpositivists do, however, cite the limitation of this paradigm.

7. Patti Lather, *Getting Smart: Feminist Research and Pedagogy With/in the Postmodern* (New York: Routledge, 1991).

8. Ibid., 108; citing John Caputo, *Radical Hermeneutics: Repetition, Deconstruction, and the Hermeneutic Project* (Bloomington: University of Indiana Press, 1987), 262.

9. Ibid., 107.

10. There are differences among postpositivists, too, on this matter, which we will discuss later.

11. Norman K. Denzin, *The Research Act: A Theoretical Introduction to Sociological Methods* (Englewood Cliffs, N.J.: Prentice Hall, 1989); Elliot W. Eisner, "Objectivity and Subjectivity in Qualitative Research and Evaluation," in *Qualitative Studies in Education,* ed. Elliot W. Eisner and Alan M. Peshkin (New York: Teachers College Press, 1989), 15–16; Patti Lather, "Research as Praxis," *Harvard Educational Review* 56 (August 1986): 257–77; Yvonna S. Lincoln and Egon G. Guba, *Naturalistic Inquiry* (Beverly Hills: Sage, 1985); Peter McLaren, *Life in Schools: An Introduction to Critical Pedagogy in the Foundations of Education* (New York: Longman, 1989); Joyce McCarl Nielsen, *Feminist Research Methods: Exemplary Readings in the Social Sciences* (Boulder: Westview Press, 1990).

12. David M. Fetterman, *Ethnography Step by Step* (Newbury Park, Calif.: Sage, 1989); Steinar Kvale, "The Qualitative Research Interview: A Phenomenological and Hermeneutical Mode of Understanding," *Journal of Phenomenological Psychology* 14 (fall 1983): 171–96; Patricia Maguire, *Doing Participatory Research: A Feminist Approach* (Amherst, Mass.: Center for International Education, 1987).

13. Steinar Kvale, "To Validate Is to Question," in *Issues of Validity in Qualitative Research,* ed. Steinar Kvale (Sweden: Student Literature, 1989), 75.

14. Jill Green, "Fostering Creativity Through Movement and Body Awareness Practices: A Postpositivist Investigation Into the Relationship Between Somatics and the Creative Process" (Ph.D. diss., Ohio State University, 1993); Susan W. Stinson, *Research as Choreography,* National Dance Association Scholar Lecture (Reston, Va.: National Dance Association, 1994).

15. Denzin.

16. See Anselm L. Strauss and Juliet Corbin, *Basics of Qualitative Research: Grounded Theory Procedures and Techniques* (Newburry Park, Calif.: Sage, 1990), for their concept of grounded theory building.

17. Lincoln and Guba, 208.

18. Charles Bazerman, "Codifying the Social Scientific Style: The *APA Publication Manual* as a Behaviorist Rhetoric," in *The Rhetoric of the Human Sciences,* ed. John Nelson (Madison: University of Wisconsin Press, 1987), 125–44; Patti Lather, "Deconstructing/ Deconstructive Inquiry: The Politics of Knowing and Being Known," *Educational Theory* 41 (spring 1991): 199–208; Laurel Richardson, "The Collective Story: Postmodernism and the Writing of Sociology," *Sociological Focus* 21 (1988): 199–208; Laurel Richardson, *Writing Strategies: Reaching Diverse Audiences,* Qualitative Research Methods Series 21 (Newburry Park, Calif.: Sage, 1990); Dan Rose, *Living the Ethnographic Life* (Newburry Park, Calif.: Sage, 1990); John Van Maanen, *Tales of the Field* (Chicago: University of Chicago Press,

1988); Harry F. Wolcott, *Writing Up Qualitative Research*, Qualitative Research Methods Series 20 (Newburry Park, Calif.: Sage, 1990).

19. Richardson, *Writing Strategies*.

20. Van Maanen.

21. Richardson, "Collective Story."

22. Lather, "Deconstructing/Deconstructive"; Magda Lewis and R. Simon, "A Discourse Not Intended for Her," *Harvard Educational Review* 56 (November 1986): 457–72; Richardson, "Collective Story"; Richardson, *Writing Strategies;* Rose; Wolcott.

23. Lather, "Deconstructing/Deconstructive"; Patti Lather, "Staying Dumb?: Feminist Research and Methodology With/in the Postmodern" (paper presented at the Beyond Ideology Critique Conference, Temple University, Philadelphia, April 1991); Richardson, *Writing Strategies;* Lewis and Simon; Daphne Patai, "Constructing a Self: A Brazilian Life Story," *Feminist Studies* 14 (spring 1988): 143–66.

24. See explanation of split-page formats in section on Deconstructive Research.

25. These include what Lather calls deconstructionist and reflexive tales. These tales tend to break down a particular theoretical stance in order to disrupt the authority and assumptions of a dominant paradigm.

26. Max Van Manen, *Researching Lived Experience: Human Science for an Action Sensitive Pedagogy* (New York: State University of New York Press, 1990).

27. Kvale, "To Validate."

28. Ibid.

29. Matthew Miles and Michael Huberman, *Qualitative Data Analysis: A Sourcebook of New Methods* (Beverly Hills: Sage, 1984), cited in Kvale, "To Validate," 78.

30. Due to limitations of space, we will not discuss these strategies here but strongly suggest that the prospective postpositivist researcher be familiar with them before entering the research setting.

31. Kvale, "To Validate," 81.

32. Ibid., 82–83.

33. Robert C. Bogdan and Sari Knopp Biklen, *Qualitative Research for Education: An Introduction to Theory and Methods* (Boston: Allyn and Bacon, 1982), 87.

34. Lincoln and Guba, 308–309.

35. Kvale, "To Validate," 87–89.

36. Patti Lather, "Issues of Validity in Openly Ideological Research: Between a Rock and a Soft Place," *Interchange* 17 (winter 1986): 63–84.

37. Robert Donmoyer, "Distinguishing Between Scientific and Humanities-Based Approaches to Qualitative Research" (paper presented at American Education Research Association annual meeting, Chicago, 1985), 4, photocopied.

38. This designation is often used in poststructuralist research to deconstruct gender conceptualization.

39. While anthropologists originated ethnographic study, variations of their methods have been used for many years by researchers in other fields, especially education, who recognize their focus of study is, in effect, its own subculture and they are outsiders. Dance ethnographers have completed a number of studies that are listed in Judith A. Gray, ed., *Research in Dance IV: 1900–1990* (Reston, Va.: National Dance Association, 1992).

40. Such material would be referred to as "data" in positivist research; no substitute has yet gained acceptance in postpositivist research.

41. See, for example, Judith Alter, "A Field Study of an Advanced Dance Class in a Private Studio Setting," *Dance Studies* 10 (1986): 49–97 (Les Bois, St. Peter, Jersey, Channel Islands, Britain: Center for Dance Studies).

42. See, for example, Susan W. Stinson, "A Place Called Dance in School: Reflecting on What the Students Say," *Impulse: The International Journal of Dance Science, Medicine and Education* 1 (October 1993): 90–114.

43. See, for example, Susan W. Stinson, Donald Blumenfeld-Jones, and Jan Van Dyke, "Voices of Young Women Dance Students: An Interpretive Study of Meaning in Dance," *Dance Research Journal* 22 (fall 1990): 13–22.

44. Some researchers who are studying a less discrete setting (such as all dance classes within one institution) do no direct observation.

45. See, for example, Green; also Karen Bond, "Dance for Children with Dual Sensory Impairments" (Ph.D. diss., La Trobe University, Melbourne, Victoria, Australia, 1992); Helen Thomas, ed., *Dance, Gender and Culture* (New York: St. Martin's Press, 1993).

46. See, for example, Donald Blumenfeld-Jones, "Body, Pleasure, Language and World: A Framework for the Critical Analysis of Dance Education" (Ed.D. diss., University of North Carolina at Greensboro, 1990); Suzanne Kathryn Oliver, "Juxtaposition and Metaphor: Personal Yearnings Toward a Deeper Dance" (Ph.D. diss., University of Illinois at Urbana-Champaign, 1994); Susan W. Stinson, "Reflections and Visions: A Hermeneutic Study of Dangers and Possibilities in Dance Education" (Ed.D. diss., University of North Carolina at Greensboro, 1984).

47. Ann Oakley, "Interviewing Women: A Contradiction in Terms," in *Doing Feminist Research*, ed. Helen Roberts (London: Routledge Kegan Paul, 1981), 37–61.

48. Green; Karen Bond, "How 'Wild Things' Changed Gender Distinctions," *Journal of Physical Education, Recreation and Dance* 65 (February 1994): 28–33; Janette M. Vallance, "Collegial Conversation: Meaning in Dance" (Ph.D. diss., University of Alberta, 1989).

49. Green; Bond, "Wild Things."

50. All relationships and their implications must be acknowledged in the research report.

51. Some helpful strategies for analysis may be found in Max Van Manen, *Researching Lived Experience*.

52. Phenomenological research is one kind of interpretive inquiry in which there is often little if any emphasis on sociocultural context. An exception is Sondra Fraleigh's work, *Dance and the Lived Body* (Pittsburgh: University of Pittsburgh Press, 1987). See also Fraleigh's "A Vulnerable Glance: Seeing Dance Through Phenomenology," *Dance Research Journal* 23 (spring 1991): 11–16.

53. Lather, *Getting Smart*, 128–29.

54. The researcher's role in emancipatory research is usually combined with that of educator. All educators, including researcher-educators, may be viewed as manipulative when they attempt to persuade students to see the world in any particular way. All researchers have an obligation to be reflexive and to seek discrepant cases that might reveal unanticipated interpretations.

55. Lather describes false consciousness in relationship to Marxist and feminist interpretations regarding "people's complicity in their own repression" (*Getting Smart*, 119).

56. Some postpositivist theorists and researchers problematize this term. There is an awareness that although many educators and researchers may attempt to "empower" people, it is possible that a hidden power dimension actually creates an opposite effect that maintains an uneven power dynamic and does not actually empower people at all.

57. Fetterman; Kvale, "Qualitative Research Interview"; Maguire.

58. Elizabeth Ellsworth, "Why Doesn't This Feel Empowering? Working Through the Repressive Myths of Critical Pedagogy," in *Feminisms and Critical Pedagogy*, ed. Carmen Luke and Jennifer Gore (New York: Routledge, 1992), 90–119.

59. Mimi Orner, "Interrupting the Calls for the Student Voice in 'Liberatory' Education: A Feminist Poststructuralist Perspective," in *Feminisms and Critical Pedagogy,* ed. Carmen Luke and Jennifer Gore (New York: Routledge, 1992), 81.

60. Patti Lather, "Feminist Perspectives on Empowering Research Methodologies," *Women's Studies International Forum* 11 (6):569–81.

61. Lather, *Getting Smart,* 137.

62. Ibid., 138.

63. Ibid.

64. For a further discussion of these limitations and problems, see Ellsworth.

65. Oliver.

66. Sherry Badger Taylor, "Reclaiming Our Bodies: Towards a Sentient Pedagogy of Liberation" (Ed.D. diss., University of North Carolina at Greensboro, 1991).

67. Sherry B. Shapiro, "Re-Membering the Body in Critical Pedagogy," *Education and Society* 12 (1994): 61–79; Sherry B. Shapiro, *Pedagogy and the Politics of the Body* (New York: Garland, in press); Sherry and Svi Shapiro, "Silent Voices, Bodies of Knowledge: Towards a Critical Pedagogy of the Body," *Journal of Curriculum Theorizing* 1 (1995): 49–72. See also Sherry B. Shapiro, ed., *Dance, Power and Difference: Critical and Feminist Perspectives in Dance Education* (Champaign: Human Kinetics, 1998).

68. Green, "Fostering Creativity"; Jill Green, "Moving Through and Against Multiple Paradigms: Postpositivist Research in Somatics and Creativity—Part I," *Journal of Interdisciplinary Research in Physical Education* 1, no. 1 (1996): 42–54; Jill Green, "Moving Through and Against Multiple Paradigms: Postpositivist Research in Somatics and Creativity—Part II," *Journal of Interdisciplinary Research in Physical Education* 1, no. 2 (1996): 73–86; Jill Green, "Choreographing a Postmodern Turn: The Creative Process and Somatics," *Impulse* 4 (1996): 267–75; Jill Green, "Somatic Authority and the Myth of the Ideal Body in Dance Education" (paper presented at the Congress on Research in Dance [CORD], 1995); Jill Green, "The Student Body: Dance Education and the Issue of Somatic Authority" (paper presented at the annual meeting of the American Alliance of Health, Physical Education, Recreation and Dance, [AAHPERD], 1996).

69. Blumenfeld-Jones.

70. Stinson, "Reflections and Visions."

71. Thomas.

72. Isabel Marques, "A Partnership Toward Art in Education: Approaching a Relationship Between Theory and Practice," *Impulse: The International Journal of Dance Science, Medicine, and Education* 3 (April 1995): 86–101.

73. Leslie Gotfrit, "Women Dancing Back: Disruption and the Politics of Pleasure," in *Postmodernism, Feminism, and Cultural Politics,* ed. Henry A. Giroux (New York: State University of New York Press, 1991), 174–95.

74. Leslie G. Roman, "Intimacy, Labor, and Class: Ideologies of Feminine Sexuality in the Punk Slam Dance," in *Becoming Feminine: The Politics of Popular Culture,* ed. Leslie G. Roman with Elizabeth Ellsworth (London, New York, Philadelphia: Falmer Press, 1988), 143–84.

75. Jane K. Cowan, *Dance and the Body Politic in Northern Greece* (Princeton: Princeton University Press, 1990).

76. Carol Martin, "Feminist Analysis Across Cultures: Performing Gender in India," *Women and Performance: A Journal of Feminist Theory* 3 (1987–88): 31–40.

77. Christy Adair, *Women and Dance: Sylphs and Sirens* (New York: New York University Press, 1992).

78. Susan Manning, *Ecstasy and the Demon: Feminism and Nationalism in the Dances of Mary Wigman* (Berkeley: University of California Press, 1993).

79. Cynthia Novack, *Sharing the Dance: Contact Improvisation and the American Culture* (Madison: University of Wisconsin Press, 1990).

80. Ann Daly, "The Balanchine Woman: Of Hummingbirds and Channel Swimmers," *The Drama Review* 31 (spring 1987): 8–21; Ann Daly, "Classical Ballet: A Discourse of Difference," *Women and Performance: A Journal of Feminist Theory* 3 (1987–88): 57–66.

81. Lather, *Getting Smart.*

82. Jane L. Parpart, "Who Is the 'Other'?: A Postmodern Critique of Women and Development Theory and Practice," 1992, unpublished manuscript.

83. See Lather and Green for examples of deconstructivist stories.

84. Lather, *Getting Smart,* 13.

85. Ibid., 136.

86. Ellsworth; Lather, *Getting Smart.*

87. See Frederick Erickson, "Qualitative Methods in Research on Teaching," in *Handbook on Teaching,* 3d ed., ed. Merlin C. Wittrock (New York: Macmillan, 1986), 119–61, for various researcher roles.

88. This term, with Marxist roots, signifies that practice is a large part of the research process. According to Lather, it is about "philosophy becoming practical" (*Getting Smart,* 11) and it has an action component.

89. Lather, *Getting Smart,* 139.

90. This postmodern word is used to describe a questioning of one's own assumptions and a displacement of one's own theoretical stance.

91. Green, "Fostering Creativity."

92. Marianne Goldberg, "Ballerinas and Ball Passing," *Women and Performance: A Journal of Feminist Theory* 3 (1987–88): 11–31; Marianne Goldberg, "She Who Is Possessed No Longer Exists Outside," *Women and Performance: A Journal of Feminist Theory* 3 (1986): 17–27.

93. Jude Walton, "The Literature of Legs: Postmodernism," *Writings On Dance* 2 (spring 1987): 23–31.

94. Sally Ann Ness, *Body, Movement, and Culture: Kinesthetic and Visual Symbolism in a Philippine Community* (Philadelphia: University of Pennsylvania Press, 1992).

95. Clyde Smith, "'Mandala' and the Men's Movement(s) in the Light of Feminism" (master's thesis, University of North Carolina at Greensboro, 1995).

96. Cynthia J. Novack, "Ballet, Gender and Cultural Power," in *Dance, Gender and Culture,* ed. Helen Thomas (New York: St. Martin's Press, 1993), 34–48.

97. Donald S. Blumenfeld-Jones, "Dance as a Mode of Research Representation," *Qualitative Inquiry* 1 (December 1995): 391–401.

98. See Karen Bond, "Dance for Children with Dual Sensory Impairments," for an example of research that includes both quantitative and qualitative methodology; also see Green, "Moving Through and Against Multiple Paradigms—Part I."

REFERENCES

Adair, Christy. *Women and Dance: Sylphs and Sirens.* New York: New York University Press, 1992.

Alter, Judith. "A Field Study of an Advanced Dance Class in a Private Studio Setting."

Dance Studies 10 (1986): 49–97. Les Bois, St. Peter, Jersey, Channel Islands, Britain: Center for Dance Studies.

Bazerman, Charles. "Codifying the Social Scientific Style: The *APA Publication Manual* as a Behaviorist Rhetoric." In *The Rhetoric of the Human Sciences,* ed. John Nelson, 125–44. Madison: University of Wisconsin Press, 1987.

Blumenfeld-Jones, Donald. "Body, Pleasure, Language and World: A Framework for the Critical Analysis of Dance Education." Ed.D. diss., University of North Carolina at Greensboro, 1990.

———. "Dance as a Mode of Research Representation." *Qualitative Inquiry* 1 (December 1995): 391–401.

Bogdan, Robert C., and Sari Knopp Biklen. *Qualitative Research for Education: An Introduction to Theory and Methods.* Boston: Allyn and Bacon, 1982.

Bond, Karen. "Dance for Children with Dual Sensory Impairments." Ph.D. diss., La Trobe University, Melbourne, Victoria, Australia, 1992.

———. "How 'Wild Things' Changed Gender Distinctions." *Journal of Physical Education, Recreation and Dance* 65 (February 1994): 28–33.

Bresler, Liora. "Qualitative Paradigms in Music Education Research." *The Quarterly Journal of Music Teaching and Learning* 111 (spring 1992): 64–79.

Caputo, John. *Radical Hermeneutics: Repetition, Deconstruction, and the Hermeneutic Project.* Bloomington: University of Indiana Press, 1987.

Cowan, Jane K. *Dance and the Body Politic in Northern Greece.* Princeton: Princeton University Press, 1990.

Daly, Ann. "The Balanchine Woman: Of Hummingbirds and Channel Swimmers." *The Drama Review* 31 (spring 1987): 8–21.

———. "Classical Ballet: A Discourse of Difference." *Women and Performance: A Journal of Feminist Theory* 3 (1987–88): 57–66.

Denzin, Norman K. *The Research Act: A Theoretical Introduction to Sociological Methods.* Englewood Cliffs, N.J.: Prentice Hall, 1989.

Donmoyer, Robert. "Distinguishing Between Scientific and Humanities-Based Approaches to Qualitative Research." Paper presented at American Education Research Association annual meeting, Chicago 1985.

Eisner, Elliot W. "Objectivity and Subjectivity in Qualitative Research and Evaluation." In *Qualitative Studies in Education,* ed. Elliot W. Eisner and Alan M. Peshkin, 15–16. New York: Teachers College Press, 1989.

Ellsworth, Elizabeth. "Why Doesn't This Feel Empowering? Working Through the Repressive Myths of Critical Pedagogy." In *Feminisms and Critical Pedagogy,* ed. Carmen Luke and Jennifer Gore, 90–119. New York: Routledge, 1992.

Erickson, Frederick. "Qualitative Methods in Research on Teaching." In *Handbook on Teaching,* 3d ed., ed. Merlin C. Wittrock, 119–61. New York: Macmillan, 1986.

Fetterman, David M. *Ethnography Step by Step.* Newburry Park, Calif.: Sage, 1989.

Fraleigh, Sondra. *Dance and the Lived Body.* Pittsburgh: University of Pittsburgh Press, 1987.

———. "A Vulnerable Glance: Seeing Dance Through Phenomenology." *Dance Research Journal* 23 (spring 1991): 11–16.

Giddings, Anthony, ed. *Positivism and Sociology.* London: Heinemann, 1974.

Goldberg, Marianne. "She Who Is Possessed No Longer Exists Outside." *Women and Performance: A Journal of Feminist Theory* 3 (1986): 17–27.

———. "Ballerinas and Ball Passing." *Women and Performance: A Journal of Feminist Theory* 3 (1987–88): 11–31.

Gotfrit, Leslie. "Women Dancing Back: Disruption and the Politics of Pleasure." In *Postmodernism, Feminism, and Cultural Politics,* ed. Henry A. Giroux, 174–95. New York: State University of New York Press, 1991.

Gray, Judith A., ed. *Research in Dance IV: 1900–1990.* Reston, Va.: National Dance Association, 1992.

Green, Jill. "Fostering Creativity Through Movement and Body Awareness Practices: A Postpositivist Investigation Into the Relationship Between Somatics and the Creative Process." Ph.D. diss., Ohio State University, 1993.

———. "Choreographing a Postmodern Turn: The Creative Process and Somatics." *Impulse* 4 (October 1996): 267–75.

———. "Moving Through and Against Multiple Paradigms: Postpositivist Research in Somatics and Creativity—Part I." *Journal of Interdisciplinary Research in Physical Education* 1 (1996): 42–54.

———. "Moving Through and Against Multiple Paradigms: Postpositivist Research in Somatics and Creativity—Part II." *Journal of Interdisciplinary Research in Physical Education* 1 (1996): 73–86.

Harding, Sandra. *Whose Science? Whose Knowledge?* Ithaca: Cornell University Press, 1991.

———, ed. *Sex and Scientific Inquiry.* Chicago: University of Chicago Press, 1987.

Kvale, Steinar. "The Qualitative Research Interview: A Phenomenological and Hermeneutical Mode of Understanding." *Journal of Phenomenological Psychology* 14 (fall 1983): 171–96.

———. "To Validate Is to Question." In *Issues of Validity in Qualitative Research,* ed. Steinar Kvale, 73–92. Sweden: Student Literature, 1989.

Lather, Patti. "Issues of Validity in Openly Ideological Research: Between a Rock and a Soft Place." *Interchange* 17 (winter 1986): 63–84.

———. "Research as Praxis." *Harvard Educational Review* 56 (August 1986): 257–77.

———. "Feminist Perspectives on Empowering Research Methodologies." *Women's Studies International Forum* 11 (6): 569–81.

———. "Deconstructing/ Deconstructive Inquiry: The Politics of Knowing and Being Known." *Educational Theory* 41 (spring 1991): 199–208.

———. *Getting Smart: Feminist Research and Pedagogy With/in the Postmodern.* New York: Routledge, 1991.

———. "Staying Dumb?: Feminist Research and Methodology With/in the Postmodern." Paper presented at the Beyond Ideology Critique Conference, Temple University, Philadelphia, April 1991.

Lewis, Magda, and R. Simon. "A Discourse Not Intended for Her." *Harvard Educational Review* 56 (November 1986): 457–72.

Lincoln, Yvonna S., and Egon G. Guba. *Naturalistic Inquiry.* Beverly Hills: Sage, 1985.

Locke, Lawrence F. "Qualitative Research as a Form of Scientific Inquiry in Sport and Physical Education." *Research Quarterly* 60 (March 1989): 1–20.

Maguire, Patricia. *Doing Participatory Research: A Feminist Approach*. Amherst, Mass.: Center for International Education, 1987.

Manning, Susan. *Ecstasy and the Demon: Feminism and Nationalism in the Dances of Mary Wigman*. Berkeley: University of California Press, 1993.

Marques, Isabel. "A Partnership Toward Art in Education: Approaching a Relationship Between Theory and Practice." *Impulse: The International Journal of Dance Science, Medicine, and Education* 3 (April 1995): 86–101.

Martin, Carol. "Feminist Analysis Across Cultures: Performing Gender in India." *Women and Performance: A Journal of Feminist Theory* 3 (1987–88): 31–40.

McLaren, Peter. *Life in Schools: An Introduction to Critical Pedagogy in the Foundations of Education*. New York: Longman, 1989.

Miles, Matthew, and Michael Huberman. *Qualitative Data Analysis: A Sourcebook of New Methods*. Beverly Hills: Sage, 1984.

Ness, Sally Ann. *Body, Movement, and Culture: Kinesthetic and Visual Symbolism in a Philippine Community*. Philadelphia: University of Pennsylvania Press, 1992.

Nielsen, Joyce McCarl. *Feminist Research Methods: Exemplary Readings in the Social Sciences*. Boulder: Westview Press, 1990.

Novack, Cynthia. *Sharing the Dance: Contact Improvisation and the American Culture*. Madison: University of Wisconsin Press, 1990.

———. "Ballet, Gender and Cultural Power." In *Dance, Gender and Culture*, ed. Helen Thomas, 34–48. New York: St. Martin's Press, 1993.

Oakley, Ann. "Interviewing Women: A Contradiction in Terms." In *Doing Feminist Research*, ed. Helen Roberts, 30–61. London: Routledge Kegan Paul, 1981.

Oliver, Suzanne Kathryn. "Juxtaposition and Metaphor: Personal Yearnings Toward a Deeper Dance." Ph.D. diss., University of Illinois at Urbana-Champaign, 1994.

Orner, Mimi. "Interrupting the Calls for the Student Voice in 'Liberatory' Education: A Feminist Poststructuralist Perspective." In *Feminisms and Critical Pedagogy*, ed. Carmen Luke and Jennifer Gore, 74–89. New York: Routledge, 1992.

Patai, Daphne. "Constructing a Self: A Brazilian Life Story." *Feminist Studies* 14 (spring 1988): 143–66.

Parpart, Jane L. "Who Is the 'Other'?: A Postmodern Critique of Women and Development Theory and Practice." 1992, unpublished manuscript.

Richardson, Laurel. "The Collective Story: Postmodernism and the Writing of Sociology." *Sociological Focus* 21 (1988): 199–208.

———. *Writing Strategies: Reaching Diverse Audiences*. Qualitative Research Methods Series 21. Newburry Park, Calif.: Sage, 1990.

Roman, Leslie G. "Intimacy, Labor, and Class: Ideologies of Feminine Sexuality in the Punk Slam Dance." In *Becoming Feminine: The Politics of Popular Culture*, ed. Leslie G. Roman with Elizabeth Ellsworth, 143–84. London, New York, Philadelphia: Falmer Press, 1988.

Rose, Dan. *Living the Ethnographic Life*. Newburry Park, Calif.: Sage, 1990.

Shapiro, Sherry B. "Re-Membering the Body in Critical Pedagogy." *Education and Society* 12 (1994): 61–79.

———. *Pedagogy and the Politics of the Body*. New York: Garland, in press.

————, ed. *Dance, Power and Difference: Critical and Feminist Perspectives in Dance Education.* Champaign: Human Kinetics, 1998.

Shapiro, Sherry, and Svi Shapiro. "Silent Voices, Bodies of Knowledge: Towards a Critical Pedagogy of the Body." *Journal of Curriculum Theorizing* 1 (1995): 49–72.

Smith, Clyde. "'Mandala' and the Men's Movement(s) in the Light of Feminism." Master's thesis, University of North Carolina at Greensboro, 1995.

Stinson, Susan W. "Reflections and Visions: A Hermeneutic Study of Dangers and Possibilities in Dance Education." Ed.D. diss., University of North Carolina at Greensboro, 1984.

————. "A Place Called Dance in School: Reflecting on What the Students Say." *Impulse: The International Journal of Dance Science, Medicine and Education* 1 (October 1993): 90–114.

————. *Research as Choreography*. National Dance Association Scholar Lecture. Reston, Va.: National Dance Association, 1994.

Stinson, Susan W., Donald Blumenfeld-Jones, and Jan Van Dyke. "Voices of Young Women Dance Students: An Interpretive Study of Meaning in Dance." *Dance Research Journal* 22 (fall 1990): 13–22.

Strauss, Anselm L., and Juliet Corbin. *Basics of Qualitative Research: Grounded Theory Procedures and Techniques*. Newburry Park, Calif.: Sage, 1990.

Taylor, Sherry Badger. "Reclaiming Our Bodies: Towards a Sentient Pedagogy of Liberation." Ed.D. diss., University of North Carolina at Greensboro, 1991.

Thomas, Helen, ed. *Dance, Gender and Culture*. New York: St. Martin's Press, 1993.

Vallance, Janette M. "Collegial Conversation: Meaning in Dance." Ph.D. diss., University of Alberta, 1989.

Van Maanen, John. *Tales of the Field*. Chicago: University of Chicago Press, 1988.

Van Manen, Max. *Researching Lived Experience*. New York: State University of New York Press, 1990.

Walton, Jude. "The Literature of Legs: Postmodernism." *Writings On Dance* 2 (spring 1987): 23–31.

Wolcott, Harry F. *Writing Up Qualitative Research*. Qualitative Research Methods Series 20. Newburry Park, Calif.: Sage, 1990.

5 SCIENTIFIC EXPLORATION IN DANCE

Steven J. Chatfield

Introduction

THE HISTORY OF SCIENCE is replete with experimentalists who, like the princes of Serendip, "were always making discoveries, by accident or sagacity, of things they were not in quest of."[1] Because of its conventional presentational format, scientific experimentation might appear to some to be an extremely orderly, even formulaic sequence of steps that all experimentalists follow in their efforts to contribute to the smoothly cumulative, linear advancement of scientific knowledge. However, in an analysis of the history of science it becomes apparent that many great discoveries were happy accidents discovered by creative and perceptive workers through absorption in inventive experimental structures. Contrary to notions of linear accumulation, advancements in scientific knowledge have often been sudden, disruptive, and revolutionary.

In the three major sections of this chapter, I make an attempt to temper the stereotypical notion of scientific methodology as a formulaic set of rules that everyone must follow. The first section describes problem solving as the fundamental basis of scientific methodology. Section two introduces background information on the philosophy and history of science in an effort to develop perspective for the third section, which includes examples of commonly used experimental designs. My presentation of strengths and weaknesses for some commonly used experimental designs is not intended to be read as a mandate for prescribed models. Rather, I hope the review of exemplary designs reads like a good text on choreography in the sense that we can examine successful works and learn from the strategies that have been employed to overcome difficulties inherent in the problems being solved. When appropriate, I try to point out how creative manifestations of experimental science parallel processes we know from our involvement in choreographic enterprises, processes such as total absorption in our pursuit, discipline and hard work, and invention and discovery. In so doing, I hope to encourage motivated dancers to develop experimental expertise and use it to benefit dance as an art form.

Many volumes have been written on the philosophy, history, and methods of science, and on the design and analysis of experiments. This chapter's humble intent is to serve as a primer to this body of literature. Throughout the chapter, the interested reader is directed to related works providing in-depth coverage of issues introduced here.

Problem Solving

Fundamental to all scientific experimentation is problem solving. The standard format for reporting experimental research reflects widely accepted problem-solving procedures. Typically, reports progress from an introduction that arrives at a clear statement of the problem being addressed to separate sections for methods, results, and discussion. The introduction contextualizes the work being reported. The methods section presents elements of the work in enough detail that an interested researcher could replicate the work in an effort to cross-validate the results. The results section presents obtained outcomes, preferably free from interpretations. This enables readers to make their own inferences. The discussion section provides a reader with the researcher's interpretation of the data in the context of the existing body of relevant knowledge.

This conventional style of presentation tends to sterilize the adventure and inner drama of experimentation. Such reports give the impression of linearity even when the research was confused and floundering. They present the process in a step-by-step fashion even when the actuality of the work was enfolding and circuitous. They may even present a theoretical stance for a deductive flow in the introduction when in fact the theoretical significance of the work was recognized inductively, after the data were analyzed.[2]

Due to the idiosyncratic processes of successful scientists, it is arguable that there is no such thing as "the" scientific method. Even without a lockstep formula for problem solving, a generally recognized pattern of activity surrounds successful experimentation. John Dewey[3] described this pattern as five phases of reflective thinking. Even though Dewey listed his analysis from phase one through phase five, he was quick to point out that the sequence is not fixed; each phase can be fed by or lead to any of the others.

Phase one is called suggestion. When we are perplexed, troubled, or confused, when we are in a hole, our natural tendency to act, to go forward, is temporarily arrested. Action is replaced by ideas, and the mind leaps toward solutions. Without this hesitation we would proceed in a routine fashion. This hesitation, or thought, is "conduct turned in upon itself and examining its purpose and its conditions, its resources, aids, and difficulties and obstacles."[4]

Phase two, intellectualization, is the formulation of a problem to be solved. In this phase we consider the perplexity we experienced. The felt difficulty is being located and defined. Genuine involvement in phases one and two could separate normal from creative scientists. If problems are ready-made and handed to us, they are nothing more than tasks. Normal scientists carry out the tasks of normal science. Perceiving confusion is an act of discovery; forming an original problem statement is a creative act. Creative scientists revolutionize knowledge through their abilities to suspend action and frame fruitful questions.

In phase one, if ideas do not spontaneously spring to mind, there simply are none. In phase two, intellectualization cultivates the ideas and prepares one of them to initiate and guide the way through observation. It is in phase three that the guiding idea or working hypothesis emerges. It is imperative that a working hypothesis be stated in testable terms so that its value as a solution can be observed. A working hypothesis directs careful use of procedures and techniques that are helpful to preliminary assessment of its tenability.

Observations guided by the working hypothesis pertain to the world around us, to objective reality, to facts, and they are the seeds for thought. Phase four, reasoning, uses observation to mentally elaborate the hypothesis. This is distinct from the fledgling suggestion that pops automatically to mind in phase one. In reasoning, the tentative working hypothesis is linked to previous experience and knowledge and its elaboration and refinement prepare the way for phase five, testing.

Decisive action characterizes phase five. Experimental corroboration or verification of the working hypothesis is sought. A critical feature of this phase is the careful design of an experiment controlling the influences of and allowing rejection of rival hypotheses. In a well-designed experiment, the results are unequivocal. Through the use of design techniques and inference, the outcome of the experiment provides evidence used to decide acceptance or rejection of the working hypothesis.

Based on his five phases of reflective thinking, some credit Dewey with codification of steps in the modern scientific method.[5] Dewey's perspective was broad in scope, however, finding more focus in the general education classroom than in a scientific laboratory. In contrast, Mario Bunge wrote with the intent to formulate a text on the scientific method for science students. He listed the following ordered sequence of eight steps in his description of scientific methodology:

1. Ask well-formulated and likely fruitful questions.

2. Devise hypotheses both grounded and testable to answer the questions.

3. Devise logical consequences of the assumptions.

4. Devise techniques to test the assumptions.

5. Test the techniques for relevance and reliability.

6. Execute the tests and interpret their results.

7. Evaluate the truth claims of the assumptions and the fidelity of the techniques.

8. Determine the domains in which the assumptions and the techniques hold, and state the new problems raised by the research.[6]

Bunge also formulated rules for adequate execution of the scientific method. At the same time, however, he cautioned that, "The asking of astute and rewarding questions, the building of strong and deep theories, and the design of delicate and original tests are not rule-directed activities. . . . Scientific methodology can give some hints and it does supply means for spotting mistakes, but is no substitute for original creation and does not spare us all mistakes."[7] Significant among the rules Bunge lists is the notion that even a confirmed hypothesis should be considered, at best, only partially true.

Before examining applications of problem solving in current research, I want to lend some perspective to problem-solving procedures from philosophical and historical points of view. A quick look at some of the rationales for and sources of today's procedures can promote a deeper understanding of their intent and provide insight into their development and current form.

Philosophical and Historical Background

In Renaissance thought, experimentation began to supplant theological fiat as a knowledge base to unlock the secrets of nature.[8] Francis Bacon (1561–1626) is credited with planting the seeds of the modern scientific method by challenging the medieval reliance on self-evident or authoritative premises as bases for conclusions.[9] He recommended building conclusions inductively, based on exhaustive data collection. Bacon was always on guard against being misled by reasoning.

He advised keeping mental abstractions, "firmly based upon the accurate observation and analysis of 'things solid and realized in matter.'"[10] Because of the dedicated primacy he placed on collecting data, his method proved too unwieldy for broad application. Galileo (1564–1642) and Newton (1642–1727) began integrating reasoned deduction and induction and thereby framed modern scientific methodology.[11]

Today, the rational development and experimental confirmation of theories (although not necessarily in that order) can be thought of as the ultimate aim of science. A theory is a parsimonious statement that explains an existing body of data in causal terms. Ideally, theories are simple statements that achieve a broad scope of explanatory power. Theories describe phenomena in terms of cause and effect relationships. At any given point in time, confirmed theories constitute scientific knowledge.

According to the assumption of the uniformity of nature, phenomena in the universe behave in predictable ways.[12] This assumption does not require a state of absolute fixity. It simply requires a relative degree of order. Change is recognized. Because theories make statements in terms of cause and effect relationships, for science to be effective, natural events cannot be purely random and unrelated. A scientific law of nature evolves from confirmed theory. Theory confirmation hinges on supporting evidence in the form of data. (*Data* is plural for *datum*. For the purposes of this chapter, a datum will refer to an observable fact.) Data are collected during experiments. Experimentation can be defined as planned observation probing a controlled set of our experiences.

An experiment is a tool used to test the value of experience. Dewey called experimentation a natural attitude of childhood that can be lost through acculturation and routine.[13] He contends that effective education preserves and perfects the imagination, the abstraction of thought necessary to see familiar experience in a new light. It is in this way that education replaces the lazy assimilation of tradition and its thoughtless acceptance of habits, routines, beliefs, and opinions. In effective education and effective science, belief in the accepted is suspended. Experiments perform critical tests that are designed to either reject beliefs and opinions or authorize conviction in them. Dewey maintains that, "Without initiation into the scientific spirit one is not in possession of the best tools which humanity has so far devised for effectively directed reflection."[14] Dewey's views and methods remain vital today and find voice in the writings of such individuals as Donald Schön.[15] What is important here is to establish that reflective thinking in the scientific method ultimately leads to inferential statements generated by experimental outcomes.

Inference is the logical derivation of conclusions through either deductive or inductive processes. While most texts will present scientific methodology as deductive problem solving in the context of theory-driven models, there is a legacy of strong support for and high yields from inductive or data-driven methods.[16] Data-driven work is most apparent during times when there is a practical problem to solve or when there is an insufficient data base in the area of interest to support theory formation.[17] Based on autobiographies of elite experimentalists, Conrad Snyder and Bruce Abernethy reported instances in which data-driven research (induction) led to theory-driven approaches (deduction) in parallel with the career development of individual researchers. Snyder and Abernethy also report an instance in which research was driven by a new methodology. It is important to recognize the contributions that method-driven research can make, particularly in times of swift technological advances. As new equipment and capabilities for measurement and analysis appear in search of problems to solve, data and theory can evolve as consequences.

Whether inductive, deductive, or method driven, progress in science has been described as theory falsification acting as a smooth, cumulative process operating on the basis of sound contradictory empirical data from even a single study.[18] As evidenced by the history of science, however, falsification does not operate in this manner at all. Instead of rejection, contradictory data are either ignored as trivial, explained away on the basis of methodological flaws, or absorbed via post hoc modification of the existing theory.

Thomas Kuhn places theories within the context of an inclusive construct he refers to as a paradigm.[19] He argues that the evolution of scientific knowledge is neither smooth nor cumulative; rather, it is disruptive and revolutionary. Sudden changes in knowledge occur when existing paradigms and theories are overthrown. Kuhn sees scientific revolution as one possible outcome of a paradigm crisis. While his critics have accused him of an overly broad conceptualization of paradigm, his underlying point is, nonetheless, important to consider because it provides insight into the relative nature of one of the fundamental assumptions of scientific inquiry: objectivity.[20] Included in Kuhn's use of paradigm is reference to a scientific community with shared metaphysical commitments, beliefs, preconceptions, theories, techniques, and model solutions to exemplary problems.[21] During a period of what Kuhn refers to as "normal science," one paradigm and its worldview dominates. Periods of "paradigm crises" and one possible outcome, "revolutionary science," provide a corrective remedy to the old worldview when a new paradigm emerges and assumes a dominant role. Unfortunately, because of the investment that many scientists have in a dominant paradigm, rational persuasion is an unlikely vehicle for paradigm shifts. Planck said that "a new scientific truth does not triumph by convincing its opponents and making them see the light, but rather because its opponents eventually die, and a new generation grows up that is familiar with it."[22]

A realistic understanding of the assumption of objectivity is that divine, absolute truth is not promised. What is promised is a state-of-the-art, contemporary understanding of the world. Unlike mythology or religion, science makes no claim of final, incorrigible truth. As stated by Bunge, the modest claims of science are quite simply: "(i) to be *truer* than any nonscientific model of the world, (ii) to be able to *test* such a truth claim, (iii) to be able to *discover its own shortcomings,* and (iv) to be able to *correct its own shortcomings.*"[23] The assumption of objectivity is justifiable on the pragmatic grounds that it is more fruitful for empirical inquiry than assuming that reality is a wholly subjective experience.[24]

According to Snyder and Abernethy, revolutionary science is induced by experimentalists who exhibit at least two common characteristics: expert problem-solving abilities, and eclectic knowledge and experience.[25] They also exhibit attunement to the deep structure of knowledge and understand the underlying theories of more than one content area. With these characteristics, innovative experimentalists look at old questions from a new perspective and they challenge established paradigms and worldviews. They find new answers to old questions, resurrect abandoned questions that were deemed anomalous or trivial, and raise new questions. They locate perplexing issues and pursue their definition and solution. Normal scientists work from exemplary problems within the dominant paradigm. Creative scientists are not shackled by model problems.

One mechanism for validating scientific knowledge generated from experimentation is through the repetition of experiments conducted in a given area, either by one researcher (or research team) or by unaffiliated researchers. In addition to accumulating evidence to support progressive theory development, this repetition provides opportunities for the sagacious researcher to notice significant anomalies, data that lie outside the explanatory power of existing theories. Where the less fastidious or more myopic researcher, the so-called normal scientist, would discount or ignore these findings, the creative, revolutionary scientist will seize them. It is in this way that serendipitous discovery can be cultivated and the seeds for revolutionary science sown. W. B. Cannon catalogues numerous instances in the history of science where chance discovery or, as he puts it, "the happy use of good fortune" has been responsible for sudden, as opposed to smoothly cumulative, advancements in knowledge.[26]

Cannon details Claude Bernard's nineteenth-century discovery of the neural control of circulation as an example of serendipity operating in biological research. Prior to Bernard's discovery, it was thought that nervous impulses were responsible for generating heat in biological organisms. Bernard set out to verify that thought by cutting the nerve leading to a rabbit's ear and expecting to record a drop in temperature. The opposite occurred: the temperature of the ear increased dramatically. Without knowing it, he had eliminated neural input that kept blood vessels in the ear constricted so that blood was shunted to other areas. Without this regulatory neural input, the blood vessels dilated, allowing blood to flood the ear and warm it. "Thus by accident appeared the first intimation that the passage of blood into different parts of the body is under nervous government—the most significant advance in our knowledge of the circulation since Harvey's proof, more than 300 years ago, that the blood does, indeed, circulate."[27]

Whether by accident or by design, expert researchers with the ability to revolutionize science introduce new paradigms of inquiry.[28] Snyder and Abernethy establish how, particularly in human action research, paradigm shifts (their terms for Kuhn's revolutionary science) have been introduced by expert researchers importing paradigms and methods from allied fields. They quote Koestler's discussion of the genesis of scientific creativity, "all decisive advances in the history of scientific thought can be described in terms of mental cross-fertilization between different disciplines."[29]

In her attempt to link the seemingly disparate fields of science and dance, Janice Gudde Plastino also cited Koestler's *The Act of Creation* when she compared "the individual act of scientific discovery with the exquisite moment of artistic insight."[30] E. Mach describes total absorption and persistent labor in the midst of systematized inquiry as the minimal necessary conditions for cultivating creativity and discovery.[31] He suggests that through intense interest and sharpened attention, discoverers appear to arrive at sudden creations through deliberate acts, when in reality a slow, gradual process prepares the way for a serendipitous occurrence to ignite a creative moment. He begins the summary of his essay with the following paragraph.

A welcome complement to the discoveries which the history of civilisation and comparative psychology have furnished, is to be found in the confessions of great scientists and artists. Scientists *and* artists, we might say, for Liebig courageously declared there was no essential difference between the labors of the two. Are we to regard Leonardo da Vinci as a scientist or as an artist? If it is the business of the artist to build up his [or her] work from a few motives, it is the task of the scientist to discover the motives which permeate reality. If scientists like Lagrange and Fourier are in a certain measure artists in the presentation of their results, on the other hand, artists like Shakespeare and Ruysdael are scientists in the insight which must have preceded their creations.[32]

He goes on to describe how individuals such as Newton and Mozart have spoken of thoughts and melodies pouring in upon them. He speculates that either consciously or instinctively, these individuals prepared themselves for inspiration by pondering their pursuit and repeating their efforts through systematic and persistent labor.

Susan Stinson attempts to draw our attention to parallel processes in choreography and scholarly research.[33] She makes a compelling argument for transferring the knowledge of process we have as choreographers to the processes involved in different kinds of research. She describes how students begin work on new choreography with some ideas, but without form or content. She develops the notion of total absorption in the work through attention to the false starts and unfinished phrases and how, through persistent labor, clarity of form and content emerges. Choreography does not proceed via a step-wise use of formulas. Choreographers proceed in a manner equivalent to that of a working experimentalist who makes disciplined use of tools of the trade. Looking retrospectively on his research career in motor control, Kelso mused, "One of the beauties and attractions of scientific endeavor . . . is that there is no telling in advance what form the product will take."[34]

Another intriguing example of how processes in choreography and scholarly research can be paralleled is seen in Paulette Shafranski's text, *Modern Dance: Twelve Creative Problem-Solving Experiments*.[35] In this text Shafranski details movement experiments to stimulate creativity and improvisation. Her method of problem solving places process demands on the dance student in much the same way that laboratory experimentation can place demands on the science student.

Creativity and dedication are hallmarks in experimental research in much the same way that they are in choreography. Consider, for example, Donald Cram's thoughts about his research group. Dr. Cram is a Nobel laureate and professor of chemistry at the University of California, Los Angeles.

> [Graduate students] bring spirit, verve, imagination, and optimism to the group. They leave with independence, mature judgment, and tolerances of differences between people, but an intolerance of sloppy results, noncontractual relationships, and of people who want something for nothing.
>
> I would judge almost all of these students to be operationally creative; that is, they can solve problems. Only about 5 to 10 percent, however, are conceptually creative. They are the ones that formulate research objectives. . . . They not only know how to get things done, but they know what *should* be done. What a rare combination![36]

In developing an appreciation for how creative individuals, artists and scientists alike, prepare themselves for the process of their work, it is important to remember that research is a special activity. It is distinct from everyday experience. In reference to the act of dancing, Sondra Fraleigh wrote, "When I dance, I am subtly attuned to my body and my motion in a totally different way than I ordinarily am in my everyday actions."[37] A scientist might say the same of the difference between observation during everyday experience and observation in an experiment. My point in pursuing the relationships between the processes of choreography and experimentation this far is to establish fundamental similarities between the two. I hope to promote an understanding of the creative side of experimentation and its applicability to research in dance. I do not perceive scientific experimentation in dance as a threat to the integrity of the art. On the contrary, I see potential benefit to the art as a result of experimental investigation of its performance and educational aspects.

Experimentation is a special form of observation. It is directed observation in a controlled setting with the aim of making statements about cause and effect relationships. Data collected without appropriate control are no different from observations occurring during everyday experience in the world. In experimentation, some level of control over the environment is required to expose the cause of the phenomenon being analyzed. This kind of control aims to eliminate sources of influence on the variable(s) selected for study.[38] Without controls, unequivocal evidence in direct support of cause and effect relationships cannot be obtained. If ten potential causes were allowed to operate on the event of interest, but only one was being accounted for, even if there was a significant effect, no accurate, logical statement regarding the relationship of the effect seen could be made in terms of the singular cause analyzed. The experimental search for cause and effect relationships has as its goal the explanation, prediction, and manipulation of naturally occurring phenomena.

Of course, resting behind concerns of experimental control is the assumption that observable phenomena have discoverable causes. Before the advent of scientific scrutiny, causation was attributed to supernatural forces. If phenomena fall outside of the assumption of causality, if supernatural forces with discretionary powers are acting on the universe, they fall outside the realm of scientific investigation. Another example of how science operates within a relative as opposed to an absolute framework can be seen in how the assumption of causality has adapted to include modern developments in physics. Instead of claiming the absolute certainty of causal connections, scientific parlance has adopted expressions such as shared variance, confidence intervals, and levels of probability.[39]

It is important at this point to make a clear separation between cause and effect relationships and statistics. Contrary to common misconceptions, statistics do not establish cause and effect. Statistics provide analytical tools that enable statements of variability, confidence, and probability. They assess the likelihood of purely random chance operating to yield the results seen during experimentation. Statistical statements of probability are used to describe the confidence placed in the findings. If there is a high probability that the same results found through experimentation could be obtained by chance, the confidence in the experimental results is low. On the other hand, if the data obtained in an experiment would be found by chance less than five in one hundred times, then the confidence that the experimental results reflect a cause and effect relationship is higher. This level of probability (that is, less than 5 percent or $p < .05$) is a commonly accepted convention in behavioral research on human subjects. As a convention, it is not, however, without its detractors.[40] Statistical significance is not synonymous with cause and effect; it is simply a probability estimate. Cause and effect is argued based on the appropriateness of experimental design and the logical analysis of interpretable data. A workable knowledge of statistics is a prerequisite for analyzing and reporting results from most experimental studies. However, related statistical concerns are beyond the scope of this chapter. The interested reader is referred elsewhere for more information.[41]

An additional consideration in the search for causality is the suitability of subject matter for experimentation. When relatively few variables surround a set of physical facts, experimentation can be readily employed to uncover the effects that one set of variables has on another. However, as the complexity of the subject matter increases, experimentation becomes less useful. Depending upon the phenomenon of interest, descriptive or qualitative research strategies might be more productive than experimentation. In their simplest form, experiments deal with a single causal factor. Multifactorial experiments and analysis of interactions begin to mimic real world settings, but even in these sophisticated and complicated experimental arenas, the control necessary for valid collection and meaningful analysis of data places limits on the complexity of the subject matter that can be studied.

Although statistics and experimental design are often thoroughly intermeshed, a beginning understanding of the strengths and weaknesses of designs is within reach of individuals without a background in statistics. As a choreographer interested in structures and their permutations, I find explorations of experimental design fascinating.

Experimental Design

Observation is an everyday activity for all of us. What sets experimental observation apart from everyday experience is planning and control. Planning and control are the primary concerns of designing valid experiments. Planning and control give purposeful direction to observation. The balance of this chapter is devoted to these concerns. Design focuses on select factors, or variables, that are components of the phenomenon of interest. Design elements are intended to isolate some variables while neutralizing others. Three principle categories of variables need definition: independent, dependent, and extraneous.

The independent variable is the cause of the phenomenon. It is the variable being studied, the experimental variable, and it is often purposely manipulated in some fashion so that the effects of its manipulation can be measured. For example, the independent variable might be a treatment such as a pharmaceutical substance or a training regimen that is administered.

The effect is the dependent variable. This is sometimes called the criterion measure. The dependent variable is the result that is being observed or measured. Independent variables can also be measured; the difference quite simply is that the independent variable causes changes in the dependent variable (for example, dance training five times a week causes x improvement in dance performance whereas training two times a week causes only y improvement).

An extraneous variable influences the dependent variable and rivals the independent variable as an explanation of any change in the dependent variable. It is because of extraneous variables that control is a requirement for valid experimentation. Without appropriate levels of control, experimental validity is threatened. In this context, validity refers to whether the independent variable actually affected the dependent variable. Concerns of validity can be separated into external and internal. External validity asks questions regarding the degree to which a given experiment can be generalized to other populations, settings, or treatments. Internal validity refers to the ability to rule out rival hypotheses for the selected cause and effect relationship(s) under study. Internal validity is the minimum requirement for an interpretable experiment. Therefore, internal validity is emphasized in this chapter. Paraphrased below are Donald Campbell and Julian Stanley's descriptions of common threats to internal validity.[42] These threats include history, maturation, testing, instrumentation, statistical regression, selection, experimental mortality, and selection-maturation interaction.

A threat to internal validity posed by history would involve a systematic change in events external to the subject and the experiment that compete with the independent variable to affect the dependent variable. For example, if the physiological effects of dance training were being investigated, exposure to new conditioning or recreational activities during the investigation could interfere with the results. If changes in aesthetic appreciation as a result of taking a particular class were being studied, accidental exposure outside the class to lectures by visiting artists or documentary films on dance could threaten isolation of the class as the only influence on the results obtained. Other historical events of concern include new fads, changes of season, breaks from school, the stress of final exams, transitions between terms in an academic schedule, and so on.

Maturation as a threat to internal validity refers to systematic change internal to the subject that is not part of the study but that affects the dependent variable. If an unaccounted-for change in maturation affects the dependent variable and the independent variable does not change, mistaken conclusions will be drawn. Even if the dependent variable is affected by both maturation and the independent variable, the competing effects disallow definitive interpretations of the outcomes in terms of the independent variable. The normal healing process of a musculoskeletal injury is an example of maturation. The effects of healing could compete with the effects of special therapeutic modalities to explain the positive outcomes of medical treatment. Other examples of maturation that can impact studies of human performance include aging, hunger, exhaustion, boredom, and the like.

In designs that use repeated measurements, a testing effect refers to the influence that participation in the initial measurement sessions has on subsequent measurement sessions. This applies to instances where the pretest is not part of the independent variable. In tests of physical performance it is common for scores to improve during the first few trials as the task being tested is learned and fine-tuned. If practice time is not allowed, in other words if the first few attempts are recorded as the pretest values, any subsequent testing within a reasonable frame of time, with or without training, would most likely show improvement as a result of learning during the pretest to better perform the task. In the psychological realm, pretesting can sensitize individuals to issues, attitudes, preferences, and so on, and thereby cause a change at retesting without administration of any feedback or training whatsoever.

Instrumentation must be monitored very closely to guarantee measurement stability. Whether the instrument is a piece of equipment or a judge's scoring sheet, changes in instrument calibration or subjective assessments can affect the measurement obtained and rival the independent variable as an explanation of any effects seen. Calibration of instruments as well as subjective ratings should be consistently checked and adjusted as necessary throughout testing. Tests that involve subjective assessments need reliability checks built into them to protect against inter- and intraobserver shifts.

All measurements contain some degree of error. An obtained measurement is accurate insofar as it reflects the true value within an acceptable range of measurement error. Regression toward the mean is a statistical phenomenon that occurs when groups selected on the basis of extreme scores show movement toward the mean upon retesting. In other words, individuals who scored extremely poorly on the pretest probably had measurement error acting to their disadvantage. Upon retest these same individuals are likely to score higher because the measurement error will not be expressed as extremely in a disadvantageous direction. This variability around the real score that results from fluctuations in and the direction of the measurement error will cause an extreme score to regress toward the mean. Studies with group assignment based on anything other than a random procedure (for example, intact groups, interest-based volunteerism, and so on) are open to threats from regression. It is particularly important not to base group assignment on extreme scores.

Selection bias refers once again to the effects of grouping by any procedure other than a random one. If comparison groups are not formed randomly there is a threat that they were different upon formation, prior to administration of the treatment variable. Even designs that provide for a pretreatment measurement of the dependent variable cannot account for the effects that unmeasured characteristics might have. A treatment group formed by volunteers may have high motivational characteristics that are outside the scope of the study. These motivational attributes might interact with the treatment to generate significant posttest changes. If, by contrast, the same treatment were given to a group with low motivational attributes, it could have a lesser effect or no effect at all. In such a case the isolation of the effect of the independent variable on the dependent variable would be insufficient to allow inference. In fact, it would not be the independent variable that was responsible for the change, it would be the interaction of the independent variable with a factor extraneous to the study (motivation, in the example above) that was the cause of the effect seen. A guarantee of equation across groups is required to protect against this threat.

As a threat to internal validity, experimental mortality refers to differential loss of subjects from comparison groups. For example, dropout could result from such things as injuries in the experimental group due to the independent variable, or loss of commitment in controls. When dropout, or mortality, occurs, a competing explanation for any effect from the independent variable immediately becomes survival of the fittest. In all group data, there are individuals in the group who score below the group mean value. If the independent variable actually acted as a screening device, as opposed to a factor that stimulated changes, it could differentially weed out the low-scoring individuals and leave only the high scorers. The posttest group mean would be higher because the low scorers were not included, not because of any effect that the treatment had on their scores.

In pre-experimental and nonequivalent control group designs, selection-maturation interaction occurs when one group differentially undergoes physiological and/or psychological changes. When this threat is operative, something internal to members of one of the groups affects measurements of that group but not the other. For example, girls who engage in heavy physical training have delayed menarche. Untrained girls of the same age enter puberty and one of the consequences is increased body fat. If someone were investigating these two groups in regard to weight changes due to training they might mistakenly conclude that the training resulted in body fat reduction. In reality, the training did not "reduce" body fat; rather, it delayed pubescent changes in the hormonal milieu that would have resulted in fat gain. Attitude changes that affect motivation during testing might also fall under this threat, as would any of the factors listed above under maturation.

Concerns of experimenter effects can be added to Campbell and Stanley's list of threats to internal validity. One such effect, expectancy, is included here.[43] Expectancy refers to the effect of anticipated outcomes on data from knowledgeable experimenters dealing with labeled groups. For example, if judges are evaluating posttest performances and they know which subjects are from the treatment group, they might award higher scores to these subjects because they *should* do better and, thus, posttest ratings *should* be higher.

Following is an analysis of various experimental designs and their capabilities to protect against these threats to validity. Campbell and Stanley's division of designs into Pre-Experimental, True Experimental, and Quasi-Experimental is used below.[44] Pre-Experimental designs contain groups formed prior to the experiment through a process other than random assignment.

Pre-Experimental Designs

Pre-experimental designs include the One-Shot Case Study, the one group pretest-posttest design, and the static-group comparison.

THE ONE-SHOT CASE STUDY

In a One-Shot Case Study a single group is examined after unmonitored exposure to an experimental treatment. For example, if a group of elite dancers is studied for the purpose of making statements of causality, the supposed treatment is dance training. This design provides no internal basis for comparison. The available data stand alone; they cannot be assessed internally in terms of any other data. Therefore, no context is available within which to interpret these data and no causal inferences can be legitimately drawn. Campbell and Stanley refer to the experimental use of this design as "misplaced precision."[45]

The point regarding misplaced precision is well taken in terms of experimentation leading to statements of causality. In that respect, One-Shot Case Studies suffer critical threats to internal validity from history, maturation, selection, and mortality. In the example above, each of these threats could provide a plausible explanation that would challenge dance training as the cause of results obtained in a One-Shot Case Study. For example, since this design involves an intact group, perhaps this group shared an usually high value for a characteristic being measured, such as flexibility, before they ever had any exposure to dance training. Perhaps individuals who are attracted to dance as a profession are genetically endowed with higher than average joint mobility. If this were the case, selection, not dance training, would be responsible for the high level of flexibility found. In this scenario, the same results could have been obtained on this group even if they had not trained in dance. Campbell and Stanley comment that, "Basic to scientific evidence . . . is the process of comparison, of recording differences, or a contrast."[46]

Numerous examples of One-Shot Case Studies can be found in the dance medicine and science literature. Outside of making causal claims, there are defensible reasons why this design might be used. Consider, for example, a first look at an unresearched area. A One-Shot Case Study could provide readily and economically obtainable information to assess whether there is any reason to invest time and money in a better study. Recognition of the limitations of this design places results in a clearly descriptive frame, without interpretations suggesting cause and effect relationships. Descriptive data obtained with this design might, however, yield hypotheses for future testing in more sophisticated designs.

Since Mark Kram's 1971 *Sports Illustrated* article, "Encounter with an Athlete," drew attention to the athleticism of ballet, numerous One-Shot Case Studies have catalogued physiologic profiles of dancers for a variety of measures.[47] Most typically, these studies have used standardized measures imported to dance from medicine and exercise physiology. These baseline data have made a valuable contribution, but their explanatory scope is severely limited.

In some instances, an operative assumption of One-Shot Case Studies is that standardization of testing and measurement procedures allow comparison to established norms. If a One-Shot Case Study were to reveal that a group possessed outstanding characteristics, a closer look would be warranted. Consider, for example, a study that has shed some much-needed light onto the confounding collection of data that surrounds dancers' performance on isokinetic tests of strength and endurance.[48] Mohamad Parnianpour et al. used a triaxial isokinetic dynamometer to profile dancers' isometric and dynamic strength and endurance.[49] Previous studies used isokinetic dynamometers with the capacity to measure isolated actions in a single plane only. Parnianpour et al. studied integrated spinal actions in three planes. When these researchers compared results obtained from thirty-five female dancers to normative data bases from other studies, dancers demonstrated less isometric strength but greater speed and power than groups representing the general female population. In addition, dancers demonstrated less accessory-plane motion during endurance testing, indicating higher levels of control and coordination. This study differs from previous efforts in its measurement of integrated spinal actions versus isolated peripheral joint actions (most typically of the ankles and knees), and its ability to assess motion control issues from a multiplanal perspective versus analyses restricted to a single plane. While integrated spinal actions and spatial control of motion are arguably central components of dance training, this study's design does not support causal inference.

It does, however, establish the need for a True-Experimental or Quasi-Experimental design that could test the hypothesis that dance training increases control, speed, and power of spinal actions.

THE ONE GROUP PRETEST-POSTTEST DESIGN

The One Group Pretest-Posttest design is an extension of the One-Shot Case Study that tests the intact group twice, once before administration of the experimental treatment and once after. This design supports statements of difference but not statements of causality. Explanations of posttest results that rival the independent variable include the internal threats of history, maturation, testing, instrument decay, statistical regression, selection-maturation interaction, and expectancy. As with One-Shot Case Studies, lack of control makes statements of causal inference hazardous at best. In the One Group Pretest-Posttest design, a threat from mortality is controlled insofar as information regarding its impact is collected and assessed. If there is little or no dropout there is no concern.

In an attempt to determine the persistence of symptoms of eating disorders among ballet students, researchers collected initial data on fifty-five students in a ballet school and follow-up data for only thirty-two of those individuals.[50] Based in part on the number of students who had high scores on the Eating Disorder Inventory (EDI) at both initial testing and follow-up, these workers contended that "environmental pressures to maintain extreme thinness may lead to sustained eating disorders."[51] However, without comparable data from those students who dropped out of the study, it is possible that the same percentage of the dropouts would have scored just as high at follow-up as they did initially. If that proved to be the case, then the ballet school would not be a factor in the sustainment of the high EDI scores at all. Without comparable information from the dropouts, there is no evidence to support causal connections between the "environmental pressures" of the ballet school and the behavior of the students. These data are purely descriptive and do not provide support for either causal inference or generalization to other groups.

These researchers take even further interpretive license when they declare that "certain subcultures [implying ballet] tend to breed particular disturbances."[52] If initial testing revealed high EDI scores, the ballet school may not have been a factor in either sustainment or development of eating disorders. An equally plausible explanation of the presence of eating disorders among these ballet dancers is that these individuals had a history of eating disorders and were drawn to this ballet school because the environment supported their already established hyperactivity and drive for thinness. In this case, high scores on initial testing should preclude the suggestion that the ballet culture "breeds" eating disorders.

This same study provides a good backdrop for the discussion of expectancy as a threat to validity. Until evidence is presented that diagnoses were given by individuals who were blind to the group association of their clients or, better yet, by individuals who were uninformed about the whole experimental endeavor, work such as this will remain open to criticisms that their expectancy to find support for their hypothesis influenced confirmation of the disorders they were looking for through diagnoses by fully informed researchers. Expectancy as a threat to validity can operate across all designs and becomes increasingly problematic when measurements rely more on subjective evaluations than objective quantities. Simple and effective procedures such as blind evaluation are required to control for this threat.

I am not attempting to minimize the serious consequences of disordered eating, nor am I trying to deny that eating disorders may be more prevalent among some categories of dancers than in the population at large. Aside from these concerns, I find the work criticized above to be a particularly good example of interpretations and conclusions that exceed the limits of the design used and the data gathered.

Any design that does not randomize group assignment only partially protects against threats to validity from selection. The One Group Pretest-Posttest design allows comparison of the pretest and posttest measures to evaluate differences. This ensures that, upon entry, the group did not possess the posttest level of the measured characteristic and allows statements regarding sameness or change to be made. However, statements of causality are questionable. Even though a researcher can be convinced that the group changed, the change cannot necessarily be attributed solely to the experimental treatment. There is no way of sorting out characteristics of an intact group that might be reacting to the treatment and therefore contributing to changes that other groups without those characteristics would not demonstrate. Without random appointments to groups, or some other way of assessing the "normal" nature of the study group, it is possible that an experimental treatment could interact with a special characteristic that members of the intact group shared in common. This uncontrolled and typically unmeasured characteristic could be responsible for the change seen and could rival the effect of the treatment on the measured characteristic as an explanation for the change. If the group had not possessed this special characteristic, it is possible that the treatment would not have resulted in the change seen.

Consider the study reported by Kirkendall and Calabrese as an example.[53] They found a significant improvement in maximal oxygen consumption in a group of female ballet dancers measured before and after an August-to-December training season for the *Nutcracker*. With this statistical finding in hand, they concluded that dance could be used as a conditioning activity to positively influence maximal oxygen consumption and work performance. However, a closer analysis underscores the fact that the "improved" maximal oxygen consumption values for these dancers were low in comparison to athletic groups and were more indicative of normal values obtained from untrained individuals. Even more importantly, the initial values for these dancers were suspiciously low, below the low end of the range of normative values for untrained populations!

With these issues in mind, it is appropriate to conclude that the change seen in the female ballet dancers they studied was due at least as much, if not more, to their initial values, not to the rigors of the training. At posttest these dancers demonstrated values for maximal oxygen consumption that fall squarely in the range of values typically categorized as normal for untrained women. It is possible that this training would not have resulted in any change at all if these female dancers had started with pretest values in the normal range. From this perspective, conclusions regarding the positive aerobic conditioning effects of ballet rehearsals would have no support. It was the low initial level of the dependent variable that was responsible for the change, not necessarily the rehearsal. Perhaps during their summer break these individuals were so abnormally sedentary that the simple demands of returning to a normal lifestyle, demands such as the repeated bouts of walking required to meet their rehearsal schedules, could account for the changes seen.

THE STATIC-GROUP COMPARISON

The last Pre-Experimental design to be covered here is the Static-Group Comparison. In this design, two or more intact groups are studied simultaneously so comparisons between groups can be made. One group serves as a control group, and the others represent "trained" groups. Each group is tested only once. The groups are typically established based on the fact that members of a group have a select characteristic in common. For example, a group of dance majors might be compared to a group of sedentary students. If causal inferences are drawn on the basis of data from studies of this design, the assumption is that the training caused any of the differences that are found by testing. In the example just given, dance majors are assumed to be "trained" while the sedentary controls are assumed to have no exposure to dance or any other training that could influence the results. This design offers protection against threats to validity from history, testing, instrumentation, and regression.

Assuming that the groups have equal exposure to the same historical events, effects from history should be equally distributed between groups. A threat from testing is nonexistent since there are no repeated tests in this design. Instrumentation is controlled insofar as instruments hold their calibration or are recalibrated throughout the testing session, or, if testing has to be scheduled for more than one day, each testing session has an equal mix of subjects from different groups. Regression toward the mean will not be a threat if the groups were not established on the basis of extreme scores.

However, Static-Group Comparisons are open to threats from selection and mortality, the two threats that are at least partially controlled by the One Group Pretest-Posttest design. In a Static-Group Comparison there is no way of knowing whether the groups were different upon formation. The experimental group could have had higher values for the dependent variable than the control group before administration of the independent variable. Maybe individuals genetically endowed with high levels of motor control are attracted to dance, and maybe dance does not really improve control at all, it just transfers its expression to the movement skills practiced. In a Static-Group Comparison where interpretations of the data exceed limitations of the design, high motor control values of dance majors compared with nonmajors would be attributed to their dance training. Differences between groups located by such a study can be legitimately discussed, but no causal inferences are supported.

Even if the groups were not different when the experimental group began exposure to the treatment, in a Static-Group Comparison there is no way of telling how many of the experimental group dropped out before the testing occurred. This kind of mortality could leave the remainder of the group intact because they began the exposure with the characteristics necessary to survive. Perhaps individuals with high and low motor control abilities are drawn equally to dance, and perhaps dance demands high motor control abilities for success but does not train participants to develop it. (I do not mean to imply that this is the case; I do not think it is. I am just trying to delimit a clear example.) In this scenario, those who could survive exposure to the training would be those who entered it with high levels of motor control. Those who entered with low levels would not develop motor control because of their participation and would drop out because they could not succeed. When those with low control abilities dropped out, the group that would get tested in the Static-Group Comparison would be left with only the genetically endowed individuals.

A group of researchers analyzed trained dancers and naive, untrained controls during performance of *dégagé à la seconde*.[54] Analyses began with the weight of the body equally distributed between the two feet. Performance of the *dégagé à la seconde* involves shifting the weight onto one leg and moving the gesture leg to forty-five degrees of hip abduction. Kinematic analysis identified two distinct neuromuscular control strategies. The dancers used a translation strategy that preserved the horizontal nature of lines drawn across the eyes, the shoulders, and the iliac crests while simultaneously preserving the verticality of the axis of the trunk. The naive subjects employed an inclination strategy that tilted the trunk away from the gesture leg and counter-rotated the head to reestablish a horizontal line across the eyes. Based on these findings, these researchers concluded that the dancers' translation strategy represented new coordination resulting from "long-term training and indicates that a new motor program has been elaborated."[55]

While the description of the dancers' translation strategy will sound familiar to dancers and dance teachers, and while dance teachers will tell us that beginners need to learn this translation strategy, the information available from within this Static-Group Comparison does not support generalizations regarding the effects of dance training. No training was administered as part of the study and no efforts to equally distribute innate movement strategy preferences across groups were made. Thus, as obvious as the results might appear in terms of establishing training as the cause of this strategy, no direct evidence to support such an inference was actually gathered. Simple statements of difference can be logically substantiated, but statements of causal inference are questionable.

Using genetic endowment to account for all differences is done here only to illustrate examples. Genetic endowment, innate movement preferences, and various other factors most probably interact with training in every way possible to produce success in dance. My point is quite simply that, as with the other two Pre-Experimental designs, the Static-Group Comparison does not provide strong evidence to support statements of causal inference. Because of the lack of control in Pre-Experimental designs, data and interpretations from them are rendered descriptive at best. At this time, a relatively substantial body of Pre-Experimental research has been done in dance medicine and science. The field could now benefit from studies using more sophisticated designs to follow up on the salient features of these descriptive analyses of dancers. As new areas are investigated or new measures are piloted, Pre-Experimental designs provide a ready, but severely limited, starting point. As an area of study matures, more attention needs to be paid to study design if we aim to decipher causality.

True Experimental Designs

The magic prescription that helps support causal inferences drawn from the results of True Experimental designs is random assignment to groups.[56] Randomization equally distributes known and unknown characteristics of participants across all of the groups. If any threats to the cause and effect relationship of the independent variable and the dependent variable exist, they should be neutralized by their equal expression across all of the groups. Campbell and Stanley detail three True Experimental designs: the Pretest-Posttest Control Group design, the Posttest-Only Control Group design, and the Solomon Four-Group design.

All of these designs facilitate control of all of the threats to internal validity listed above except expectancy. If expectancy could threaten the validity of any given project, special steps must be taken to control it.

THE PRETEST-POSTTEST CONTROL GROUP DESIGN

This design combines the repeated testing of the One Group Pretest-Posttest design with the between-group comparison of the Static-Group design. At least two groups are studied simultaneously. Both groups are pretested and posttested. The experimental group is exposed to the treatment but the control group is not. The key feature that sets this design apart from the Pre-Experimental designs is the equation of the groups at pretest through random assignment.

An extension of this design commonly used in educational and physical training settings is to repeat the posttesting. Consider, for example, a study that was done to test the effect of auditory feedback on foot pronation.[57] This report included three experiments, two of which were Pretest-Posttest Control Group designs with repeated posttesting. In the first experiment, auditory feedback triggered by a pressure transducer placed on the arch of the foot was used as the independent variable or the experimental treatment. Ten untrained women volunteered to participate and were randomly assigned to either a control or an experimental group. Control and experimental groups were treated equally. Both groups were outfitted with a pressure transducer and an auditory feedback unit. The control group was outfitted with a dummy auditory unit and did not receive any auditory feedback. The testing sessions were composed of a *battements tendu en croix* barre exercise that took forty seconds to complete at the prescribed tempo. During each testing session the exercise was repeated four times. Data were collected during three testing/training sessions. For the experimental group, an auditory signal was generated whenever they pronated during bouts 2 and 4 of each testing/training session. In addition to being connected to an auditory signal generator (or a dummy unit in the case of the controls), the pressure transducer was connected to a device that recorded the total amount of time spent in pronation.

In this design, bout 1 of the first testing session served as the pretest. Both groups averaged approximately thirty seconds of pronation during this bout of testing. For day 3, bout 3, mean pronation times were 21.8 and 3.1 seconds for the control and experimental groups respectively. Statistical analysis confirmed the significance of the difference ($p < .05$) and supported the conclusion that auditory feedback during performance of *battements tendu* can reduce the frequency of pronation in beginning dance training. The auditory feedback was administered for two bouts of the exercise over each of the three days of testing/training. This totaled only 240 seconds of treatment and presented rather dramatic evidence to support the inference that auditory feedback can cause reduced pronation.

Since this work used a mechanical device to quantify the number of seconds spent in pronation, the threat of expectancy would seem to have been controlled. However, it is important in designs such as this to make certain that treatment of the control and experimental groups differs only with respect to administration of the independent variable. In all other respects, handling of the groups must be equal. If these groups reported for testing on separate days, and if the administration of the testing differed, it is possible that things said, even the way in which things were said, could have been different between groups and the experimenters could have unwittingly biased the outcome.

Rosenthal gives exhaustive treatment to potential experimenter effects even in well-designed experiments.[58] I am not suggesting that the foot pronation study encountered this difficulty, but consider the ramifications of experimenters in such a situation who unconsciously alter the tones of their voices as they deliver the same message to two different groups. For the controls their message might imply that pronation does not really matter; whether pronated or not, just concentrate on accomplishing the *tendus*. To the experimental group, however, the vocal intonation might imply that nothing else matters; regardless of what else might occur, remain focused on eliminating pronation at all times during testing. If this had been the case, then the degree of emphasis placed on elimination of pronation would compete with the auditory feedback as an explanation for the improvement seen.

Common remedies to this sort of a threat to validity include keeping members of the research team responsible for subject contact blind to the group affiliation of the subjects, or finding a way to ensure standardization or equation of the testing environment. If, as an example, test instructions are recorded on videotape, and the video is used for test administration, every subject will receive exactly the same message in the same way. Mixing controls and experimentals in testing/training sessions could also help equate treatment across groups.

If assurances of protection are provided against threats not covered by design, the Pretest-Posttest Control Group design can be used to gather data supporting casual inference. If there is an influence from the pretest that affects the posttest results, the Posttest-Only Control Group design can eliminate the effect and the Solomon Four-Group design can factor out the effect as a component of the study.

POSTTEST-ONLY CONTROL GROUP DESIGN

In a Posttest-Only Control Group design, no pretest data are collected. This True Experimental design is the same as the Pre-Experimental Static-Group Comparison with the single, but ultimately critical exception that in the Posttest-Only Control Group design, group assignment is made by a random procedure.

In terms of valid causal inference, randomization frees this True Experimental design from the tangled web of competing inferences inherent in a Static-Group Comparison. In the Posttest-Only Control Group design, random group assignment helps assure that the factors of concern are isolated and manipulated, and that extraneous variables are neutralized by their equal expression among groups. Campbell and Stanley comment that this design is not commonly recommended by research texts because it is often confused with the Static-Group Comparison and because equation through randomization is distrusted.[59] They also comment on this design's appropriate use by Fisher in his seminal experimental work in agriculture and suggest this design's utility in educational and legal research.

THE SOLOMON FOUR-GROUP DESIGN

The Posttest-Only Control Group design actually accounts for the last two groups of the Solomon Four-Group design. The Solomon Four-Group design combines the two groups formed in the Pretest-Posttest Control Group design with the two groups from the Posttest-Only Control Group design. The final design yields four groups in all: two experimental groups, one that receives the pretest and the posttest, and one that receives only the posttest; and two control groups, one that receives the pretest and the posttest, and one that receives only the posttest. As with all of the True Experimental designs, group assignment is decided by a random procedure. With the testing manipulations of the Solomon Four-Group design, the magnitude of a testing effect can be assessed. The investment is rather considerable, but it is, nonetheless, the most efficient way available to sort through the information required to assess the magnitude of a testing effect.

Quasi-Experimental Designs

Throughout the history of experimentation, Quasi-Experimental designs have arisen in response to the needs of field research. In Quasi-Experimental designs, some of the control possible through True Experimental designs is sacrificed in favor of operating within more applied settings. To illustrate this point and to move forward in this chapter to other issues, only two of the many Quasi-Experimental designs covered by Campbell and Stanley are discussed. They are the Nonequivalent Control Group design and the Time Series design.

THE NONEQUIVALENT CONTROL GROUP DESIGN

The Nonequivalent Control Group design mimics the True Experimental Pretest-Posttest Control Group design. Instead of using a random procedure for grouping, however, intact groups are studied. Even with the use of intact groups, incorporation of a control group constitutes a vast improvement over the Pre-Experimental One Group Pretest-Posttest design. The Nonequivalent Control Group design facilitates control of history, maturation, testing, instrumentation, selection, and mortality as threats to validity. Any effects from history, maturation, testing, and instrumentation should be equally expressed by both groups. Analysis of the effects of selection is facilitated by appraisal of group equivalence, at least on the variable(s) of interest, by comparative analysis of pretest results. Through this design information to assess the potential effects of subject dropout, or mortality, can be gathered. As the groups become increasingly similar, the control over each of these threats to validity becomes increasingly stronger. In instances where application of True Experimental designs is impossible, Campbell and Stanley recommend this Quasi-Experimental design as a viable and worthwhile alternative.[60]

However, in the Nonequivalent Control Group design, protection against regression hinges on the procedure followed during selection, and protection against selection-maturation interaction is weak. If an attempt to match constituency within either of the groups is made on the basis of extreme pretest scores, regression of scores at posttest could interfere with analysis of the effect of the independent variable.

To illustrate the potential effects of a selection-maturation interaction, imagine a scenario in which two intact ballet classes are used to analyze the benefits of supplemental strength training. With the long-term hope of intervening in injury patterns typical of male ballet dancers who are regularly required to perform lifts, this imaginary research team wants to assess the effects of a particular strength training program on a group of dedicated and promising young boys. The ballet school they approached for their subjects had two classes for boys, one in the early afternoon and one in the evening. The early afternoon class was chosen as the experimental group and the evening class as the control group. In this way the strength training could be conveniently conducted in the afternoon, following the ballet class. To give the strength training a reasonable chance to show measurable improvements, it was designed as a six-month training program. No difference was seen on the pretest scores, and for posttest, the experimental group showed significant strength gains.

At first glance the researchers thought they had confirmed the benefits of their strength training program. But when they discussed the results with the director of the ballet school, they learned that the boys in the early afternoon class were just slightly older and attended this class because they were released from school earlier than the younger boys who had to attend the evening class. The director commented that more than changes in strength, she had noticed changes in classroom behavior in the early afternoon group. The suspicious researchers mounted follow-up interviews and found that 75 percent of the early afternoon class, their experimental group, were in the throes of puberty. At this point the researchers realized that their design contained a critical flaw that did not allow them to attribute the posttest strength gains (the dependent variable) to the strength training (the independent variable) that they administered. Because male sex hormones positively affect neuromuscular coordination and muscular strength, pubescence competed with the strength training program to explain the strength gains seen.

Such a disastrous waste of time and energy could have been avoided with improved planning and design. The above example used an obvious effect of maturation acting differentially across groups (a classic selection-maturation interaction) to make a point. Less obvious effects should also be considered. Hunger and fatigue can have a significant impact on the quality of participation in training sessions and on test performance. Attitude changes and socialization resulting from advancement through short- and long-term cycles within a training or academic system fall under the heading of maturation effects, as do all biological or psychological processes within individuals that vary with time.

THE TIME SERIES DESIGN

The last design to be examined here is the Time Series design. In this design repeated observation sessions are scheduled before and after administration of the treatment. For example, four pretests might be conducted before an experimental treatment is administered and four posttests used to follow up. The Time Series is an extension of the One Group Pretest-Posttest design in which only one group is studied, but repeated observations before and after introduction of the independent variable provide enough information to formulate plausible arguments against maturation, testing, instrumentation, regression, selection, mortality, and selection-maturation interaction as threats to validity. However, because this design is extended over time, history presents a threat to internal validity.

To control or explain the threat that history presents over time, the experimenter needs to demonstrate an acceptable degree of isolation from events external to the experiment that could affect the dependent measure. Limitations placed on the subjects and confirmed through interviews or activity logs could help accomplish this. Limitations placed on the testing and training environments might also be necessary. An experimenter aware of intervening historical events might be able simply to explain them away. That is, she or he might present a compelling argument that the results seen could not be explained by the intervening event.

Campbell and Stanley qualify the control that the Times Series design has over maturation as a threat by reasoning that it would be highly unlikely to see sudden shifts in behavior resulting from maturation that would coincide with administration of the experimental treatment.[61] Maturation typically causes slow, incremental change. Even if maturation were to cause a sudden, dramatic shift, it would only be by chance that it would occur with the treatment as opposed to during the baseline observations preceding introduction of the independent variable. However, spontaneous remission of illnesses (both biological and psychological), the normal temporal progression of healing, and the abrupt onset of changes such as menarche pose exceptions to this argument. For reasons such as these, Otto Payton describes clinical variations to the Time Series design including an A-B-A design, and, yes, it is the equivalent of an A-B-A choreographic structure in experimental terms.[62] The A phase is a control phase of repeated observations before administration of the experimental treatment (B). After repeated measures during B, treatment is withdrawn, there is a return to A, and measurements are again repeated as a posttraining control phase. Before proceeding with an example of this design from the literature, I want to introduce the concept of single-subject experimentation.

Up to this point, this chapter has dealt specifically with the application of experimental designs to group analyses. Another important application of experimental design is to single-subject research, which is the ultimate form of within-subjects designs. Any design that can be applied to groups can be modified for within-subjects use. Applications of within-subjects designs date back to the 1800s and include pioneering efforts in physiology by Ivan Pavlov and in psychology by Hermann Ebbinghaus. Within-subject designs have a distinct disadvantage in terms of external validity (generalization beyond the immediate experimental setting), but, as has been the case with Pavlov and Ebbinghaus, this disadvantage can be remedied by multiple efforts that replicate results.

Geoffrey Keppel summarizes the difference between group and within-subject experiments by clarifying that in the analysis of groups, also referred to as between-subject analysis, the information of interest represents differences between subjects.[63] In within-subjects designs, analysis considers differences in the information gleaned from repeated measurements on the same subject. Keppel goes on to describe within-subjects designs as particularly efficient and sensitive and "the obvious choice to study such behavioral changes as learning."[64] When an intensive investment in training is required to generate measurable outcomes, and when individuals within a group respond differentially to training, use of within-subjects designs and analyses not only makes sense, it becomes imperative. Barry Bates, Janet Dufek, and Howard Davis state that differential responses between members of a group threaten validity of group analysis and "not only justify but dictate" the use of within-subject designs.[65]

Consider, for example, the application of experimental research to issues of motor control in dance. J. A. Scott Kelso and Betty Tuller described performance of the same movement using different muscle ensembles and performance of different movements using the same muscle ensemble as common features of motor systems.[66] Reports by Ryman and Ranney, and Chatfield, Barr, Sveistrup, and Woollacott suggest that variability among dancers may be more the norm than the exception.[67] Because of issues such as these, between-groups designs for movement analysis in dance could, at best, mask information of interest and, at worst, suffer critical threats to validity.

Body therapists using variations of Karel and Berta Bobath's neurodevelopmental treatment (NDT) to rehabilitate injured dancers have stimulated incorporation of NDT practices into some forms of dance training.[68] A study utilizing an A-B-A single-subject design examined the hypothesis that NDT could inhibit abnormal and facilitate normal postural reflexes.[69] A normal equilibrium reaction to a posterior perturbation is ankle dorsiflexion. In a child with spastic quadriplegia, this normal and corrective dorsiflexion response is replaced by an inappropriate plantar flexion response that exacerbates the disturbance to equilibrium. Researchers used electromyography (EMG) to measure the response of ankle dorsiflexors to posterior perturbation in a child with spastic quadriplegia. They collected baseline or control data for seven days (phase A). For each of the next nine days they administered NDT and, after NDT, collected data on each of these days (phase B). Finally, they withdrew the NDT and collected data for seven more days (return to phase A). The relative amount of dorsiflexor activity was roughly equivalent across the two A phases, whereas phase B showed a marked increase in relative dorsiflexor activity.

This example presents convincing evidence that NDT facilitated incorporation of a normal equilibrium reaction into an individual's reflexive response repertory where it was previously absent. The repeated observations in all phases of the design replace the need for a control group (or control subject) in the sense that they establish measurement variability and stability within each condition. Graphic and statistical analyses support clear separation of the stable magnitudes of the data from its variations during A and B phases. The evidence gathered by repeating phase A after withdrawal of NDT provides a convincing argument against healing as a plausible explanation for the change seen in B.

For more information on within-subjects research designs refer to Thomas Welsh and Steven Chatfield.[70]

Additional Concerns

In the final analysis, it must be remembered that no experiment is perfect. Experimental designs do not necessarily have to provide protection against each and every threat to validity. Points to keep in mind include: understanding the weaknesses and strengths of a design selected for use, incorporating means of protection outside of design concerns when necessary, and placing appropriate limits on interpretation of data and formulation of conclusions. Even when exerting control over the experimental situation to address design weaknesses, it is important to understand the ultimate limitations of a design and to construct studies that address the research question at hand in the best way possible.

In this chapter I deal primarily with concerns of internal validity. In Keppel's analysis of the advantages and disadvantages of within-subjects designs, he discusses forfeiture of external validity or generalizability in favor of in-depth analysis of the unique.[71] As experiments are structured to provide greater generalizability, sacrifices are typically made to protections against threats to internal validity.[72] It is most important to remember that designs should serve to answer the research question asked in the best way possible. There are many important questions, particularly in dance science and medicine, that can be answered without a need to infer broadly ranging external validity. By contrast, in some instances the only answer sought might be one of generalizability. Creating an appropriate design for the question at hand is crucial to success.

Another relevant design issue is design complexity. This chapter deals, for the most part, with single factor designs, studies in which the effects of one independent variable are studied. Such a reduction of operative influences on the phenomenon of interest can lead to findings that might not hold true in applied settings where numerous influences act simultaneously. If an experimental design uses a laboratory setting to reduce the multiple variables that would normally act on the dependent variable in an applied setting to an isolated single independent variable, interpretation of the outcomes may be limited to the laboratory setting and have no real explanatory power in applied settings. The complexity of the phenomenon of interest can play an important role in deciding on an appropriate level of reduction.

Chemists and physicists sometimes have the luxury of dealing with singular entities in purely isolated situations. Their search for basic information does not necessarily require application in complex, real world settings where multiple causes interact simultaneously to affect the dependent measure.

By contrast, multifactorial designs are extensions of single-factor designs that incorporate two or three independent variables (or multiple levels of the same independent variable). Using multiple testing conditions for data collection can constitute a new independent variable. For example, consider Donna Krasnow et al.'s study of the effects of special training on alignment under static and dynamic testing conditions.[73] The design of this study could be noted as 4 x 2 x 2, where there were four groups (one control and three different treatment groups), two testing conditions (static versus dynamic posture preceding measurement), and two different testing sessions (pretraining and posttraining). The three training groups included one group given only imagery training, a second given only conditioning training, and a third given both imagery and conditioning training. In an inclusive analysis of all of the data, no posttest differences were found between groups. However, a significant difference between testing conditions was located. Follow-up analyses suggested that the moment of greatest difficulty during testing, return to vertical alignment after an off-center torso roll, was handled best by and showed most improvement in the group that received combined imagery and conditioning training. If the study had only analyzed alignment from a static vertical perspective, this finding would have been missed. The static vertical perspective is typically used in laboratory measurements of alignment, yet much of the movement performed in dance can be classified as off-center (that is, movement that requires the line of the body to deviate from the vertical line of gravity). Extension of this design enabled analysis under a condition that mimicked a real world setting.

In his assessment of future directions for research in movement behavior, Jeffery Summers states that there is an increased interest in real-world tasks and the use of more natural research settings.[74] Keppel discusses an important advantage of multifactorial experiments as the degree to which they can approximate the actual setting in which behavioral phenomena naturally occur.[75] Beyond their simulation of real-world settings and their sensitivity to individual uniqueness, multifactorial designs allow analysis of interaction effects as protection against threats to validity.[76] Keppel provides comprehensive coverage of interactions.[77] One of several ways in which Keppel defines interaction is: "An interaction is present when one of the independent variables does not have a constant effect at all levels of the other independent variable."[78] Interactions themselves could be the phenomenon of interest in some research questions.

One final concern deserving emphasis is measurement (or test) validity and reliability. We have dealt with issues surrounding the validity of designs. It is also critically important to be assured that measurements employed within the designs are both valid and reliable. This point returns to Bunge's eight-step problem-solving sequence discussed above. Stages three through five suggest clarification of the constructs being measured and the appropriateness of the measures. A valid test measures what it is supposed to measure. A reliable test yields acceptably reproduced results upon repeated administration. Reliable tests are not necessarily valid, however. Test construction and validation are crucial stages in experimentation that cannot be taken for granted. Without a valid measure, the most astounding results are rendered uninterpretable and the best design is rendered purposeless. This is important in dance science because the specificity and sensitivity of standardized measurements in sport and medicine are questionable when it comes to analysis of the subtle changes that occur in dance training that very well could be pivotal to increasing expertise. In terms of assessing the benefits of dance as an educational vehicle in a general education curriculum, standardized tests such as the SAT may not even test intelligence in the domain where the benefits of dance reside.[79]

Closing Thoughts

This chapter moves quickly from problem solving and the philosophy and history of science to experimental applications of scientific methodology in dance and related areas. For some, the juxtaposition of dance and science will forever suggest antithetical worldviews. Even with such a perspective it is important to appreciate how science has made and will continue to make significant contributions to dance. Scientific contributions to our understanding and practice of dance are many and varied. John Weaver's "Anatomical and Mechanical Lectures Upon Dancing" dates back to 1721.[80] Today, articles reporting experimental research in dance appear regularly in the journals of professional organizations. The broad array of topics under investigation promise to identify the effects of dance training and the demands of performance, confirm training preparation for the demands of performance, and assist with screening and intervention prior to the onset of medical problems. When medical problems do arise, research can help assess the efficacy of therapeutic protocols and the level of rehabilitation necessary for a safe return to dancing. Plastino was hopeful that dance science could provide a forum through which everyone involved in the art and practice of dance could share a common bond: "We all need information from Dance Science, because ultimately, we want to keep the dancer moving at full capacity safely and sanely for the longest period of time regardless of the dance medium."[81]

My excitement in wedding dance and science stems from my experiences as both a dancer and an experimenter. I see very clear similarities between processes involved in the two pursuits. The way that dancers and choreographers learn to solve problems has direct links to the reflective thinking required for good science. The well-developed perceptual and movement analysis capabilities of choreographers can transfer seamlessly to experimental venues, and the creative abilities that an artist might bring to scientific endeavors could be revolutionary! What a dance scientist needs is expertise in an allied field. Martha Eddy provides a comprehensive list of scientific fields related to dance. She includes the disciplines of biology, physics, medicine, anatomy, physiology, and psychology; as well as the specialized fields of biomechanics, exercise physiology, motor learning, kinesiology, physical therapy, athletic training, nutrition, and rehabilitation.[82]

In the arena of liberal arts education, experimental research could prove very helpful in promoting a broader understanding of the contribution that movement can make to education. It would be advantageous to have information available to us that addresses the general education benefit of accessing and developing movement intelligence. Information regarding the transfer of movement intelligence to other forms of intelligence could also be helpful.

A review of the outcomes of the 1977 conference, "The Arts and Aesthetics: An Agenda for the Future," makes apparent our lack of progress on several research fronts that might aptly be addressed through a variety of modes of inquiry, including experimentation.[83] Stanley Madeja's report itemizes seven priority areas of research for arts and aesthetics in education. Some pose organizational and data base challenges, others could be addressed through experimentation. Consider the following items from Madeja's list: testing and revising theories of aesthetic development in students, optimizing the learning experience within the schools through aesthetic education and the arts, investigating the relationship of cultural values to aesthetic learning, and improving evaluation in the arts and aesthetics.

Donald Schön's article offers an excellent example of how such work could be mounted in an easily doable fashion.[84] Another marvelous example is a quasi-experimental study that was begun in 1933 and published in 1942.[85] Both the scope and the findings of this study are incredible. Arrangements were made with colleges and universities to admit students from high schools that had been given license to modify their programs in any way they chose. One of several fundamental premises of their curriculum revisions was a doubt that success in college required study of certain subjects for a certain length of time. Upon entry into colleges and universities, students from these experimental curricula were matched with counterparts on their college campus who graduated from conventional preparatory programs. More than 1,400 matched pairs were involved in the study. Performance in college provided the basis for analysis. Peter Oliva summarized the results as follows.

> The graduates of the experimental schools, as it turns out, did as well as or better than their counterparts in college in all subjects except foreign languages. The graduates of the experimental schools excelled their counterparts in scholastic

honors, leadership positions, study habits, intellectual curiosity, and extraclass activities. The eight-year study showed rather conclusively that a single pattern of required courses is not essential for success in college.[86]

To be clear, I am not suggesting that experimentation promises a panacea. Campbell and Stanley devote a section of their text to "Disillusionment with Experimentation in Education."[87] In the end, the results of experimental research are only as good as the researcher. Deep understanding and appropriate application of the tools of the trade are prerequisites to success. My intent in this chapter is to promote a rudimentary understanding of and to provide some insight into experimental processes. I hope interested readers find the various works cited herein to be helpful in their pursuit of more comprehensive treatments. Finally, I also hope to encourage the use of experimentation. I firmly believe that our experiences in and our knowledge of dance and choreography have prepared us well for, and are at least partially transferable to, experimentation in the scientific spirit.

Study Questions

1. Describe the differences between "normal" and "creative" scientists. Discuss issues surrounding their personal characteristics as well as their working processes. Be sure to directly address how each might deal with the impact of contradictory data on theory falsification.

2. Explain the statement: "Threats to validity compete with the working hypothesis to explain the results of an experiment." Include coverage of every threat to internal validity covered in this essay.

3. Compare and contrast the One Group Pretest-Posttest design, the Pretest-Posttest Control Group design, and the Nonequivalent Control Group design in terms of their protection against threats to internal validity.

4. Select a problem of interest, propose an experiment, and fabricate results. Interpret your results and form conclusions based on your hypothesis(es). Evaluate the strengths and weaknesses of your imaginary work in terms of its ability to provide a convincing explanation of the cause and effect relationship between your independent and dependent variables.

NOTES

1. Horace Walpole, letter to Horace Mann, n.p., 1751, quoted in W. B. Cannon, "The Role of Chance in Discovery," *Scientific Monthly* 50 (1940): 204.

2. Induction is reasoning that proceeds from the particular to the general, from data to theory. By contrast, deduction is reasoning that proceeds from the general to the particular, from theory to expected experimental outcomes in a given instance.

3. John Dewey, *How We Think* (Boston: D. C. Heath, 1933), 107–17.

4. Dewey, 108.

5. Deobold B. Van Dalen, *Understanding Educational Research* (New York: McGraw-Hill, 1979), 12.

6. Mario Bunge, *Scientific Research I: The Search for System* (Berlin: Springer-Verlag, 1967), 9.

7. Bunge, 10–11.

8. Edwin G. Boring, "The Nature and History of Experimental Control," *The American Journal of Psychology* 67 (1954): 577.

9. Van Dalen, 12.

10. See William A. Armstrong's introduction to Francis Bacon, *The Advancement of Learning: Book 1*, ed. William A. Armstrong (London: Athlone Press, 1975), 23.

11. Van Dalen, 12; see also E. Mach, "On the Part Played by Accident in Invention and Discovery," trans. Thomas J. McCormack, *The Monist* 6, no. 2 (January 1896): 171, where he refers to Galileo's *Dialogues* and Newton's *Optics*.

12. For comprehensive treatments of the assumptions underlying scientific inquiry see Van Dalen, 17–24; and Paul L. Dressel and Lewis B. Mayhew, *General Education: Explorations in Evaluation* (Washington, D.C.: American Council on Education, 1954), 112–13.

13. Dewey, *How We Think*, 202.

14. John Dewey, *Democracy and Education* (New York: Macmillan, 1926), 223.

15. See Donald A. Schön, "The Theory of Inquiry: Dewey's Legacy to Education," *Curriculum Inquiry* 22, no. 2 (1992): 119–39.

16. In addition to Bacon, see also: T. C. Chamberlin, "Studies for Students: The Method of Multiple Working Hypotheses," *Journal of Geology* 5 (1897): 837–48; John R. Platt, "Strong Inference," *Science* 146, no. 3642 (16 October 1964): 347–53; and Conrad Wesley Snyder Jr. and Bruce Abernethy, eds., *The Creative Side of Experimentation: Personal Perspectives from Leading Researchers in Motor Control, Motor Development, and Sport Psychology* (Champaign, Ill.: Human Kinetics, 1992), 9–11, 208.

17. Snyder and Abernethy, 208.

18. Karl R. Popper, *The Logic of Scientific Discovery* (New York: Basic Books, 1959).

19. Thomas S. Kuhn, *The Structure of Scientific Revolutions*, 2d ed. (Chicago: University of Chicago Press, 1970); and Thomas S. Kuhn, "Second Thoughts on Paradigms," in *The Structure of Scientific Theories*, ed. Frederick Suppe (Urbana: University of Illinois Press, 1974), 459–82.

20. Margaret Masterman, "The Nature of a Paradigm," in *Criticism and the Growth of Knowledge*, ed. I. Lakatos and A. Musgrave (Cambridge: Cambridge University Press, 1970); cited in Kuhn, "Second Thoughts on Paradigms," 460. By Kuhn's own counting, Masterman tallied at least twenty-two different uses of paradigm in Kuhn's original work, the 1962 edition of *The Structure of Scientific Revolutions* (see also the 1970 edition cited in note 19, above).

21. Kuhn, *The Structure of Scientific Revolutions*, 174–210; Kuhn, "Second Thoughts on Paradigms," 459–82.

22. Max Planck, *Scientific Autobiography and Other Papers*, trans. Frank Gaynor (New York: Philosophical Library, 1949), 33–34, cited in Bruce Abernethy and W. A. Sparrow, "The Rise and Fall of Dominant Paradigms in Motor Behaviour Research," chap. 1 in *Approaches to the Study of Motor Control and Learning*, ed. Jeffery J. Summers (Amsterdam: North Holland, 1992), 12.

23. Bunge, 29.

24. Van Dalen, 18. See also D. C. Phillips, "After the Wake: Postpositivistic Educational

Thought," *Educational Researcher* 12 (May 1983): 4–12. In particular, note Phillips's discussion regarding the Vienna Circle's adoption of the "Verifiability Principle" (p. 5) in an attempt to expunge the influence of metaphysics from science and philosophy, a thrust not unlike that of Bacon and others in the Renaissance who attempted to separate theological fiat from empiricism.

25. Snyder and Abernethy, 216–21.

26. W. B. Cannon, "The Role of Chance in Discovery," *Scientific Monthly* 50 (1940): 204.

27. Cannon, 205.

28. Snyder and Abernethy, 214.

29. Snyder and Abernethy, 214; quoting Arthur Koestler, *The Act of Creation* (New York: Macmillan, 1964), 230.

30. Janice Gudde Plastino, *Dance and Science: Melding, Molding, and Moving* (Reston, Va.: National Dance Association, 1991), 4–5.

31. Mach, 168–74.

32. Ibid., 173–74.

33. Susan W. Stinson, "Research as Choreography," *Spotlight on Dance* 20, no. 3 (spring–summer 1994): 1, 8.

34. J. A. Scott Kelso, "Autobiography," in Snyder and Abernethy, 63.

35. Paulette Shafranski, *Modern Dance: Twelve Creative Problem-Solving Experiments* (Glenview, Ill.: Scott, Foresman, 1985).

36. Donald Cram, "Commentary: Tribe and Leader," *Notice,* a publication of the Academic Senate, University of California, vol. 13, no. 5 (March 1989): 3.

37. Sondra Fraleigh, "Good Intentions and Dancing Moments: Agency, Freedom and Self-Knowledge in Dance," Emory Cognition Project with the Mellon Foundation, Colloquium on the Self, Emory University, Atlanta, Georgia, May 5, 1989; quoted in Sondra Fraleigh, "A Vulnerable Glance: Seeing Dance Through Phenomenology," *Dance Research Journal* 23, no. 1 (spring 1991): 13.

38. Boring, 573–89.

39. Van Dalen, 21.

40. B. Don Franks and Schuyler W. Huck, "Why Does Everyone Use the .05 Significance Level?" *Research Quarterly for Exercise and Sport* 57, no. 3 (September 1986): 245–49.

41. Good introductions include Jerry R. Thomas and Jack K. Nelson, *Introduction to Research: In Health, Physical Education, Recreation, and Dance* (Champaign, Ill.: Human Kinetics, 1985); and George A. Ferguson, *Statistical Analysis in Psychology and Education,* 5th ed. (New York: McGraw-Hill, 1981). More advanced treatments can be found in Geoffrey Keppel, *Design and Analysis: A Researcher's Handbook,* 3d ed. (Englewood Cliffs, N.J.: Prentice Hall, 1991).

42. For a comprehensive treatment of external and internal threats to validity with specific reference to sixteen variations of commonly used pre-experimental, true-experimental, and quasi-experimental designs, see Donald T. Campbell and Julian C. Stanley, *Experimental and Quasi-Experimental Designs for Research* (Chicago: Rand McNally, 1963).

43. For a comprehensive treatment of this realm of threats to validity see Robert Rosenthal, *Experimenter Effects in Behavioral Research,* enlarged ed. (New York: Irvington Publishers, Halsted Press, 1976). Thomas and Nelson (see note 41 above), p. 220, were first to cite Rosenthal (the 1966 edition) and incorporate expectancy into Campbell and Stanley's list.

44. Campbell and Stanley, 6–64.

45. Ibid., 7.

46. Ibid., 6.

47. Mark Kram, "Encounter with an Athlete," *Sports Illustrated* (September 27, 1971): 92–94, 96–98, 100, 103.

48. For a review of this issue see Steven J. Chatfield, "Electromyographic Response of Dancers to Isokinetic Work and Select Dance Movements," *Kinesiology and Medicine for Dance* 16, no. 1 (fall–winter 1993–94): 60–82.

49. Mohamad Parnianpour, Mohsen Davoodi, Mindy Forman, and Donald J. Rose, "The Normative Database for the Quantitative Trunk Performance of Female Dancers: Isometric and Dynamic Trunk Strength and Endurance," *Medical Problems of Performing Artists* 9 (June 1994): 50–57.

50. David M. Garner, Paul E. Garfinkel, Wendi Rockert, and Marion P. Olmsted, "A Prospective Study of Eating Disturbances in the Ballet," *Psychotherapy and Psychosomatics* 48 (1987): 170–75.

51. Garner, Garfinkel, Rockert, and Olmsted, 173.

52. Ibid., 174.

53. Donald T. Kirkendall and Leonard H. Calabrese, "Physiological Aspects of Dance," *Clinics in Sports Medicine: Symposium on Injuries to Dancers* 2, no. 3 (November 1983): 525–37.

54. Laurence Mouchnino, Roselyne Aurenty, Jean Massion, and Antonio Pedotti, "Strategies for Simultaneous Control of Equilibrium and Head Position During Leg-Raising Movement," *Comptes rendus de L'Academie des Sciences* (Paris) t. 312, Série III, no. 5 (1991): 225–32.

55. Mouchnino, Aurenty, Massion, and Pedotti, 225.

56. Randomization is not a perfect remedy to all threats, however. There is a set of threats to internal validity beyond the scope of this chapter that is not controlled by randomization of group assignment. The interested reader is referred to Thomas D. Cook and Donald T. Campbell, *Quasi-Experimentation: Design and Analysis Issues for Field Settings* (Chicago: Rand McNally College Publishing Co., 1979), 53–70.

57. Priscilla M. Clarkson, Robert James, Andrea Watkins, and Peter Foley, "The Effect of Augmented Feedback on Foot Pronation During Barre Exercise in Dance," *Research Quarterly for Exercise and Sport* 57, no. 1 (March 1986): 33–40.

58. See Rosenthal in note 42 above.

59. Campbell and Stanley, 25.

60. Ibid., 47.

61. Ibid., 41.

62. Otto D. Payton, *Research: The Validation of Clinical Practice*, 2d ed. (Philadelphia: F. A. Davis, 1988), 120–21.

63. Keppel, 329.

64. Ibid.

65. Barry T. Bates, Janet S. Dufek, and Howard P. Davis, "The Effect of Trial Size on Statistical Power," *Medicine and Science in Sports and Exercise* 24, no. 9 (September 1992): 1059–65.

66. J. A. Scott Kelso and Betty Tuller, "A Dynamical Basis for Action Systems," in *Handbook of Cognitive Neuroscience*, ed. Michael S. Gazzaniga (New York: Plenum Press, 1984), 321–56.

67. Rhonda S. Ryman and Donald A. Ranney, "A Preliminary Investigation of Two Variations of the Grand Battement Devant," *Dance Research Journal* 11 (1978–79): 2–11; Steven J. Chatfield, Sherrie Barr, Heidi Sveistrup, and Marjorie H. Woollacott, "Electromyo-

graphic and Kinematic Analysis of Movement Repatterning in Dance," *Impulse* 4, no. 3 (1996): 220–34.

68. For a historical overview and applications to dance see Rita Honka, "Body Therapy Repatterning and the Neuromotor System" (master's thesis, University of Oregon, Eugene, 1992).

69. Claire Anne Laskas, Sheila L. Mullen, David L. Nelson, and Marnee Willson-Broyles, "Enhancement of Two Motor Functions of the Lower Extremity in a Child With Spastic Quadriplegia" *Physical Therapy* 65, no. 1 (January 1985): 11–16.

70. Thomas M. Welsh and Steven J. Chatfield, "Within-Subject Research Designs for Dance Medicine and Science," *Journal of Dance Medicine and Science* 1, no. 1 (1997): 16–21.

71. Keppel, 329–43.

72. Payton, 79.

73. Donna H. Krasnow, Steven J. Chatfield, Sherrie Barr, Jody Jensen, and Janet Dufek, "Imagery and Conditioning Practices for Dancers," *Dance Research Journal* 29, no. 1 (spring 1997): 43–64.

74. Jeffery J. Summers, ed., "Movement Behaviour: A Field in Crisis?" in *Advances in Psychology 84: Approaches to the Study of Motor Control and Learning* (Amsterdam: Elsevier Science Publishers B. V., 1992), 551–62.

75. Keppel, 481.

76. Campbell and Stanley, 27–29.

77. Keppel, chap. 9, 187–202.

78. Keppel, 197.

79. For comprehensive coverage of measurement validity and reliability, see American Psychological Association, *Standards for Educational and Psychological Tests* (Washington, D.C.: American Psychological Association, 1985); Steven J. Chatfield, "Concerns of Validity and Reliability in Dance Science Research," *Kinesiology for Medicine and Dance* 14, no. 1 (fall/winter 1991–92): 44–56; Margaret J. Safrit, *Introduction to Measurement in Physical Education and Exercise Science* (St. Louis: Times Mirror/Mosby College Publishing, 1986); and Margaret J. Safrit, ed., *Reliability Theory* (Washington, D.C.: American Alliance for Health, Physical Education, and Recreation, 1976).

80. See Richard Ralph, *The Life and Works of John Weaver: An Account of His Life, Writings and Theatrical Productions, with an Annotated Reprint of His Complete Publications* (London: Dance, 1985), 143–49.

81. Plastino, 5.

82. Martha Eddy, "An Overview of the Science and Somatics of Dance," *Kinesiology and Medicine for Dance* 14, no. 1 (fall–winter 1991–92): 20–28.

83. Stanley S. Madeja, "Research in the Arts: Agenda for the Future," *Journal of Physical Education and Recreation* 48 (November–December 1977): 55–57.

84. Schön, see note 15 above for the full citation. Relevant points are in the sections titled "A Homely Example of Designing" and "Some Implications for Educational Research" on pages 127–37.

85. See Wilford M. Aikin, *The Story of the Eight-Year Study* (New York: Harper and Bros., 1942).

86. Peter F. Oliva, *The Secondary School Today,* 2d ed. (New York: Harper and Row, 1972), 120.

87. Campbell and Stanley, 2–4.

REFERENCES

American Psychological Association. *Standards for Educational and Psychological Tests.* Washington, D.C.: American Psychological Association, 1985.

Bates, Barry T., Janet S. Dufek, and Howard P. Davis. "The Effect of Trial Size on Statistical Power." *Medicine and Science in Sports and Exercise* 24, no. 9 (September 1992): 1059–65.

Boring, Edwin G. "The Nature and History of Experimental Control." *The American Journal of Psychology* 67 (1954): 573–89.

Bunge, Mario. *Scientific Research I: The Search for System.* Berlin: Springer-Verlag, 1967.

Campbell, Donald T., and Julian C. Stanley. *Experimental and Quasi-Experimental Designs for Research.* Chicago: Rand McNally, 1963.

Chamberlin, T. C. "Studies for Students: The Method of Multiple Working Hypotheses." *Journal of Geology* 5 (1897): 837–48.

Chatfield, Steven J. "Concerns of Validity and Reliability in Dance Science Research." *Kinesiology for Medicine and Dance* 14, no. 1 (fall/winter 1991–92): 44–56.

Cook, Thomas D., and Donald T. Campbell. *Quasi-Experimentation: Design and Analysis Issues for Field Settings.* Chicago: Rand McNally College Publishing Co., 1979.

Ferguson, George A. *Statistical Analysis in Psychology and Education.* 5th ed. New York: McGraw-Hill, 1981.

Keppel, Geoffrey. *Design and Analysis: A Researcher's Handbook.* 3d ed. Englewood Cliffs, N.J.: Prentice Hall, 1991.

Kuhn, Thomas S. "Second Thoughts on Paradigms." In *The Structure of Scientific Theories,* ed. Frederick Suppe, 459–82. Urbana: University of Illinois Press, 1974.

Platt, John R. "Strong Inference." *Science* 146, no. 3642 (16 October 1964): 347–53.

Safrit, Margaret J. *Introduction to Measurement in Physical Education and Exercise Science.* St. Louis: Times Mirror/Mosby College Publishing, 1986.

———, ed. *Reliability Theory.* Washington, D.C.: American Alliance for Health, Physical Education, and Recreation, 1976.

Snyder, Conrad Wesley, and Bruce Abernethy, eds. *The Creative Side of Experimentation: Personal Perspectives from Leading Researchers in Motor Control, Motor Development, and Sport Psychology.* Champaign, Ill.: Human Kinetics, 1992.

Thomas, Jerry R., and Jack K. Nelson. *Introduction to Research: In Health, Physical Education, Recreation, and Dance.* Champaign, Ill.: Human Kinetics, 1985.

Van Dalen, Deobold B. *Understanding Educational Research.* New York: McGraw-Hill, 1979.

Welsh, Thomas M., and Steven J. Chatfield. "Within-Subject Research Designs for Dance Medicine and Science." *Journal of Dance Medicine and Science* 1, no. 1 (1997): 16–21.

6 DANCE IN THE HERMENEUTIC CIRCLE

Joann McNamara

CONSIDER HOW MEANING and its interchanges with interpretation thread through the following dance moments:

- A researcher reads two different books about the meaning of dance and tries to make sense out of the conflicting interpretations.
- Discussing the Judson Church Dance Theatre in a dance history class, a student wonders: What was it like to dance in New York in the early 1960s, and to be part of the social milieu of that time?
- Observing a cross-cultural dance, an audience member grapples with its meaning.
- Talking in the dressing room after a contact improvisation performance, dancers are struck by the diverse personal experiences of their individual performances.

In each of the above instances the meaning of some sort of dance phenomenon is brought forward, and in these initial acts of questioning, one enters the hermeneutic dialectic circle of interpretation. Philosopher Martin Heidegger sheds light on the reciprocal interaction of human questioning and investigation when he writes, "Every questioning is a seeking. Every seeking takes its direction beforehand from what is sought. Questioning is a knowing search for beings in their thatness and whatness. The knowing search can become an "investigation," as the revealing determination of what the question aims at."[1]

I begin this essay, then, with a question, a signpost toward an enhanced understanding of hermeneutic inquiry and perhaps dance as well: What is hermeneutics and how can it facilitate an understanding of dance phenomena?

Hermeneutics is a tradition, an approach used to examine the meaning of a text and how its meaning is constructed. The term *text* here refers to all symbolic constructs of meaning which, in the world of dance, may include dances, the social and cultural activities surrounding dance, books about dance, the language of dance, and so forth. Consequently, discourses such as Susan Foster's post-structural investigation, *Reading Dancing: Bodies and Subjects in Contemporary American Dance,* and Cynthia J. Novack's anthropological analysis, *Sharing the Dance: Contact Improvisation and American Culture,* are both hermeneutic in a general sense in that each is concerned with the meaning of dance and how that meaning is constructed.[2]

Yet as an interpretation *theory,* contemporary hermeneutics provides a specific approach for investigating the interchanges between the meaning of a text and how that meaning is constructed. There are two primary branches of hermeneutics, both of which are rooted in the work of the nineteenth-century philosophers Fredrich Schleiermacher and Wilhelm Dilthey and, to some extent, the phenomenology of Edmund Husserl.[3] The objectivist theory, led by E. D. Hirsch and his proponents, contends that meaning resides within the text itself and that a valid interpretation is one that accurately discerns the meaning of the text.[4] Accuracy is derived first and foremost through an objective examination and analysis of the text and its historical context. Hirsch posits that the hypothetical-deductive method usually employed in the natural sciences is also appropriate for the interpretation of phenomena in the human sciences. Drawing strongly as it does from logical positivism, this branch of hermeneutics is referred to as positivistic hermeneutics.

In contrast, Hans-Georg Gadamer argues that methodology relevant to the natural sciences is not at all applicable to the human sciences. The meaning of a text actually emerges from the process of interpretation itself.[5] Therefore the interchanges among one's own pre-understandings, the text, as well as the traditions and cultural context of the text, combine to construct the meaning of any particular text. It is this second branch of anti-objectivist hermeneutics, phenomenological hermeneutics, that scholar/writers in the field of dance most often employ.[6] Unlike methods focusing on correct methodology or the "true" interpretation of a text, phenomenological hermeneutics emphasizes the value of understanding the very essence of the subject itself, within its various settings.

Linking the interpretation theory of hermeneutics with phenomenology, a philosophy that offers a reflective approach to the description of everyday lived experiences, provides the researcher a form of inquiry capable of embracing limitless problems, issues, and themes. Aesthetic issues and dance phenomena in general lend themselves particularly well to hermeneutic phenomenological inquiry.[7] Gary Madison writes, "Hermeneutical theory is a veritable crossroads where tendencies as diverse as phenomenology and linguistic analysis, semantics and the critique of ideologies, structuralism and conceptual analysis, Marxism and Freudianism come together. Hermeneutics is a subject as central to theology as it is to jurisprudence, as central to philosophy as it is to literary criticism."[8]

Also well suited to this type of investigation are the interactions that so often occur among the people involved in dance. Sociologist Janet Wolff notes that phenomenological hermeneutics "is able to work on any level, from the individual, to the small group or the whole society."[9] Wolff notes that "If we accept the fact that there is a single horizon of all human life, then common humanity is in itself enough guarantee that the hermeneutic circle will work as well in the study of the primitive tribes of New Guinea as it does in European history, or the sociology of contemporary Britain."[10] Although the interpreter's own historical situation must be embraced in a hermeneutic inquiry (as discussed below), this type of investigation is not limited to phenomena of a historical nature. Writes Wolff, "The hermeneutic method, in short, is not restricted to historical investigation, but applies also in the cultural sciences where continuity of single tradition is not a defining characteristic."[11]

What Assumptions Are Inherent in Hermeneutic Inquiry?

According to fundamental notions of phenomenological hermeneutics, to exist is to interpret; our presence in the world propels us into a continual interpretation of our own existence and that of the world around us. One cannot perceive, think, speak, or write about a situation from outside the network of symbols that make up our culture. These symbols may include, but are not limited to, dances or other works of art, language, nonverbal body movement, texts, objects, or social interactions. Since *Being* (Heidegger's term for human presence) is inseparable from acts of interpretation, one's own ontological existence and situation, in relation to that which is (or will be) interpreted, is a necessary part of any hermeneutic phenomenological negotiation. Heidegger writes, "All ontology, no matter how rich and tightly knit a system of categories it has at its disposal, remains fundamentally blind and perverts its innermost intent if it has not previously clarified the meaning of Being sufficiently and grasped this clarification as its fundamental task."[12]

Another major premise of phenomenological hermeneutics is that as one comes to understand the phenomenon of investigation, the very process of understanding is also clarified. An analysis of *Dasein* (a term used by Heidegger referring to the type of existence that is always attempting to understand its own existence) must therefore begin with a clarification of one's own presence.

My own interest in phenomenological hermeneutics began to evolve in 1988 when I worked as dance critic for the *Ann Arbor News*. Frustrated with the cursory nature of the newspaper review, I began to examine forms of inquiry that supported a more in-depth analysis of the meaning and interpretation of a dance. Although at first I considered this journey a way to enhance my interpretive and evaluative skills as a dance critic, it soon became evident that too many aspects of the newspaper review format hindered interpretations of integrity. Time and space limitations; a well-cemented hierarchy of dance artists in the community, formed in part by the writings of other dance critics; and my own culturally derived working habits were all situations I began to examine more closely and question.

Heidegger suggests that *Being*, an embodiment of preunderstandings, is always already existing, or there. In other words, one is capable of understanding, to some extent, any text—such as a dance at a concert, or one's own performance of an improvisation—simply because one is capable of understanding in the first place. For example, all humans exist in a space and a culture and know that space and culture in a fundamental way. Humans are *of* a space and culture, and this way of knowing is always part of one's consciousness, long before one acquires knowledge or becomes familiar with the realm of ideas. In this way most people have a practical experience with movement that is readily drawn upon when they observe a dance. As humans we know the feeling of moving on, around, or through different spaces. There is a difference in the way our bodies may feel, for instance, when walking on a crowded boulevard flanked by skyscrapers compared to wandering through chaparral under a stretch of southwestern sky. It is also part of the human situation to experience the physiological and muscular changes that take place when one exerts varying levels of energy during one's everyday activities. With these types of experiences we can relate to the qualitative expressions of dancers as they perform with varying levels of energy in their spatially created worlds. We bring a precognitive experience of movement with us to a dance concert that enables us to personally relate to the dances. When one makes an assertion, no matter what it may be, it is always from this perspective.

Another dimension of preunderstanding is the unique formal, perhaps informal, understandings about life that all humans embrace. This realm of consciousness embodies those understandings against which one is constantly validating one's perceptions of the world. For instance, if one attends a modern dance concert and is familiar with that genre, one may assume that the dances on the program will most likely be closely aligned with other contemporary mediums such as music, set designs, costumes, and perhaps text. One would expect to see dancers moving with flexible, articulated torsos, using gravity, and so forth. If, however, in the opening piece dancers appeared on stage in pointe shoes and an evening-length fairy tale began to unfold, one would immediately call into question those preunderstandings. Is this a spoof? An experiment? What is happening here?

Observations and interpretations are also made from a vantage that often, already, embraces certain theories. This does not mean that when one interprets phenomena that a theoretical framework or method will automatically be attached to that observation, but rather that these theories subtly precondition our observations and interpretations to begin with. For example, as critic for the *Ann Arbor News,* I realized that I automatically began interpreting dances as aesthetic objects. I attended primarily to the formal attributes of the dance such as its movement, energy, rhythm, and spatial relationships and then discerned how these attributes worked together to form the content and meaning of the dance.

As evident in the above discussion, interpreters are biographically situated; they are a composite of their unique personal experiences as well as their historical and sociocultural situations. This presence in the world cannot be denied but instead must be examined as part of their interpretation. To understand the meaning of a text is to understand the historically and culturally determined self. Like Heidegger, Gadamer suggests that interpretation is founded in the notion of understanding and the explication of that which is, or has been, understood.[13] Clarifying Gadamer, Weinsheimer writes, "The consciousness of the interpreter is no more pure, no more transparent to itself, than is the artwork. We too are historical and in need of interpretation. We, too, need to understand ourselves. Just as art is more than art, so also is the experience of art more than pure aesthetic experience; it is a mode of self-understanding."[14]

Gadamer writes extensively of the influence of our prejudices (a word that has accrued negative connotations but actually means to prejudge) on the act of interpretation, and of the necessity of examining how those prejudices affect one's interpretation. Gadamer writes that, "Actually 'prejudice' means a judgment that is rendered before all the elements that determine a situation have been finally examined."[15] Since prejudices, assumptions, and preunderstandings are part of any interpretive process acted out in a consciously engaged present, there is no beginning or ending point to interpretation.

The hermeneutic phenomenological tradition views interpretation as a circular endeavor that may be entered at any point since one always, already, brings one's own biographically situated context to the situation. Whatever the entry point of the hermeneutic circle may be, Heidegger, Edmund Husserl, and Gadamer all suggest the necessity of embracing these pre-existing understandings, prejudices, and assumptions prior to and during an interpretation.[16] Gadamer writes, "The circle then is not formal in nature, it is neither subjective nor objective, but describes understanding as the interplay of the movement of tradition and the movement of the interpreter."[17]

To Heidegger, *Being* is primarily a temporal experience. The interpretation of existence or reality starts with understanding, which generally consists of explaining that which is already understood. When one questions or interprets something (including existence itself), one cannot dissociate oneself from the past, present, and future temporality of that comprehension. Therefore one necessarily understands existence from a temporal and historical position. Consequently, an action, or practical application of a theory, must correspond to the reflective consciousness. Yet this transcendence is both toward the world and temporal, rather than focused on reflective consciousness alone, such as is the case with a pure phenomenological approach. This idea of *Being* takes into account the extenuating contexts of the world that influence one's comprehension of reality, moving beyond the reflection and description of experiential transcendence. Thus, a conversation with the multiple social, cultural, and historical ways of knowing a phenomenon is essential to a hermeneutic phenomenological dialectic circle of interpretation.

An interpreter's presence, then, is one that embodies her or his inner world of perceptions, preunderstandings, lived body space, time, relations, and those thoughts and ideas not yet expressed or written, as well as an outer world, comprising the space where all actions expand into a social realm through written or verbal and nonverbal communication. Both of these realms are experienced in the lived moment. As Valerie Malhotra Bentz writes:

> The hermeneutic phenomenologist insists that the premises, perceptions, and judgments of the researcher/writer not be falsely "hidden" or objectified, but clarified. They are interwoven throughout the research process. Research from this perspective is neither "objective" nor "subjective." Knowledge is the result of a dialectical process between our experiences and our interactions with others in the lifeworld.[18]

These two realms of experience—those of the inner and outer worlds—form one's *horizon,* a hermeneutic phenomenological term used to distinguish the line at which anticipations and preunderstandings intersect with lived time, joining the unfamiliar with the known. Husserl's phenomenological ideology suggests that all human customs take place within *horizons,* which are essential to our perception and understanding of the world. Therefore, the relationship between consciousness and the world is not merely a spatial one but one that is enmeshed in determinacy and indeterminacy. An indeterminate *horizon* is necessarily a part of a determinate act, embracing a spatio-temporal aspect. Pre-given conscious life is essentially the combined horizons of the perceived world and the cultural world. Together these form the *horizon* of the existential, or lived consciousness, and it is from this consciousness that an object and its expression exist.

It is also by means of the horizon that one comes to know the parts as well as the whole of a phenomenon. This notion is illuminated by Van Pursen, who writes:

> The word "horizon" connotes something fleeting and at the same time denotes, in the most disparate senses, a kind of reference point. The horizon is tied to an observer; there is something subjective about it. On the other hand, it seems that the horizon encompasses everything. The horizon has a problematic character. Prosaic space, which is encircled by the horizon, becomes mysterious.[19]

In reality, of course, the horizon is not actually there. Nevertheless, it acts as a subjective pivotable anchor to our position on earth.

Another notion fundamental to phenomenological hermeneutics is the meaningfulness of language in the interpretive process. Language is the interpreter's situation and it is out of this relation to language, along with one's relation to one's particular history and society, that one's impressions and experiences of the world emerge and take form. As Heidegger writes, "Language is the house of Being. In its home man dwells."[20] Not only do the conceptions of the world emerge from the interpreter's particular language, but in turn the interpreter shapes the meaning of the world around her or him through its usage. The actual meaning of a text, as described by the interpreter, is never truly concrete but rather recreated through language, grammar, and syntax, which form the underpinnings of its multilayered partners, discourse, and text.

It is often said that dance is particularly difficult to put into words because of its fleeting quality, yet all of life is really remembered moments. By the time one thinks about or acknowledges the present moment, no matter what that moment may hold, it has already flowed into the past. Although the dance initially impacts one at a precognitive, experiential level, one cannot begin to think about or interpret a dance without using language.

By means of our various realms of consciousness, which are one with the existentials of lived body, space, time, and relations, our experiences and language concurrently unfold to recreate each other. Through spoken and written discourse the meaning of one's lived world is conveyed to others. In its transmission of messages, language is indeed an intentional act and therefore meaningful. The meaningfulness of language is at the core of the debate between those linguists who consider language a mere system of codes that can be deconstructed to meaningless signs, and the hermeneutic phenomenological position that language is meaningful. The codes of a language may consist of the grammar and system of rules that make up that particular language, yet it is through language that meaningful expressions are conveyed in the form of either spoken or written discourse.

The concept that meaning is conveyed through discourse and therefore an intentional act—forming the foundation of our very consciousness, the stepping stones to our apprehension and way of knowing the world around us—is essential to the hermeneutic dialectic circle. Once an interpreter perceives and becomes aware of a dance, for instance, that dance becomes the object of the interpreter's intention or what Husserl refers to as the *noema*.[21] The noema, as in the situation of a dance experienced, is an act of consciousness, the dance's meaning. And *noesis,* or the process of experiencing and interpreting the noema, becomes the actual act. Alfred Schutz sheds light on the concept of noema and noesis when he writes of "the double manner" of describing cogitations:

> the first, the noematic, dealing with the "cogitatum," that is, with the intentional object of our specific thought as it appears in it, for instance as a certainty, possibly, or presumable existent object, or as a present, past, or future object; the second, the noetic, dealing with the acts of cogitation, with the experiencing itself (noesis) and with its modifications as: with perceiving, retaining, recollection, etc., and their peculiar differences of clarity and explicitly.[22]

Corresponding to Husserl's notion that discourse is intentional, philosopher Paul Ricoeur contends that discourse is an event that conveys meaning.[23] The concept of discourse as an event has its germination in the idea that discourse is conducted by a speaker and is propositional, with various levels of sentence structure. According to Ricoeur, discourse consists of three parts. First, it requires a different kind of understanding than a sentence, which is much shorter. Second, it includes *codification,* or a system of rules that shape the work into its unique literary form. Third, it has a *style.*[24]

Meaning, then, emerges from the grammatical interaction of these three levels of speech actions, which can be discerned and examined again and again. Discourse as event thus has its roots in the notion that "to mean is what the speaker does" and this takes place in part by means of the three levels of sentence structure.[25] In turn these three levels of structure form a discourse through the grammatical dimensions of language.

The propositional content of one's discourse merges with the situation of the speaker to provide structure for the specific words and language one draws upon to convey one's message. Joined together in this manner, words employed by a speaker or writer are not open to numerous interpretations, or polysemous, any longer. Rather they have specific meaning formed by the speaker's or writer's intent. Expressions unfold as one strives to complete one's intended acts; one's conscious involvement with others and the world contribute to the formation of consciousness as meaning is conveyed through discourse. The importance of this to the hermeneutic phenomenological approach is suggested by Ricoeur, who writes:

> the notion of the speech event is not cancelled, rather it is submitted to a series of dialectical polarities summarized under the double title of event and meaning and sense and reference. These dialectical polarities allow us to anticipate that the concepts of intention and dialogue are not to be excluded from hermeneutics, but instead are to be released from the one-sidedness of non-dialectical concept of discourse.[26]

In light of this and the other hermeneutic phenomenological principles discussed above, any investigation of a dance phenomenon is not only about understanding what the meaning of that phenomenon is, but also about the processes of the investigator's own construction of meaning as well. As one interacts with and comes to understand the phenomenon of investigation, one's inner and outer worlds form an intersection—a horizon joining the unfamiliar with the known. This lived moment can then be shared with others through language, which is usually meaningful.

What are the Strengths and Weaknesses of Hermeneutic Inquiry for Dance Phenomena?

In many ways the world of hermeneutics parallels the world of dance. The dancer is well aware that the body/being is the expressive dance tool. The body/being is not an instrument that is put on and taken off at will but is, rather, always the lived experience of the dancer. This situation is similar to that of the hermeneut, who, by the nature of the hermeneutic tradition, does not merely employ a methodology for purposes of interpretation but actually lives and experiences the phenomenological hermeneutic tradition moment to moment in her or his everyday life. For dancers who have experienced and understand the sense of integration made possible through their unique situation, it is probably not difficult to understand the fulfillment one can derive from a total immersion into the intuitive/logical/reflective consciousness, as is often experienced with phenomenological hermeneutics.

This, of course, is also one of its greatest weaknesses. One does not merely learn and then apply a paradigm, although that too is part of the hermeneutic interpretive process. Learning how to employ this approach takes a long "training" period because the interpreter must learn how to reflect upon and describe her or his own lived experiences and prejudices. One must also learn how to examine the sociocultural and historical situation of the phenomenon of investigation, as well as the phenomenon itself. In the case of phenomenological hermeneutics the interpreter must learn how to grasp the very essence of the experienced text and then convey that through language. In short, this is an approach that requires a thorough training of the body/being—of the lived and reflective consciousness —as well as the development of the skills necessary to discern the sociocultural and historical contexts of a phenomenon.

Hermeneutics is an unusually flexible paradigm, allowing for much creativity on the part of the interpreter. The hermeneut does not attempt to reproduce or objectively represent reality but, rather, builds an interpretation via a blueprint of her or his own design, and through logical argumentation. Unrestrained by rigid methodological underpinnings, the interpreter has the freedom to make numerous choices during every loop of the interpretive process. By constructing an *understanding* of meaning, rather than adhering to an exacting method, hermeneutics allows for the transient and mobile features of dance and its connected areas of inquiry to be more finely discerned.

The investigation of meaning through dance interpretation methodology is particularly complicated when the dance to be interpreted is a new work. American dance, located on the edge of its own varied forms, as well as those of the culture within which it resides, acts as an initiator and perpetuator of change, thriving and evolving on experimentation. From community-based dance events to internationally acclaimed dance companies, the American dance terrain is a spectacle of the unfamiliar and changing. Diverse styles, disparity of forms, variety of content, and obtuse differences among choreographers, who may or may not represent distinct cultural orientations, characterize American dance. Making sense out of these can be a challenge for even the most seasoned interpreter/writer. In its ability to accommodate the aesthetic, sociocultural, and historical contexts of a work—and the personal viewpoints and biases of the interpreter—it is a method particularly well suited for the interpretation of new and changing dance forms and related phenomena.

Hermeneutics is also a valuable method when understanding has been obscured by ideology or false consciousness.[27] Gadamer writes, "The best definition for hermeneutics is: to let what is alienated by character of the written word or by the character of being distantiated by cultural or historical distances speak again."[28] Dreyfus suggests hermeneutics is particularly useful as a means of understanding reality when differing methods of explanation exist or when a breakdown in communication between opposing discourses has occurred.[29]

What Processes Are Employed in Hermeneutic Research Methods?

The phenomenological hermeneutic investigation begins with a question or notion about a phenomenon that the interpreter finds particularly intriguing and significant to her or his own life and interests. In the world of dance, questions may arise about phenomena as diverse as a dance, the rehearsal habits of a choreographer, or the funding trends of various government and nonprofit groups, to name a few. The phenomenological aspect of this approach turns the interpreter's attention to the lived experiences of the people connected to the phenomenon of investigation. What did it mean to be a dancer with the Judson Church Dance Theatre in New York during the 1960s? What does it mean to be a writer/scholar and to write a dance interpretive text? What does it mean to be a contact improvisation dancer? What does it mean to be a choreographer? The hermeneutic tradition will necessarily bring forward the historic and sociocultural contexts both of the phenomena and the interpreter herself/himself. What is the meaning of this dance interpretive text within its (and my own) historic and sociocultural context? What is the meaning of that dance, performed at that particular place and time? What is the meaning of the Judson Church Dance Theatre group to that time in history, and what is its meaning to us now? What is the social and historical significance of the contact improvisation dancer's performance? The phenomenological hermeneutic approach emphasizes both the internal and external contexts of the phenomenon so that the interpreter is free to work with and negotiate both realms of the phenomenon.

As already noted, the process of interpretation also begins with clarification of one's own position within the interpretive process, since interpretation is considered a subjective rendering. Pre-understandings and prejudices must be ferreted out and the historic and sociocultural situation of the interpreter addressed, since these contexts play a vital role in the interpreter's perspective and construction of knowledge.

The researcher does not begin the investigation with a preconceived hypothesis, seeking then to demonstrate and explain the phenomenon, based on that predetermined view. Instead, as the researcher gathers data (which is discussed below) the essences of the phenomenon are discerned and described, forming a foundation for the construction of themes and a later analysis of the data. Just as the choreographer's initial idea may change during the choreographic process, so too may the hermeneut's ideas and choices shift and change during the process of interpretation. As the interpreter comes to understand the phenomenon of investigation, new and changing knowledge of the phenomenon itself may lead the interpreter into different interpretive directions. What is important is that whatever new turn along the way the interpreter may make, the primary aim of any hermeneutic inquiry—to discover the significant meaning of the phenomenon—be kept in mind.

A spiral or circle is sometimes used by the interpreter at the outset of inquiry, as a metaphoric framework to the hermeneutic dialogue. In this way as the parts and contexts of the phenomenon are observed, organized, and described, the simultaneous wholeness of the phenomenon is never far from view. Indeed, the whole of the phenomenon and its parts are examined throughout the interpretive process, moving back and forth into the foreground and background as the interpreter proceeds. As the dialectic hermeneutic circle embraces the insights of others and the multidimensional contexts of the phenomenon, it becomes better known to the interpreter. In this way the interpreter begins to understand the phenomenon as an insider. Understanding is enhanced and truth is approached, though never fully acquired, since the inner and outer worlds of the interpreter are continually changing. Many meanings may emerge, based upon the changing nature of the phenomenon, the interpreter, and the unique observations and choices made during the interpretive process.

Data collected and discovered by the hermeneut is both qualitative and experiential. The interpreter strives to discover the essence and themes of the phenomenon through her or his own lived experiences, the experiences of others, and the historical, sociocultural constructs of the phenomenon. The sources the investigator may turn to are as bountiful as her or his imagination. Interviews; rehearsal notes; informal discussions; reflections of audience members: this is just a small sample of the types of data embodied in the personal experiences of others, which the interpreter may draw from. Additional data may be gathered from sources such as dance reviews; photographs or videos of dance; program notes; the written discourses of historians or philosophers, and so forth.

Often the interpreter goes out into the natural environment of those connected to the phenomenon of investigation to gather data. This may include a dance studio, nightclub, outdoor performance space, the private study of a dance writer, or other places where the people of dance gather or live. Sometimes the natural environment emerges as one of the contexts of the data, a part of the hermeneutic dialogue that the interpreter chooses to examine more closely. This, in addition to the other data selected for closer discernment, will, of course, shape the final interpretation.

As the interpreter collects, describes, and mediates the data, themes—which emerge from the attributes or essential qualities of the phenomenon—may become apparent. These themes are integral to the phenomenon, made up as they are by the core attributes of the phenomenon. If the themes are taken away, the phenomenon will no longer be what it truly is. Max Van Manen suggests that:

In determining the universal or essential quality of a theme our concern is to discover aspects or qualities that make a phenomenon what it is and without which the phenomenon could not be what it is. . . . In the process of apprehending essential themes or essential relationships one asks the question: Is this phenomenon still the same if we imaginatively change or delete this theme from the phenomenon? Does the phenomenon without this theme lose its fundamental meaning?[30]

Since themes are fundamental to the structure of the phenomenon, they may actually act as signposts to their own organization and written presentation. Van Manen notes five ways the researcher may organize the presentation of themes: *thematically, analytically, exemplificatively, exegetically or existentially.*[31] There may be overlapping among these approaches and new ones may be invented. Whatever the interpreter chooses, the organization of the emerging themes should direct one to the essential nature of the phenomenon.

According to Van Manen, *thematic* organization of the themes themselves requires division of the phenomenon's emerging themes into chapters, sections, or parts, followed by an in-depth examination of each of these sections. Thematic organization thus defined is evident in a proposal made by sociologist Janet Wolff in her book, *Hermeneutic Philosophy and the Sociology of Art,* which is one of the earliest recognitions of dance as a phenomenon capable of phenomenological hermeneutic interpretation.[32] Wolff proposes a hermeneutic interpretation of four major themes integral to

modern dance in contemporary Western society. . . . I have divided the analysis, somewhat arbitrarily, into four basic sections: (1) the hermeneutic grasp of the society of genesis of the modern dance; (2) the nature of modern dance itself; (3) the perspective of choreographer, dancer, and, perhaps audience; and (4) the hermeneutic-phenomenological comprehension of the dynamics of changing dance-forms.[33]

Wolff states that the first section is the most problematic since the *society of genesis of the modern dance* must be reasonably delimited. Yet, according to Wolff, hermeneutic inquiry is particularly suitable for mediating the complexity inherent in an investigation such as this. She proposes to begin her analysis with an examination of those features of social life in America and Great Britain that influenced the development of modern dance. Wolff notes that some may not consider this initial analysis to be objective but suggests that its strength is that it allows one to examine *any* aspect of society that may be considered significant to the genesis of modern dance.[34]

Section 2 of Wolff's investigation—the nature of modern dance—is a thorough, descriptive, rendering of modern dance from several angles: as a technique, as an expressive dance form, in its relationship to other contemporary art forms and within its social context. The third section of Wolff's investigation is a phenomenological examination of the people involved in modern dance, and last, section 4 is a phenomenological hermeneutic negotiation of modern dance in contemporary Western society. Of this fourth section, Wolff notes that it is capable of discerning all the aspects of social life that have either influenced the dance or are embraced by the dance.[35]

Another approach to the organization of thematic material is through *analysis*. One mode of analysis is to reconstruct the collected data, then examine the themes rendered by that reconstruction, as the means of discerning the significance of the phenomenon. One could, for instance, conduct interviews with modern dancers of several major American companies, transcribe the interviews, and then reconstruct the transcribed interviews into stories about their careers. From these reconstructed stories, then, major themes that point to the significant meaning of a modern dancer's career would be selected for further exploration. Van Manen suggests other ways of analyzing stories, such as examining embodied *anecdotes* or using examples of life situations to build "*fictionalized antinomous accounts*" that bring out contrasting ways of seeing or acting in concrete situations."[36] Or, one may choose to analyze all three—reconstructed stories, anecdotes, and fictionalized antinomic accounts—selecting themes from all of these realms for further discernment.

Another way to organize and present themes through analysis is to describe the phenomenon or situation of investigation in a way that demonstrates its complex or enigmatic nature, and then address through a hermeneutic dialogue those concerns that the description evokes. The opening paragraph of Selma Jeanne Cohen's *Next Week, Swan Lake: Reflections on Dance and Dances*, alludes to this type of approach: "So you are going to see *Swan Lake*, the great and long-admired classic. I hope you enjoy it. But what, precisely, are you going to see?"[37] Following a description of events leading up to the 1895 production of *Swan Lake*, Cohen raises questions regarding subsequent performances that directly point to the complexity and puzzling nature of *Swan Lake*:

> Because *Swan Lake* can be experienced only in performance, what the audience encounters each time is a realization of—of what? The intentions of the choreographer? How do we know them? No conveniently detailed diaries provide this information. From the notated score of the dance? Most often, for works created prior to this century, there is no such score, but it happens that for *Swan Lake* there is one. Or rather, there are several. Which only complicates the problem.[38]

Cohen's text also reflects another analytical organization of themes discussed by Van Manen, which is the demonstration of how a traditional interpretation fails to render the significant meaning of a phenomenon, followed by a hermeneutic investigation that does describe such meaning. Traditional perspectives of numerous philosophers weave throughout Cohen's text, sometimes offering support, but often in stark contrast to Cohen's thorough dialogue on the identity and meaning of *Swan Lake* and dance in general. According to Van Manen one may complete this particular form of analysis by demonstrating "how certain themes emerge from considering etymological and idiomatic sources, from examining experiential descriptions, literary and phenomenological material, and so forth."[39]

In contrast to thematic or analytic presentations of data, a study conducted by Valerie Malhotra Bentz demonstrates a decidedly *exegetic* approach, weaving as it does her own experiences and interpretation of a dance with the notions and themes of philosophers renowned for their work in the tradition of phenomenological hermeneutics.[40] Van Manen writes:

> The exegetical approach orients itself first or primarily to the available phenomenological human science literature and organizes itself in terms of a discussion of those texts and the structural themes that their authors have already identified and discussed. The exegetical approach treats the works of other authors as incomplete conversational scripts that require a strong reading in order to overcome the limits of those texts.[41]

The process of interpretation actually begins for Bentz with strong intuitions about the significance and meaning of a dance. These initial impressions, which are experienced physically throughout her entire body, begin to connect and link up with one another. Following these initially felt experiences of a work, she begins to receive images of the dance, and these images then naturally connect up to ideas. In a discussion of her interpretation of the dance *Soul Gatherers,* Bentz recalls, "first of all when I saw it I had a powerful emotional experience and then I thought about, and felt, what I saw as Heidegger just came right to me because all of the messages of Heidegger just float around in that dance; the Being, the earth and the soul. It's almost like they generated Heidegger's philosophy in their dance."[42]

Bentz notes that once she is clear about the philosophical perspective she feels the dance connects with, she turns to the texts that negotiate those ideas. So in writing her interpretation of *Soul Gatherers,* she scanned Heidegger's writings (which she has studied extensively) for passages that were particularly relevant to various sections of the dance.

An interpreter may also choose to present her or his thematic material *exemplificatively*. This organizing framework requires discerning the core structure of a theme, followed by examples that offer diverse perspectives on that theme. In an investigation of teaching dance, for example, the interpreter may examine the various experiences of teaching as a graduate assistant or seasoned professional;

at a community college, a dance studio, or in a home basement; or perhaps the experiences of teaching dance to various student populations.

Lastly, *existential* presentation of thematic material calls upon an examination of phenomena in relation to the lived existentials of time, space, body, and others. Selecting this particular approach may move the phenomenological component of phenomenological hermeneutics into the foreground, as is the case with Sondra Horton Fraleigh's *Dance and the Lived Body: A Descriptive Aesthetics.* Fraleigh merges phenomenology with existentialism, offering a concept of the dancer's experienced, *lived body* as the central juncture for an aesthetics of dance.[43] Fraleigh writes, "When the dancer succeeds, neither body nor mind is held at a distance; they are the same action." At that moment the dancer is not aware of her self or her movement in space, but rather she is experiencing a spontaneous and holistic fusion of movement and self in time. According to Fraleigh, "To experience the dance is to experience our own living substance in an aesthetic (affective) transformation. To express the dance is to express the lived body in an aesthetic form. The body, understood in its lived totality, is the source of the dance aesthetic."[44]

The notions of lived time and lived space are also integral to Fraleigh's presentation. She agrees with Maurice Merleau-Ponty's view that our lived bodies are *of* space and time rather than *in* space and time. *Time-space* are lived dimensions of life, indistinguishable from movement:

> In dance we live the poetry of time and space as we actually embody time and space in our movement, imbuing them with an aesthetic form. It is in this sense that we can speak of moving time-space in dance. We are in fact, in all our movements, moving time-space; but in dance we give these specific aesthetic form. We create them as we formulate the time-space qualities of the dance, its envisioned poetry and rhythmic music.[45]

As the organization of emerging themes is presented and the historical and sociocultural situations of both the interpreter and the phenomenon of investigation examined, the dialectic hermeneutic circle of inquiry begins to take shape. In its final form it emerges as a discussion, or as Richard Rorty writes, "the conversation of mankind."[46]

What is the Role of Language and Style in the Hermeneutic Dialogue?

As discussed above, the meaningfulness of language is central to the hermeneutic tradition; spoken and written discourses are considered integral to all phases of a hermeneutic inquiry. Discourse is considered, at some level, to be expressive, since it is always an expression of a human being about something both meaningful and contextual to that being. This notion of hermeneutic text as expressive is also rooted in notions about the exchanges among one's consciousness, one's language, and one's culture.

Self, according to this linguistic perspective, is a composite of several kinds of consciousness, some of which are intricately linked to one's use of language and which may shift into a foreground or background position of significance, depending on the purpose of one's discourse. One realm of consciousness is that which is aware of its separateness from the world. Thus, the world must be present for the consciousness to be aware of its existence. Jean Paul Sartre suggests that this consciousness *(For-Itself)* embodies the past, present, and future of existence. "As present, the For-Itself is constituted by its presence of the world; as past, the For-Itself is constituted by what it has made of itself in its previous actions and expressions; as future, the For-Itself is what it is working on to make itself—it is its possibilities."[47]

Removed from the language of the actual phenomenon of interpretation, one discerns and constructs or reconstructs meaning, which draws upon one's prior experiences, one's anticipations, and the connections between the actual experience and the expression of that experience. Words are selected and the shape of the sentence is formed as one anticipates the expression to be conveyed. In this manner both the parts and the whole of the phenomenon—or for Ricoeur, the semiotics and semantics—play a simultaneous and significant role in the temporally oriented process of discourse.

Whether mediating or recreating the world through discourse, the preliminary processes of language engagement are similar whether one speaks or writes. Using language to convey the meaning of a dance, for example, one must apprehend the lived experience of the dance and then express, through language, that experience as it arises. The temporal nature of language is acknowledged as all of *Being;* all interpretations are realized to unfold in a temporal realm. Schutz writes, "It is of the essence of language that normally any linguistic communication involves a time process; a speech is built up by sentences, a sentence by the step by step articulation of successive elements (polythetically, as Husserl calls it)."[48] This part of consciousness is that which linguistically deals with the existentials of lived body, space, and time.

Another part of consciousness, *Being-for-Others,* is that which understands lived relations as separate consciousnesses, different from one's own consciousness yet upon whose existence one depends for the very awareness of one's own ability to know. The significance bestowed upon relations with others in the philosophical tradition of phenomenological hermeneutics is unique among philosophical systems.[49] This is due in part to the central phenomenological notion that humans, in their inability to actually share or transfer their lived experiences directly to one another, are destined to an all-encompassing isolation.

It is the *meaning* of an experience that one shares with another when one speaks or writes, rather than the actual experience itself. Language, discourse, and text evolve as, and simultaneously construct, our social and temporal world. As Ricoeur writes, "Communication in this way is the overcoming of the radical noncommunicability of the lived experience as lived."[50] Communication is an enigma because "being-together, as the existential condition for the possibility of any dialogical structure of discourse, appears as a way of trespassing or overcoming the fundamental solitude of each human being."[51] Since communication of one's own experiences is transmitted through one's language, those experiences necessarily unfold in a public sphere. In this way knowledge and understanding are socially derived and created.

The third realm of consciousness or self from which expression emerges is that consciousness *(Being-in-the-World)* that experiences its own consciousness, as well as those of others, through the use of signs, and these experiences unfold and are realized within a worldly context, specific to that individual and moment in time. In a sense, the speaker or writer becomes a tool of his or her cultural language, thrust as one is into a pre-existing system of symbolic codes that have been handed down from generation to generation. Nevertheless, changes are made—however small, however slow—as expressions are fixed into discourse and the human element kneads a linguistic system of traditions. Rooted in language, as well as a particular historical and social situation, human expressions communicate what has been, what is, and what can be. Interpretation or other human expressions can be acknowledged as a never-ending process of being. One's use of language reflects a tradition and is the product of a certain time in history.

Style, as addressed by James Kinneavy's phenomenological communication model, unfolds as a condition of these various genuine parts of consciousness that embrace at once the writer's past, present, and future situation and project, as well as her or his interactions with others. These overlapping realms of presence (For-Itself, Being-for-Others, Being-in-the-World, and style) form the consciousness from which actions of language usage originate. Style, according to phenomenological hermeneutics, is regarded as subjective expression fused with the culturally bound structure and codes of one's language, which correspond to the purpose of one's method and discourse. Thus, the phenomenological hermeneutic writing style will be primarily expressive, since the writer's own feelings, thoughts, and intuitions are embodied in the discourse. Van Manen suggests, "The writer produces text, and he or she produces more than text. The writer produces himself or herself."[52]

In writing about the meaning of a dance or other text, one becomes removed from the living, breathing phenomenon; the thing itself. As one begins to write, one's lived world becomes instead the computer screen or paper in front of one, and perhaps one's notes about the dances one has attended to. Van Manen states that, "Writing fixes thought on paper. It externalizes what in some sense is internal; it distances us from our immediate lived involvements with the things of our world. As we stare at the paper, and stare at what we have written, our objectified thinking now stares back at us."[53] No longer are nonverbal gestures, voice, and the actual presence of the one who conveys the message part of the information-exchanging process. Instead, signs themselves, the marks on the writer's page, become the discourse, promoting a natural distancing of the writer from the message and the reader. Whereas spoken discourse disappears when one speaks, when one writes the discourse becomes fixed on paper, captured through the use of language. "The human fact disappears. Now material 'marks' convey the message."[54]

The message of the interpreter's text, removed now from the original meaning of the author, becomes a work independent of its creator. The reader of the text is unable to have questions answered or misunderstandings clarified. At the heart of phenomenological hermeneutics is the notion of distancing, or "What the text means now matters more than what the author meant when he wrote it."[55] Thus the text enters the world with semantic independence, now existing outside of the horizons and temporal realm of the writer. What the writer meant when writing the text may not be at all what the reader discerns now as the text's meaning. Ricoeur writes: "When the text no longer answers, then it has an author and no longer a speaker. The authorial meaning is the dialectical counterpart of the verbal meaning, and they have to be construed in terms of each other."[56]

Although a distancing from the actual phenomenon or situation occurs as one processes one's impressions and expressions through written discourse, at the same time the interpreter also gets close again to that experience. One comes to know it again, in part as a recreation but often with renewed and greater clarity than one's original observation of the phenomenon. Through reflection, writing, editing, and rewriting, the phenomenon of investigation becomes better known. One's first thoughts and reflections about the phenomenon of investigation, which were private inner experiences, now enter the social realm of one's world, as the interpreter puts these thoughts into language, transforms them into discourse, and fixes them into writing. Through one's use of language, reflection, speaking, and writing, the act of interpretation necessarily moves beyond the interpreter's own inner world of associations to become a complex social act in her or his outer world; one which is deeply enmeshed in and perpetuated by the traditions of the culture within which one resides.

By means of the hermeneutic dialectic circle, the interpreter passes on his or her experiences to others, and the existential solitude of existence is bridged.

Through written discourse those experiences are saved and passed from generation to generation in what Ricoeur refers to as "archives available for individual and collective memory."[57]

How Is Hermeneutic Discourse Evaluated?

So, given the rather arbitrary nature of this approach, is there a means of verifying the quality of a phenomenological hermeneutic interpretation? What criteria are used to evaluate its adequacy? It is probably no surprise that an important means of assessing the value of a hermeneutic phenomenological interpretation is derived from the reader's own new and changed understanding of the text of interpretation. After all, according to hermeneutic phenomenological principles, the germination of all interpretation is consciousness; and so it is back to conscious reflection that one must first turn in order to assess the value of an interpretation.

The following questions may act as signposts: Do I now have a better understanding of this text of interpretation? Has what once seemed distant and remote to me now become more accessible and familiar? Are the relations among its parts and whole apparent to me now? Do I understand the extenuating sociocultural and historical contexts of this text? And last, but perhaps most importantly: Having read this interpretation, do I have a better understanding of myself and thus the human condition? For it is, after all, enhanced understanding, rather than an objective explanation, for which hermeneutics aims.

As one reads a hermeneutic discourse, horizons that were once disjoined now merge. New horizons form as points of departure, and truth is approached although, as already noted, never fully attained. Rather than arriving at a *true* or *correct* interpretation through objective methodology, the interpreter instead shares the value of understanding the very essence of the subject itself, within its various settings. As noted at the beginning of this chapter, according to Gadamer objective methodology is in itself diametrically opposed to the study of human sciences:

> But the specific problem that the human sciences present to thought is that one has not rightly grasped their nature if one measures them by the yardstick of a progressive knowledge of regularity. The experience of the sociohistorical world cannot be raised to a science by the inductive procedure of the natural sciences. Whatever "science" may mean here, and even if all historical knowledge includes the application of experiential universals to the particular object of investigation, historical research does not endeavor to grasp the concrete phenomenon as an instance of a universal rule.[58]

Although a precise means of measuring the reliability and validity of a hermeneutic investigation is fundamentally opposed to the conceptual core of this tradition, scholars and writers have nevertheless discerned several components essential to this type of study. Madison, for example, has extrapolated from Gadamer's texts several principles of methodology that most interpreters employing this approach adhere to.[59] These he lists as: coherence, comprehensiveness, penetration, thoroughness, appropriateness, contextuality, agreement (both with the author and with the other interpreters of the author's work), suggestiveness, and potential. Madison writes:

> Interpretation should be viewed as a mode of practical reasoning and of persuasive argumentation. The model for interpretation should therefore be looked for in the theory of argumentation and not in what is called the logic of (scientific) explanation. It is not to science but to *rhetoric or the theory of persuasive argumentation that interpretation* should look for its theoretical and methodological grounding. For what, throughout its long history, as long as that of science itself, to which it has always opposed an alternative conception of rationality, rhetoric has taught is that while in the realm of human affairs and action we can never be absolutely certain of anything, we can nevertheless have legitimate grounds for believing that some things are clearly better than others.[60]

In summary, phenomenological hermeneutics provides a significant venue through which both personal and sociocultural traditions of diverse dance phenomena may be examined, interpreted, and reconstructed. Rigorous principles of interpretation merging intuitive comprehension with thoughtful argumentation—characteristic of the hermeneutic phenomenological approach—are favorable for the investigation of phenomena that are changing, yet culturally situated. The grafting of phenomenology with hermeneutics offers a rich comprehension of the intuitively, subjectively grasped essence of many types of dance phenomena, without diminishing the significance of their sociocultural and historical constitution.

Study Questions

1. Select a dance-related phenomenon of interest and discuss your preunderstandings of and prejudices about that phenomenon. How might these shape your interpretation and understanding of its meaning?

1A. Discern the primary themes of your selected phenomenon. Organize the themes either thematically, analytically, exemplificatively, exegetically, or existentially. What about this phenomenon suggests that it be organized in this way? Does overlapping occur? If yes, why, and in what ways?

1B. What is the historical and sociocultural significance of this phenomenon?

2. Using your thoughts and answers from 1, 1A, and 1B above as a framework, interpret your selected dance-related phenomenon.

3. Discuss the phenomenological hermeneutic notions of the meaningfulness of language and discourse. Do you agree or disagree with these primary premises? Why? As an interpreter, what are the advantages and disadvantages, if any? How do these notions about language compare with other forms of inquiry?

4. Select and read a current dance review from a daily journal, then consider a phenomenological hermeneutic interpretation of the same work. What are the differences and what are the advantages and disadvantages of both approaches?

5. Select a dance with which you are familiar (it may be one you have choreographed). Examine and write about (or discuss) its meaning from one or several of the following perspectives:

- your own, as choreographer (or observer)
- the dancer's or dancers'
- other observers'

If discussing the perspectives of others, design your interview questions to grasp the essential meaningfulness of the interviewee's experiences.

6. Select one of the following and examine its meaning both at the time of its initial performance/usage/writing/production, and now. In your discussion address its historic and sociocultural significance as well as your own position in relation to your interpretation.

- *Strange Fruit,* choreographed by Pearl Primus
- the text *Orchesography,* written by Thoinot Arbeau
- the costumes designed for *Parade* by Pablo Picasso
- the Feuillet dance notation system
- a dance review written by Edwin Denby
- the choreography of Bronislava Nijinska
- the Academie Royal de Musique et Danse

NOTES

1. Martin Heidegger, *Being and Time,* trans. J. Macquarrie and E. Robinson (New York: Harper and Row, 1962).

2. Susan Leigh Foster, *Reading Dancing: Bodies in Contemporary American Dance* (Berkeley: University of California Press, 1986); Cynthia Novack, *Sharing the Dance: Contact Improvisation and American Culture* (Madison: University of Wisconsin Press, 1990).

3. See Gary Madison, *The Hermeneutics of Postmodernity* (Bloomington and Indianapolis: Indiana University Press, 1988).

4. E. D. Hirsch Jr., *Validity in Interpretation* (New Haven and London: Yale University Press, 1967). Also see Madison, *The Hermeneutics of Postmodernity,* 3–39.

5. Hans-Georg Gadamer, *Truth and Method,* 2d ed., trans. Joel Weinsheimer and Donald Marshall (New York: Continuum, 1993).

6. Valerie Malhotra Bentz, "Creating Images in Dance: Works of Hanstein and Ziaks," in *Women's Power and Roles as Portrayed in Visual Images of Women in the Arts and Mass Media,* ed. V. Bentz and P. Mayes (New York, Mellon Press, 1993), 171–97; Selma Jeanne Cohen, *Next Week, Swan Lake: Reflections on Dance and Dancing* (Middletown, Conn.: Wesleyan University Press, 1982); Joann McNamara, "From Dance to Text and Back to Dance: A Hermeneutics of Interpretive Dance Discourse" (Ph.D. dissertation, Texas Woman's University, 1994); Susan Stinson, "Reflections and Visions: A Hermeneutic Study of Dangers and Possibilities in Dance Education" (Ph.D. dissertation, University of North Carolina at Greensboro, 1984).

7. For texts that discuss the relevance of hermeneutic inquiry for addressing aesthetic issues, see Hans-Georg Gadamer, *Truth and Method* and *The Relevance of the Beautiful and Other Essays,* trans. Nicholas Walker, ed. Robert Bernasconi (Cambridge: Cambridge University Press, 1986); Janet Wolff, *Hermeneutic Philosophy and the Sociology of Art* (London: Routledge Kegan Paul, 1975). For texts that discuss the relevance of hermeneutic inquiry for examining social action, see Janet Wolff, *Hermeneutic Philosophy and the Sociology of Art;* Paul Ricoeur, *Freedom and Nature: The Voluntary and the Involuntary,* trans. Erazim V. Kohak (Chicago: Northwestern University Press, 1966); *The Conflict of Interpretations: Essays in Hermeneutics* (Evanston, Ill.: Northwestern University Press, 1974) and *From Text to Action* (Evanston, Ill.: Northwestern University Press, 1991).

8. Gary Madison, *The Hermeneutics of Postmodernity* (Bloomington and Indianapolis: Indiana University Press, 1988), 26.

9. Wolff, *Hermeneutic Philosophy and the Sociology of Art,* 137.

10. Ibid., 121.

11. Ibid.

12. Martin Heidegger, *Basic Writings,* trans. D. F. Krell I (San Francisco: Harper San Francisco, 1977), 53.

13. Gadamer, *Truth and Method.*

14. J. Weinsheimer, *Gadamer's Hermeneutics: A Reading of Truth and Method* (New Haven and London: Yale University Press, 1985), 97.

15. Gadamer, *Truth and Method,* 270.

16. Gadamer, *Truth and Method;* Heidegger discusses the notions of fore-having, fore-conception, and fore-sight in *Being and Time,* 199; Edmund Husserl, *Ideas,* trans. W. R. Boyce Gibson (New York: Collier Books, 1931).

17. Gadamer, *Truth and Method,* 293.

18. Valerie Malhotra Bentz, *Becoming Mature: Childhood Ghosts and Spirits in Adult Life* (New York: Aldine de Gruyter, 1989), 2.

19. C. Van Peursen, "The Horizon," in *Husserl: Expositions and Appraisals,* ed. F. Elliston and P. McCormick (Notre Dame, Ind.: University of Notre Dame Press, 1977), 183.

20. Heidegger, *Basic Writings,* 193.

21. Husserl, *Ideas.*

22. Alfred Schutz, *On Phenomenology and Social Relations,* ed. R. W. Helmut (Chicago: University of Chicago Press, 1970), 59.

23. Paul Ricoeur, *Interpretation Theory: Discourse and the Surplus of Meaning* (Fort Worth: Texas Christian University Press, 1976).

24. Paul Ricoeur, *From Text to Action* (Evanston, Ill.: Northwestern University Press, 1991).

25. Ricoeur, *Interpretation Theory: Discourse and the Surplus of Meaning*, 19.

26. Ibid., 23.

27. Gary Shapiro and A. Sica, eds., *Hermeneutics* (Amherst: University of Massachusetts Press, 1985).

28. Hans-Georg Gadamer, "Practical Philosophy as a Model of the Human Sciences," *Research Phenomenology* 9 (1980).

29. H. L. Dreyfus, "Holism in Hermeneutics," in *Hermeneutics and Praxis*, ed. R. Hollinger (Notre Dame, Ind.: University of Notre Dame Press, 1985), 229.

30. M. Van Manen, *Researching Lived Experience: Human Science for an Action Sensitive Pedagogy* (New York: State University of New York Press, 1990), 107.

31. See Van Manen, *Researching Lived Experience*, 168–73.

32. Wolff, *Hermeneutic Philosophy and the Sociology of Art*.

33. Ibid., 134.

34. Ibid., 136.

35. Ibid.

36. Van Manen, *Researching Lived Experience*, 170.

37. Cohen, *Next Week, Swan Lake*, 3.

38. Ibid., 4.

39. Van Manen, *Researching Lived Experience*, 171.

40. Bentz, "Creating Images in Dance: Works of Hanstein and Ziaks."

41. Van Manen, *Researching Lived Experience*, 172.

42. Valerie Malhotra Bentz, interview with Joann McNamara (Santa Barbara, California, 28 May 1993). In "From Dance to Text and Back to Dance: A Hermeneutics of Dance Interpretive Discourse," 335.

43. Sondra Horton Fraleigh, *Dance and the Lived Body: A Descriptive Aesthetics* (Pittsburgh: University of Pittsburgh Press, 1987).

44. Ibid., xvi.

45. Ibid., 183.

46. Richard Rorty, *Philosophy and the Mirror of Nature* (Princeton: Princeton University Press, 1979), 389.

47. James Kinneavy, *A Theory of Discourse* (New York: W. W. Norton, 1971), 398.

48. Schutz, *On Phenomenology and Social Relations*, 205.

49. Kinneavy, *A Theory of Discourse*.

50. Ricoeur, *Interpretation Theory: Discourse and the Surplus of Meaning*, 16.

51. Ibid., 15.

52. Van Manen, *Researching Lived Experience*, 126.

53. Ibid., 125.

54. Ricoeur, *Interpretation Theory*, 26.

55. Ibid., 30.

56. Ibid.

57. Ricoeur, *From Text to Action*, 107. Also see Wolff, *Hermeneutic Philosophy and the Sociology of Art*. Wolff contends that understanding a culture's language is fundamental to understanding how various dimensions of meaning shape that culture's worldview.

58. Gadamer, *Truth and Method*, 4.

59. Madison, *The Hermeneutics of Postmodernity*, 29–30.

60. Ibid., 35.

REFERENCES

Bauman, Z. *Hermeneutics and Social Science.* New York: Columbia University Press, 1978.

Bentz, V. *Becoming Mature: Childhood Ghosts and Spirits in Adult Life.* New York: Aldine de Gruyter, 1989.

———. "Romance Gone Bad: Simmel's Sociology of the Dyad and a Dance Work." Paper presented at the Midwest Sociological Association annual meeting, Chicago, 1990.

———. "Creating Images in Dance: Works of Hanstein and Ziaks." In *Women's Power and Roles as Portrayed in Visual Images of Women in the Arts and Mass Media,* ed. V. Bentz and P. Mayes, 171–97. New York: Mellon Press, 1993.

Carr, D. "Husserl's Problematic Concept of the Life-World." In *Husserl: Expositions and Appraisals,* ed. F. Elliston and P. McCormick, 202–12. Notre Dame, Ind.: University of Notre Dame Press, 1977.

Cohen, S. J. *Next Week, Swan Lake: Reflections on Dance and Dancing.* Middletown, Conn.: Wesleyan University Press, 1982.

Dreyfus, H. L. "Holism in Hermeneutics." In *Hermeneutics and Praxis,* ed. R. Hollinger, 227–47. Notre Dame, Ind.: University of Notre Dame Press, 1985.

Foster, S. 1986. *Reading Dancing: Bodies and Subjects in Contemporary American Dance.* Berkeley: University of California Press, 1986.

Fraleigh, S. "A Vulnerable Glance: Seeing Dance Through Phenomenology." *Dance Research Journal* 23, no. 1 (1981): 11–16.

———. *Dance and the Lived Body: A Descriptive Aesthetics.* Pittsburgh: University of Pittsburgh Press, 1987.

Gadamer, H. *Truth and Method.* New York: Seabury Press, 1975.

———. "Practical Philosophy as a Model of the Human Sciences." *Research in Phenomenology* 9 (1980): 74–86.

Garvin, H. R., ed. *Phenomenology, Structuralism, Semiology.* Lewisburg, Pa.: Bucknell University Press, 1976.

Heidegger, M. *Being and Time.* Transl. J. Macquarrie and E. Robinson. New York: Harper and Row, 1962.

———. *Basic Writings.* Trans. D. F. Krell. San Francisco: Harper San Francisco, 1977.

Hirsch, E. D., Jr. *Validity in Interpretation.* New Haven and London: Yale University Press, 1967.

Husserl, E. *Ideas.* Trans. W. R. Boyce Gibson. New York: Collier Books, 1931.

———. "The Phenomenological Theory of Meaning and of Meaning Aprehension" In *The Hermeneutics Reader,* ed. Kurt Mueller-Vollmer, 165–86. New York: The Continuum Publishing Company, 1900–01.

———. *The Phenomenology of Internal Time-Consciousness.* Ed. Martin Heidegger, trans. James S. Churchill. Bloomington: Indiana University Press, 1964.

———. *Logical Investigations.* Trans. J. Findlay. New York: Humanities Press, 1970.

Kinneavy, J. *A Theory of Discourse.* New York: W. W. Norton, 1971.

Madison, G. B. *The Hermeneutics of Postmodernity.* Bloomington and Indianapolis: Indiana University Press, 1988.

McNamara, J. "From Dance to Text and Back to Dance: A Hermeneutics of Interpretive Dance Discourse." Ph.D. dissertation, Texas Woman's University, 1994.

Novack, C. J. *Sharing the Dance: Contact Improvisation and American Culture*. Madison: University of Wisconsin Press, 1990.

Ricoeur, P. *Husserl: An Analysis of His Phenomenology*. Evanston, Ill.: Northwestern University Press, 1967.

———. *The Conflict of Interpretations: Essays in Hermeneutics*. Evanston, Ill.: Northwestern University Press, 1974.

———. *The Rule of Metaphor*. Toronto: University of Toronto Press, 1975.

———. *Interpretation Theory: Discourse and the Surplus of Meaning*. Fort Worth: Texas Christian University Press, 1976.

———. *Hermeneutics and the Human Sciences: Essays on Language, Action and Interpretation*. Cambridge: Cambridge University Press, 1981.

———. *Time and Narrative*. Vol. 2. Trans. K. McLaughlin and D. Pellauer. Chicago and London: University of Chicago Press, 1985.

———. *Time and Narrative:* Vol. 3. Trans. K. McLaughlin and D. Pellauer. Chicago and London: University of Chicago Press, 1988.

———. *From Text to Action*. Evanston, Ill.: Northwestern University Press, 1991.

Rorty, R. *Philosophy and the Mirror of Nature*. Princeton: Princeton University Press, 1979.

Schutz, A. *The Phenomenology of the Social World*. Evanston, Ill.: Northwestern University Press, 1967.

———. *On Phenomenology and Social Relations*. Ed. R. W. Helmut. Chicago: University of Chicago Press, 1970.

Schutz, A., and T. Luckmann. *The Structures of the Lifeworld*. Trans. R. M. Zaner and H. T. Engelhardt. Evanston, Ill.: Northwestern University Press, 1973.

Shapiro, G., and A. Sica, eds. *Hermeneutics*. Amherst: University of Massachusetts Press, 1985.

Stapleton, T. 1983. *Husserl and Heidegger*. Albany: State University of New York Press, 1983.

Stinson, S. "Reflections and Visions: A Hermeneutic Study of Dangers and Possibilities in Dance Education." Ph.D. dissertation, University of North Carolina at Greensboro, 1984.

Tugendhat, E. "Phenomenology and Linguistic Analysis." In *Husserl: Expositions and Appraisals,* ed. F. Elliston and P. McCormick, 325–37. Notre Dame, Ind.: University of Notre Dame Press, 1977.

Van Breda, H. L. "A Note on Reduction and Authenticity According to Husserl." In *Husserl: Expositions and Appraisals,* ed. F. Elliston and P. McCormick, 124–25. Notre Dame, Ind.: University of Notre Dame Press, 1976.

Van Manen, M. *Researching Lived Experience: Human Science for an Action Sensitive Pedagogy*. New York: State University of New York Press, 1990.

Van Peursen, C. "The Horizon." In *Husserl: Expositions and Appraisals,* ed. F. Elliston and P. McCormick, 182–201. Notre Dame, Ind.: University of Notre Dame Press, 1977.

Weinsheimer, J. *Gadamer's Hermeneutics: A Reading of Truth and Method*. New Haven and London: Yale University Press, 1985.

Wolff, J. *Hermeneutic Philosophy and the Sociology of Art*. London: Routledge Kegan Paul, 1975.

7 WITNESSING THE FROG POND

Sondra Horton Fraleigh

> The old pond
> a frog jumps in
> Plop!
>
> BASHO

Why Do Frogs Jump So High?

DO FROGS JUMP HIGH because they have great hip extensors? Do they jump high because of some reflex stimulus? In order to experience themselves in the jump? For fun? For food? For protection? Or is the jump an incredible air moment in a dance, a sprightly surprise contrast to unblinking stillness? If this were true, the height of the jump might find its reason in human delight.

The latter does not speak to the frog's point of view, but rather to a matter of *human perception.* Accordingly, it poses an aesthetic question. Are frog jumps delightful to humans especially on account of their height and suddenness and maybe other aesthetic qualities—the gangly shape of the frog's body in the jump, its flight against the sunny shimmer of the pond? These are questions of perceptual awareness, aesthetic questions, because aesthetics derives from sense perception. The word *aesthetic* has its etymological roots in "sense perception," from the Greek *aesthesis* or *aisthesis.*[1]

Our example describes aesthetic values including "height and suddenness" (as qualities of the jump) and ascribes the aesthetic valuation of "delight" (as an affective experience in the awareness of the human perceiver). Qualities of the jump are located in the jump, the object of attention, but only as the jump is perceived and qualified in the awareness of the subject. Aesthetic qualities arise as a matter of attention and in relation to an object, frog movement in this case. Aesthetic values have objective status as describable properties, but only as these properties are actualized (valued) in the subjective life (the experience) of a perceiver.[2] This view of objective/subjective relational factors in aesthetic experience is described in more detail in theories of "objective relativism"[3] and also in philosophies that understand aesthetics as a matter of human engagement.[4]

The Frog's Intentions (A Short Study in Five Parts)

Now to the frog's point of view: its intentions. Speculations on why frogs jump high from their own vantage point elicit a much-debated question in aesthetic discourse. Are the intentions of the author of an act or art important in the aesthetic reception and critical evaluation of that act or art? If the frog jump is a movement in a spontaneous dance (an act) or, even more to the point, part of an elaborate choreography (an art), these debates would apply. In philosophical aesthetics, they rage under the tame rubric of "intentional fallacy" or "intentionalism," as Berys Gaut discusses and Larry Lavender further explores in relation to the teaching (and critiquing) of choreography.[5]

Questions concerning interpretation of artworks according to the intentions of the artist cross over the boundaries of philosophical aesthetics and contemporary criticism, providing a cornerstone for the emergence of "the new criticism" about fifty years ago.[6] In terms of frogs, we might wonder about their intentions in general, whether frogs wish to communicate with us in any way. Although I know at least one—to my delight—who jumps to say good-bye to me (I am certain of its intent) when I leave my favorite pond.

I. On Intention and Interpretation

Because artists have intentions when they create works (even though we know certain artists like Merce Cunningham try to purge themselves of certain kinds of intentions), issues concerning interpretation arise. How are we to know what a choreographer intends the movement to convey (to express, to symbolize, or exemplify) if we cannot just ask? Indeed, what notions of meaning may human movement fulfill? What are the limits of the ways that movement can mean? Aestheticians and critics, not to mention dancers, choreographers, and audiences, have already created (and described) a wide range of ways that movement can be meaningful, embodied in styles from expressive to formal, narrative to abstract.

Ritual dance also communicates meaning, from the symbolic to the esoteric and immanent; although aesthetics as a philosophical discipline has not typically been applied to a study of ritual. Interpretation is at the heart of aesthetic discourse, as we seek to understand what aesthetic phenomena are, and how they function.

Aesthetic phenomena, we should notice, embrace much more than art. They are the qualitative dimensions we recognize as such all around and within us. Most basically, aesthetic values are the intrinsic good, that which is founded as good in our experience, and also the affective. This definition states the subjective bodily-lived aesthetic relative to perceptual awareness, but it is still not a full account. Our skin, that organ where the brain begins, connects us to a large world of aesthetic possibilities beyond its boundaries.[7] We may recognize these as potential in nature, in conversation, in cooking, in memories, in children, in animals, in the dances of all people, in rocks, rivers, and frog ponds. Aesthetics is founded in our senses, realized through our living body in its wholeness, actualized in our words, our works, and daily life.

Whatever its purpose in performance, all dance is embodied; it contains the complexities of intentional human movement and presents unique descriptive/interpretive challenges. Rooted in art, ritual, and play, dances are creative endeavors that produce (actually bring into being) aesthetic values involving human skill, imagination, and intentionality. As human artifacts (products), we can distinguish the aesthetic properties of our dances from those we ascribe to material nature. The blazing colors of a morning sky over the rocky pinks of Utah's Bryce Canyon differ from similar qualities in a dance—even though human movement and skies can both blaze. We can also distinguish our (sitting and leaping) dances (or relate them) to those of nonhuman creatures (such as frogs). Interpretation of particular dance events (and of the dancing) requires a conscious leap of the imagination from movement to language. Moreover, the movement of human dance is not just any movement. It displays very specialized behaviors and appears in circumstances that are often set apart from the ordinary—theaters cut into mountainsides (like Colorado's Red Rock Theater), and torchlit caves, as in the Butoh dance of Yumiko Yoshioka (through her work at Bröellin Castle International Theatre Research outside Berlin). When we interpret a dance, we exercise our ability to discern what continuities movement, image, and language have, especially since these arise through the-body-as-utterance, poiesis, or expression.[8]

Interpretation is not a unidimensional act. In dance it is more a process of weaving together various threads: discerning and describing aesthetic qualities (of form and expression), comparing and relating works or dance events, describing movement signature or style, deciphering whether representational or symbolic content plays a part, relaying the tensions and resolutions of myth and narrative that often appear unannounced,[9] and considering political, social, or historical context. Aesthetic values (perceptual qualities), like color values in a painting or movement values in a dance, may be defined in the process. Thus aesthetic values may function in a twofold sense; they may refer to relational properties intrinsic to a dance, or they may imply aesthetic worth. Dances bear the marks (aesthetic values) of their makers. As we interpret and value these human marks, we carry the dance from movement into language. According to perspective, several different interpretations of the same dance event are possible. It is through such varied perspectives that we share the dance event.

Some would argue that dancing is to be appreciated spontaneously and not interpreted. Indeed it could also be argued that the attempt to find "meaning" in a dance can obscure its affective (aesthetic) function, and that one does not find meaning in a dance the same way one does in a book, for instance. These are thorny issues in dance and art criticism. Critic Susan Sontag argues against interpretation in an influential article that views art as an intrinsic matter.[10] In defence of late modernist nonrepresentational art, she is against interpretation as a function of deciphering what a work represents or means. But hers is a narrow definition of interpretation that (when imported to dance) cannot account for varying choreographic intentionality. The significance of art (especially dance) is seldom literal. In any case, dance works will always convey signature or style, as the root of *significance* and *signature* (sign) indicates: In other words, interpretation is not always about finding representational or symbolic significance in a work. This is what makes interpretation interesting.

For instance: Doug Elkins's Bessie award–winning work, *Center My Heart* (1996), a joyful confluence of hip-hop, capoeira, kung fu, and modern dance techniques (with traces of ballet) is a dance visualization of Pakistani party music by Nusrat Fateh Ali Khan. Its generous unfoldings of geometric centering designs break and reassemble in the exciting rhythms of the kinky movement. Much of its aesthetic interest is created through its amalgamation of disparate global influences. It reminds me of the centering principles at work in the designs of early Turkish carpets (twelfth and thirteenth century), as architect Christopher Alexander brought these designs to attention through his collection and exhaustive study of their formal (and magical) centering principles.[11] The carpets are pictures of God. So why would I associate them with a secular dance?

Center My Heart is human in its play and passion, an exuberant and irreverent mixture of movement worlds and styles, one of the marks of postmodernism (should we still call it this?), although more challenging than the early ease of minimalist postmodern. His dance goes to the heart of technical challenge—in strong and supple movement, in polyrhythms and swift closures, brief and rebounding. Where movement is surrendered, as in the performance of Lisa Nicks, dance is also a picture of God. She reminds me that the centering this work involves is not just revealed in its geometry. I told Elkins that his dance reminded me of Turkish carpets and their fascinating centers-within-centers. (Sometimes we do talk to choreographers about their work, but is the work's meaning established this way?) He said he had the intricate designs and mandelas of mosques in mind. Does it matter that the dance maker was inspired by mosques and the witness related his work to her recent study of magic carpets? I do not think so. Interpretation is translation, an enrichment of perceptual exchanges between the work, the performer, and the witness.

When understood as *an explanation or translation* of something, interpretation is related to perception and description. To claim that dances cannot or should not be interpreted is to disavow the intelligent intersection of language, imagination, and movement. Dancing teaches us about the mind-body connection in a way that no other art can.

II. On Intention, Interpretation, and Nature

As expressions, language and dance both stem from human agency, the freedom to move forth the pleasure and power of ourselves in word and action. Human agency implies movement—intention, purpose, and freedom in action—hence, choices to be made. Indeed, choice is the very basis of culture. Nature is often contrasted to culture (as frogs to humans) in aesthetic discourse, because nature unfolds its own order of action, moving according to its own causal and accidental factors. Nature has its own aesthetic design, one we interact with all the time, as surely as day and night follow upon one another and the seasons condition our biorhythms. Physicists interpret nature, typically asking what events in nature "mean" as they seek scientific verification of nature's coherent and chaotic patterns. Although aestheticians might also consider natural phenomena, their interpretive task is less concerned with facticity than the scientist's and more with qualitative description. If nature and culture can be contrasted, they also have continuities, and human creativity (we need to understand) can be considered within the scope of nature. We work and play with nature, and sometimes against it, in producing the acts and arts of culture. We can also anthropomorphize nature (as in our Frog Pond), although we might recognize when we are doing this.

I hold that dance (all dance) expresses our given body-of-nature and at the same time our acquired body-of-culture.[12] The bodily synthesis of nature and culture in dance makes it an intriguing locus for research. Future studies might investigate just how our natural and cultural bodies coalesce in dance. If this were even charted, where would it lead? Certainly across science and anthropology, art and aesthetics, and perhaps it would raise the illusive study of "intrinsic value":

pleasure in movement and its bodily basis in dance. It is increasingly apparent that our survival depends upon our moving with (and not against) nature, and that we need to rediscover the original project of dance modernism: our bodies, our movement, and ourselves as a part of that nature.

III. On Aesthetic Intention and Ritual

Human intentions are embodied in human actions, even though some actions, like slipping on a banana peel, are unintentional. Dance is a special instance of human action according to intention. All dance is aesthetic action at some point, although it may in addition to its aesthetic intention exhibit other root intentions as well. Consider the social and ritual functions of dances such as the *Navajo Squaw Dance* with its doubled purpose of courtship and mythopoetic reprise (of celebration after the war on Taos). Its aesthetic intentions (of special movements heightened by rhythm) are poetically contained in its wider purposes of courtship and celebration, and the secular and sacred are not separated: "The movement is timed to the appropriate verse and done with a finish and clarity of intent that elevates the act above ordinary movement."[13] We can speak of the function of a dance in its cultural context (play, art, ritual, etc.) and at the same time identify basic aesthetic intentions embodied in the movement. To return to our frog: height and suddenness of jumping are aesthetic properties that could be intended in any movement—ritual dance, theater dance, drama, or basketball. It is total context that establishes purpose. We can properly speak of an aesthetics of basketball, its jazz rhythms, darting passes, and the heart-stopping feints and flourishes of star players even though basketball is not primarily motivated by aesthetic intention. Its primary purpose is established in its cultural context as competitive play.

Aesthetic properties are not extrinsic elements, pretty or decorative flourishes tacked onto dance movement. Aesthetic properties *belong* to movement, as the word *property* indicates. Aesthetic properties (also called qualities and values) are discerned as qualitative dimensions that inhere in movement: syncopated and overlapping rhythms, space (where inner meets outer), and efforts—light, languorous, and explosive. Aesthetic qualities belong to the structures of movement, in other words. Here I have added "qualitative discernment" to my definition of aesthetics. In dance this aspect is tied to structural elements of movement that can be identified and described. If the process of identification seems somewhat objective as elements are singled out and named, it nevertheless relates directly to the subjective/affective source of aesthetic experience as founded in sense perception and emotional responsiveness. The pond brings reflections in the water, visiting blue jays and hummingbirds, shadowy shapes at twilight, firefly neons, and a chorus of frogs at night—nature's (unintentional?) cosmos, green-eyed trees to sit in, *imago,* and darkness.

Concerning ritual, it would be surprising if all peoples had categorical concepts of aesthetics or equivalent words for it, but that does not mean they do not have "aesthetic intentions" as engaged in action (the attempt to jump high for "the joy" of it, for instance, or the development of heightened rhythm). Aesthetic intentions are embedded in material structures, and the materials vary with each medium of expression. Aesthetic intentions are human marks, the purposeful marks of invention and creativity. The Yup'ik masks of southwestern Alaska that inspired the structural anthropology of Claude Lévi-Strauss and surrealism in art bear such purposeful creative marks. They were carved for ceremonial masked dancing, for ritual.

Lévi-Strauss saw carved into the masks evidence of "deep structures" of the human mind that he later spent his life's work elaborating. For the Yup'ik, the mask dances are a way of making prayer and seeking an abundant future. The masks are also carved with aesthetic care for their expressiveness and shamanic powers: to facilitate communication among humans and animals and the living and the dead. The aesthetics of the masks inhere in their objective structure and their psychological affect. As intrinsic to the dance, the masks are visually and kinesthetically affective, even though traditionally, they were often discarded after use. Now the collection of masks serves as a touchstone of cultural pride.[14] Aesthetic intentions are actions that are oriented toward some qualitative outcome, be it carving or dancing. While ritual dances function beyond aesthetic intent to serve magical and religious purposes, they nevertheless also embody aesthetic intentions in their expressiveness. The line between ritual and art has permeable boundaries. Dance as theater art descends from ritual and may still reflect the magic and therapeutic of ritual, even in a secular setting.[15] Ritual, like art, has been created qualitatively—for the eye, the ear, and the heart. I am suggesting that the boundaries between art and ritual may not be as tightly drawn in experience as they are in our verbal explanations, as aesthetic inquiry could take up.

IV. Phenomenology and Intention in Dance

Interpretation and intention (especially aesthetic intention) are major conceptual categories in aesthetic discourse. They are also key concepts in phenomenology, a branch of modern philosophy that has guided much of my research and writing. As a phenomenologist, my process leads me to research intentionality through a specific method that seeks to get to the core of a phenomenon, assuming nothing as definitively given. The descriptive method of phenomenology aims to be simple (even if it is not) and seeks to uncover and describe what is most obvious, however hidden or assumed in our perception. The phenomena of description can be anything. If I ask what dance is, for instance, I need to conjure particulars. Otherwise my definition will be abstract and general. I may get to theory and eventually to general definitions, but first I appeal to the concrete.

The concrete image that comes to mind when I consider the term *dance* is that of a human being engaged in some special kind of human action or behavior. If (as a phenomenologist) I assume that I do not know what the person is doing, I become curious. First I notice that the person is moving in unusual ways. (This assumes that I know what "usual" ways of moving are, but how far back need I go?) This thing called "dancing" is not the way people move in general as they go about their daily lives. (And what is "daily life"?) I travel back to the word *usual*, which suggests *use* at its root, because I am aware that the dancer is not using her movement to accomplish any ordinary task, nor does s(he) appear to be moving toward a particular destination. Indeed, the dancer's movement seems set apart for some special purpose, not a utilitarian one. The movement seems to serve no purpose outside of its own requirements. (Yes I would have to know a lot about movement and purpose to get to this, or would I?) But my scope may be too limited and abstract. I begin to conjure every example of dance I can think of, from the Argentine tango to Japanese butoh and passing through postmodern contact improvisation. I think also of the traditional Hawaiian hula and children skipping to music. I am struck in all these cases by how the dancers are invested in their movement, and that they do not seem to be going anywhere. They move for the dancing.

If I want to go somewhere (to the store or the bank), dancing (of any kind) might be a very strange way of getting there, and it would certainly take a long time. But what the heck, I say, I like to make interesting patterns in space and snappy rhythms. Maybe I could just slow my dance down a little, tuck the rhythm inside my walk, and mark the turns in my imagination; then I could dance to the bank without having people stare at me.

The dancer I conjure might dance down the street sometimes (like I do), but not for long. She sees that someone is looking and remembers she has to get to the store before it closes. Speed and economy enter her walk. Now she is getting into a car, and I notice how the stretch of her arm in opening the door, her stepping up, and the turning of her body as she sits are all well suited to her purpose of getting into the car. I think to myself that her movement has a certain kind of functional elegance, and I suddenly see it as a part of her everyday dance.

When I watch a dance at some special event, I begin to notice that its steps fall in rhythms, shapes jut and flow into one another in arresting ways, and I respond to the expressive dynamics of the movement. If I watch dances of many different kinds, over the years I might come to the conclusion that they all have some common features much like those I just mentioned.[16]

When I turn my attention to the dancer/performer, I begin to understand that the dynamics or qualities of the dance ensue from the dancer's intentions in terms of actual movement. So I might focus a theoretical problem here, one of describing (defining) intention as revealed in voluntary motion—intention as embodied volition—not as a mental decision to be carried out after the fact. The latter would be another use of the word: intention toward future action, not as contained in or accomplished in movement itself. Intentional movement is movement that is done on purpose, not accidentally or involuntarily. Except in trance dances, dance movement is performed on purpose. Dance presents a special case of voluntary motion, imbued with the aesthetic intentions of performers and the larger intentionality (purposes) of each particular dance.

V. Through Intention Back to Interpretation

The dancer embodies aesthetic intention creating the discrete properties of intentional movement (like height and suddenness). Still further in dance, these discrete properties coalesce in a total event; internal coherence becomes apparent as properties and parts become a whole. Consider the problem of language here. Singular properties are only discrete in description; a human jump, like the frog's jump, is perceived whole. Its height cannot manifest apart from its spring and trajectory, its suddenness, shape in space, its relation to the pond beneath and the splash landing. Neither can it be separated from the jumper, the frog itself, or the perceptive witness of the pond.

With intentionally created human jumps that are part of a dance, the task of interpretation becomes very complex as we notice what precedes and follows the jump. For it is not singular movements that establish meaning. Meaning arises within the entire context of the movement and its perceived purpose. No single movement in a dance means anything by itself. A jump is just a jump until it is contextualized within a community of dance makers, performers, and audience-participants. The aesthetic properties of a dance (its qualitative values), its aesthetic essence (its subject), its symbolic and metamorphic powers are created and interpreted within a cultural context. The dance *meaning* (I believe we can use this word when speaking of nonverbal phenomena) is established through interpretation and communication, engaging our thinking through the body.

In its many varieties, dance contains our cultural heritage, the very constructs of our historied body. Aesthetics and criticism stem from culture (including embodied culture) even as they also become cultural products. Thus, the aim of aesthetic and critical theory is *to illuminate culture:* to define, to interpret, to evaluate, to challenge custom and convention from outside the frog pond, being inside at the same time. Consider how we manufacture our cultural values, make aesthetic choices, and how these may become politicized.[17]

If we spiral back to the beginning of this short study on intention—to "bracket in" taste, touch, sight and sound, to intuit where intentions (of all kinds) arise in consciousness—we may feel them gestating viscerally, pulsing in muscle and seeding in the bone of our whole-body consciousness. ("Bracketing in" is the inclusive reverse of "bracketing out" that I borrow from the innovative pedagogy and dance phenomenology of Andrew Cornish.) Some intentions find their way out in our freely chosen movements of making and doing and in our acts of speech. Perhaps intentions live more than once as they recede, then make sudden reappearances. In other cases we become aware of how they grow like plants, steadily from inception to fruition.

Of interest to dance is how our intentions are finally actualized in the conscious orientation of movement. At some point they become synonymous with movement; the forms and energies of our efforts coalesce in time and space. Dissolved in decision and consent, we become the dance.

In dancing as in life, our intentions may be forceful or yielding, and intentionality regularly slips into movement beyond any effort or control of the will. Bypassing thought, movement is taken for granted, because it is of our own nature or has become second nature (as we commonly say of something that has sedimented in the nervous system). Phenomenologist Paul Ricoeur recognizes the importance of movement that lives many times, settling into our second nature through repetition. Learning, habit, and skill all lie in this area, even as second nature requires a first. If "our body becomes the form of our will," as Ricoeur holds, then our body-of-dance is being formed hourly, as is our body-of-life. What butoh dancer Akira Kasai calls "the community body"[18] is the larger result of our dancing. Reflecting the body of the pond, we become what we dance. What forms do we want to practice?

How High? (Theory of Relativity)

Interpretations of movement in both frogs and humans require keen observation. When you think of it, frogs only jump high in proportion to their size. Here is a relativity: frogs can jump higher than their own height by a long shot, but I cannot. This I know through observation of frogs and my own experience. But should I press this relativist tact further, I may wonder if frogs really do jump so high, because I am not the only measure here. There are, after all, humans who do exceed their own height, now by at least a foot, in high jumps, and more than this in broad jumps. But they are exceptional humans, not the norm, and frogs who jump high (and far) are not exceptions. The answer to my original inquiry (as it contains my philosophic commitment, the points I am making, the values I am deriving and inventing) is: I believe frogs jump high because they are frogs, and for all of the reasons first speculated. The answers are in the questions. I am obligated to explain frogness at this point, but I will let it go for now, lest we be led into a discussion regarding instinct and into speculations on nature you might have felt lurking in the original question the minute you saw it.

Why frogs jump high or how high they jump might call for a scientific investigation, if we wish to understand frog anatomy and kinesiology—their excitation patterns and manner of extension. However, one can see from the rash of questions following upon the original that the query is more inclusive, because it elicits broader concerns about movement—its relativity in human perception and its contrasting qualities in frogness. Indeed, the question elicits interpretation, even interpretations that frame (notice and ascribe value to) frog movement as dance. We can investigate the term *high* in our question about frog "high jumps" as *quantitative value* (measure) or *qualitative value* (aesthetic).

Why Are Frogs Such Excellent Jumpers?

This is an altogether different question. Now we are in the realm of critical value, asking what makes for excellence and good performance. Still we are dealing with frogs here, so the question of intentionality that informs our judgments about human performance (does the performance fulfill its intention?) does not enter the picture. We would need to account for the difficulty of getting in touch with intentionality in nonhuman creatures. Granted, there may be some people who are gifted in communication outside the human sphere. I do well with frogs, some do better with whales and porpoises, and those who have communed with wolves and horses are legendary.

When we ask questions about excellence in human performance, we are using our critical faculties and exercising judgment. We seek to know what constitutes successful performance. In dance criticism, we are engaged in ascertaining what constitutes "the good" performance, the good being a standard of value defined or implied in the criticism. For when we praise anything, we are identifying a qualitative dimension and singling it out as valuable. (Notice how that word *quality* is creeping back in.) If we believe that jumping or leaping high is praiseworthy, as in virtuoso moments of the ballet, we have singled out a quantitative dimension and ascribed qualitative value to it. If we are captivated by the frog's ability to jump up wildly from complete stillness, this becomes another valued characteristic. The critical standard here is a quality of our own experience relative to the jump.

Not only do we enter into critical valuing when we praise, we return to the overarching category of the aesthetic, based in affective life and sense perception. We have categorical names for some aesthetic responses like excitement and surprise, pleasure and anguish, but others are difficult to pin down with words. Affective life is revealed and sometimes named in our dances. The sentient basis in feeling precedes our naming. We name the responses that arise in the body —"delight" in the frog's leap, for instance. Critical evaluation implies explicit judgment and exists within the larger context of aesthetic valuation—the naming and describing of qualitative properties. We cannot critique what we cannot describe. The task of identifying kinds and qualities of movement comes first. Thus a leap might "take flight," and a fall could seem "sequential" or "collapsed." We can speak of a turn as "full and flowing," implicating critical as well as aesthetic valuing if we employ these qualifiers to indicate something successful in the performance. Certainly many of our aesthetic descriptions are also critical evaluations, but technically speaking, critical evaluations are explicit judgments. They take a stand (as I am just about to do).

Are Frogs Beautiful Dancers?

Now you may not think that frogs are beautiful dancers, or that they dance at all. I happen to believe that frogs are beautiful dancers, and that they are always dancing. Let me defend this thesis. Frogs are beautiful dancers because *they are not divided from their movement.* That is: their movement displays none of the splits of attention that I often see dancers struggle with as they seek to become one with the movement they are intending to do. In the process of learning a particular dance, however, or even an entire dance form, dancers may reach a frog level of excellence—

> moving totally in tune with intention, achieving
> a wide range of expression, amazing speed, and a superb
> level of stillness when they want it. In short, they may become
> unselfconsciously graceful, moving with nature.

Inculcation of form in dance is a matter of practice; moreover, it seeks an excellence often termed "grace," whether the formative properties are ethereal, as in the airborne (European-romantic) ballet, or earthy, as in the stamping (Muslim-Hindu) north Indian *kathak*. Grace is another word for beauty in dance, and beauty is another word for the aesthetic. At least this is the history of these terms.[19]

As a phenomenologist, I am sometimes concerned with describing grace as a matter of *intention and consciousness* in dance (not to be confused with "intentionalism," the aforementioned argument about whether the intentions of artists determine the meaning of works). My definition of grace rides on intentionality, being so in tune with intent that all consciousness of it disappears. Moreover, this is not a purely mental phenomenon I wish to locate. It is the entire body consciousness of intentionality. In the personalized terms that phenomenology often uses, I could describe this phenomenon as realizing the movement (making it real) as you become the dance, dissolving your intentions (to jump, turn around, look toward your partner, or back over your shoulder, etc.). These are those times when you become absorbed into your body's consciousness, your intentions dissolve, and movement becomes easily commensurate with body. No element of the movement is foreign to you; you claim it as yours. It is your dance, your body. You might even call it second nature at a certain point. It becomes your nature, as natural as the frog's leap.

This is just as true in everyday life as it is in dance:

> When my intentions are realized in action, they are no longer intentions.
> They disappear (as they manifest) in all I do effortlessly. Here nothing is held
> in the past as what I intended to do but now find left over. There is no
> residual wish for something unfulfilled, nor forward spill; no body, no mind,
> no limit. Grace is life lived in the present, moving of its own accord. I feel
> life's temporal aspect "nowing" in my bones when I experience the pleasurable
> spontaneity of present-centered dancing or witness that of others.

This description of grace is both phenomenological (a matter of consciousness) and metaphysical (concerned with describing grace as transcendence of intent). This is a description and also a definition. It uses the familiar first-person voice to ground an abstract explanation, but it is not idiosyncratic. It stems from a universalizing impulse, a desire to communicate, but even more to create a voice for intersubjective understanding.

To shift from phenomenology to value theory, I could view my core definition of grace as an aesthetic standard—that which I value as an aesthetic good. If I employed it as a standard of judgment in evaluating dancing, that good dancing relies on (clear) realization of intention, I would be using it as a critical standard. To this point, I remember Mary Wigman's caution when I studied with her. "Never show the audience what you can't do," she said. "They want to see what you *can* do." I understood her to mean that good dancing is about "can do." It is satisfied in being what it is, not overtaxing itself for effect and risking falsity. It seems too simple to say, thus all the more needs saying. My briefly stated theory uses "can do" (realization of intent) as a dance denominator (essence, or phenomenological reduction) and employs it in a definition of grace. Consider further what the *can* in "I can dance" or "he can dance" involves in view of bodymind integrity, since ability in dance is both fulfillment and transcendence of intention and is not a purely physical or mental phenomenon. Expressive-psychological factors enter in. What constitutes great dance is often the next question, one involving a pyramid of critical values and standards I try to avoid. For I find more pleasure in contemplating a metaphysics of grace than in climbing patrician ladders. Value theory and normative discourse are philosophical disciplines that allow me to understand how my theses and arguments function, and how my phenomenological descriptions and definitions also state my values.[20]

I believe frogs are beautiful dancers because they move with nature, never a false move, nothing over or underdone, always just enough. Children at play often have these qualities. Intention is not apparent when it is at one with effort; neither does effort itself surface to attention. Not all dance is about such innocent grace, however. But the best (and maybe even the greatest) is in some sense equally spontaneous and unself-conscious. Simple dances can be graceful. The dances of the physically and mentally handicapped can be graceful. They also move within the complexities of human intentionality. I love to witness the incredibly fragile, elusive grace of the elderly. Slow dances, fast dances, earth dances, and spirit dances all can be graceful. Graceful (beautiful) movement is not simply the province of professional dancers. Theirs, however, are special cases (but not the only ones) in which we can witness the complexities of intentionality—our possible and implausible dances, transforming, transcending intent. In some sense, the audience does want to see "can't do," to glimpse what they cannot do (but might), and what the dancer once could not do, but now can.

Reading by the Pond

In his famous short story written at the beginning of the nineteenth century, *Uber das Marionettentheater*,[21] Henrich von Kleist also considers the metaphysical problem of consciousness in graceful movement: that humans do not have the perfect consciousness of God, nor the complete lack of consciousness of a marionette. He reasons that graceful movement is more difficult for humans in their intentional willing and self-reflexivity. Humans deal with an awkward level of consciousness in movement that gods and marionettes (and frogs I would contend) escape in their unself-consciousness.

The power of philosophic/linguistic interpretation will become apparent if we continue to press this question of grace and beauty further. Deconstructions of Kleist's view have attributed sinister meanings to his seemingly innocent story

—that his idealism recommends a Nazi state repressing signs of difference and dissent—and that his logical conclusion (though not explicitly stated) would justify puppetlike mechanization and mutilation of dancers.[22] Maybe these include anorexia and cosmetic surgery, and addiction to sylphlike perfection (or comparable affectations for Kleist's time)?

Perhaps the fierce conformity of women in another of Kleist's texts, *Penthesilia* (1807), his mythic play about the Amazon warrior-queen and her army, would qualify as mechanization?[23] But all armies are mechanized formalization. National formalism at the Nuremberg rallies and the Munich Olympics would undoubtedly qualify as political warrior formalization—mass control war machinery—culminating in the attempt to eliminate a people considered "unaesthetic" by the Nazis. Is all group mechanization so sinister? What about conformity and mechanization in the classical corps de ballet? Erick Hawkins called the toe shoe "a machine."[24]

I wonder about the toe shoe as mutilation. Is it a form of foot binding? How about the reshaping of the natural form of the arms in Javanese dance? The tortures of self-effacement and sublimation that Indian classical dancers are compelled to undergo?[25] Excruciating physical torture endured by youths in training for the classical Chinese opera?[26] The corset as mutilation (remember Isadora)? Ritual mutilation of the one-breasted Amazons to better shoot their arrows? The widespread practice, both ancient and modern, of scarification, including ear and nose piercing? Gothic-Rock-Death-Punk body piercing (arising in Britain with Gothic Club Dancing in the early 1980s and enduring through punk subcultures)?[27] *Castrati,* castration of young boys to maintain the "boy soprano" voice? Ritual sexual aesthetics (enslavement through genital mutilation and clitorectomy of 90 million African women, now outlawed in Kenya)?[28] The terrible beauty of idealized bodies in dance and modeling when the standard distorts nature and spurs eating disorders?

Kleist's marionette story is well-known since its English translation and inclusion in a book of readings on philosophies of dance.[29] Undertake your own reading and see whether you agree with the following deconstructive conclusion: "There is indeed a persuasive parallel between the coercive formalism of dance, and the totalitarian formalism of the Nazis' aesthetic State. Just as the performance of mechanized dance steps might be improved by mutilation, as in Kleist's tale."[30] This reading (interpretation) sees beyond the centering principles involved in graceful movement that provide the metaphysical thematic in Kleist's story. Does his idealism support Nazi totalitarianism? Would *any* idealization or aesthetic manipulation of the body imply suppression of its freedom and nature?

These are questions of interpretation, and interesting ones for aesthetics (especially as it applies to politics of nations and of human bodies). Mikhail Bakhtin's view of interpretation, *diologism,* is similar to the viewpoint of phenomenology. It conceives of ideas and words as *intersubjective.* Their meaning is established within a context, and between people.[31] I submit that language and dances live as embodied voices, and even conflicting voices. They are not absolutes—as relativist views, quantum physics, and existential phenomenology would affirm.[32] One need not abandon the notion of truth to embrace the validity of multiple viewpoints, conflicting perceptions, experiential truth, and truths that arise through interpretation as culturally shared meaning. Indeed, such truths as aesthetics and history claim are not invariant. They are multivalent and arise through interpretation. Since the appearance of T. S. Kuhn's *The Structure of Scientific Revolutions,*[33] it is well established that the truths of science are also historically contingent. There are many possible interpretations of texts, dances, and life. The latter turns us toward a history of the pond, where the question of whether frogs are beautiful dancers appears in a fuller context.

The Old Pond

Beauty has been the historic ingredient of the aesthetic. But what does it mean? Its definition from classical philosophy until the eighteenth century revolved around issues of harmony and proportion according to the golden mean, that the smaller part is to the larger what the larger is to the whole. The ratios could be mathematically calculated in architecture and in music, as demonstrated in the overtone series. We still use *beauty* as an aesthetic modifier, but we mean many things less quantifiable when we say it. Often we are expressing our pleasure in something, its expressive eloquence, or its power to move us. The history of the term *beautiful* contains the history of aesthetics.[34] We constantly invent new ways of applying it. Just as we evolve new understandings of grace—as we must—if it continues to have any meaning in dance.

Questions concerning grace and beauty in dance are historic aesthetic questions. Contemporary dance is often more concerned with questions about expression (or its absence) and embodiment of ideas. The identification of gender issues, especially if these represent aesthetic trends, is of increasing concern in dance aesthetics. In theater dance, the female inheritors of Isadora Duncan and Mary Wigman explore healing as magic (Anna Halprin), ritual transformation (Urban Bush Women), community engagement (Ann Carlson), intrinsic animal pleasure (Marie Chouinard), dance as life (Deborah Hay), risk and danger (Elizabeth Streb), risk and rapture laced with emotional violence (Pina Bausch), even cruelty and ugliness (Susanne Linke). Joan Laage has imported butoh, Japan's indigenous modern/postmodern dance, to the West, and she has infused her choreography with the "concrete," "hanging," and "adorned" butoh body, tapping the body's unconscious in the manner of Zen emptiness.[35] Sun Ok Lee's Zen Dance presents the body directly through the Zen mind and ritual chanting. In contrast to the expressive concreteness of these female choreographers are the more abstract works of George Balanchine and Merce Cunningham, two of the most influential male choreographers of the twentieth century.[36]

We inherit formalist/autonomist aesthetics from arguments about the nature of art descended through the male philosophical tradition beginning in the classical age with the philosopher-poets (philosopher-kings). Central questions for Plato and Aristotle concerned man's participation in the universe in his power to make and respond to beautiful things. Early inquiries did not separate aesthetics and ethics. Theories of the beautiful and the good were intermixed with concerns for the cosmos, nature, and man. In *Laws VII,* Plato considers art as "appearance" and of the essence of God, as he cautions humility for the artist. Aristotle concerns us with art as "imitation," in his *Poetics.* Through Plotinus's *Enneads* we learn of ideal form and beauty in dance as an image of cosmic order.[37] From Roman antiquity, we gain the only classical history and aesthetics of dance, *On Dance* by Lucian. Francis Sparshott outlines aesthetic questions on dance posed by Lucian that are still under debate.[38]

Not, however, until the eighteenth century did Art (with a capital *A*) and the term *fine art* in its modern sense originate. Likewise the term *aesthetics* is coined in that time by Alexander Gottlieb Baumgarten (which suggests that we use it with reservation in reference to preceding periods). He conceives of aesthetics as a "theory of sensuous knowledge, as a counterpart to logic as a theory of intellectual knowledge."[39] Questions about art shift to matters of taste, genius, imagination, and creativity.

In 1760, choreographer Jean-George Noverre calls for a unity of expression and action in ballet, advocating incorporation of pantomime and gesture and praising the productions of Bathyllus and Pylades, two celebrated mimes famous about 22 B.C. during the reign of Augustus. The imitative dance termed *Pantomimus* was one of the most popular public amusements in Rome until the fall of the empire. Noverre's aesthetic is classic (Platonic and Aristotelian) in its valuing of dance as representation and imitation. Noverre calls for adding ballet choreographers to the celebration of what he identifies as the tradition of "great men."[40] About twenty years later, through Immanuel Kant questions about the relativity of perception in terms of art and taste evolve, signaling a shift in understanding and the beginning of contemporary subjectivist aesthetics.[41] In his aesthetics, Benedetto Croce, whose life spans the nineteenth and twentieth centuries (1866–1952), moves aesthetic discourse from eighteenth-century matters of taste and formal judgments of the beautiful toward *intuition and expression.* He identifies beauty with expression in his philosophical linguistics, paving the way for critical reception of abstract expressionism in art and aesthetics. In an article in 1930, the same year that Mary Wigman first performed in America, John Dewey introduced experiential themes concerning art as interaction with and reconstruction of the environment ("From Absolutism to Experimentalism" in *Contemporary American Philosophy*). His aesthetics, *Art as Experience* (1934), influenced American education as it mapped the experiential ground of art from a pragmatic stance.[42] At the same time through Mary Wigman and Martha Graham, concert dance became overtly expressive of emotion, influencing the growth of modern dance (also known as "expressive dance") in education.

New Streams in an Old Pond

Relativist concerns arising in the late eighteenth century take on a different character in the modern/postmodern world where cultural multiplicity requires concrete aesthetics. This could involve the scholarship of anthropology, since global awareness through mass communication and easy transit makes the world smaller (and ethnically richer) today. In addition, the intimate politics of gender, power, and gendered bodies in art (especially in dance) has barely been touched upon in aesthetics. This may be linked to the mythic equation of dance and body with woman and nature,[43] and to Western philosophy's devaluation of woman in her association with the body and nature. Aristotle, often credited as the father of biology and a major source of aesthetic theory, sees woman as a lower species, her body simply a vessel for the sperm of the male who is the true parent. Woman is passive and emotional, and there is nothing valuable about her body as bearing and nurturing life. Women are "monsters . . . deviated from the generic human type."[44]

From Plato and Aristotle to Dewey, from classical views of art as appearance and imitation to modern outlooks on art as expression and experience, aesthetics has been written by men. Until recently, the only woman contributing to mainstream contemporary aesthetics was Susanne Langer, with her study of symbolism and reason in its relationship to rite and art (*Philosophy in a New Key*, 1942).[45] Her perspective was not feminist, but she was the first contemporary philosopher to write an aesthetics of dance (in *Feeling and Form*, 1953). Of interest to dance is that she continued to weave aesthetic problems with bodymind issues (*Mind: An Essay on Human Feeling*, 1967). Later Sparshott devoted a lot of his attention to philosophical issues in dance in two of his works (1988 and 1995).[46] His work concentrated on general philosophical questions of classification, identity, and context without building an aesthetics of dance per se.

Now there are many new voices in philosophical aesthetics, and feminism is a major influence as it questions the formalist/autonomist tradition of patriarchal philosophy. Feminist and gender-based aesthetic research calls for relevant aesthetic discourse that does not "outlaw" emotions but focuses more concretely on the integrity of emotion and intellect. Three recent works focussing on concrete aesthetic issues are *Dancing Female,* edited by Sharon E. Friedler and Susan B. Glazer (1997), *Dancing Women* by Sally Banes (1998), and *Alien Bodies* by Ramsay Burt (1998).[47] The new aesthetics being written by both men and women is exposing the devaluation of women in philosophy, the exclusion of feminine voices in aesthetic discourse, and the objectification of women in art for power and profit. It proposes new models of thought and action that valorize the feminine.[48]

Feminist scholars have discovered a gender bias in aesthetics that associates "woman" with "emotion," then devalues them both. Rather than deny the association (since emotions are human traits and belong to both sexes) feminist scholarship is opening major debates on the very nature and importance of the emotions[49] and challenging aesthetic standards that evolved as reasoned universals through traditional philosophy. This scholarship encourages women to value their own experience, "the personal as political." Thus feminism is criticizing the cannons of "great art,"[50] even as performance communities spring up in dance where participation is encouraged and the master model is deconstructed.

The latter tendency in dance is fueled by improvisatory and somatics practices abridging aesthetic questions of hierarchy and excellence with egalitarian concerns. For example: when dance techniques develop within particular idioms, some performers will inevitably excel. With challenges in technique, there are obstacles to overcome, stated standards of excellence, sometimes ranking, ordering, and teaching of essentials, all the marks of hierarchy. Are hierarchy and excellence inevitably linked, then? Is hierarchy necessarily a bad thing? We might logically ask, what kind of aesthetic hierarchy (or choice) is being honed in any given dance practice? Such questions apply to the study of various performance communities and their aesthetic values, from classical ballet to contact improvisation and folk dance. All of these create performance values of well-doing and excellence, but the context and treatment of these values may vary greatly.

Feminist aesthetics holds much in common with the critiques of pragmatism and existentialism in their focus on experience and "the-life-world," but feminism is developing a new and gender-wise perspective on experience as a major existential category. It is even exhuming an unlikely theoretical source employing the psychosexual insights of Freudian psychoanalysis (on ways of "seeing" such as voyeurism, fetishism, and scopophilia) to shift aesthetics to a gendered perspective.[51]

Out of such work comes the feminist aesthetic concept of "the male gaze," or the assertion that the prevalent way of seeing the world (and art) is through an objectification of woman that puts her in a passive (and dehumanized) position, a concept that has not gone unquestioned in terms of its assumptions, its possible ethnocentrism, and its failure to account for erotic pleasure.[52] Laura Mulvey, who introduced the aesthetic problem of the active/male and passive/female positions in film theory, continues to defend the theoretical stance of feminist practice that aims to present an alternative to dominant ways of looking. She believes we should learn from the past while transcending outworn forms, conceiving a "new language of desire."[53] Ramsay Burt is similarly motivated in his well-researched book on the male dancer.[54]

Antecedent to the concept of the male gaze is the feminism of Simone de Beauvoir (1905–1980) and her identification of woman as the objectified "other." Beauvoir is the first major philosopher in contemporary feminism. Her breakthrough book, *The Second Sex* (1949), introduces feminism as a philosophical endeavor and becomes a classic.[55] Her works also contribute to the early development of existential phenomenology. She develops a philosophy of femininity as learned behavior, holding that "biology is not destiny." The controversial work of Camille Paglia, *Sexual Personae: Art and Decadence from Nefertiti to Emily Dickinson* (1990), later questions this thesis. She believes that feminism has exceeded its proper mission of seeking political equality for women and has ended by rejecting human limitations imposed by nature and fate.[56] In *Who Stole Feminism? How Women Have Betrayed Women* (1994), philosopher Christina Hoff Sommers voices related (but more conservative) concerns. She believes that "equity feminism," identified with the advancement of women, is being displaced by what she calls "gender feminism," an elitist intellectual movement sustained in the academy that denies differences between the sexes and discriminates against women who do not fit into its agenda.[57] Clearly, feminism is no longer a single movement with a unified purpose. We might more aptly speak of feminisms within a field of difference. Ecofeminism is a recent response to such diversity. It affirms our relationship to the earth, the spirituality of nature, and the partnership of men and women in the larger bio-dance.[58]

Phenomenology, with its concerns for the body, also introduces new streams of thought to the growing field of dance aesthetics. Maxine Sheets-Johnstone builds upon Langer's dance aesthetics and brings phenomenology into aesthetic discourse on dance in *The Phenomenology of Dance* (1966).[59] From the perspective of existentialism and also employing phenomenology, I later develop a descriptive aesthetics in *Dance and the Lived Body* (1987).[60]

As Anglo-American analytic philosophy becomes more enamored with scientific justification (or "physics envy" as it has been called), existentialism and phenomenology explore emotional life and the irrational as philosophic themes, just as feminism later identifies an ethics of care as a viable alternative to an ethics of justice.[61] The combination of existentialism and phenomenology (termed "new existentialism" by Colin Wilson) evolves a philosophy of the body in protest against essentialist views.[62] Its descriptive psychological stance, searching out the truth of the body-as-lived, develops a unique method for investigation in dance aesthetics and somatic studies. Sparshott feels the work of defining a field of dance aesthetics takes on new significance within phenomenology's repudiation of body/mind dualism.[63]

Phenomenology's nondualist project as originally set out by Merleau-Ponty is still unrealized in philosophy. His ideas have nevertheless been subsumed (and updated) by cognitive science on one hand[64] and hermeneutics on the other. In France, his direct heirs are Michel Foucault and Jacques Derrida, imported to America more as literary theorists on deconstruction than as philosophers.[65] The respect for the body that is a key concept in emerging feminist aesthetics draws upon the rejections of dualism first incorporated in the "lived body" paradigm of phenomenology but now extends this to concerns for how our bodies mediate culture and may be used to sustain oppression.[66] Dance aesthetics, we might understand, is either explicitly or implicitly an aesthetics of the body. We can also read it as a discourse and history of the body.[67]

A Drop of Pond Water

Logocentric philosophy redraws the outlines of continuing arguments in hopes of "getting it right." If it succeeds, will that be the end of philosophy (and thus of aesthetics)? Isn't "getting it right" the limiting supposition behind every discipline, as deconstructive theory would argue?[68] Would we want to "get it wrong," then? Is this where we are headed? No, not necessarily, but we are going in the direction of risk. Aesthetic inquiry is not about having the last word. It engages us in a process of discoveries, frustrations, and realizations. At best these can be recorded, built upon, tested over time, and shared with others as one's best efforts. I employ the descriptive method of phenomenology as it intends to make a clean break with positivist philosophical analysis. When phenomenology is true to its stated purposes, it begins with present time consciousness, not depending on previous theory but starting from scratch. Phenomenology would hope to yield studies of ourselves as embodied in history. It cultivates an alertness most like the code of the samurai, the clearing process of meditation, and the witnessing of frog ponds: "Expect nothing, be ready for anything."

If a path of inquiry opens certain views, it also imposes limits. As streams in philosophy and literary criticism still developing in the latter half of the twentieth century, phenomenology and its relatives, deconstruction and postmodern criticism, risk maintaining a focus on Eurocentric aesthetic values, redrawing its rankings and outlines, rather than substituting new maps. Feminism also risks ethnocentrism and a joining of the patriarchal culture it hopes to expose, deconstruct, and overcome politically, entering the "battleground" on prevailing terms.[69] We are coming to a time when intellectuals and artists outside the white mainstream will broaden the base of dance aesthetics, as a recent publication of the Dance Critics Association demonstrates.[70] Today's multicultural upheaval and shifting gender relationships are among the central challenges for contemporary dance aesthetics.

Sparshott sees that a central project for dance aesthetics is to develop ways of talking about the body's intelligence. Sarah Fowler would like dance aesthetics to develop a full exposition of kinesthetic intelligence.[71] As Sparshott outlines a history of dance aesthetics and speculates on its future, he produces a linear bibliography of sources beginning with Plato and Plotinus, extending to the eighteenth century's exclusion of dance (in the idea and system of what we presently call "fine art"), and ending with identification of sources for present-day aesthetics of dance.[72] Concerning the frog pond of which we are speaking, dance aesthetics is a drop of water within the history of the pond as a whole. Using our microscopic vision, we can nevertheless understand the relative importance of this teeming drop—as did Beverly Brown in her dance, *Life in a Drop of Pond Water*.

Ugly Dances

So how about it? Do you think frogs are beautiful dancers? Perhaps frogs "can't dance"? Maybe they are not graceful by some standards? Or maybe frogs do ugly dances? They can move in sudden spurts not commensurate with balletic grace, and their legs and eyes are so disproportionate to body size. (But maybe not to them?) Besides (in human terms), they have no necks. Maybe dancing is not what they are doing even if they could be proven graceful and well turned out? (And I think they can.)

My frog friend, a relativist and mystic, taught me something in this regard. She said that my favorite frog pond, which is also her home, becomes a theater whenever I sit beside it. That the pond and all its creatures are always dancing. The movement of my attention toward the expressive dynamic of the pond had allowed me to understand this, she told me. But, she cautioned that I was allowed this understanding as a moment of grace, a return to my childhood perfection that had since been muddled by false sophistications and living in haste. The dance of the pond was of my consciousness, but not of my doing, she told me, since the *doer* in me had to be given up for the dance to appear.

A Frog Jumps In

The moment I said the words a soft wind enveloped me and bore me to the pond. There I learned to observe, and even more to witness, to absorb the events of the pond without judging them. As their witness, I let them be. But I know now that a witness also affirms what s(he) sees, hears, and otherwise senses, calling forth her experience, and should acknowledge this. A witness clears her attention in order to carefully observe. In this sense, she gets rid of herself (what she knows already) so that the world may write itself upon the clarity of her consciousness. Finally, a witness attests and supports what she perceives.

This may happen out loud, in writing, or exist in the unstated affirmations or creations of her consciousness. Her original stance of unbiased attention is what allows the ontological status of anything (its being) to appear in consciousness. But here is the inevitable question: is unbiased attention really possible? The nearest example I can think of is the kind of attention attained by experienced meditators who have actually practiced nonjudgmental attitudes (toward self and others) so that thoughts may pass away without getting stuck in repetitive patterns. This process eventually clears the mind, if only for a while; wherein, the witness (the watcher herself) also disappears.

There is an analogous process in philosophy. Although not so pure, this process can be mystically akin to meditation. Some philosophers have even named their works meditations. Descartes's *Meditations* is contemplation dwelling within a thesis. As a modern philosophical method, phenomenology broke with philosophical thesis building. Its meditative stance was to clear consciousness of habitual ways of looking (experiencing), which is a certain kind of disappearing. Phenomenology holds this in common with modern somatic methods that seek to release human potential through revealing movement habits and impressing neurological pathways with new movement choices.[73] The aim of phenomenology is to allow the essence of things to appear (to consciousness) and to identify habits of thought and action. Its purpose is finally to describe the contents of consciousness. In this it echoes the purpose that philosophy has historically reiterated: to distinguish and describe the features of life. Plato held that philosophy was born in love—the love of wisdom— and saw philosophers as seekers.

Quantum Witness

The witness as "one who beholds" is at the foundation of philosophy. The witness who "attests" is entering into philosophical creativity at another level. He examines what he sees (sight is taken here to represent sensing and experiencing) and finally says what he understands of it. He is the seeker Plato spoke of. His quest is knowledge and wisdom. In his creativity, he backs away from himself to question his insights, to change his mind when new insights cancel the old, to clear his attention, to think in unbiased and nonhabitual ways. The father of phenomenology, Edmund Husserl, eventually evolved his philosophy toward a transcendental outlook, believing he had constructed a scientific manner of removing the observer from the observed (once more demonstrating the desire to "get it right"). Existential phenomenology through Martin Heidegger, Jean Paul Sartre, and Merleau-Ponty held that the observer and the observed cannot be separated, that we are a part of that which we behold and attest. Ontology, or the study of being, for them, became the study of our subjective intermingling with the objects of perception.[74] Through existential phenomenology, I understand that: the frog pond I witness is one I construct in my perceptual intermingling with the world I behold.

Philosophy has developed theories of "disinterestedness" to describe appreciation of aesthetic phenomena. Immanuel Kant laid the groundwork for aesthetic formalism and the autonomy of art when he used "disinterestedness" to explain the aesthetic attitude, an attitude that does not seek to possess the object of attention but remains "indifferent" to its existence.[75] This does not mean that the viewer is not perceptually involved, just that such involvement is not grasping. But this is implicit in the receptivity of the appreciative witness—more positive and less distant. I think of aesthetic perception as active receptivity. "Disinterested" is such a pale and dreary term. Even my husband's spotted blue ceramic frog, witnessing the pond of my writing from a nearby shelf, is not disinterested. The audience for art and other aesthetic phenomena (such as sunsets, friendly faces, earthquakes, and frog ponds) is actively attentive and receptive—even sometimes a critical agent. This we have just been able to touch upon.

A philosopher seeks to understand things, so s(he) asks questions and follows through with her investigation employing her experience, thought, and reason. But there is something enigmatic that propels her through and past these. She knows that her questions will guide her thought, and that her reasoning will build her understandings. A philosopher is a creative artist within this process. Ultimately, she seeks an insight that will move her understanding beyond mental habits and assumed authority. She wants to know more when she finishes than she did at the beginning. In short, she seeks to surpass her self, that bundle of bodymind habits that identifies with a limited ego, a separate self. She seeks to release what her understanding holds in its limitlessness but hides from her in the moment of her grasp. For the very act of grasping brings about a limit, a habit, the familiar and safe knowns. Her problem is to move her consciousness beyond the obvious familiar to capture the obvious that is present but unplumbed. A philosopher wants to learn what lies beneath the surface of the pond in its inseparability from her own mind, as this may teach her about the larger mind of which she is a part—her boundless thought, her fluid body.

> Plop!
> In the silence—
> the muted morning lifts
> a rainbow from the pond.

A Dip in the Pond (The Pleasure Principle)

I have tried here to engage students in aesthetic inquiry in dance in five interrelated ways: by involving them in my own philosophical process, introducing some major (historical) questions in aesthetic and critical theory, offering a critique of the style and content of traditional (logocentric) aesthetics, posing some questions of my own, and building a bibliography of resources along the way. I have not included educational theory, which is an important field of philosophical inquiry, and I have only briefly touched upon literary theory, which often crosses over into philosophy in its probing questions of language, signs, symbols, and theories of meaning. I might have focussed this chapter on "philosophical inquiry" per se, but thought within its generalities (of inductive and deductive reasoning) that I might more productively narrow my considerations of dance to aesthetics, the branch of philosophy that studies the arts and other aesthetic phenomena. I felt the necessity to define aesthetics and to sketch the history of aesthetics; to place dance in this historical stream as well as to explore some aesthetic questions (What is grace? for instance). I have tried to show how dance criticism relates to aesthetic theory through the intersection of interpretation with aesthetic and critical valuation. Issues of interpretation are continuing concerns in aesthetic and critical inquiry and have occupied a large part of my exploration. From entirely different perspectives, interpretation and valuation also provide the basis for Judith Lynne Hanna's and Janet Adshead's investigations in dance aesthetics.[76]

I have included value theory, the philosophical discipline that supports our understanding of qualitative questioning and reasoning. I have used phenomenology as a first-person mode of description, inviting my immediate conscious-ness into play in weaving strands (on aesthetics and criticism) together. Students may notice that I have also used phenomenology as a definitional tool. The latter is a matter of style. It aims to valorize experience and is opposed to the logocen-tric style of traditional aesthetics, which separates the physical and emotional from the verbal and intellectual.

Because I have not considered inquiry in philosophies of education, I refer students to an excellent issue of *Studies In Art Education* for three articles—espe-cially as these clarify the nature and aims of philosophy (including feminist/gen-der perspectives)[77]— and also to Susan Stinson's defense of "Interpretive Inquiry in Dance Education."[78] According to value theory, educational theory explicates instrumental theories of art. When the arts are used for educational purposes, they are by definition instrumental. The instrumental nature of educational val-ues renders them part of the category of extrinsic value.[79] This does not imply that educational uses of dance are inferior (although we sometimes use extrinsic as a pejorative). Rather it designates a "use" beyond intrinsic value, a unique ap-plicability of dance. I have felt it more important here to introduce the (eidetic and substantial) matter of intrinsic value in dance, that aesthetic experience of the body in motion upon which all other values rely—pleasure (move over Freud!) and its beloved companions: grace, joy, and freedom.[80]

Research Questions, Problems, and Exercises

Why Do Frogs Sit So Quietly?

(a) They are paying attention.
(b) They have beginner's minds.
(c) They are good phenomenologists.
(d) They have reached a still point in their dance.
(e) All of the above
(f) None of the above
(g) Other reasons?
(See answer at end of chapter.)

On Aesthetic Questions and Aesthetic Values

1. Write an essay on changing concepts of beauty in dance.
2. Write an essay on changing concepts of grace in dance.
3. Write an essay on aesthetic values.

4. List as many meanings for the aesthetic as you can find, and see what they may have in common. Give examples of how aesthetic values are created and perceived in dance. Bring the abstract into the concrete by using examples of actual dances or dance processes (such as choreography and performance). Tap into your own experience and extend it through research.

5. Read "Autonomist/Formalist Aesthetics, Music Theory, and the Feminist Paradigm of Soft Boundaries," by Claire Detels in the *Journal of Aesthetics and Art Criticism* 52, no. 1 (winter 1994). Consider her identification and critique of masculinist/formalist theory and its logocentric subordination of experience to intellect. Consider what her notion of "soft boundaries" might mean for dance theory and aesthetics.

6. Read Alison Jagger's article, "Love and Knowledge: Emotion in Feminist Epistemology," in *Gender/Body/Knowledge: Feminist Reconstructions of Being and Knowing*, ed. Alison Jagger and Susan Bordo (New Brunswick: Rutgers University Press, 1989). How have the emotions been misunderstood and "outlawed" in theories of knowledge? How might feminist and gender-based dance theory contribute to a better understanding and healthy valuing of human emotions? What are the implications of this for dance aesthetics?

7. Read the chapter on dance ethnography in this book (chapter 9) and consider how points of aesthetic inquiry may intersect with inquiry in ethnography. How might the inclusion of cultural concerns make aesthetic discourse more concrete? What are some cultural/social/political issues that need to be addressed in dance aesthetics?

On Criticism

How is a description a definition? When does a definition become a critical standard? Study a piece of critical writing in dance (a concert review or an article). What are some critical questions that arise? How are they answered? What aesthetic standards are either explicitly stated or implicit in the descriptive text? What does a careful reading reveal as noticeably absent?

Voicing Experiential Values

We dance to experience ourselves more abundantly, to focus and clarify aesthetic experience—on the skin, in the brain, in every intelligent cell. We turn to the arts to understand what experience is. Explore your own voice of experience. Write an essay on aesthetic values as experiential values. Use examples of dances you have choreographed, seen, or performed. These might be class studies, concert dances, traditional lineage-based dances, folk or social dances. Be clear about whether you are developing the voice of the choreographer, the dancer, the community, the audience-participant, or the critic. In other words, who are you in this essay?

In what sense do all of the above cultural agents imbue value? What subjects arise as "existentials" in your examination? These will be the crucial topics (subjects) derived from philosophical examinations of (descriptions of) experience.

The Spiral Dance: Phenomenology as Method

Decide what you want to find out. Break a coconut (your ego). Write quickly and fearlessly without editing or censoring. Let time pass. Revisit your writing, spiral in to extract the core thoughts. Develop these descriptively using "I" statements to let your consciousness speak. This is a way to probe your awareness. Ask what you are conscious of in the experience of the phenomenon you are describing. A phenomenon is anything that appears to consciousness: a person, a feeling, an experience, an event, an idea, a perception, or in the case of research—a question. When your description is complete, you have core existential values that you can expand philosophically. Here thoughts spiral outward from the core as you examine its components and elaborate core values. You might find the spiral expanding to become inclusive of what you excluded before, but now from another vantage point. You will have asked "does this really belong?" and reentered the thought from an examined perspective. Or you may surprise yourself with new insights or see relationships that were not apparent to you before. *Intuition* guides the original spiral into the core. The outward spiral develops *theory*.

The above is a suggested phenomenological method, not *the* method, since there could be various approaches. It may yield an insightful article that can lead to further inquiry or be complete as a philosophical investigation on its own. Your insights might also be used within other research paradigms to bring an experiential view to a historical question, or perhaps one in ethnology, feminist analysis, or movement analysis. The existentials you extract and develop are core experiential values and may be verified (or questioned) by points raised through other methods.[81] This would require some comparative study on your part according to the subjects raised in your inquiry. You might also find that your experiential descriptive research supports or fills out points at issue raised by authors coming from other research paradigms. This is another way of verifying your work. It does not establish irrevocable truth, but this is not the point. Rather, it respects experiential truth and our ability to make points of contact with others that are arrived at independently.[82]

Study Your Experience

Complete the following with short, single-paragraph descriptions:

When I dance, I . . .
When I choreograph, I . . .
When I watch a dance, I . . .

Say what you do in these cases, what you experience, what you feel, what you think about if this applies. Speak of your process if this applies. Be simple. Describe what is essential for you without resorting to analogy. Say what *it is*, the process itself, not what it is like. Go into your immediate consciousness, write quickly, asking your experience to speak. Do not edit your feelings. Ignore your internal critics, those voices in your mind that say "that's not it," or "not good enough," or "so-and-so won't like it." This exercise is not about recalling definitions of others, but rather tapping into your own experience. These are descriptive definitions. A description is a definition in its own way, and it can lend fresh perspective to tired formula definitions.

Do this exercise a few more times, at different times, forgetting your previous descriptions.

Finally compare them all, and *study your experience.*

NOTES

1. For a fuller consideration, see Richard Griffith and Erwin Strauss, eds., *Aisthesis and Aesthetics* (Pittsburgh: Duquesne University Press, 1970).

2. For a fuller discussion of relational factors in aesthetic valuing from the point of view of value theory, see Sondra Fraleigh, *Dance and the Lived Body: A Descriptive Aesthetics* (Pittsburgh: University of Pittsburgh Press, 1987), 43–48.

3. Ibid., 97.

4. See Arnold Berleant, *Art and Engagement* (Philadelphia: Temple University Press, 1991).

5. See Berys Gaut, "Interpreting the Arts: The Patchwork Theory," *The Journal of Aesthetics and Art Criticism* 51, no. 4 (fall 1993): 587–609.

For a discussion of both sides of the debate in terms of dance, see Larry Lavender, "Intentionalism, Anti-Intentionalism, and Aesthetic Inquiry: Implication for the Teaching of Choreography," *Dance Research Journal* 29, no. 1 (spring 1997): 23–42.

6. See Noël Carroll, "Anglo-American Aesthetics and New Criticism: Intention and the Hermeneutics of Suspicion," *The Journal of Aesthetics and Art Criticism* 51, no. 2 (spring 1993): 245–52.

7. For a comprehensive study of whole body consciousness in the interrelatedness of all the body's systems and scientific explanations of the brain's workings throughout, see Deane Juhan, *Job's Body: A Handbook for Bodywork* (New York: Station Hill Press, 1987). Skin as surface of the brain, 35–37. "The search for organizational factors of purposeful muscular control—whether it be action or relaxation takes us deeper and deeper into the

---

The correct answers are (e), (f) and (g): They are sitting zazen. Next question: can (e) and (f) both be true?

central nervous system, where we find that every muscular response is built up, selected, and colored by the totality of our neural activity, both conscious and unconscious. . . . And the patterns of stimulation that are passed on by the nerves contacting the muscle cells are the ongoing summations of all of our sensory and mental events," 144.

8. For a study of the body as the foundation for language, see Mark Johnson, *The Body in the Mind* (Chicago: University of Chicago Press, 1987).

9. See Claude Lévi-Strauss on "tension of oppositions" in myth: "myth always progresses from the awareness of oppositions toward their resolution." "The Structural Study of Myth," in *Structural Anthropology* (New York: Basic Books, 1963).

10. As a critic, Sontag calls for a descriptive rather than prescriptive approach to looking at forms in art, but she fails to make a distinction between works that have symbolic or representational intent and those that are formalist in conception. See Susan Sontag, "Against Interpretation," in *Against Interpretation and Other Essays* (New York: Farrar Straus Giroux, 1966).

11. Christopher Alexander, *A Foreshadowing of 21st Century Art: The Color and Geometry of Very Early Turkish Carpets* (New York: Oxford University Press, 1993).

12. The feminist complexities of the woman/nature parallel are well represented in Susan Griffith's *Woman and Nature: The Roaring Inside Her* (New York: Harper and Row, 1978). For how the body-of-nature and the body-of-woman become related through mythology, see Fraleigh, "Mythic Polarity," in *Dance and the Lived Body,* 141–58.

How are mythic polarities treated in psychology through the work of C. G. Jung and feminist analysts from that school, such as Marion Woodman in *Addiction to Perfection: The Still Unravished Bride* (Toronto: Inner City Books, 1982). For further feminist perspectives on nature-culture dualism, see Ynestra King, "Healing the Wounds: Feminism, Ecology, and Nature/Culture Dualism," in *Gender/Body/Knowledge: Feminist Reconstructions of Being and Knowing*, ed. Alison Jagger and Susan Bordo (New Brunswick: Rutgers University Press, 1989), 115–41. See also Donna Wilshire, "Uses of Myth, Image, and the Female Body," ibid., 92–114.

13. David McAllester, "A Paradigm of Navajo Dance," in *Parabola: Myth and the Quest for Meaning* (issue on Sacred Dance) 4, no. 2 (May 1979): 28–35.

14. Ann Fienup-Riordan, *The Living Tradition of Yup'ik Masks: Agayuliyararput, Our Way of Making Prayer* (Seattle and London: University of Washington Press, 1996), 261–305.

15. Jamake Highwater, *Dance: Rituals of Experience,* 3d ed. (New Jersey: Princeton Book Company, 1978).

16. See also the "irreducible structure of dance" in Fraleigh, *Dance and the Lived Body,* 48–49.

17. On the creation of political values, see Noam Chomsky, *Manufacturing Consent.* Sound recording: analog. Recorded at Cambridge, Mass., Jan. 22, 1993.

18. Akira Kasai, butoh workshop at the *San Francisco Butoh Festival* (August 1997). For a description of Kasai's workshop and festival performance see Sondra Fraleigh, *Dancing into Darkness: Butoh, Zen, and Japan* (Pittsburgh: University of Pittsburgh Press, in press).

19. For a history of "The Beautiful," see Wladyslaw Tatarkiewicz, "The Great Theory of Beauty and Its Decline," *The Journal of Aesthetics and Art Criticism* 31, (winter 1972): 165–72.

20. For a comprehensive treatment of value theory and normative discourse including definitions of intrinsic, extrinsic, and inherent values, how values become standards, categories of values (including aesthetic and critical values), and what establishes criteria of "importance" in values, see Paul W. Taylor, *Normative Discourse* (Englewood Cliffs, N.J.:

Prentice Hall, 1961). See also Resieri Frondizi, *What Is Value: An Introduction to Axiology*, 2d ed., trans. Solomon Lipp (Lasalle, Ill.: Open Court, 1971).

21. Heinrich von Kleist, *Über das Marionettentheater* (Wiesbaden: Insel Verlag, Insel-Bucherei Nr. 481, 1954), 5–13.

22. Ian Mackenzie, "Terrible Beauty: Paul de Man's Retreat from the Aesthetic," *The Journal of Aesthetics and Art Criticism* 5, nos. 1–4 (fall 1993): 551–60.

23. Heinrich von Kleist, *Penthesilea: Ein Trauerspiel* (Stuttgart: Philipp Reclam, 1963).

24. Erick Hawkins, "The Body Is a Clear Place," *Focus on Dance* 5 (1969): 34–39.

25. Avanthi Meduri, "Western Feminist Theory, Asian Indian Performance, and a Notion of Agency," *Women and Performance* 5, no. 2 (1992): 93.

26. As seen in *Farewell My Concubine*, a film by Chen Kaige, 1993.

27. See Tricia Henry Young, "The Politics and Aesthetics of Gothic Club Dancing," in *Proceedings, 30th Annual Conference, Congress on Research in Dance*, ed. Nancy L. Stokes (Tucson: University of Arizona Press, 1997), 469–84.

28. See Alice Walker's novel on this subject, *Possessing the Secret of Joy* (New York: Simon and Schuster, 1992).

29. Heinrich von Kleist, "Puppet Theater," in *What Is Dance?* ed. Marshall Cohen and Roger Copeland (New York: Oxford University Press, 1983), 178–84.

30. Mackenzie, "Terrible Beauty: Paul de Man's Retreat from the Aesthetic."

31. Mikhail Bakhtin, *Problems of Dostoevsky's Poetics*, ed. and trans. Caryl Emerson (Minneapolis: University of Minnesota Press, 1984), 40.

32. I do not include here the postpositivist literary movements of "structuralism" ("death of the subject") and its outgrowth "deconstruction" ("death of the author"), because they moved attention from the existential individual (thus the "embodied voice") to systems of meaning giving priority to universal structures in which the individual and society were both subsumed. For a further treatment of these developments, see Norman F. Cantor, *Twentieth-Century Culture: Modernism to Deconstruction* (New York: Peter Lang, 1988), 345–69.

Existentialism and deconstruction have a common ancestor. Nietzsche's philosophical poetry inspired both ("Is there still an above and below?"). He foresaw the decentering of values and search for meaning that was to occupy both existential individualism and deconstruction ("Does not empty space breathe upon us"?). See also Nietzsche's influence on Foucault's postmodern concern with "the mechanisms of power, the effects of truth," discussed in Cantor, *Twentieth-Century Culture,* 364.

33. T. S. Kuhn, *The Structure of Scientific Revolutions* (Chicago: University of Chicago Press, 1963; 2d ed. enlarged 1970).

34. Tatarkiewicz, "The Great Theory of Beauty and Its Decline."

35. See Joan Laage, "Embodying the Spirit: The Significance of the Body in the Contemporary Japanese Dance Movement of Butoh" (Ph.D. dissertation, Texas Woman's University, 1993).

36. My sampling is too small to state a gender trend. The better comparison would be George Balanchine and Merce Cunningham with Martha Graham and Mary Wigman, as the noted male and female greats of the twentieth century. In this comparison the male/abstract and female/expressive parallel still holds.

The question of Rudolph Laban's influence comes up as well. The primary influence of his work (as it survives today) has been in the area of dance theory, notation, and analysis. Wigman was once his student, but she carried his theories far more successfully into aesthetic practice than he himself did, influencing American concert dance directly through her tours and her student Hanya Holm, who established a Wigman school in the United

States before evolving her own. Wigman is still present in the late-twentieth-century surge of expressionist Japanese butoh. Butoh founder Kazuo Ohno studied with Takaya Eguchi who studied with Mary Wigman and imported her expressionist style and its probings of the subconscious to Japan.

37. Plotinus, *Ennead*. 3rd. ed., rev. (London: Farber & Farber, 1966).

38. Francis Sparshott, "The Future of Dance Aesthetics," *The Journal of Aesthetics and Art Criticism* 51, no. 2 (spring 1993): 227–34.

39. Paul Oscar Kristeller, "The Modern System of the Arts," in *Problems in Aesthetics*, 2d ed., ed. Morris Weitz (New York: Macmillan, 1970), 108–64; on Baumgarten, 151–55.

40. "Poetry, painting and dancing, Sir, are, or should be, no other than a faithful likeness of beautiful nature. It is owing to their accuracy of representation that the works of men like Corneille and Racine, Raphael and Michelangelo, have been handed down to posterity, after having obtained (what is rare enough) the commendation of their own age. Why can we not add to the names of these great men those of the *maitres de ballet* who made themselves so celebrated in their day?" Jean-George Noverre from *Letters on Dancing and Ballets*, Letter 1 (1760, rev. 1803), reprinted in *What is Dance?* ed. Marshall Cohen and Roger Copeland (New York: Oxford University Press, 1983), 10–15.

41. Immanuel Kant, "Critique of the Aesthetical Judgement," first division, first book, "Analytic of the Beautiful," in *Critique of Judgement*, trans. James Creed Meredith (Oxford: Clarendon Press, 1952), 1781: "The judgment of taste is therefore not a judgment of cognition, and is consequently not logical but aesthetical, by which we understand that whose determining ground can be no other than subjective." For an analysis and brief presentation of Kant's aesthetics, see Albert Hofstader and Richard Kuhns, eds., *Philosophies of Art and Beauty* (Chicago: University of Chicago Press, 1964), 277–343.

42. John Dewey, *Art as Experience* (New York: Minton, Black, 1934). George Plimpton Adams and William Pepperell Montague, eds., *Contemporary American Philosophy: Personal Statements* (New York: The Macmillan Company, 1930), II, 13–27.

43. For a treatment of these mythical parallels, see Fraleigh, *Dance and the Lived Body*, 141–58. For the hatred of the body deeply embedded in traditional Western philosophy, see David Michael Levin, "Philosophers and the Dance," in *What Is Dance?* ed. Marshall Cohen and Roger Copeland (New York: Oxford University Press, 1983), 85–94. Consider also the fear and ridicule of women in philosophy (from Aristotle to Schopenhauer and Nietzsche), and the problems that some forms of Christianity have had with the sensuousness of dance.

44. Aristotle, *De Generatione Animalium* (*G.A.*), in *The Works of Aristotle*, trans. J. A. Smith and W. D. Ross (London: Oxford, 1912), I, 4:2, 767B5–B15. Women are merely "mutilated males" (*G.A.* II, 3:737a). Men are "more divine" (*G.A.* II, 1:732a).

45. Susanne Langer, *Philosophy in a New Key: A Study in Symbolism of Reason, Rite and Art* (Cambridge: Harvard University Press, 1942). See also *Feeling and Form* (1953) and *Mind: An Essay on Human Feeling* (1967).

46. Francis Sparshott, *Off the Ground: First Steps to a Philosophical Consideration of the Dance* (Princeton: Princeton University Press, 1988), and *A Measured Pace: Toward a Philosophical Understanding of the Arts of Dance* (Toronto: University of Toronto Press, 1995).

47. Sharon Friedler and Susan B. Glazer, *Dancing Female: Lives and Issues of Women in Contemporary Dance* (Amsterdam: Harwood Academic Publishers, 1997). Sally Banes, *Dancing Women: Female Bodies on Stage* (London: Routledge, 1998). Ramsay Burt, *Alien Bodies: Representations of Modernity, Race, and Nation in Early Modern Dance* (London: Routledge, 1998).

48. See *The Journal of Aesthetics and Art Criticism* 48, no. 4 (fall 1990), special issue on

"Feminism and Traditional Aesthetics." See also Peggy Zeglin Brand and Carolyn Kors-meyer, eds., *Feminism and Tradition in Aesthetics* (University Park: Pennsylvania State University Press, 1995).

49. Alison Jagger, "Love and Knowledge: Emotion in Feminist Epistemology," in *Gender/Body/Knowledge: Feminist Reconstructions of Being and Knowing*, ed. Alison Jagger and Susan Bordo (New Brunswick: Rutgers University Press, 1989), 145–71.

50. Carolyn Korsmeyer, "Pleasure: Reflections on Aesthetics and Feminism," *The Journal of Aesthetics and Art Criticism* 51, no. 2 (spring 1993): 199–206.

51. On scopophilia, see Korsmeyer, "Pleasure: Reflections on Aesthetics and Feminism," 199–206.

52. For several articles concerning "the male gaze," see *The Journal of Aesthetics and Art Criticism* 48, no. 4 (fall 1990), on "Feminism and Traditional Aesthetics." For a critique of "the male gaze" from the point of view of phenomenology, see Sondra Fraleigh, "A Vulnerable Glance: Seeing Dance Through Phenomenology," *Dance Research Journal* 23, no. 1 (spring 1991): 11–16. For a critique of "the male gaze" as an ethnocentric concept that belies a "representation anxiety," see Avanthi Meduri, "Western Feminist Theory, Asian Indian Performance, and a Notion of Agency," 91.

53. Laura Mulvey, "Visual Pleasure and Narrative Cinema," *Screen* 16, no. 3 (1975): 6–18.

54. Ramsay Burt, *The Male Dancer: Bodies, Spectacle, Sexualities* (London: Routledge, 1995).

55. Simone de Beauvoir, *The Second Sex,* trans. H. M. Parshley (New York: Alfred A. Knopf, 1957).

56. Camille Paglia, *Sexual Personae: Art and Decadence from Nefertiti to Emily Dickinson* (New York: Vintage Books, 1991), 3.

57. Christina Hoff Sommers, *Who Stole Feminism? How Women Have Betrayed Women* (New York: Simon and Schuster, 1995).

58. See *Ecofeminism and the Sacred,* ed. Carol J. Adams (New York: Continuum, 1993).

59. Maxine Sheets-Johnstone, *The Phenomenology of Dance* (Madison: University of Wisconsin Press, 1966).

60. Sondra Fraleigh, *Dance and the Lived Body* (Pittsburgh: University of Pittsburgh Press, 1987).

61. See Carol Gilligan, *In a Different Voice: Psychological Theory and Women's Development* (Cambridge: Harvard University Press, 1982); also Joan C. Tronto, "Women and Caring: What Can Feminists Learn About Morality From Caring?" in *Gender/Body/Knowledge: Feminist Reconstructions of Being and Knowing*, ed. Alison Jagger and Susan Bordo (New Brunswick: Rutgers University Press, 1989), 172–87.

62. See Colin Wilson, *The New Existentialism* (London: Wildwood House, 1980).

63. Sparshott, "The Future of Dance Aesthetics."

64. See Francisco Varela, Evan Thompson, and Elanor Rosch, *The Embodied Mind: Cognitive Science and Human Experience* (Cambridge: MIT Press, 1991). "When Merleau-Ponty undertook his work—the potential sciences of mind were fragmented into disparate, noncommunicating disciplines: neurology, psychoanalyses, and behaviorist experimental psychology. Today we see the emergence of a new interdisciplinary matrix called cognitive science, which includes not only neuroscience but cognitive psychology, linguistics, artificial intelligence, and in many centers, philosophy" (xvi–vii). See also *The Mind's I: Fantasies and Reflections on Self and Soul,* composed and arranged by Douglas R. Hofstadter and Daniel C. Dennett (New York: Basic Books, 1981); Sherry Turkle, *The Second Self: Computers and the Human Spirit* (New York: Simon and Schuster, 1984); Ray S.

Jackendoff, *Consciousness and the Computational Mind* (Cambridge, Mass.: MIT Press, 1987). Phenomenology as ethnomethodology has been recently pursued in the studies of improvisation by David Sudnow, *Ways of the Hand: The Organization of Improvised Conduct* (Cambridge, Mass.: Harvard University Press, 1978).

65. For deconstructive criticism, see Jonathan Culler, *On Deconstruction: Theory and Criticism After Structuralism* (Ithaca: Cornell University Press, 1982). See also Jacques Derrida, "Form and Meaning: A Note on the Phenomenology of Language," in Jacques Derrida, *Speech and Phenomena* (Evanston, Ill.: Northwestern University Press, 1973), 106–60; and Michael Foucault, *The Order of Things* (New York: Pantheon Books, 1970).

66. See Part I: "The Body, The Self," especially Susan Bordo, "The Body and the Reproduction of Femininity: A Feminist Appropriation of Foucault," in *Gender/Body/Knowledge: Feminist Reconstructions of Being and Knowing*, ed. Alison Jagger and Susan Bordo (New Brunswick: Rutgers University Press, 1989), 13–145. See also Fraleigh, Part I: "Dance and Embodiment," in *Dance and the Lived Body*, 3–77.

67. See Susan Leigh Foster, *Reading Dancing: Bodies and Subjects in Contemporary American Dance* (Berkeley: University of California Press, 1986).

68. "Any discipline must suppose the possibility of solving a problem, finding the truth, and thus writing the last words on a topic. The idea of a discipline is the idea of an investigation in which writing might be brought to an end." Jonathan Culler, *On Deconstruction: Theory and Criticism after Structuralism*, 90.

69. Avanthi Meduri provides a critique of "the Western feminist gaze" and its cultural oversights regarding Indian classical dance in "Western Feminist Theory, Asian Indian Performance, and a Notion of Agency." Her critique raises (aesthetic) questions about the supposition that the use of "less space" in a dance necessarily implies "less freedom" for the dancer. The more, the bigger, the better? We need to notice that we often use the language of dominance in our aesthetic valuing, not to mention our tacit acceptance of power as conquest (of space, of nature, of ourselves, of others)—thus our perpetuation of what we seem to criticize. The "inner space" of the dancer's consciousness (in dance as in life) is a more complex study than the dancer's actual occupancy of the space around her body.

70. *Looking Out: Perspectives on Dance and Criticism in a Multicultural World*, ed. David Gere (New York: Schirmer Books, 1995).

71. Sarah Fowler, "Review of *Dance and the Lived Body* by Sondra Fraleigh," *Journal of Aesthetics and Art Criticism* 47, no. 1 (winter 1989): 89–90.

72. Sparshott, "The Future of Dance Aesthetics," 227–34.

73. Somatic movement methods contribute to a holistic somatic therapy (and an implicit phenomenology) that allows spontaneous emergence of bodily expressions—facilitating the habitual thinking of the body and noticing the kinesthetically ingrained features or patterns. Somatic therapies awaken new levels of awareness as the therapist guides the client toward change through somatic movement/dance classes and in hands-on body work.

Major somatic studies include: the Feldenkrais Method of Awareness Through Movement (used in movement lessons) and Functional Integration (hands-on facilitation of movement and the nervous system), the Alexander Technique (hands-on reeducation of movement for postural improvement and enhanced functioning), and Bonnie Bainbridge Cohen's Body/Mind Centering (accounting for the movement of the total organism's interrelated systems). Others based on the premise of the fuller functioning of the human being through movement and touch are: Craniosacral Therapy, Rosen Breathwork, Rolphing, Yoga therapy, Trager Mentastics, Pilates, Holotropic Breathwork, and Polarity Balancing. Most of these lead to certification, and some practitioners combine modalities.

74. For a fuller account of the intersection of existentialism and phenomenology and its significance for dance, see Fraleigh, chapter 1, *Dance and the Lived Body*, 3–21.

75. Immanuel Kant, "The Satisfaction Which Determines the Judgement of Taste Is Disinterested," second section of the first book of *The Critique of Judgement*, 1781.

76. Hanna utilizes anthropology, sociology, and semiotics in her approach. See Judith Lynne Hanna, *The Performer-Audience Connection* (Austin: University of Texas Press, 1983). Adshead and her collaborators approach interpretation as a matter of interactions and relationships among various elements of dance works, promoting Laban movement analysis as a means of describing movement in time and space—with an emphasis on internal context. See *Dance Analysis: Theory and Practice*, ed. Janet Adshead (London: Dance Books Ltd., 1988).

For a thorough analysis of the aesthetic theories of Hanna and Adshead, see Joann McNamara, "From Dance to Text and Back to Dance: A Hermeneutics of Dance Interpretive Discourse" (Ph.D. dissertation, Texas Woman's University, 1994). In her dissertation, McNamara also analyzes the dance-based aesthetic theories of Susan Leigh Foster (semiotics), Ann Daly (feminism), Cynthia Novack (ethnography), Valerie Malhotra Bentz (hermeneutic phenomenology), and Sondra Fraleigh (existential phenomenology), including interviews with the authors.

77. Wanda T. May, "Philosopher as Researcher and/or Begging the Question(s)," E. Louis Lankford, "Philosophy of Art Education: Focusing Our Vision," and Elizabeth Garber, "Feminism, Aesthetics, and Art Education," all in *Studies in Art Education: A Journal of Issues and Research* 33, no. 4 (summer 1992): 226–43, 195–200, 210–25.

78. Susan W. Stinson, "Interpretive Inquiry in Dance Education," *Impulse* 1, Human Kinetics Publishers (1993): 52–64.

79. For a study of instrumental values as extrinsic, see Paul Taylor, *Normative Discourse*.

80. I believe that at its most fundamental and healthiest level dance derives from the pleasure we take in our bodies, analogous to the erotic pleasure released in what Freud called "the pleasure principle." He saw this as conditioned by a "life instinct" against which he postulated a "death wish," which enters less obtrusively into consciousness. Sigmund Freud, *Beyond the Pleasure Principle*, trans. James Strachey (New York: Bantam, 1959), 109.

At age sixty-five, Freud speculated as "a starting point for fresh investigations" that life and death (instincts) are integrated in bewildering tensions, but that on balance "the pleasure principle seems to serve the death instinct" (102–10). (The death of orgasm, the return to the womb?) I would argue that death is not an "instinct" but an occurrence, and that what Freud studied somewhat inconclusively were powerful interactive elements of consciousness, those same (intrinsic aesthetic) phenomena that compose dancing. For the reliance of all extrinsic values on intrinsic values ("pleasurable qualities of experience"), see Taylor, *Normative Discourse*.

81. Freedom and agency are existentials that often come up for me. This leads me to look at how they arise in other contexts—the implications of "bound movement" or "free and flowing movement" in movement analysis, for instance. An existential account of freedom and agency would not simply consider the observable characteristics of a movement but should account for the experience of the mover and place the movement in context, culturally and historically.

82. For example: consider the "dialectical relationship" between the performer as a person and the role the performer portrays. Jane Desmond explores this in a historical-feminist critique of Ruth St. Denis: "Dancing Out the Difference: Cultural Imperialism and Ruth St. Denis's 'Radha' of 1906," *Signs* 17, no. 1 (autumn 1991): 28–49. I develop this in *Dance and the Lived Body* as a crossing point between the dancer, the dance role, and tech-

nical challenges. I describe this as a dialectic that moves the dancer beyond the personalized self (and self-expression) toward an embodiment of ideas and images in the dance, the personal/universal dialectic inherent in dancing (23–30). Much of Desmond's article takes up complexities of St. Denis's incorporation of ethnic otherness in her dancing and the aesthetic results. I can compare my perspective with Desmond's study and others. This personal/universal dialectic is also explored in still another way in Frank Hoff's study, "Killing the Self: How the Narrator Acts," a study of the performer's conscious denial of self in Kabuki and Noh. Here the performer seeks to become aware of a difference between himself and his role. *Asian Theater Journal* 2, no. 1 (spring 1985): 1–25. Might this dialectic also arise in various guises in ritual dance? Or is ritual an avenue for dissolving difference?

REFERENCES

Adams, Carol J., ed. *Ecofeminism and the Sacred.* New York: Continuum, 1993.

Adshead, Janet, ed. *Dance Analysis: Theory and Practice.* London: Dance Books Ltd., 1988.

Alexander, Christopher. *A Foreshadowing of 21st Century Art: The Color and Geometry of Very Early Turkish Carpets.* New York: Oxford University Press, 1993.

Berleant, Arnold. *Art and Engagement.* Philadelphia: Temple University Press, 1991.

Burt, Ramsay. *The Male Dancer: Bodies, Spectacle, Sexualities.* London: Routledge, 1995.

Cantor, Norman F. *Twentieth-Century Culture: Modernism to Deconstruction.* New York: Peter Lang, 1988.

Carroll, Noël. "Anglo-American Aesthetics and New Criticism: Intention and the Hermeneutics of Suspicion." *The Journal of Aesthetics and Art Criticism* 51, no. 2 (spring 1993): 245–353.

Culler, Jonathan. *On Deconstruction: Theory and Criticism After Structuralism.* Ithaca: Cornell University Press, 1982.

Dissanayake, Ellen. *What is Art For?* Seattle: University of Washington Press, 1988.

Fraleigh, Sondra. *Dance and the Lived Body.* Pittsburgh: University of Pittsburgh Press, 1987.

———. "A Vulnerable Glance: Seeing Dance Through Phenomenology." *Dance Research Journal* 23, no. 1 (spring 1991): 11–16.

———. *Dancing into Darkness: Butoh, Zen, and Japan.* Pittsburgh: University of Pittsburgh Press, in press.

Friedler, Sharon, and Susan Glazer, eds. *Dancing Female: Lives and Issues of Women in Contemporary Dance.* Amsterdam: Harwood Academic Publishers, 1997.

Frondizi, Resieri. *What Is Value: An Introduction to Axiology.* 2d ed., trans. Solomon Lipp. Lasalle, Ill.: Open Court, 1971.

Gere, David, ed. *Looking Out: Perspectives on Dance and Criticism in a Multicultural World.* New York: Schirmer Books, 1995.

Griffith, Susan. *Woman and Nature: The Roaring Inside Her.* New York: Harper and Row, 1978.

Hawkins, Erick. "The Body Is a Clear Place." *Focus on Dance* 5 (1969): 34–39.

Highwater, Jamake. *Dance: Rituals of Experience.* 3d ed. New Jersey: Princeton Book Company, 1978.

Jagger, Alison, and Susan Bordo, eds. *Gender/Body/Knowledge: Feminist Reconstructions of Being and Knowing.* New Brunswick: Rutgers University Press, 1989.

Johnson, Mark. *The Body in the Mind.* Chicago: University of Chicago Press, 1987.

Korsmeyer, Carolyn. "Pleasure: Reflections on Aesthetics and Feminism." *Journal of Aesthetics and Art Criticism* 51, no. 2 (spring 1993): 199–206.

Kristeller, Paul Oscar. "The Modern System of the Arts." In *Problems in Aesthetics,* 2d ed., ed. Morris Weitz. New York: Macmillan, 1970.

Kuhn, T. S. *The Structure of Scientific Revolutions.* Chicago: University of Chicago Press, 1963; 2d ed. enlarged 1970.

Laage, Joan. "Embodying the Spirit: The Significance of the Body in the Contemporary Japanese Dance Movement of Butoh." Ph.D. dissertation, Texas Woman's University, 1993.

Lavender, Larry. "Intentionalism, Anti-Intentionalism, and Aesthetic Inquiry: Implication for the Teaching of Choreography." *Dance Research Journal* 29, no. 1 (spring 1997): 23–42.

Mackenzie, Ian. "Terrible Beauty: Paul de Man's Retreat from the Aesthetic." *The Journal of Aesthetics and Art Criticism* 5, nos. 1–4 (fall 1993): 551–60.

May, Wanda T. "Philosopher as Researcher and/or Begging the Question(s)." *Studies in Art Education: A Journal of Issues and Research* 33, no. 4 (summer 1992): 226–43.

Meduri, Avanthi. "Western Feminist Theory, Asian Indian Performance, and a Notion of Agency." *Women and Performance* 5, no. 2 (1992): 93.

Sheets-Johnstone, Maxine. *The Phenomenology of Dance.* Madison: University of Wisconsin Press, 1966.

Sommers, Christina Hoff. *Who Stole Feminism? How Women Have Betrayed Women.* New York: Simon and Schuster, 1995.

Sontag, Susan. *Against Interpretation and Other Essays.* New York: Farrar Straus Giroux, 1966.

Sparshott, Francis. "The Future of Dance Aesthetics." *Journal of Aesthetics and Art Criticism* 51, no. 2 (spring 1993): 227–34.

Tatarkiewicz, Wladyslaw. "The Great Theory of Beauty and Its Decline." *The Journal of Aesthetics and Art Criticism* 31, (winter 1972): 156–80.

Taylor, Paul W. *Normative Discourse.* Englewood Cliffs, N.J.: Prentice Hall, 1961.

Young, Tricia Henry, "The Politics and Aesthetics of Gothic Club Dancing." In *Proceedings, 30th Annual Conference, Congress on Research in Dance,* ed. Nancy L. Stokes, 469–84. Tucson: University of Arizona Press, 1997.

8 THE SENSE OF THE PAST

Historiography and Dance

Shelley C. Berg

> With her foot on the threshold she waited a moment longer in a scene which
> was vanishing even as she looked, and then, as she moved and took Minta's
> arm and left the room, it changed, it shaped itself differently; it had become
> she knew, giving one last look at it over her shoulder, the past.
>
> Virginia Woolf, *To the Lighthouse* (1927)

IN HER NOVEL, *To the Lighthouse,* Virginia Woolf allows her character, Mrs.
Ramsey, a flash of unusual insight and illumination; the past is shaped by the
present and the present is reshaped by the past. At any given instant, we both live
history and live in history. For the dance historian, struggling with questions of
historiography, the relationship of past and present is doubly complex. Theories
of writing about history become more problematic in light of the ephemeral nature of what theater historian Joseph Roach calls the "transcendental signified";
the act of performance.[1] Because dance history is both enacted and lost at the
moment of performance, we are continually documenting the past even as we
create the present; dance perpetually exists, as Marcia Siegel has noted, at the
vanishing point. For the dance historian, this evanescent state is both a challenge
to our persistence and accuracy in research, and a gift to our ingenuity and imagination in documentation.

The discipline of historical scholarship is a threefold endeavor; it requires
both research and writing, with the act of interpretation forming a critical link
between the two. Using textual and iconographic materials and other artifacts,
the historian seeks to understand and explain the events of the past. But because
"the past itself is beyond reach, the historian is always reading the shadowy remains," a task made more difficult when the subject of the search is as transient

225

as dance.[2] In creating this evocation of the past, each element of the historiographic project—research, writing, and interpretation—continually reshapes and modifies the others; each is a part of a constantly changing and evolving constellation of apprehension, knowledge, and meaning. In the course of tracing evidence and providing documentation, the historian may uncover an unlooked-for date or an unexpected occurrence that illuminates a host of previously unconsidered possibilities. In writing a narrative of events, or in creating a biography, the historian may, on a broad scale, clarify concepts and establish contextual connections that reveal new areas for further investigation or even uncover missing links in existing documentation. Thus, the act of historiography is itself a process, an active engagement in the performance of history.

Indeed, the production of a formal work of textual historiography has much in common with the act of performance. Each requires the selection of a time frame, genre, or work for historical study or for performance. The selection process is followed by an intensive period of research and investigation; this is often a time of the acquisition of a technique, performance style, or specialized skills in the case of the performer, and the development of an organizational strategy, research methodology, and bibliography for the historian. Just as the performer must endure the rigors of creating or learning and then rehearsing a work for presentation, so the historian must assemble evidence, establish connections, and essay various rhetorical strategies and methods of configuration to define and shape the writing of the historical narrative. The historian's process of writing "gives shape to what went before," in much the same way that the artist is linked to a living and vital performance tradition.[3]

In the course of this essay, I consider the role of the dance historian, discuss questions of methodology in dance history research, and offer examples of dance historiography in action, namely, the creation of the biography of a dancer/choreographer from a variety of written and visual sources and the reconstruction of a dance work, in terms of its written history and description and in terms of the performance of choreography.

The tasks and responsibilities of the dance historian are continually being invented and expanded, reconsidered and revised. We have been chroniclers of events and biographers of personalities, detailing the who, what, when, and where that are part of the foundation of historical inquiry. We have analyzed form and interpreted content in our attempts to articulate the slippery concept of "why." We have described motion, movement, and formal choreography, grappling with the problems of linguistic representation of a symbolic form. We have also struggled with questions of canonical texts and authenticity, debated problems of reconstruction and revival, and discussed concerns of political relevance and historical evaluation. In brief, we have addressed many of the traditional concerns of the historian, albeit sometimes in nontraditional fashion. The task of the historian, to redescribe and reinterpret "what the traces from the past delineated, illustrated, exhibited, described and interpreted," must be central to the mission of the dance historian as well. But just as the terms *describe* and *interpret* appear with added emphasis in the preceding sentence, the core of the dance historiographer's mandate is discovered in the nexus of depiction and exegesis.[4] Both description, in the textual evocation of the past, and explanation, the hermeneutic analysis of a body of historical research, play key roles in the performance of dance historiography; just such an example is discussed below.

In her book, *Writing Dance in the Age of Postmodernism,* dance historian Sally Banes includes a selection of her essays on the Euro-American avant-garde. In "Balanchine and Black Dance," Banes describes the trajectory of the choreographer's fascination with jazz in general and African American vernacular dance in particular.[5] She creates a broad canvas for her discussion by developing a historical context for Balanchine's interest in African American culture, ranging from his initial work with Stravinsky on *le jazz hot* elements in *Apollo* to his work on Broadway for musicals such as *Cabin in the Sky* and the Ziegfeld Follies. Banes also details the choreographer's collaboration with African American dancers such as Buddy Bradley and the Nicholas Brothers, which broadens her field of inquiry to include the arenas of popular entertainment, film, and vernacular dance. Having established a firm historical precedent for Balanchine's adoption of African American stylistic elements throughout his career, Banes concludes her essay with a description and analysis of one of his masterpieces, *The Four Temperaments*. She integrates the observations of both dancers and critics, in quotes and paraphrases, with her own description and assessment of the choreography, thus giving the reader a kaleidoscopic perspective of the ballet. Her discussion is always buttressed by her incorporation of supporting materials in the study of African American culture by dancers, choreographers, critics, and music and art historians and anthropologists. In her conclusion, Banes makes a compelling argument for her interpretation of the inclusion of African American stylistic elements in the choreography of George Balanchine; she presents a case carefully built through the collation and analysis of both primary and secondary source material.

While dance historians have need of the conventional modes of description, analysis, interpretation, and evaluation, the standard formulas for the practice of historiography often require adjustment, negotiation, or even inspired reinterpretation. Indeed, the process of reenvisioning and retooling the orthodoxies of historical inquiry is continually taking place; the emerging emphasis in American and literary studies, often called the "new historicism" or the "poetics of culture," is just one example of the dialectic at work.

The desire to create more flexible and elastic methodologies has encouraged scholars to cross the boundaries separating disciplines such as anthropology, art, music, politics, literature, women's studies, and economics, and their enterprise has yielded refreshing results. Practitioners of the "new historicism" have fractured conventional paradigms of historical study and sought novel and less limiting means "to expose the manifold ways in which culture and society affect each other."[6] Jane Marcus, for example, looks at the overlapping effects of militant suffragette street demonstrations in England and the appearance of the "hobble" skirt presented by the Parisian fashion house of Worth in the same era. She examines the contributions of women writers to the literature of World War I and considers the concomitant influence of the poster art and political dress of the British suffragette to create a fascinating account of the development of feminist fetishism in Britain during the Great War.[7] Marcus here incorporates a diverse collection of unusual primary source material with her feminist analysis of both the fiction and the memoirs of women authors of the time. The impacts of literature, fashion, and contemporary popular art, considered and examined in concert, help define what Marcus terms the "semiotics and somatics" of women's suffrage in England.

In his essay, "Image, Text, and Object in the Formation of Historical Consciousness," Stephen Bann uses what he terms a "rhetoric of evocation, in which objects, texts and images all contribute to the materialization of the past."[8] He examines a variety of techniques used by nineteenth-century antiquarians, painters, historians, and novelists to achieve a sense of authenticity and historical evocation. In one example, Bann discusses the effect of the display of ancient artifacts in their "fragmented and abraded states" to draw the viewer's attention to their "pathos" as incomplete relics. He then contrasts this with the presentation of antique statuaries "restored" to their presumed timeless and flawless perfection; the first approach invests the historical fragment with "age-value," while the latter highlights the "picturesque" quality of the work displayed.[9] For historians such as Bann, the history of a work of art and the work itself are symbiotic texts inextricably linked in a rich historical narrative.

Both Marcus and Bann have appropriated and integrated a diverse collection of sources and techniques to create their analyses, venturing well outside the traditional methodologies for historiography. In challenging the assumptions that compartmentalize academic disciplines, "new historicists" may be good role models for dance historians. Increasingly, dance historians have found that the freedom to traverse disciplines has fostered the development of rich and varied historical perspectives. In her study of German choreographer Mary Wigman, *Ecstasy and the Demon*, Susan Manning has incorporated contextual materials that treat issues of the politics of German nationalism and feminism; these constructs, in turn, help illuminate elements of the choreographer's aesthetic that had been obscured in more traditional biographies.[10] Ann Daly's extensive work on the American tours of Isadora Duncan includes a consideration and assessment of Duncan's ability to connect the experience of her dancing with some of the most urgent social discourses of her time: the American obsession with creating a "national selfhood, a cultural identity and a means of self-expression."[11] She considers reviews of Duncan's work by critics of the time to illustrate the impact, both positive and negative, engendered by her dancing. Daly then discusses Duncan's work in the light of literary critic Julia Kristeva's theory of semiotic and symbolic representation and the idea of the chora, which she uses to frame her analysis of the cultural significance of Duncan's dancing. Through this multilayered approach to Duncan as dancer, choreographer, and cultural icon, incorporating elements of literary theory within the process of historiography, Daly has offered a revised perspective of her place in our collective historical consciousness.

The selection of an artist for biographical study offers the dance historian an array of opportunities for exploration in terms of both research and writing. The historian may choose to focus on specific aspects of the artist's life: his or her individual achievements in dance, or his role in the development of a choreographic style or genre, for example. As noted in the two examples above, a biographical narrative may be enriched by incorporating material that can illuminate the artist's relationship to the culture in which his art was created, flourished, or even expired. A compelling and comprehensive biographical account will interweave all the threads of the artist's life to render a vivid and expressive portrait. A biography should give the reader a sense of sympathy with the subject, as well as provide a broad contextual landscape in which to view the central figure of the study.

Just as there is no single manner in which historical understanding may be applied or comprehended, multiple narratives and perspectives on a biographical subject are both valid and valuable. In dance, the lives of such diverse artists as Isadora Duncan, Martha Graham, and Vaslav Nijinsky have been studied by numerous biographers. Some accounts have been highly detailed and scrupulously documented, such as Richard Buckle's biography of Nijinsky and Keith Money's study of Anna Pavlova.[12] Other chroniclers have focused on analyzing and interpreting data to portray the artist in relation to his era: Suzanne Shelton's *Divine Dancer*, a biography of Ruth St. Denis, and Marcia Siegel's work on the life of Doris Humphrey, *Days on Earth*, are exemplary studies of this kind.[13]

Case Study: Research on Sada Yacco

How, then, can a dance historian design the research for a biographical narrative and construct a portrait that is both historically accurate and coherent in narrative? In order to illustrate a variety of methodological approaches, I present a case study of my research on the Japanese dancer and actress Sada Yacco. Yacco is an appropriate subject in this regard, as the process of my pursuit and discovery of her history parallels a similar journey in my own growth in understanding of the practice of historiography.

While many renowned dancers and choreographers are well represented in biographical studies, there remain artists whose stories have yet to be told. I first encountered one such little-documented figure in the course of my contextual research on Serge Diaghilev's Ballets Russes; she was the Japanese dancer Sada Yacco. She again appeared in the mise-en-scène of my academic research in a doctoral seminar on Ruth St. Denis. St. Denis first saw Yacco perform at the Paris Exposition of 1900, as did Isadora Duncan. The Japanese dancer was the undoubted "star" of the Japanese Players, a dramatic troupe organized and directed by her husband, Otojiro Kawakami. It was through Yacco, St. Denis asserted, that she first beheld and understood "the beautiful austerities of Japanese art."[14] Yacco was then performing under the auspices (and at the theater named for) American dance pioneer Loïe Fuller. Duncan, who toured in Europe with Fuller and Yacco from 1901 to 1902, styled Yacco "a great tragedian," and the Japanese dancer clearly had Fuller's implicit imprimatur through the latter's sponsorship at the Exposition.[15]

There was little information available on Yacco herself, and even less on what she did and how she performed. A few dance histories briefly noted her appearances in Paris and adduced her influence on St. Denis. In terms of the larger scope of dance history, Yacco remained an enigma, her impact obscured by a combination of factors; the emphasis on Western dance forms, choreographers, and dancers in most dance histories, the difficulties in determining sources for and locating contemporaneous reviews of her performances in the West and, simply, the passage of time. It seemed logical that any major biographical studies of Yacco would be in Japanese, which would make it difficult to access and translate. I could find no biography available in English, and no account that treated, comprehensively, her performance career outside Japan. Sada Yacco appeared only briefly in the West, in the years between 1899 and 1902, with a fleeting visit to Paris in 1907. I believed she was a significant figure in twentieth-century dance and drama whose story had not been told.

Here was a pocket of dance history that had not yet been fully explored; therefore, I determined that my work should focus on the documentation of her

European and American tours and her influence on the pioneers of American modern dance. Yacco appeared on European and American stages at a strategic moment in twentieth-century dance and theater. Dancers such as Duncan and St. Denis were soon to be pioneers of a new dance aesthetic. A symbol of the expressivity of another culture, Yacco's artistry was a testament to their belief in the interpretive power of dance. If Yacco had fired the imaginations of St. Denis, Duncan, and Fuller, it seemed probable that she had an equally powerful effect on the actors, directors, artists, and writers who saw her perform in the West and that it would be possible to find accounts of her performances. In limiting my study of Yacco to her appearances in Europe and America, I believed that I had set manageable chronological and geographical limits for my inquiry, but I knew that further research would gradually refine the shape of my investigation.

I began my research by constructing a series of basic questions with which to frame my inquiry. Who was Sada Yacco and what, where, and how did she perform? As the answers to these basic initial questions began to appear, I started to formulate a second set of questions designed to add depth and contextual perspective to the study, and which concerned denser and more complex issues of identity, influence, and interpretation. How did Western audiences and critics perceive Sada Yacco; as their image of a Japanese woman at the turn of the century; as one of the select coterie of brilliant and glamorous actresses of the era; or as the prototype of their perception of the enigmatic geisha? How did she choose to convey her personae, both onstage and off, and how was this complex kaleidoscope of roles made manifest in her acting and dancing?

The scope of my inquiry was continually enlarged as I uncovered new sources and amassed new information. At strategic intervals, I stepped back from the enterprise of gathering and collecting materials in order to review, reconsider, and reflect on old information in the light of new knowledge. This component of the historiographic process is crucial to the development of a coherent and meaningful narrative of interpretation. Although research seldom takes a clearly defined and linear path, the periodic reassessment of the parts of an inquiry in terms of what one knows and understands of the whole will ultimately produce a richer, more complete historical picture. Just as a choreographer assesses his work holistically, considering all the aspects and elements of movement, music, and decor as they coalesce in performance, so the historian must continually reappraise her material and her perspectives as new information is uncovered. How then to begin the process itself? I will again use my study of Yacco as a paradigm to illustrate key elements and issues in the discussion.

The historian may follow numerous organizational strategies for her research and often each project will, at least in part, dictate its own strategy. Although attempts have frequently been made to establish specific professional procedures, there has been "little agreement among historians upon a systematic mode of inquiry, analysis, and reporting."[16] However, as the theater historian Joseph Donohue notes, there are fundamental tenets and guidelines that should be observed.

> In order to produce sound scholarship, a scholar's obligations consist in producing the evidence necessary to substantiate an argument and in documenting that evidence clearly and with reasonable fullness. As a result, it is held to be incumbent on the working scholar to keep precise track of the ground that has been covered during research and, in writing, to provide enough signposts to allow a fellow scholar to retrace the path, or any segment of it, for purposes of verification or other, independent purposes.[17]

In other words, it is incumbent on the dance historian to collect her research materials, her evidence, and clearly indicate her sources or provide sufficient documentation of her process for those who follow. The evidence itself may consist of virtually any types of artifacts and materials that are relevant to the scope of the inquiry and may be divided into the two categories of primary and secondary sources. Secondary sources, usually books written about a specific subject or that cover a more general topic, are removed from the historical time and event in question and present another historian's view of that topic. In general, books that cover broad themes in a more general fashion are good starting points for more specific and in-depth research. Look at the bibliographies and footnotes of your secondary sources for clues to locating primary sources. These include all manner of visual and oral evidence contemporaneous with the period of inquiry, such as articles in newspapers and periodicals, letters, diaries, contracts, music scores, photographs, statuary and objets d'art, programs, and costumes. It is these primary sources that give a historical study its contextual web, allowing for multiple strands of articulation and interpretation. Each strand should be connected to the central subject of the study but also attached to the other threads in the design in a clear and logical configuration.

The process of designing a search may have parallels to the creation of a work of choreography. The researcher must continually observe, question, develop, modify, and synthesize her material in much the same manner as a choreographer constructs and clarifies the shape and structure of a dance. Just as there are primary or central motifs in a choreographic plan, a research project should foreground the work(s) or person(s) to be examined. Initially, various strategies to focus and amplify the inquiry can be essayed. A dancer or choreographer, conversant with the interplay and navigation of form and pattern, might find visual or graphic devices especially useful. For example, the researcher may devise a conceptual map as a constellation, with the main subject, work, or question at the center, surrounded by a field of related topics or queries. This schema can help to identify and elucidate connections and relationships for both immediate investigation and later contextual interpretation. The creation of timelines that detail dates critical to the subject, together with strategic cultural, political, and social events, could help establish the parameters of a search and suggest the scaffolding for a written analysis. While the precise configuration of each quest may vary, it is vital that the researcher be bold and imaginative as well as thorough in constructing her investigative design.

In beginning my research on Sada Yacco, I made a preliminary bibliography to track any references to her, or to the Japanese Players, the troupe with which she performed at the Exposition. I started the process with both primary and secondary sources; while books on Japanese theater history composed most of the latter category, I scanned newspapers, magazines, and other periodicals devoted to theater, the visual arts, and society, both in the hope of finding critical reviews of her performances and to get a flavor of the tastes, conventions, and mores of the period. I knew that a knowledge and understanding of Japanese theater, and Yacco and Kawakami's place in it, would be material to my assessment of their reception in the West. They were often identified as Kabuki performers, although few Kabuki scholars recognized them as such. I organized these sources into an annotated bibliography, which functioned as a research log, allowing me to keep a written record of the sources I had consulted, what information I had found, and how those sources contributed to the study as a whole.[18] One source often led to several others, and the process helped stimulate new ideas for further exploration.

This chain of evidence and documentation soon began to clarify the themes I would find most valuable in delineating Yacco's impact within the framework of the larger cultural and historical context of her era. I discovered that she became, in effect, the embodiment of a constellation of contemporaneous artistic and cultural discourses; the fin de siècle vogue for *japonisme* and Art Nouveau, the complex image of the female performer at the beginning of the twentieth century, and the Symbolist fascination with the exotic and fantastical. Yacco was able to entrance audiences with her dancing, so unusual and exotic to Western eyes, and then galvanize them with the emotional power of her acting. It was this unexpected fusion of dance and drama that so powerfully affected that first generation of American modern dancers. Even in the first phases of research, the definition of these threads of interpretation became visible; a description of the methodology I employed to identify each of these threads will serve as illustration.

As Sada Yacco's appearances at the Paris Exposition were undoubtedly her most celebrated, and possibly best documented, performances, I examined books and periodicals devoted to this extraordinary world's fair. Without exception, every source noted that the Exposition had been the apotheosis of the style in the visual arts known as Art Nouveau; indeed, Martin Battersby, in his book *The World of Art Nouveau*, declares the Exhibition "the apogee and the finale of Art Nouveau."[19] Battersby remarks on the variety of mediums and artistic forms that embraced the Art Nouveau aesthetic, including Tiffany and Gallé glass, Majorelle furniture, the sculpture of Charpentier and Daumpt, Lalique jewelry, Meissan and Sèvres porcelain, and the poster art of artists such as Toulouse-Lautrec and Alphonse Mucha.[20] Much of the subject matter of Art Nouveau was inspired by the organic curves and arcs found in nature, with flowers and the female form becoming the most popular themes. Practitioners of the style often drew their inspiration from two primary sources; the elegance of French eighteenth-century furniture and objets d'art and the spare, stylized, and asymmetric design emphasized in Japanese art.

Further research on the confluence of Japanese art and Art Nouveau led me to descriptions of one of the most notable, and best documented, sights at the Exposition, L'Art Nouveau Bing. This was a pavilion designed and created by Siegfried Bing, which featured six ornately decorated rooms in a style of voluptuous elegance. Bing, a French art dealer, had begun his career as a promoter of Japanese art objects in France and accrued a fortune through *japonisme*, "the French fascination with anything Japanese."[21] Clearly, the appreciation of both Art Nouveau and *japonisme* were central to one's experience of the Exposition.

Many sources that documented the fair also described the Théâtre Loïe Fuller, where Yacco performed, which was designed for the American dancer by architect Henri Sauvage. The facade was sculpted by Art Nouveau artist Pierre Roche and took the form of "draperies flowing from two lifesize figures of the dancer which flanked the entrance."[22] By 1900, Fuller had become the darling of Art Nouveau artists, creating phantasmagorical images reminiscent of birds, butterflies, and flowers in her dances. Thus, Yacco was performing in a milieu devoted to the celebration of the major visual arts movements of the era. This information helped hone and delineate new questions about Yacco's reception in Paris. How had the dance elements in Yacco's performances resonated with the themes of Art Nouveau and *japonisme* in art and visual design, and was their popularity partly responsible for her success? It was these questions that led to the definition of the first strand of interpretation in the web of context for my study of Yacco.

In researching sources for information on the Paris Exposition to learn more about the visual and performing arts presented there, I came across a book entitled *1900*, by French essayist Paul Morand.[23] A book that took its title from the year, written by a Frenchman, would surely discuss the fair. Morand, who was twelve at the time of the Exposition, nevertheless recalled it vividly. In his poetic and episodic descriptions of the people and events that crowded the Exposition, he writes eloquently of Yacco and refers, in an offhand way, to an essay on the Japanese artist by André Gide, which appeared in a periodical called *La Vogue*. I knew that at the time Morand was writing Gide would soon become an influential critic, essayist, and playwright, and I believed his assessment of Yacco would be central to my understanding of her effect on the critics and literati of her time. The fact that Gide had reviewed Yacco's performances opened up new avenues for exploration; if he wrote about Yacco, who else among his friends and contemporaries might have done the same?

I thought it crucial to obtain a copy of the review and began the search by consulting the National Union Catalog for libraries holding *La Vogue*. The catalog listed the New York Public Library, which did not have any holdings for 1900. They, in turn, referred me to the Elmer Holmes Bobst Library at New York University, which did have issues of *La Vogue* from 1899–1901 on microfilm. I scanned each issue page by page but could find no articles on Yacco written by André Gide; I did, however, discover a lengthy and evocative review of her performances by Henri Detouche entitled "Une Mime Japonaise."[24] I also noted that the periodical covered the performing arts in some detail, devoting an entire issue to the great French actress Sarah Bernhardt. Detouche wrote frequently, and with knowledge and authority, on theater, which led me to believe that his interest in and admiration for Yacco was based on considerable experience of theater-going. Would critics in other periodicals, especially any devoted to theater, be equally enthusiastic? Would Yacco bear comparison to other contemporary actresses such as Bernhardt, Eleanora Duse, and Ellen Terry? The André Gide conundrum was still unsolved, but I had begun to develop evidence and produce documentation that Yacco was indeed viewed as a significant artist by notable critics of her era. The next stage of my research took me in three different, yet interrelated directions; I wanted to find and evaluate the Gide article, which could lead to a clearer understanding of Yacco's impact in Paris; I needed to locate and then scan newspapers and periodicals that covered theater in Paris in 1900 for reviews, to create a fuller picture of her style as both an actress and a dancer; finally, I planned to survey analyses of the art of other actresses of the fin de siècle in order to compare Yacco's performances with those of her contemporaries.

As at least two of my objectives would be served by research in many of the same sources, I decided to focus on French journals and daily papers that covered either the Paris theater or the Exposition. Newspapers often provide the most immediate and compelling material in terms of primary sources, and many major daily papers are accessible through interlibrary loan. The Library of Congress, major city libraries, and state historical societies are often able to facilitate newspaper research in the United States, while major collections abroad, such as the British Library and the Bibliothèque Nationale in Paris, can help guide the researcher to available and useful sources.

Through interlibrary loan, I surveyed three major Paris daily newspapers, *Le Temps, Le Figaro,* and *Le Gaulois,* for the months of June through November 1900; these dates covered the time span of the Exposition. The papers listed the attractions of the Exposition theaters and gave me the dates and times of Yacco's performances at the Théâtre Loïe Fuller. The schedules revealed that she played at least one drama, complete with an elaborate dance section and death scene, three times a day! As I discovered later, this grueling schedule had a significant impact on her performing style, possibly forcing her to adapt her histrionic style to incorporate cruder, more "Western" theatrical "effects." In July, a well-informed front-page editorial appeared in *Le Gaulois.*[25] The writer outlined his views on Yacco's salutary effect on Japanese theater and noted that she faced a "predicament" as a Japanese woman performing with an all-male theatrical troupe. In turn of the century Japan, it was forbidden for a woman to appear onstage with men, and vice versa. In assessing this material, the researcher must take into account the Western image of the actress at the turn of the century, when actress and prostitute were still often synonymous. Both onstage and off, Yacco brought together the audience's implicit and explicit expectations of the possibilities inherent in the life and customs of the exotic "Other." At a time when American and trans-European feminism was in the ascendant, Yacco, both Japanese and a former geisha, was seen in Europe as a feminist phenomenon. The editorial also made plain that members of the Parisian press were aware of Yacco's status in her homeland, and that they took both her position in Japan and her efforts as an actress and dancer abroad with serious consideration.

An extensive article in *Le Temps* by Adolphe Brisson, who was an enthusiast of Sarah Bernhardt, described Yacco as a "genius" and "incomparable." His description of her dancing persuasively linked the spiraling arcs and visual design of her movement with the curvilinear style and floral themes of Art Nouveau. He observed that she "bends like a spray of cut flowers . . . imitates the coiling of a liana (and) . . . the leaps of a hummingbird on a branch."[26] For Brisson and many of his colleagues, the potent amalgam of the visual images of *japonisme* and Art Nouveau encouraged the proliferation of poetic, even hyperbolic metaphors to describe Yacco's dancing; this type of expressive language was typical of French theatrical and literary criticism of the era. As I collected more critiques describing the performances of Yacco and the Japanese Players, I discovered how sensitive I needed to be to the nuances and details of language in order to clearly understand their meanings.

An interview with Yacco herself was printed in *Le Gaulois* in September in which she told the romantic and colorful story of her life.[27] As she was becoming an international celebrity, Yacco was creating her own legend, fashioning her own image in much the same manner as did her famous contemporaries. She carefully reveals herself as modest but assured, and she is anxious to see the performances of her fellow actresses, including Eleanora Duse, who, the Japanese actress states, is reported to be very like Yacco herself in her ability to portray death. It is evident then, that there will be more comparisons of Yacco's performances with those of her fellow "Player Queens." How would the Parisian theater critics react to the unusual combination of dance and drama in Yacco's performances, which seemed central to the creation of her onstage personae, that of the exotic and enigmatic geisha?

A check of my research log revealed that Martin Battersby mentioned a journal entitled *Le Théâtre* in connection with the use of the term *art nouveau,* citing the October 1900 issue's illustrations of the offerings at the Théâtre des Varietés. That citation proved serendipitous; the October issue of *Le Théâtre* had a thoughtful essay on Yacco by its editor, Henri Fouquier, while the September issue carried another review, "Pantomimes Japonaises," by Arsène Alexander, the art critic for the newspaper *Le Figaro.*[28] Here again was evidence that Yacco was considered a serious and important artist by critics with a sophisticated perception of theater and the arts. Alexander quotes the British actress Ellen Terry, who remarked of Yacco, "I never had an idea of such acting," thus bestowing on Yacco an imprimatur from one of her peers. If a writer such as Alexander described her as "a feline and passionate dancer," surely the art and drama critics who so admired Loïe Fuller would come to the latter's theater at the Exposition to see the Japanese performer. Had other art critics written about Yacco? I planned a broader survey of periodicals, including those devoted to the fine arts and literature, which I hoped might provide more materials.

I returned to both my research log and my growing collection of articles and reviews to try and elicit more clues from my sources. I noted that in his brief quotation from André Gide's review of Yacco, Paul Morand had included a sentence that included the phrase "chère Angèle." It seemed unusual for an author to use a proper name in such an article, and I hoped it would provide a clue to finding Gide's elusive commentary, as indeed it did. In a bibliographic collection of Gide's complete works in the Library of Congress, I discovered a series of essays entitled "Lettres à Angèle," first published in 1900 and then reprinted as part of an anthology of his writings called *Prétextes* in 1903 and 1929.[29] Gide's article proved to be something of a Rosetta stone in the development of the research process. His description of Yacco's performance included a vivid account of both her dancing and her famous death scene, noting that Yacco "gives us, in her rhythmic and measured outbursts of passion, the sacred emotion of the great ancient dramas."[30]

Gide not only gave an extraordinary sense of Yacco's performance, he indicated yet another source for more research material.

Gide noted that another author, Emile Verhaeren, had written an excellent account of the Exposition in the journal *Mercure de France*. Who, then, was Verhaeren and had he too written about Yacco? I obtained the 1900 issues of *Mercure de France* on microfilm and looked for works by and about Verhaeren in author indexes and bibliographies. Emile Verhaeren was a Belgian poet and essayist of the "cult of humanity" at the turn of the century, who frequently wrote on theater and literature. His critique of the Exposition proved to be a literary meditation on art and exoticism, and it painted an extraordinarily detailed and evocatively written picture of the dance attractions at the fair, including a discussion of Yacco in her two most famous roles. In addition, in an anthology of Verhaeren's poems, I found a list of writers, artists, and intellectuals who were instrumental in the development of the literary and theatrical aspects of a movement known as Symbolism; the list included Gustave Kahn, the founder of *La Vogue,* and I learned that Gide, too, was in sympathy with the movement's precepts. I knew that the *maître* of the Symbolist movement in theater, the poet Stéphane Mallarmé, had considered Loïe Fuller's dancing as "l'incorporation visuelle de l'idée." Perhaps Yacco's dancing had enthralled other Symbolists besides Verhaeren. Thus, my reading of Gide and Verhaeren prompted, if indirectly, an investigation of the evolution of Symbolist theater in France.

Research revealed that Symbolist theater, as it emerged from Mallarmé's aesthetic, emphasized drama as a "revelation of the soul," a "synthesis of the arts," and called for an actor who could become the embodiment of the symbol itself; hence Mallarmé's fascination with Loïe Fuller. Here, my research on Japanese theater, especially Kabuki, became germane. In Japanese theater, evocation, suggestion, mystery; the synthesis of music, dance, and visual design; the actor as hieroglyph—are all central to the performance of Kabuki, where the intent is to "present to the audience not the thing itself, but the designed impression of the thing."[31] The plays presented in Paris by Yacco and Kawakami presented a distillation of this aesthetic. The stylized movement and gesture, the hieratic designs, the strange and exotic stories of Japanese myths and legends all spoke to the Symbolist blueprint for a new kind of theatrical experience. I was able to mine this very rich vein of associations by expanding the scope of my research to include a variety of journals, such as *La Revue Blanche* and *La Revue Independente,* which were organs of Symbolist rhetoric, and whose articles helped me establish a literary and theatrical context in which to place Yacco's appearances in Paris.

This seemed an auspicious moment to step back from my research and review my materials. The quality and the quantity of critical essays I had uncovered concerning Yacco's performances at the Paris Exposition led me to conclude that she was more than a momentary sensation; she was considered a serious and exceptional artist. The strands of my research had become more complex but also more clearly defined. I had found descriptions of her performances that allied her dancing with Art Nouveau and the French rage for *japonisme,* and comparisons of her art with that of the great actresses of the time, and I had discovered parallels in the aesthetic espoused by Symbolist writers and artists with the tenets of Kabuki theater. More research, which took more than five years and included work in the Library of Congress, the Dance Collection and the Billy Rose Theatre Collection of the New York Public Library, the Theatre Museum and the British Library in London, and the Bibliothèque Nationale in Paris, deepened my interpretations and enhanced my insights, while strengthening the contextual web of meaning I had initially constructed.

Recreating a "Lost" Dance

Another facet of historiographic endeavor relates, of course, to performance. Can a "lost" dance work be subjected to a historiographic process through which it might be "recalled to life"? In the last ten years, there have been several successful examples of the reconstruction and revival of ballets that had seemed irretrievable. Vaslav Nijinsky's *Le Sacre du printemps* and Balanchine's *Cotillion* have both been restaged by Millicent Hodson and Kenneth Archer for the Joffrey Ballet. Nijinsky's *L'Après-midi d'un faune* was reenvisioned and scored in Labanotation, translated from Nijinsky's original movement notation, by Ann Hutchinson Guest, and had its American debut at the Juilliard School under the direction of Jill Beck. Hodson and Archer have detailed the methodology of their process in their excellent essay, "Ballets Lost and Found."[32] An issue of *Choreography and Dance* entitled *A Revival of Nijinsky's Original L'Après-midi d'un faune,* with exegesis by both Guest and Beck, is devoted to the extraordinary story of this ballet's rebirth.[33]

In a coda to this discussion of historiography, I include examples from both of these sources in my case study of the revival of Sir Frederick Ashton's 1933 ballet *Les Masques.* The ballet was revived by Elizabeth Schooling, a member of the original cast, and performed by students of the Dance Division of Southern Methodist University.

Why did we consider *Les Masques* as a significant work for revival? We must first look briefly at the work's performance history, its place in the Ashton canon and as part of the larger frame of twentieth-century ballet. Ashton originally choreographed *Les Masques (Ou Changement de Dames)* in 1933, a year that clearly marked a watershed in ballet history. Two ballets that exemplify the currents of change that define the era, George Balanchine's *Cotillion* and Leonide Massine's

Les Présages, have been revived by the Joffrey Ballet, and it seemed important to complete this trilogy of "lost" works by restoring an Ashton ballet of the same period.[34] Both Balanchine and Massine explored romance and destiny as themes for their ballets; how did Ashton work with similar motifs? In terms of Ashton's own ballets, *Les Masques* seemed an important antecedent of his more widely known works such as *Apparitions* (1936) or ballets still in repertory such as *Les Rendevous* (1933). The ballet, designed in an elegant black and white Art Deco style by the choreographer's close friend and collaborator, Sophie Fedorovitch, is a scintillating comedy of manners. A favorite Ashton subject, romantic love, with its vicissitudes and follies, was illustrated in the ballet's slight plot. Two masked couples meet at a nightclub; they switch partners, and discover that the husband and wife have again fallen in love, and the lover has found his intended inamorata.

Our initial efforts in the reconstruction process were twofold; first, we needed to discover what source materials were available to begin our research. We then needed to become immersed in the Art Deco sensibility and period of the ballet itself. As Hodson and Archer note, each work will "demand its own method of reconstruction, according to the information available and the style of the work."[35] While the importance of the primary research on the ballet itself may seem self-evident, the significance of contextual research as an indispensable component of the reconstruction process should be recognized. The dynamic relationship of an artwork to its time is essential in decoding its significance in the cultural canon; problematic and elusive elements such as performance style (which in the case of *Les Masques* included manners, deportment, and etiquette) can be more readily identified and described when placed in a specific historical framework.

The research on the ballet itself began with the collection and assembling of source materials from reviews, photographs, programs, and music scores, as well as costume and set designs in the archives of the Theatre Museum and Ballet Rambert in London and the Dance Collection of the New York Public Library. Both Rambert and the Dance Collection had fragments of film from 1934 and 1938, respectively, although no complete film of the ballet existed. The Rambert tape, which showed only a few dance moments, would prove valuable as a model of performance style and stage and costume design, while the Dance Collection film was essentially a filmed photo call. The archivist for Ballet Rambert provided a thorough *catalog raisonne* of artists who had danced the ballet while it was in the Rambert repertory from 1933 to 1953. This served as the primary resource for the gathering of oral histories.

Many dancers who performed *Les Masques,* and who worked frequently with Ashton, continue teaching and coaching and can actively communicate the *elan vital* of the Ashton repertory. The testimony of such performers is an invaluable resource in the reconstruction process, and a variety of testimonies can often provide the fullest picture of the work. Clearly, it is difficult to obtain every detail necessary for a revival from one artist; few dancers can recall everyone's steps, entrances, exits, and cues in a long or complex work. Yet multiple recollections can lead to contradictions, which must then be resolved. Hodson and Archer note their solution to the problem. "Our method on these occasions is to re-evaluate the sources and place them in hierarchical order. We ask which document or documentor has the greatest authority and use the information accordingly."[36]

The artists who created a given ballet, or worked closely with its choreographer, are usually considered the most authentic sources; their evidence should be carefully considered when it is available. There are dancers, of course, who remember little of the actual steps of movements of a ballet but can convey important information concerning its sensibility, quality of movement, or atmosphere, and their contributions to the "authenticity" of a revival can be invaluable.[37] Each detail remembered, every nuance recalled will help the reconstructor build the layers of evidence that will support the restaging of the ballet. In the case of *Les Masques*, one artist vividly recalled one movement she felt was key to understanding the vivacious, flirtatious manner of her character; the pose was pure Art Deco and revealed Ashton's preoccupation with the details of the style. Helpful auxiliary information can often be gleaned from costume, stage, and lighting designers, or even from audience members, but this should be incorporated into the revival only when corroborated by additional supporting documentation.

The contextual research on *Les Masques* was crucial to capturing the air of witty sophistication and mystery to which many critics had alluded; the critic Lionel Bradley remarked that the ballet had the flavor of a "salted almond."[38] In order to familiarize ourselves with Ashton as a choreographer, we initially read general books on his life and work, as well as accounts of the early years of the British Ballet. We then created annotated bibliographies for the music, theater, film, art, and fashion of the early 1930s in England and America. What information could we discover on the fashion and art of the thirties that would help the dancers with their body posture and deportment? What were the popular themes in the plays and films of the period, and how were they reflected in the ballet? Had Ashton's work in the musical theater, especially his collaborations with the African American dancer and choreographer Buddy Bradley, influenced his choreography for *Les Masques* and if so, would we be able to see the crosscurrents in the ballet? A broader picture of the ballet and its milieu began to emerge.

Through our investigations, we became acquainted with the stylistic conventions of Art Deco, with its emphasis on sleek, angular lines and sculptural form; this background would give the dancers references for the beautiful period look of the ballet. The fashion mannequins and starlets of the thirties provided models for the elegant and glamorous look of the women who perform the ballet's two principal female roles. We discovered the felicitous nature of creative synchronism. Ashton's gift for devastating parody is well documented, yet the scenario for *Les Masques* prefigured many parallel plots and devices in the early Astaire-Rogers musicals. Here was an example in dance history where we could valorize the achievements of the ballet stage over the popular cinema.

The act of research into the past brought both historical and contemporary social issues into high relief. The contribution of African American culture to the development of twentieth-century music, dance, art, and theater has been an important theme in recent scholarship. Certainly Ashton's work with Buddy Bradley during the early thirties influenced his early choreography. As a choreographer himself, Bradley brought together the dynamic body movements of African American vernacular dance with the tap dance steps and rhythms of jazz improvisation to create a bold and inventive style.[39] In ballets such as *High Yellow* (1932) and *Les Masques*, Ashton's collaboration with Bradley was evident. While the blending of material from black dance with the ballet idiom was clearly manifest in *High Yellow*, with movements such as "snakehips" being readily recognizable, we found that Ashton's use of black vernacular forms in *Les Masques* was both more subtle and more theatrical.[40] Yet there are hints in the ballet that the role of the Lover was meant to be a black man. In oral histories with dancers who performed the ballet, however, they thought that in Ashton's conception of the part, the emphasis should be placed more on the manner in which the character appropriated African American vernacular movement as part of his effort to disguise his identity. If there was anything "shocking" for audiences in the original *Les Masques*, it came from the frisson of eroticism rather than miscegenation. Nonetheless, it became clear that in casting and teaching the ballet, we would need to be sensitive to the social climates of the 1930s and the 1990s and make clear Ashton's great admiration and respect for Buddy Bradley and the African American dance tradition.

The initial staging of *Les Masques* was undertaken by Peter Franklin-White, a dancer who had often seen the ballet when he studied with Marie Rambert but who had never danced the ballet himself. Although some of the artists who performed in Ashton's original cast recalled the work in some detail, they were somewhat reluctant to undertake a reconstruction. In recent years, Ashton himself had decided not to have the ballet revived, probably believing the work to be too "stylized" and dated to appeal to contemporary audiences. We believed, however, that the opportunity for student dancers to learn and perform the work of a master choreographer was an important facet of their education as artists, and we staged a "first draft" of *Les Masques* for comment by those who both originally saw and performed the ballet.

Even in these preliminary learning and rehearsal stages, the students found their involvement in all aspects of the reconstruction valuable. Although the performance and analysis of masterpieces of dance repertory are central to the tradition of dance history, we have not fully explored the educational potential of the process of reconstruction and revival. The process should be accompanied by critical learning activities that can enhance the dancer's performance, enrich contextual information on the ballet, and help both performers and directors develop critical insights that will make the performance experience more meaningful. Such activities could, for example, make use of interactive computer technology. As the dancers and director research the ballet, information on its performance and contextual history could be placed on a multimedia "bulletin board." In the initial stages of learning about the ballet, the dancers could share their impressions and feelings about the task of mastering and interpreting a work physically and musically; this could take the form of an electronic "journal." By giving the dancers a formal arena in which to share and analyze their responses to the work and their roles, they literally share in the ballet's recreation. While the work is in performance, the dancers and the director could use the technologies already developed to hone details of execution and interpretation. Finally, audience reactions and comments could be added to the performers' own commentaries, and a concluding analysis of the ballet would be written by the director. This material, in addition to a notated score and videotape of the work in revival, would represent a full-scale exegesis of the process and realization of the ballet's reconstruction and assure the lasting value of the project as a historiographic record beyond performance.

We took a videotape of our first draft of Les Masques to a conference celebrating the choreographer's work and received an enthusiastic response. Although we discovered that details of the choreography and staging were indeed missing, the members of the conference, many of whom were dancers who had long worked with Ashton, found that the dancers had captured something of the mood of the ballet and the sensibility of the early Ashton "style." As a direct result of our conference presentation, Elizabeth Schooling, a member of the original cast of Les Masques, agreed to complete a final restaging of the work for performance and documentation. The performers' conviction, their commitment to the spirit of the ballet, had transcended even vexing questions of authenticity. If the ballet was not yet Les Masques, it had nevertheless begun to develop its "aura," to borrow Walter Benjamin's useful term.

For the dancers who had participated in the first phase of this revival, the unusual combination of performance problems in theory, dance "archaeology" in practice, and ballet history in action had presented a series of intriguing puzzles to be solved. They noted choreographic details that improved their execution of the steps; three ladies who are never without their fans, for example, observed that the lines of their movements were always extended by their fans, and this made them more aware of the shapes described by their arms and hands. The flirtatious "little girls" realized that their *bourrées* had different meanings in different sections of the ballet, and they began to experiment with varied dynamics and attack in each sequence. In short, the dancers had discovered that the artist who learns about the disciplines of the past is most fully immersed in her history when she affirms it through performance. It is this communion of the interpreter and the work, of "performance as sacramental act," which binds the performer to the canon and creates an ever-renewing and dynamic tradition.[41] In "de-constructing" a work such as *Les Masques,* the student dancers came to understand the value of artistry and virtuosity as holistic concepts, and that the meaning of a ballet is embedded in both its choreography and its cultural context, if only they know how to look and to learn.

❀

In a most extraordinary and satisfying way, both Sada Yacco and *Les Masques* seem recalled to life through the process, through the performance of dance historiography. Both dancer and dance will, in a sense, be reborn to speak to succeeding generations of dancers, critics, audiences, and historians. They have helped make us aware of how history and culture define each other, and that if the dance culture of the past seems a dead and distant relic, we must imaginatively recreate it in order to retrieve it. Like Virginia Woolf's *Orlando* and Ralph Pendrel in Henry James's *The Sense of the Past,* we can be time travellers, stepping through the door that propels us into the past to renew our perception "not only of the pastness of the past, but of its presence."[42]

Study Questions

1. In framing a topic for historical research, what are the first elements of the research process to be identified? How are they then developed and incorporated into the ongoing investigation?

2. What types of strategies can historians employ to create and write a historical narrative?

3. What strategies and methodologies can the historian devise to document evidence during the research and writing process?

NOTES

1. "Introduction: Theatre History and Historiography," in *Critical Theory and Performance*, ed. Janelle G. Reinelt and Joseph Roach (Ann Arbor: University of Michigan Press, 1992), 293.

2. Thomas Postlewait, "History, Hermeneutics and Narrativity," in *Critical Theory and Performance*, ed. Janelle G. Reinelt and Joseph Roach (Ann Arbor: University of Michigan Press, 1992), 356.

3. Ibid.

4. Ibid.

5. Sally Banes, "Balanchine and Black Dance," in *Writing Dance in the Age of Postmodernism* (Hanover and London: Wesleyan University Press/University Press of New England), 53–69.

6. H. Aram Veeser, introduction to *The New Historicism*, ed. H. Aram Veeser (New York and London: Routledge, 1989), xii.

7. Jane Marcus, "The Asylums of Antaeus: Women, War and Madness—Is There a Feminist Fetishism?" in *The New Historicism*, ed. H. Aram Veeser (New York and London: Routledge, 1989), 132–51.

8. Stephen Bann, "Image, Text and Object in the Formation of Historical Consciousness," in *The New Historicism*, ed. H. Aram Veeser (New York and London: Routledge, 1989), 104.

9. Ibid., 103, 108.

10. Susan A. Manning, *Ecstasy and the Demon: Feminism and Nationalism in the Dances of Mary Wigman* (Berkeley: University of California Press, 1993).

11. Ann Daly, "Reconsidering Isadora Duncan and the Male Gaze," in *Gender in Performance: The Presentation of Difference in the Performing Arts*, ed. Laurence Senelick (Hanover, N.H.: Tufts University/University Press of New England, 1992), 254.

12. Richard Buckle, *Nijinsky* (New York: Simon and Schuster, 1971); Keith Money, *Anna Pavlova: Her Life and Art* (New York: Alfred A. Knopf, 1982).

13. Suzanne Shelton, *Divine Dancer: A Biography of Ruth St. Denis* (Garden City, N.Y.: Doubleday, 1981); Marcia B. Siegel, *Days on Earth: The Dance of Doris Humphrey* (New Haven and London: Yale University Press, 1987).

14. Ruth St. Denis, *An Unfinished Life* (New York and London: Harper and Brothers, 1939), 40.

15. Allan Ross MacDougall, *Isadora: A Revolutionary in Art and Love* (New York: Thomas Nelson and Sons, 1960), 59.

16. Postlewait, "History, Hermeneutics and Narrativity," 357.

17. Joseph Donohue, "Evidence and Documentation," in *Interpreting the Theatrical Past: Essays in the Historiography of Performance*, ed. Thomas Postlewait and Bruce McConachie (Iowa City: University of Iowa Press, 1989), 177.

18. There are many different systems for developing, organizing, and keeping research logs. Some researchers prefer note cards, other keep notebooks. I often keep a loose-leaf notebook or spiral binder for citations and cross-references but usually keep my bibliographic materials and research log on yellow legal pads. I can then make notations next to references as a kind of series of running annotations, noting which sources were helpful, whether there appeared to be material for further investigation, and so on.

19. Martin Battersby, *The World of Art Nouveau* (New York: Funk and Wagnalls, 1968), 25.

20. Ibid., 11–25.

21. Gabriel P. Weisberg, *Art Nouveau Bing: Paris Style 1900* (New York: Harry N. Abrams, Inc., 1986), 9.

22. Battersby, *World of Art Nouveau,* 15.

23. Paul Morand, *1900* (Paris: Flammarion, 1931).

24. Henri Detouche, "Une Mime Japonaise," *La Vogue* 7 (1900): 119–20.

25. M. Fourcaud, "Japonisme," *Le Gaulois,* July 23, 1900, 1.

26. Adolphe Brisson, "Promenades et Visites à l'Exposition: Madame Sada Yacco," *Le Temps,* August 1, 1900, 2.

27. "Sada Yacco: Racontée par Elle-Même," *Le Gaulois,* September 9, 1900, 1.

28. Henri Fouquier, "Sada Yacco," *Le Théâtre* 44, no. 2 (October 1900): 9; Arsène Alexandre, "Pantomimes Japonaises," *Le Théâtre* 1, no. 42 (September 1900): 16–19.

29. André Gide, *Lettres à Angèle* (Paris: Editions de Mercure de France, 1900), reprinted in *Prétextes* (Paris: Mercure de France, 1903; reprint 1929).

30. Ibid., 140.

31. Earle Ernst, *The Kabuki Theatre* (Honolulu: University of Hawaii Press, 1974), 178.

32. Millicent Hodson and Kenneth Archer, "Ballets Lost and Found," in *Dance History: An Introduction,* 2d ed. (revised and updated), ed. Janet Adshead-Lansdale and June Layson (London and New York: Routledge, 1994), 98–116.

33. Jill Beck, "A Revival of Nijinsky's Original *L'Après-midi d'un faune.*" In *Choreography and Dance,* vol. 1, part 3, ed. Jill Beck (London and New York: Harwood Academic Publishers, 1991). With video.

34. *Cotillon,* revived by Hodson and Archer, received its reconstruction premiere on October 26, 1988, by the Joffrey Ballet at City Center, New York. "Ballets Lost and Found," 114; *Les Présages* was reconstructed for the Joffrey Ballet by Tatiana Leskova and Nelly Laport. Janice Ross, "Joffrey Ballet, War Memorial Opera House, San Francisco, July 2–12, 1992," *Dance Magazine* 66, no. 11 (November 1992): 94.

35. Ibid., 101.

36. Ibid., 100, 109.

37. For a fuller discussion of issues of authenticity and dance, see Shelley C. Berg, "The Real Thing: Authenticity and Dance at the Approach of the Millennium," in *Dance Reconstructed:* Proceedings of the Society of Dance History Scholars, Mason Gross School of the Arts (New Brunswick: Rutgers University Press, 1993).

38. Lionel Bradley, "Ballet Rambert and London Ballet, October 29," Dance Diaries, October 20–November 27, 1940, Theatre Museum, London. The Bradley diaries are an excellent example of unusual but informative and interesting primary source material.

39. Banes, "Balanchine and Black Dance," 59.

40. Markova performed the "snakehips" in *High Yellow.* David Vaughan, "Conversations with Markova," *Dance Magazine* 51, no. 6 (June 1977): 60.

41. Richard Taruskin, "The Pastness of the Present," in *Authenticity and Early Music,* ed. Nicholas Kenyon (Oxford and New York: Oxford University Press, 1988), 156.

42. T. S. Eliot, quoted in ibid., 156.

REFERENCES

Adshead-Lansdale, Janet, and June Layson, eds. *Dance History: An Introduction.* 2d ed. London and New York: Routledge, 1994.

Arendt, Hannah. "The Concept of History." In *Between Past and Future*. New York: Viking Press, 1981.

Banes, Sally. *Writing Dance in the Age of Postmodernism*. Hanover and London: Wesleyan University Press/University Press of New England, 1994.

Beck, Jill. "A Revival of Nijinsky's Original *L'Après-midi d'un faune*." In *Choreography and Dance*, vol. 1, part 3, ed. Jill Beck. London and New York: Harwood Academic Publishers, 1991. With video.

Benjamin, Walter. "Theses on the Philosophy of History." In *Illuminations*, ed. Hannah Arendt, trans. Harry Zohn, 253–64. New York: Schocken, 1969.

Berg, Shelley C. "The Real Thing: Authenticity and Dance at the Approach of the Millennium." In *Dance Reconstructed:* Proceedings of the Society of Dance History Scholars, Mason Gross School of the Arts. New Brunswick, N.J.: Rutgers University Press, 1993.

———. "Sada Yacco: The American Tour." *Dance Chronicle* 16, no. 2 (1993): 147–96.

———. "Sada Yacco: Le Rêve Realisé." *Dance Chronicle* 18, no. 3 (1995): 343–404.

Carr, David. *Time, Narrative and History*. Bloomington: Indiana University Press, 1986.

Carr, Edward Hallett. *What Is History?* New York: Random House, 1961.

Collingwood, Robin G. *The Idea of History*. London: Oxford University Press, 1946.

Desmond, Jane C., ed. *Meaning in Motion: New Cultural Studies of Dance*. Durham and London: Duke University Press, 1997.

The Drama Review 26, no. 1 (T93) (spring 1982). Issue devoted to Historical Performance.

The Drama Review 28, no. 3 (T103) (fall 1984). Issue devoted to Reconstruction.

Edel, Leon, et al. *Telling Lives: The Biographer's Art,* ed. Marc Pachter. Washington, D.C.: New Republic Books, 1979.

Foster, Susan. *Reading Dancing: Bodies and Subjects in Contemporary American Dance*. Berkeley: University of California Press, 1986.

Hernandi, Paul. "Clio's Cousins: Historiography as Translation, Fiction, and Criticism." *New Literary History* 7, no. 2 (1976): 248–57.

Holroyd, Michael. "History and Biography." *Salmagundi* 46 (1979): 13–26.

Kenyon, Nicholas, ed. *Authenticity and Early Music: A Symposium*. Oxford and New York: Oxford University Press, 1988.

Manning, Susan. *Ecstasy and the Demon: Feminism and Nationalism in the Dances of Mary Wigman*. Berkeley: University of California Press, 1993.

Mink, Louis O. *Historical Understanding*. Ithaca, N.Y.: Cornell University Press, 1987.

Morris, Gay, ed. *Moving Words: Re-writing Dance*. London and New York: Routledge, 1996.

Postlewait, Thomas, and Bruce A. McConachie, eds. *Interpreting the Theatrical Past: Essays in the Historiography of Performance*. Iowa City: University of Iowa Press, 1989. Contains an excellent and comprehensive bibliography on historiography by Postlewait.

Reinelt, Janelle G., and Joseph Roach, eds. *Critical Theory and Performance*. Ann Arbor: University of Michigan Press, 1992.

Senelick, Laurence, ed. *Gender in Performance: The Presentation of Difference in the Performing Arts*. Hanover, N.H.: Tufts University/University Press of New England, 1992.

Steffens, Henry J., and Mary Jane Dickerson. *Writer's Guide: History.* Lexington, Mass., and Toronto: D. C. Heath, 1987.

Veeser, H. Aram, ed. *The New Historicism.* New York and London: Routledge, 1989.

Wedgwood, C. V. *The Sense of the Past: Thirteen Studies in the Theory and Practice of History.* New York: Collier Books, 1967.

9 DANCE ETHNOGRAPHY

Tracing the Weave of Dance in the Fabric of Culture

Joan D. Frosch

> Is the concept dance useful in studying either our own culture or others?
>
> Adrienne L. Kaeppler, 1985

DEPENDING UPON THE weaver of the tale, the story of the study of dance in cultural context is woven of varying threads. This version is a discussion of the practice of dance ethnography within the weave of history, method, and current concerns.[1]

A caveat . . . "Is the concept dance useful in studying either our own culture or others?"[2]

Historically, the very concept of dance has been a thorny theoretical patch in the practice of dance ethnography. What do we mean when we call a movement behavior "dance"? How do the researcher's assumptions embedded in "dance" help or hinder ethnographic studies? Adrienne L. Kaeppler warns that the concept "'dance' may be masking the importance and usefulness of analyzing human movement systems by introducing a Western category" ("Structured Movement"). She explains, "In many non-Western societies there is no indigenous concept comparable to 'dance' and a larger view of structured movement systems is *de rigueur*."[3] When Kaeppler asks, "What are the components in our society that make it possible to classify together ballet, rock and roll, square dancing, and the waltz but separate them from ice skating, cheer leading, and a church processional?" she makes clear that we can assume little when we invoke the English word *dance*.

My day-to-day cultural environment—a university theater and dance department—certainly does not classify rock and roll, square dancing, and the waltz together with ballet. Sally Ann Ness reports that the *sinulog*—a varied choreographic phenomenon researched by Ness in Cebu City, Philippines—was criticized by some American scholars as "not dance" when they watched video footage of the event.[4] Postmodern sensibilities nourished by Judson Church and described by Cynthia Novack in *Sharing the Dance* fueled similar questions in U.S. dance circles.[5]

Context, then, is the defining component of ethnographic research. While Kaeppler is concerned with what she has termed "structured movement systems" as dimensions of "various activities [that] should be recognized as an integral part of that activity," Margaret Drewal argues that it is only because of the limited scope of specialist researchers that performance is broken down into such component parts, and she calls for a holistic understanding of performance.[6] Indeed, the *Akan* word *agor* encompasses dance, music, and play. If we wish to study "dance" in cultural context, then, we may begin by adopting a broader understanding than typically embedded in the word *dance,* or *movement,* for that matter. For example, in my research with an expatriate Ghanaian community, the synergy of dance, music, and performance was revealed as a dynamic process of meaning-making: a way of creating social space and defining its boundaries.[7]

Striving to understand indigenous categories, rather than superimposing categories of our own, leads to the potential to understand the cultural intentions of the practitioners. Taking the cue from the practitioners, we can determine what dance/movement and correlated activities are considered as important, and how they are categorized by their contextual particulars. As we set out to trace the weave of dance in the fabric of culture, it is reassuring to note Joann W. Keali'inohomoku's thoughts on why we would want to: "Dance should be studied because it is important to the people involved."[8]

What objectives might a contextualized approach to the study of dance include?

1. To define approaches to the study of dance in culture "on its own terms," examining what and *how* dance means in relation to the context of which it is a part.

2. To examine performance traditions as expressions of values and ways of knowing.

3. To investigate how performance constructs and mediates societal notions of gender, status, spirituality, and agency.

4. To explore the interplay of ethics and aesthetics in performance and society.

5. To examine the relationship of dance to ways of organizing life experi-

ence, for example, ritual, courtship, education, recreation, aesthetic expression, healing, rites of passage, work.

6. To examine the dynamics of dance within the tensions of continuity and change.

7. To examine the roles of the performer in society and to explore the creative process of performance and dance-making.

8. To recognize the role of the researcher in shaping research, and to explore the changing relationships between performer and researcher in a postcolonial world.

9. To chart paths to constructing a movement ethos through a variety of modalities: observation, embodiment, kinesthetic empathy, writing, discussion, collaboration, and performance.

10. To determine whether and how study and participation in performance modes and motivations other than our own awaken new understandings of the forms familiar to us. To determine how the particularities of ethnographic practice can help us to develop socially responsible research for the twenty-first century. To determine what role an enhanced intercultural perspective can play for the future in both the arts and an increasingly connected, though not unified, world.[9]

Invoking the Ancestors . . . and Others

Tracing the early study of dance in culture, Kaeppler cites Curt Sachs's 1933 volume, *Eine Weltgeschichte des Tanzes,* as "the first publication about dance that had any real relevance to anthropology." Yet Sachs's notion that "non-western dance represents earlier stages of western dance," Kaeppler asserts, has "no place in the study of dance in anthropological perspective."[10] According to Kaeppler, Franz Boas, pioneer of American anthropology, "laid a foundation for the possibility of examining dance and responses to it in terms of one's own culture rather than as a universal language."[11]

In 1942, Franziska Boas, performer of early modern dance and daughter of Franz, created a symposium entitled "The Function of Dance in Human Society." It broke ground for the serious discussion of dance in cross-cultural contexts. In her introduction to the publication of the symposium papers in 1944, she explains, "This seminar on the Function of Dance in Human Society was presented simply as an introductory investigation of the relationship between dance and the way of life. Primitive and exotic cultures were turned to, because in them the dance has a really vital function, and its meaning is accepted by the community."[12] Applying a "functionalist approach"[13] to dance, Franz Boas presented a paper on "Dance and Music in the Life of the Northwest Coast Indians of North America

(Kwakiutl)"; Geoffrey Gorer presented "Function of Dance Forms in Primitive African Communities"; Harold Courlander presented "Dance and Dance-Drama in Haiti"; and Claire Holt and Gregory Bateson presented "Form and Function of the Dance in Bali."

Boas's work and her *The Function of Dance in Human Society* planted seeds for both the development of cultural studies in dance, and the study of dance as healing, or dance therapy. However, Drid Williams speculates that Franziska Boas's goal was to stimulate further discussion on the application of the functionalist paradigm to non-Western dance and not to create a model or set up "authority," as the book was more widely interpreted.[14]

Fascination with knowing the other through movement finds resonance in the zeitgeist of the early twentieth century. In an era of travels and "artistic" quests for exotica, a reframing of the Western psyche is evident in the theatrical dance of the time. Fokine reveled in Orientalism: he became enamored of iconoclast Isadora Duncan and created over twenty "Oriental" ballets. Photography and film also fueled fascination with the Other. For Ruth St. Denis, a poster advertising Egyptian Deities cigarettes inspired new explorations in self-concept as Radha and later as Isis "the mysterious": "I knew that my destiny as a dancer had sprung alive in that moment." Without apology she remarked: "I did not go to India. India came to me," at the Durbar of Dehli—at Coney Island's fun-park simulation of an Indian court.[15] Between 1925 and 1926, and on successive occasions, luminaries St. Denis and Ted Shawn toured and traveled widely. Shawn hungrily reaped "the exotic" for entertainment and art, returning with complete dances learned with their appropriate costumes in tow. He brought back literally hundreds of films from his travels in Australia and Southeast Asia. Recognized for his expertise in the cross-cultural study of dance, Shawn was invited to review Gertrude Prokosch Kurath's "Panorama of Dance Ethnology." His review chided Kurath for overlooking La Meri's contributions to the field of cross-cultural dance studies.[16] La Meri formed the Ethnologic Dance Institute, which was according to Shawn "the finest clearinghouse for knowledge and information on ethnic dance that ever existed."[17]

Although extremely active, pioneering non–European American dance researchers were relegated to the margins of a marginal area of scholarship. As an undergraduate, Katherine Dunham piqued the interest of anthropologist Melville J. Herskovits, who was himself a student of Franz Boas. In preparation for her fieldwork she studied for nine months with him at Northwestern University in 1935.[18] Herskovits became a mentor to Dunham. As she embarked on her fieldwork in the Caribbean, which focused on Haiti and included Jamaica, Martinique, and Trinidad, Herskovits wrote key letters of introduction to assist her transition into research.[19] Renowned primarily as a performer, choreographer, and teacher,

Dunham published her research on Haitian dance in a monograph entitled *Las Danzas de Haiti* in 1947.[20] The book was published in French in 1950 and for the first time in English in 1983. In 1941 Herskovits commented, somewhat obliquely, on the significance of her early work: "To the present time, the most important result of Miss Dunham's field investigations has been in her own creative dancing."[21] Mary Kawena Pukui, a linguist, studied and wrote essays about the hula beginning in 1936. Pukui's work is now considered classic,[22] and Katherine Dunham's and Pearl Primus's scholarly contributions are being evaluated anew.[23]

Dancer, musician, and art historian by training, Gertrude Prokosch Kurath considered herself to be "a dancer first and foremost."[24] She turned from dance performance to research in the mid-1940s, "enjoying the teamwork of her research methods as much as any theatrical production." Kurath's 1960 essay, "Panorama of Dance Ethnology," was pivotal in weaving the diverse threads of cross-cultural dance research into a field of study, presumably to be called dance ethnology.[25]

It is interesting to note that in "Panorama" Kurath recognized the term *ethnic dance* as controversial. Further, she was not satisfied with limiting the scope of dance ethnology to "ethnic dance" and suggested that "a culturally complete picture" should include "all dance," including ballet, jazz, and "modern creative dance." Kurath's perspective lays the foundation for Keali'inohomoku's well-known piece, "An Anthropologist Looks at Ballet as a Form of Ethnic Dance."[26] Kurath wrote, "Any dichotomy between ethnic dance and art dance dissolves if one regards dance ethnology, not as a description or reproduction of a particular kind of dance, but as an approach toward, and a method of, eliciting the place of dance in human life—in a word, as a branch of anthropology."[27]

Kurath detailed her methods in "Research Methods and Background of Gertrude Kurath," an essay originally prepared for use in a seminar at Indiana University and included in the proceedings at the 1972 CORD conference in Tucson.[28] Her methods included preparation and various stages of fieldwork; laboratory study; search for "stylistic peculiarities"; exegesis with the help of a "well-informed native"; graphic representation and classification of body movement, posture, gesture, and steps; analysis or recognition of the basic movement motifs in combination with associated musical rhythms and meters; synthesis or graphic display of complete dances with formations, steps, music, and words; a consideration of the musical aspects; theoretical conclusions, and comparison with the dances of other cultures. Frisbee notes Kurath as one of the early researchers to consider native experts consulted in research as active collaborators in the research process rather than "informants": for example, the 1970 *Music and Dance of the Tewa Pueblos* is authored by Kurath with Antonio Garcia.[29]

Yet Kurath readily admits that "Despite all of the field work and experimentation, the goal always seems out of reach. I really haven't figured out a clear device for integrating the artistic and cultural factors."[30] Indeed, Kaeppler maintains that she and her contemporaries, excepting Keali'inohomoku and, later, Jill Sweet, were little influenced by Kurath's work. In a review of *Half a Century of Dance Research: Essays by Gertrude Prokosch Kurath,* Kaeppler reveals what she considers to be "probably unknown": "Kurath had very little influence on anthropology graduate students of the 1960s and 1970s."[31] In her 1978 review of the field for the *Annual Review of Anthropology,* Kaeppler noted that "Kurath's primary contribution to the study of dance ethnology was her amassing of empirical detail and her presentation of this information in such a way that other researchers and the descendants of the peoples from whom she obtained the information could actually use it."[32]

Keali'inohomoku, who trained in cultural anthropology at Indiana University, took up the thread of Kurath's work. She has written extensively, with particular interest in Hopi and Hawaii, and has done several comparative studies.[33] Having taught for fourteen years in the Department of Anthropology at Northern Arizona University, Keali'inohomoku cofounded Cross-Cultural Dance Resources, the first research institute of its kind, in 1981. The inaugural publication of CCDR was *Half a Century of Dance Research: Essays by Gertrude Prokosch Kurath.*

As an undergraduate at Bennington, "in classes with Edward T. Hall of Proxemic fame," Allegra Fuller Snyder first began to think about dance in relation to culture. Dance ethnologist Elsie Ivancich Dunin reports that in 1965–1966, Dr. Alma Hawkins, then chair of dance at UCLA, asked graduate students Dunin and Snyder "to recommend courses that would develop an 'ethnic' component of the curriculum"; eventually Dunin and Snyder "labeled this fledgling curriculum 'Dance Ethnology.'" For many years Snyder was head of the Dance Ethnology program at UCLA and chairperson of the Department of Dance (1974–1980, and acting chair 1990–91), training, together with Dunin, several generations of dance ethnologists at the master's level. Snyder enthusiastically acknowledges the influence of Franziska Boas and Kurath upon her thinking.[34] Her early theoretical work sprang from a concept she has termed "the dance symbol," which is "the dancer, the outer and observable aspects of the dancer built of three distinct and very simple factors: the movement (mimetic movement primarily), costume, and paraphernalia."[35] She later developed a concrete model of examining dance through eight levels of event patterns, moving the researcher's awareness from "'Geertzian' attention to world view to Kaeppler's kinemic attention."[36] Yvonne Daniel has built her analysis of Cuban rumba, in part, upon Snyder's framework.[37]

Kaeppler, who does not consider herself in line for inheritance from either Franziska Boas or Kurath, is Curator of Oceanic Ethnology at the Smithsonian Institution. Her fieldwork has centered in Polynesia, especially Tonga and Hawaii, examining dance as an integral part of social structure and as a surface manifestation of deep structure. Kaeppler's contributions in the area of linguistic analogies are regarded as some of the most outstanding scholarship in the field.

Drid Williams's touching revelation may resound deeply for many dance scholars: "All my life, I have wanted to talk about dancing and moving as well as I once danced and moved."[38] Williams developed *semasiology,* a theory based on semiotics intended to move dance study away from an examination of function to an understanding of human beings as meaning-makers. Semasiology is the study of meaning in signification, or human signs. Dancer turned anthropologist, Williams apologizes for all her writings on dance and culture prior to her exposure to anthropological thought.[39]

Judith Lynne Hanna is a prolific author on the subject of dance in cultural context. Anya Peterson Royce directly addressed the subject of the anthropology of dance with her book of the same name. Judy Mitoma of UCLA, Jill Sweet, Suzanne Youngerman, former head of the Laban Institute for Movement Studies, and Judy Van Zile of the University of Hawaii, are active contributors to diverse approaches in the field. Authors who have paved pathways in the research of dance as cultural practice include Daniel, Drewal, Farnell, Ness, Novack, Azzí, Baird N'Diaye, Browning, Cowan, Savigliano, Sklar, and Quigley, among others.

The Search for a System

In 1967, in Riverdale, New York, participants at the Preliminary Conference on Research in Dance—the first CORD conference—investigated the state of dance research. A look through the conference proceedings demonstrates the unformed state of the study of dance in cultural context at that time. The artist Matteo, a dancer, educator, and author, presented a list of essentials for research in "ethnic dance," including enthusiasm, inquisitiveness, having time, and a quick eye.[40]

In 1972, the Committee (later, Congress) on Research in Dance held a conference on the "Anthropology of Dance," in honor of Gertrude Kurath and founder/editor of *Impulse* Marian Van Tuyl. The conference committee included Joann Keali'inohomoku and Allegra Snyder as co-chairs, and Adrienne Kaeppler, Anya Royce, Carl Wolz, and ethnomusicologist Alan P. Merriam, who gave the keynote address. Merriam's address highlighted the major concern of the time—to find a system of research. Notably, Royce presented "Choreology Today: A Review of the Field," a comprehensive review of the literature demonstrating the development in thinking about dance over time. Keali'inohomoku presented her most recent revisions of three field guides: "Dance Data Guide," "Check List: Material Traits Associated with Dance," and "Dance Compendium Questions." Her work was intended to guide and encourage non-dance-based ethnographers to "see dance."

Alan Lomax (student of R. Birdwhistell) presented Choreometrics with dance specialists Irmgard Bartenieff and Forrestine Pauley at the 1972 CORD Conference.[41] Based on Laban Effort/Shape theory, Choreometrics is a study of cross-cultural movement styles using filmed "data," with no native exegesis. For Lomax, the data confirmed the existence of distinct movement style traditions, which appeared to supersede complexities of context, gender, language, history, and meaning. The world's movement style traditions, according to Lomax, are: "1) the primitive Pacific, 2) black Africa with Melanesia and Polynesia, 3) high culture Eurasia, 4) Europe. There also seems to be an Arctic style tradition that links northern Europe across Siberia to aboriginal North America."[42]

Attempting to correlate style with technological development and various aspects of social structure, Lomax claimed to discover that as a culture works so it sings and dances. His film "Dance and Human History" illustrates the resulting Choreometrics system. In 1990, Lomax debuted a CD-ROM program titled "Global Jukebox" based, in part, on the same Choreometrics findings.[43]

The tidy categories reducing the dancer to a relatively neat object of study may have seemed an attractive systematic approach to some at the time.[44] But one might have asked, "Whose system?" Fostered, in part, by studies like Choreometrics, cultural study is still commonly thought of as the study of objectifiable "other" cultures. Following general trends in anthropology, however, numerous dance ethnographers have demonstrated that the Other is us.[45]

New Pathways

An often voiceless, nonmaterial activity, improvisational at times—you cannot hear it, you cannot hold on to it, you may not even be able to repeat it—dance is perhaps the most ephemeral aspect performance. Drewal argues that because objectivist research methodologies value, and therefore reify, static products to study as objects, dance has not generally been considered a serious subject of study.[46] Among other influences, Puritan values negatively associate the body further with the subjective, the emotional, the sensual, and the sexual.[47] Deeper societal assumptions and fears may undergird the conceptualization of woman, sex (and homosex), body, movement, and dance to create craters of unexamined experience into which students and scholars of culture may stumble. Yet Euro-America's body-mind split appears to continue to value the disembodied mind at the expense of the body. Neither the centrality of the body to human experience nor the body's ability to act as spiritual vehicle appears to attract serious attention. In fact, the body is often trivialized and (dis)regarded as the domain of women and other historically marginalized groups, including nonwhites and children.

Such thinking hinders the development of theoretical frameworks to facilitate the study of embodied experience. The complexity of dance is glossed over as frivolous, and the dance experience is relegated to the domain of the obvious. Cartesian logic persists and dance remains unseen, unacknowledged, and, ultimately, left out of most scholarship. Even anthropology, which purports to take the whole of human existence as its field of inquiry, has, with few exceptions, ignored this aspect of human experience. Threads of anti-intellectualism in the field of dance itself have also undermined its development as a serious subject of inquiry. Furthermore, a diverse and uneven dance literature compounded by the difficulty of uncovering newer scholarship,[48] and the unfortunate tendency, by some, of tying dance to outmoded theory[49] renders a troubled foundation upon which to build new knowledge. Finally, the field claims only a handful of Ph.D. programs in which to nurture new scholars.

What Shall We Name the Baby?

The study of dance in the weave of culture, then, has a broad and uneven lineage. Accordingly, the very name of the study presents some confusion. What shall we name the baby? Keali'inohomoku finds the term "dance ethnology" to imply "a limitation of the study to cultural parameters, particularly descriptive."[50] Rather, she alternates use of "anthropology of dance" with "ethnochoreology" (suggested by Kurath as an analog to ethnomusicology), preferring "anthropology of dance."[51] Kaeppler finds the term "choreology" to be "anthropologically unfortunate because it appears to put the emphasis on dance content rather than on the contextual elements of social relations and the philosophical associations with a culture's deep structure and aesthetics."[52] Williams does not use the term "dance anthropology" in relation to her own work, and she writes, without apology, of "the dance" and human movement.[53]

Kaeppler alternately describes herself as an anthropologist with an interest in dance and an anthropologist of human movement.[54] She has also carefully separated out anthropologists with an interest in movement from dance ethnologists. According to Kaeppler, anthropologically-based studies foreground how the dance may help us to understand society, whereas ethnological studies use context to illuminate the dance.[55] Yet as Ness has pointed out, "There is something essentially anthropological about choreographic phenomena."[56] In the United States, contributions to the study of dance as a cultural practice have come from practitioners of dance performance, anthropology, the anthropology of human movement, performance studies, ethnochoreology, and dance ethnology, among others. "Dance ethnography" has emerged as a popular reference to the study of dance in cultural context by some dance researchers trained in the four fields of anthropology, and by other dance researchers as well. More importantly, the practice of ethnographic research is particularly well suited to dance.

Dance Ethnography

At its most basic, ethnography is "writing" about people (from the Greek *ethnos,* folk, people; and *graphein,* write).[57] Descriptive in nature, ethnography pursues understanding through the layering of the specific and highly complex contexts of human experience. The idea of ethnography may be best introduced by its primary research methodology: participant observation. Participant observation typically takes place in the "field." The field may be a social situation well-known, in fact "native," to the ethnographer, or an alien situation. In either case, attempting to set aside their own preconceived notions, ethnographers immerse themselves in the particular cultural setting. With the help of consultants and local experts, the ethnographer examines culture in context. Working to develop a cultural understanding through the points of view of both "insider" (by learning the language, dance, music, and native categories, participation, interviews, embodiment, and so on), and "outsider" (by observation, reading, reviewing field notes, and so forth), the ethnographer attempts to come to an understanding of culture on its own terms, an ideal that may prove to be elusive.

As the concept of ethnography has been revised and reinvigorated in its home territory of anthropology,[58] it has found itself reaching beyond the parameters of anthropology into other disciplines. Overflowing its origins, ethnographic inquiry is currently employed in fields as diverse as ethnomusicology, sociology, education, comparative literature, gender studies, health, criminal justice, and, of course, dance, among others. "Ethnography is a tool with great promise: it offers the educator a way of seeing schools through the eyes of students; health professionals the opportunity of seeing health and disease through the eyes of patients from a myriad of different backgrounds; those in the criminal justice system a chance to view the world through the eyes of those who are helped and victimized by that system; and counselors an opportunity to see the world from their clients' points of view."[59] Ethnomusicologist Anthony Seeger demonstrates the flexibility of the method: "Ethnography should be distinguished from anthropology . . . since ethnography is not defined by disciplinary lines or theoretical perspectives."[60]

Dance ethnologists are among those who have appropriated the use of ethnographic methods. In an address to UCLA's Twelfth Annual Dance Ethnology Forum entitled "Invigorating Dance Ethnology," Deidre Sklar shared a lengthy field excerpt from her dissertation entitled "Enacting Religious Belief: A Movement Ethnography of the Annual Fiesta of the Tortugas, New Mexico." Sklar concludes that "Dance ethnography depends upon the postulate that cultural knowledge is embodied in movement, especially the highly stylized and codified movement we call dance."[61]

Indeed, ethnography's hallmark practice of participant observation (or "observing participant"[62]) is extraordinarily well suited to dance study: the core of dance practice also assumes participation and observation. "Like the dancer, the ethnographer must learn by participation, through repeated interaction, with the help of those around him or her, such as they have to contribute. Attempting to defer consistently to the designs of an initially alien way of living, the hope of the ethnographer is like that of the performing artist: eventually, some competence will be gained; eventually, some audience or readership will benefit from and be inspired by whatever atonement the ethnographer has achieved within this culture through his or her trial-and-error experiences."[63]

The phenomenological experience of self within the context of the research arena is facilitated by something to which many dancers (researchers and subjects) are highly attuned: kinesthetic empathy or "empathetic kinesthetic perception," as Sklar has refined the term.[64] While some researchers may have the advantage of either native competence or significant cultural familiarity with which to enter the world of the researched, others, like Sklar, may be guided, in part, by kinesthetic empathy, or using the "body and feelings as a research tool." Sklar explains, "My research went back and forth between mimesis and conceptualization, combining the empathic kinesthetic techniques I'd developed with more traditional methods of participant observation."[65] For example, the researcher examining the lives of female ballet dancers in the New York City Ballet may enter into a slice of these dancers' lives through "moving with" their dancing in rehearsal and on stage, their movement interactions in the cafeteria and the dressing room, and, for example, their walk from subway to theater and back. These impressions become part of the ethnographic record, in much the same way as photographs or other documentary devices would. Clearly, this felt "data" must be analyzed and checked against the native experience. Alternatively, in my research with the Ghanaian community of greater Washington, D.C., my dancing was closely scrutinized by my consultants to see "if I understood the [Ewe] culture."[66] While my kinesthetic empathy with the community helped me to more effectively study *Ewe* immigrant dance experiences, *their* kinesthetic empathy with me, grounded in my *Ewe* dance ability, allowed them to take me seriously as a researcher.[67]

Ethnography attempts to reveal cultures as dynamic processes, made up of individual actors who represent a complex weave of voices and viewpoints. Further, it attempts to demonstrate the multidimensional texture of the subject of study, rather than flatten it to an ahistorical, unchanging, or mythical portrayal. Ethnography is not neat or easy to package. In fact, ethnographers will talk about the importance of messiness and the suspicions raised by work that is "too neat."[68] In other words, if we fully engage in detail-oriented study, we will not emerge with a tidy, reified stereotype that assumes homogeneity. We will more likely emerge with a contradictory, multidimensional and, perhaps, conditional understanding of a particular slice of time and space. For this reason, the results of ethnographic research may elude generalization. "The strength of ethnography and ethnographic criticism is their focus on detail, their enduring respect for context in the making of any generalization, and their full recognition of persistent ambiguity and multiple possibilities in any situation."[69]

A Humanizing Enterprise

Ethnographic research involves being with and getting to know people in many aspects of their lives. It affords particular opportunities and responsibilities, including interacting with the researched in long-term, complex, and, at times, committed relationships. How do ethnographers consider those upon whom they depend for their research—as mentors, informants, assistants, consultants, colleagues, teachers, friends, or some combination? And how do these considerations affect the efficacy and integrity of ethnographers' participant-observation? Certainly the defining spaces between researcher and researched are not static and may converge and realign anew at a later stage of research. In addition to race, such issues as culture of origin, nationality, power, privilege, skill, sex, and gender further define the field experience. For example, much research tends to "study down" either socially or economically; and in many cultures, although women may be primary culture bearers, men may control access to information.

What gives us the right to speak for others? Native status? Pragmatic connections? Education? Color? Sex? Culture of origin? Good intentions? Is there one voice that is the definitive voice of authenticity? Each study endeavored—by native and nonnative researchers alike—must be carefully negotiated with the subjects of study. It appears that the very negotiation across the differing points of view of researched and researcher can lend significant dimensions to the process.

Sandy Arkist, Ghanaian theater specialist of the Institute of African Studies at the University of Ghana, related an example of negotiating across the boundaries of privilege. After researching performance practices in a small town in rural Ghana, Arkist returned to the town with a gift of an electric generator. Overcome by feelings of remorse, his consultants revealed to him that they had not been truthful to him during his research and proceeded to correct the numerous inaccuracies they had "fed" him during his research. They had been pulling the leg of the "big man" from the university. Arkist's consultants had not taken his questioning seriously until they understood the sincerity of his intentions through his gift of gratitude.[70]

Who is the research for? Who will benefit? Who will gain? Will anybody lose? How does the research advance the goals or answer the needs of the community? Questions such as these foreground the value of a collaborative research design —one in which the research process and/or the product of the research concurrently benefit the community *and* enhance the researcher's understanding. Such an approach may intensify the involvement with and commitment to the success of the research for both parties.[71] Collaboratively structured research designs may lead one down an uncharted path of discovery. Such a pathway may newly assess the value of dance research, an assessment best articulated by the members of the community who have guided it. Obviously the goal does not reside in expressly altering people's process, or doing away with the traditional products of research, but in realizing the cognitive ideal of the people we study together with the people we study. Clearly the humanizing effect of such a perspective is one advantage of such research. Ultimately, however, there may be something greater. Through defined involvement and exchange, the researcher may gain a better perspective on the cognitive and affective processes under study —rendering research of greater significance to both academic and researched communities.

Spiraling Steps: Creating an Ethnography

Beginning by selecting and negotiating an ethnographic project, entering the spiral of asking ethnographic questions, collecting ethnographic data, making an ethnographic record, analyzing ethnographic data, and writing (or performing, or producing) an ethnography, James Spradley suggests that "ethnography is usually done with a single general problem in mind: to discover the cultural knowledge people are using to organize their behavior and interpret their experience."[72] He explains that the generality of this goal "encourages the ethnographer to study whatever informants feel is important in a particular cultural scene."[73] Kaeppler cautions us to put the same value on movement events as members of the group one is studying; and Keali'inohomoku reminds us that: "Dance should be studied because it is important to the people involved."[74] Through "the ethnographic research cycle" (see figure 9.1), Spradley has rendered a helpful picture of the nature of ethnographic research. General guidelines such as these will assist dance re-

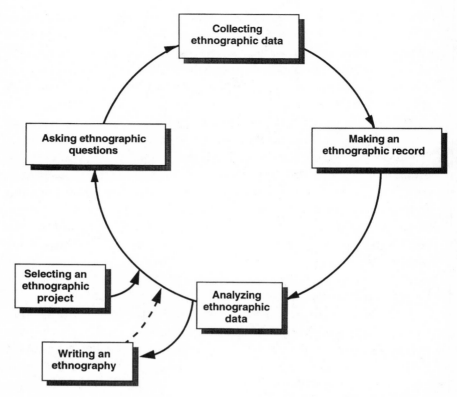

FIG. 9.1. The ethnographic research cycle. From *Participant Observation* by James P. Spradley, copyright © 1980 by Holt, Rinehart and Winston. Reproduced by permission of the publisher.

searchers as they "try on" ethnography as a method. Like the research itself, these guidelines are cyclical in nature. Dancelike, we may find ourselves performing parts of them, moving on to other parts, and returning to revisit earlier steps.

Significantly, ethnography reveals not only the weave of the cultural tapestry studied, but the weave of the ethnographer's cloth as well. It asks the researcher—native and nonnative—to explicitly position self and biases. Dance researchers have followed varying threads through their ethnographic research. The research project—especially if collaboratively conceived—can define broadly divergent and, often, innovative approaches. Each endeavor may yield a different set of requirements for study and, therefore, a different set of contributions to the field. Ethnographic research by its very nature is not formulaic.

Selecting a Project

How does a dance ethnographer select a project? Any number of factors may draw the researcher to the study of dance in a particular social situation or community: native or other personal experience; convenience or accessibility; a defined need within a community; the recognition of a "discrete, self-defined unit";[75] or trusted counsel, among others. Sally Ann Ness, with "no particular interest in Asia" but with determination to apply Laban Movement Analysis to an ethnographic study, chose her field site and topic through the counsel of her advisor, who suggested the Philippines, and a preeminent Filipino literary and culture expert, who suggested the *sinulog*.[76] In the early months of her study she revealed uncertainties about what her choice might bring: "it seemed I'd come halfway around the world to study a meaningless event."[77] Ultimately, through her self-described "ethnographic waltz" with the *sinulogs* of Cebu City, Ness found "that the choreography of each *sinulog* variant became ethnographically meaningful," providing "a form of symbolism that should always be of central value to the discipline of ethnography: the uniquely human act of dancing."[78]

On the other hand, Cynthia Novack's ethnographic work began quite confidently. On the lookout for a subject for an anthropological study of a dance form, she found it in contact improvisation. At the 1980 American Dance Guild conference on improvisation, Novack "realized that contact improvisers constituted a clear social and artistic group, distinct from all the other improvisers at the conference."[79]

Selecting a project includes defining its scope. Most dance ethnographies tend to be either topic-oriented, focusing the study on "one or more aspects of life known to exist in the community," or comprehensive, seeking "to document a total way of life,"[80] as can be viewed through the lens of movement or dance. In addition to finding focus, it is also important to shift focus when appropriate. For example, Yvonne Daniel recounts: "I had planned to study dance in Cuba, but not rumba."[81] Indeed, she had planned "to look at Haitian dance in Cuba."[82] But while in Cuba, she refocused her attention from Haitian dance to rumba, realizing that "rumba could be viewed as an indicator of social conditions and perhaps [as an indicator] of governmental efforts to change attitudes."[83]

Gaining access to a group is central to the viability of the ethnographic project. Often mediated through the personal intervention of another researcher or other personal or professional contacts, seeking and securing permission from appropriate sources is key. Who makes up the community? Who can give "permission"? What are the power relations that will not only affect how a study may be conducted, but the dissemination of the findings, as well? Securing permission from a ministry of culture, a board of directors, a council of elders, a school principal, or simply an individual or group of dancers is a foundational step in the process. Because the level of complexity of a project will impact not only the researcher's involvement but the involvement of the hosts as well, it is essential to consider the value of preliminary explorations, or planning studies, as precursors to more complex studies.

Participant Observation or the Observing Participant

Many dancer-researchers have used the dance experience to traverse the insider-outsider continuum of participant observation. Daniel found that "it is by dancing that one can fully understand dance. By dancing Cuban dance traditions as an observing participant, by sharing critiques of Cuban dance, and by interviewing Cuban dancers, I accumulated basic understandings of Cuban dance, rumba in particular. In these ways, discussions and evaluations were evoked, not only of dance criteria but simultaneously of expressed concerns in Cuban life. These methods, the mainstay of my investigation, verified discoveries made as a result of the more traditional anthropological approach as a participant observer."[84]

Effective participant observation calls for a distinct heightening of awareness. By training ourselves to observe what we may not otherwise note, we see more of the mundane and the extraordinary. In part through her training in Laban Movement Analysis, Ness developed a particularly acute reading of Cebu City and its daily life.

Weaving through insider and outsider perspectives, Novack studied how contact improvisation was taught and learned in a variety of settings, including classes, workshops, and contact jams, with a goal "to describe and analyze the history of a way of life and a way of dancing as part of culture." Novack "attended performances and lectures, and observed dancers in these settings." She progressed to conducting "extended interviews" with a broad range of participants, observers, "and also with people who have only watched it or heard about it." Further, she "consulted written materials about contact improvisation and studied and analyzed videotapes of performances in different stages of the development of the form."[85]

As a true participant and observer, the researcher in the field takes on simultaneous and sometimes contradictory roles. In the course of a year in the field, the researcher may be insider and outsider, friend and stranger, educated researcher and uninformed novice, cultural "appreciator" and cultural illiterate, inquisitive guest and persistent pest, respected person and hopeless clown.[86] Traveling across a diverse range of perspectives can prove to be a genuinely valuable (if, at times, unsettling) strategy, allowing the researcher to see and understand from multiple points of view.

Finally, moving from the general to the particular with the help of valued consultants includes critical assessment of the evolving relationship between researcher and researched. In addition to clarifying the debt owed to the people with whom we work, we can assess the impact upon our research of collaborative practices, including the co-review of fieldwork and of making available copies of papers, presentations, writings, photos, and videos to the people studied, thus enhancing the participation for all concerned.

Talking Back: Field Notes, Notation, Recording

Documentation is critical to effectively utilizing our research. Not only does it record information, situations, and findings, but it speaks back to the ethnographer once the dust of participation has settled. Documentation creates the opportunity to re-search material from the perspective of time and distance. However, research must be documented in accordance with the wishes of the study's consultants. Any recording or note-taking should be cleared with the consultants before beginning. The level of documentation with which consultants feel comfortable is not necessarily constant. In addition to other variables, it may change with the topic, the place, or the growing trust placed in the researcher. About two years into my research with the Volta Ensemble, member Gladys Vodi exclaimed, after I had asked permission to make a recording, "Oh, you can do anything! We're used to you by now!"[87] The courtesy of the question did not appear to go unappreciated, however, and helped to maintain an atmosphere of openness and choice.

Field notes can serve two purposes. A primary purpose of field notes is to document observations of a situation. A secondary purpose is to document inner responses to observations. By recording observations on one side of the page, and simply drawing a line down the outer quarter of the page, we create a space to record our responses to what we observe and experience, including our questions, concerns, and uncertainties. These meta notes can prove helpful when we return to interpret and analyze our observations. They may hold clues missed in outright observations, which can be picked up in a softer way through the use of a meta section. In some instances it may not be possible to record any notes during an event or interview. In these cases, we should make a point of putting pencil to paper as soon as possible. The more we use the language of our consultants without filtering it through our own, the closer we may come to an understanding of their perceptions of their world, and an ability to check our interpretations of their perceptions.

Field notes will multiply as we progress and will require organization. By recording specifics: correct names, exact locations, accurate dates, and, as precisely as possible, what people do and say, field notes can become a veritable reference dictionary of the group with which we are working. When possible, taped interviews should also be recorded in notes. Tape recording an interview without note taking consumes substantial time in transcription, and precludes the opportunity to record key concepts helpful to subsequent transcriptions.

Where does notation fit in? A challenging system to grasp, Labanotation is not "commonly" used although it is the most widely used of any movement notation system. Computer programs, such as Labanwriter developed by the Laban Center at Ohio State University and those developed at Iowa State University and by Dunin at UCLA, render the writing of symbols less time-consuming and somewhat less painstaking. Benesh notation, a somewhat simpler system, was developed primarily for the recording of ballet, although it has been used for other forms.

Williams and Farnell have reexamined Labanotation in the attempt to make it user-friendly, hoping to encourage more practitioners of cultural studies to attend to movement through movement notation. The Laban Script, as Williams and Farnell have called the notation, remains complicated but creates more opportunities for notating "ordinary movement." Farnell does not apologize for the level of complexity of notation because the human body in motion *is* complex.[88]

What place does the precise notation of a performance have in the study of dance in cultural context? This question confronts us with a basic assumption of Labanotation: that the performer wants to do her dance the same way twice. Margaret Drewal argues that "Labanotation was designed for Western dance styles that are more concerned with rendering clear, precise shapes in space. It does not translate well for documenting [for example] African dance styles that are more concerned with subtle transfers in weight through time. It also presumes unimprovised, repeatable dances."[89]

Would Labanotation have contributed to our understanding of the intention of the *tindera's sinulog* which is, as Ness describes the dance, to take the dancer from a tightened to a loosened or freer heart through the sincerity of her prayer?[90] Laban Movement Analysis appears to have offered, in this case, a closer fit.[91]

What can film and video documentation offer? In addition to its usefulness as a tool to learn about the other, video has the potential to inform the researcher about self and biases: for example, what, because of our training and orientation, we may fail to see. A discussion of women dancing is conspicuously absent from John Miller Chernoff's *African Rhythm and African Sensibility: Aesthetics and Social Action in an African Musical Idiom.*[92] Yet in the related video made by

Chernoff with Ibrahim Abdulai, Chernoff's primary consultant from the tradition, it is clear to the eye that dance is valued and performed by the people, especially women, of Dagbon. Indeed, Abdulai's eloquent comments on the place of dance in Dagamba are relegated to the endnotes of Chernoff's book. Chernoff prefaces Abdulai's commentary by "informing" the reader that "dance is the metaphor for participation." Yet just as he demonstrated by video, Abdulai tells Chernoff that dance itself is central to the Dagbon experience:

> Music and dancing help us to be happy.
> There is someone and his somebody dies,
> and as his somebody dies, his heart will be spoiled.
> And if they are able to play and dance, his heart will come to the dance
>   and he will throw away his spoiled heart.
>
> ... The sickness of the heart is hard.
> But if they dance,
> he can collect the worried heart and throw it away.
> It is inside the dance that laughter laughs.
> And the time there is laughter, it is from the dance
> that the laugh comes.
>
> Somebody can come out to dance,
> and his dance you will be watching.
> As he is dancing, you will say that if you watch him,
> maybe you too will be able to dance like him.
> Everyone has got the dance his heart likes,
> and that is why the dances are many in Dagbon.
> And if you have some worry and you look at all this,
> you'll see that your worry will become a bit small.
>
> That is why we like dancing,
> and that is why we give it to our children. ...
> It is something that adds to us, and it makes everyone
> happy.[93]

A recent meeting of the Society for Ethnomusicology demonstrates how video recording and interpretation of the recording can distort emphasis. A young researcher used the video he made of pubescent Balinese youngsters dancing to discuss what he considered to be their emphasis on sexuality in their movements. It was evident to the audience, but not to the researcher—until it was pointed out to him—that he had focused the camera almost exclusively on the pelvises of the girls.[94]

John Blacking cautions that "Films, videotapes, and various notations such as Laban and Benesh are all useful tools for referring to the object of study, but they cannot describe or explain what is happening as human experience, because dance as a topic of anthropological study is about subjective action and conscious human intentions, not only about observed behavior."[95] Rather than objectify or reify the human experience or supersede the complexities of context, good documentation will help the researcher to deepen understandinig about "the uniquely human act of dancing."[96]

Product: The Woven Cloth

Ethnographic research may follow the needs and desires of the researched, or it may follow the perceived needs and desires of the researcher, independent of the researched. In academia, for example, the traditional emphasis may be on writing for an academic audience. This bias may differ from, be unresponsive to, or be at odds with the goals and needs of the community studied. A reciprocal research pattern considers what one will return to the community in one's work and may question, for example, the more typical products of research—the traditional yardsticks of academic success—such as findings published in books or journals versus community-defined or process-oriented projects. A reciprocally structured or interactive ethnographic project may call for a special product tailored to, or expressive of the goals and needs of, the community studied. Reaching beyond the standard notions of research product to include consideration of products as diverse as film, video, article, performance, festival, interactive project, conference paper, lecture-demonstration, and so on may yield results that expand the significance of ethnographic research. A "final" product may, in fact, combine several modalities and identify both researchers and research communities as creative ethno-activists.

For example, "A Moving Community: Dance in Contexts of Culture and Power," a CORD Network Conference held at the University of Maryland at College Park in October 1992, "examined the ways dance functions to create communities in the diverse landscape of internationalism, ethnicity, and power" and used greater Washington, D.C., as a point of focus. Emphasizing first voice scholarship, participants and researchers of diverse cultural systems joined with nonnative researchers to present multiple voices in research. By demonstrating through varied modalities how the "margins" could redefine and enhance the mainstream of the dance community, the conference sought to encourage greater public and self-recognition among immigrant and nonmainstream performing groups to expand their audiences, and to enhance their opportunities for receiving funding and critical press coverage.

Without the support of grants, opportunities to present one's work, and the general support of the academic environment, it would be extraordinarily challenging to conduct research. Therefore, it is important to effectively articulate both the value and the ethical underpinnings of such revised models within artistic, academic, and funding settings. Pre-Boas, cultural studies in the discipline of anthropology were often attempts to explain and justify colonialism to its perpetrators. Early research on dance in culture emerged from this past and is tainted with notions of subjugation, otherness, exotica, and cultural superiority. In a world where so many have capitalized on others in the name of research, assessing the return to the communities we study may be increasingly considered de rigueur. As a practice, ethnography can shift emphasis in the research from the sole needs of the researcher and his or her cultural system (most often, the academy), to serving a broader set of purposes. By reconfiguring the notion of product our work can respond with integrity to calls for socially responsible research for the twenty-first century.

Ethical Practice: Not Poisoning the Well

What are our responsibilities to the people whose lives and cultures we study? Although an explicit study of the ethics of dance ethnography is not yet in print,[97] the American Anthropological Association has provided a set of guidelines that can inform dance research.[98] What steps are necessary to take to protect the interests of the participants in the research project? Are the voices of the researched heard and valued as determined by consultants—or is valuing left entirely to the researchers? Have the researchers clearly communicated who they are, what their plans are, and how they will act upon what they learn?

Among multiple responsibilities to the public and the profession, the American Anthropological Association asks researchers:

- to be truthful but also consider the social/political ramifications of information disseminated; confidences are to be held without compromise;
- to contribute professional expertise to the formation of grounds upon which public policy may be founded;
- to bear responsibility for the good reputation of the discipline and its practitioners. Not to jeopardize the future research or employment of themselves or others;
- to give full credit to all who have contributed to the work.[99]

Practical Concerns

Research costs money. Ethnographic research is no exception and, in fact, may be more costly than other methods. Budgeting expenditures of time and money can be crucial to the success of the ethnographic project.

In addition to possible language study and extensive library work, ethnographic research involves a significant commitment of time in the field; and language study, literature research, and fieldwork may all include travel. Ethnographic research may require becoming competent with operating equipment—under potentially unfamiliar conditions—in order to document and preserve fieldwork and to review it in playback with consultants.[100] Access to equipment requires planning to purchase or borrow. Advance planning is essential for locating a research community, corresponding with a consultant or government official to plan research access, and submitting proposals to fund the research. Medical and political concerns need to be taken into consideration and assessed with care, including evaluating the need for emergency evacuation and other travel insurance. The Society for Ethnomusicology has published a concise and practical handbook that dance ethnographers may find useful as they develop practical strategies for their research: *A Manual for Documentation, Fieldwork and Preservation for Ethnomusicologists.*[101]

Beginning with Self

How can we take up the thread of culture to weave our own tapestry of ethnographic research? How can we learn to enter the arena fully engaged and participating and, on cue, step back to observe not only the self participating, but the whole context of study? How can we develop the particular ability to see dance as a part of culture and culture as a part of dance? Perhaps by beginning with ourselves.

We can start here—anywhere we are. The notion of the field has long since transformed from the perceived exoticism of far-off lands to the tangible and, often, local arena. An exercise I call "Knowing Self as Other" is designed to introduce the notion of studying dance and movement in an important cultural context —our own. The goal of the exercise is simple: to create (through writing, choreographing, improvising, map-making, or a combination of modalities) "a personal movement ethnography," that is, an inscribing (graphy) of our movement within the context of a group of people (ethno) with whom we identify ourselves. The exercise assumes that as dance researchers—writers, historians, philosophers, performers, choreographers, and teachers of dance—we are all engaged to some degree in the study of dance as cultural practice. The exercise further assumes that, through our own lived experience, we are already experts in a cultural movement system—our own.

The creation of a personal movement ethnography asks us to turn the lens on ourselves. Each of us has a voice and experience of what it means to be part of, in harmony and dissonance with, a "nation," a "people," a "we." Within the context of a defining group, we reveal ourselves to ourselves as part of a movement culture. We see ourselves situated in the mainstream and/or the margins of a movement culture, negotiating across its boundaries. As we situate ourselves in time, place, and movement, our own life experiences demonstrate the pervasiveness of culture in our lives. Such awareness may lift the fog of self and help us to focus beyond our own cultural expectations. We may experience firsthand that ethnography reveals its object through the lens of the researcher's interpretation of the object—as a dialogue between researcher and researched. Making explicit our understanding of ourselves in cultural context, then, may not only reveal our own biases to ourselves but enhance the empathy, accuracy, and urgency with which we portray the other in our texts.

Ethnographic research connects the researcher to a wide range of interdisciplinary discussions. In addition to creating important studies in dance ethnography and the anthropology of movement, ethnographic methods have the potential to enhance many other areas of dance research. Increasing numbers of choreographers, historians, and movement analysts, among others, appear to find ethnography's "enduring respect for context and detail"[102] a valuable research tool. Tracing the weave of dance in the fabric of culture is potentially the work of not only dance ethnographers, but dance researchers of all kinds. Follow the thread.

Study Questions

1. How much detail do you perceive in a given situation? Practice describing: physical settings in detail, movement worlds, sound worlds, olfactory worlds, touch worlds, both separately and together.

2. Can you see yourself as part of a culture? Write a two-page mini-ethnography based on a specific social situation in which you play a part.

3. Name five possible ethnographic projects in dance or movement. How do they compare? Assess the likenesses and differences of the projects in terms of: accessibility, protocol for permission, level of familiarity desired or required, requirements for preparation, opportunities for active participation, possibility for

long-term study, potential ethical problems, and other factors appropriate to the particular studies.

As a class, share your assumptions or preconceived notions about the suggested projects. What do your assumptions reveal about yourselves and the perspectives you bring to research?

4. Consider alternative models for conducting ethnographic research and corresponding alternative "end-products." How do these models compare with other ethnographic studies?

5. Prepare a two-page letter of inquiry to seek funding for an ethnographic project. Include statement of problem, description of methods and goals, proposed timeline of research, and preliminary budget.

NOTES

1. I am grateful to Joann W. Keali'inohomoku for her thoughtful comments on an earlier version of this chapter.

2. Adrienne L. Kaeppler, "Structured Movement Systems in Tonga," in *Society and the Dance,* ed. Paul Spencer (New York: Cambridge University Press, 1985), 92 (hereafter "Structured Movement").

3. Adrienne L. Kaeppler, "American Approaches to the Study of Dance," *1991 Yearbook for Traditional Music* 13:11–21 (hereafter "American Approaches").

4. Sally Ann Ness, *Body, Movement, and Culture: Kinesthetic and Visual Symbolism in a Philippine Community* (Philadelphia: University of Pennsylvania Press, 1992), 89 (hereafter *Body, Movement and Culture*).

5. Cynthia Novack, *Sharing the Dance: Contact Improvisation and American Culture* (Madison: University of Wisconsin Press, 1990) (hereafter *Sharing the Dance*).

6. Kaeppler, "Structured Movement," 92; Margaret Thompson Drewal, "The State of Research on Performance in Africa," in *African Studies Review* 34, no. 3 (December 1991): 1–64 (hereafter "The State of Research").

7. Joan D. Frosch, "Things of Significance Do Not Vanish: Dance and the Transmission of Culture in a Ghanaian Community," *UCLA Journal of Dance Ethnology* 15 (1991): 54–67 (hereafter "Things of Significance").

8. Joann W. Keali'inohomoku, "Theory and Methods for an Anthropological Study of Dance" (Ph.D. diss., Indiana University, 1976a), 10–11 (hereafter "Theory and Methods").

9. James Clifford, *The Predicament of Culture: Twentieth Century Ethnography, Literature, and Arts* (Cambridge: Harvard University Press, 1988) (hereafter *The Predicament of Culture*).

10. Adrienne L. Kaeppler, "Dance in Anthropological Perspective," *Annual Review of Anthropology* 7 (1978): 33 (hereafter "Anthropological Perspective").

11. Kaeppler, "Anthropological Perspective," 33.

12. Franziska Boas, *The Function of Dance in Human Society* (Brooklyn: Dance Horizons, 1972), 1. In her preface to the second edition of *The Function of Dance in Human Society,* Boas makes explicit her awareness of the inappropriateness and imprecision of the terms *primitive* and *exotic* by encasing them in quotation marks.

13. "The overall aim of this type of explanatory paradigm was to describe danced and

ritual behaviors in terms of social needs and social equilibrium, such that both were viewed primarily as adaptive or adjustive responses either to the social or the physical environment. Functionalism was mainly an heuristic device: an indicator only for describing the *role* of the dance (and ritual) in society." Drid Williams, *Ten Lectures on Theories of the Dance* (Metuchen, N.J.: Scarecrow Press, 1991), 119 (hereafter *Ten Lectures*).

14. Williams, *Ten Lectures,* 149.

15. St. Denis in Deborah Jowitt, *Time and the Dancing Image* (New York: William Morrow, 1988), 130.

16. La Meri was the stage name of Russell Merriweather Hughes.

17. Shawn in Gertrude Kurath, "Panorama of Dance Ethnology," *Current Anthropology* 1, no. 3 (1960): 33 (hereafter "Panorama").

18. Ruth Beckman, *Katherine Dunham: A Biography* (New York: Marcel Dekker, 1979), 30. Jeannine Dominy, *Katherine Dunham* (New York: Chelsea House, 1992), 39.

19. Katherine Dunham, *Island Possessed* (Chicago: University of Chicago Press, 1969), 3, 5, 6.

20. See also Katherine Dunham, "Form and Function in Primitive Dance," *Educational Dance* 4, no. 4 (1941): 2–4; and Katherine Dunham, *Journey to Accompong* (New York: Henry Holt, 1946).

21. Melville J. Herskovits, *The Myth of the Negro Past* (Boston: Beacon Press, 1958), 270.

22. See Dorothy B. Barrère, Mary Kawena Pukui, and Marion Kelly, *Hula, Historical Perspectives* (Honolulu: Department of Anthropology, Bernice Pauahi Bishop Museum, 1980).

23. At the 90th annual meeting of the American Anthropological Association in Chicago, the contributions to anthropology of Katherine Dunham and Dr. Pearl Primus were the focus of a session entitled "African American Dance in Research and Applied Theory: Katherine Dunham and Pearl Primus." The session was chaired by Joyce C. Aschenbrenner and Yvonne Daniel.

24. Personal communication, Joann W. Keali'inohomoku, 1998.

25. Kurath is generally considered by dance scholars to be the founder of the field of "dance ethnology." For example, Kaeppler refers to her as "the parent of dance ethnology" in Kaeppler, "Anthropological Perspective," 31; and Allegra Fuller Snyder cites 1960, the year of the publication of "Panorama of Dance Ethnology," as the year the field of dance ethnology was born, in Snyder, "Past, Present, and Future," *UCLA Journal of Dance Ethnology* 16 (1992): 1–28.

26. Joann W. Keali'inohomoku, "An Anthropologist Looks at Ballet as a Form of Ethnic Dance," *Impulse* 20 (1970): 24–33 (hereafter "An Anthropologist Looks at Ballet").

27. Kurath, "Panorama," 250.

28. Gertrude Prokosch Kurath, "Research Methods of Gertrude Kurath," in *CORD Research Annual VI, New Dimensions in Dance Research: Anthropology and Dance—the American Indian.* Proceedings of the Third Conference on Research in Dance, ed. Tamara Comstock (New York: Committee on Research in Dance, 1974), note 35 (hereafter "Research Methods").

29. Frisbie in Joann W. Keali'inohomoku, "Honoring Gertrude Kurath," *UCLA Journal of Dance Ethnology* 10 (1986): 5 (hereafter "Honoring Gertrude Kurath").

30. Kurath, "Research Methods," 38.

31. Adrienne L. Kaeppler, "Review of Half a Century of Dance Research by Gertrude Kurath," *Dance Research Journal* 20, no. 1 (1988): 47–49 (hereafter "Review").

32. Kaeppler, "Anthropological Perspective," 47.

33. See Joann W. Keali'inohomoku, "A Comparative Study of Dance as a Constellation

of Motor Behaviors Among African and United States Negroes," in *Reflections and Perspectives on Two Anthropological Studies of Dance, CORD Research Annual 7*: 1–179; Joann W. Keali'inohomoku, "Music and Dance of the Hawaiian and Hopi Peoples," in *Becoming Human Through Music: The Wesleyan Symposium on the Perspectives of Social Anthropology in the Teaching and Learning of Music* (Reston, Va.: Music Educators National Conference [Symposium Papers], 1985), 5–22; and Joann W. Keali'inohomoku, "Hopi and Hawaiian Responses to Cultural Contact" (paper presented to the Quincentenary Program, Smithsonian Institution, Washington, D.C., 1988).

34. Allegra Fuller Snyder, "Past, Present, and Future," *UCLA Journal of Dance Ethnology* 16 (1992): 5 (hereafter "Past, Present and Future"). Snyder also stated that "leading into the current views of our body of knowledge was Franziska Boas' publication, *The Function of Dance in Human Society* [1944]," 7.

35. Allegra Fuller Snyder, "The Dance Symbol," in *CORD Research Annual VI, New Dimensions in Dance Research: Anthropology and Dance—the American Indian*. Proceedings of the Third Conference on Research in Dance, ed. Tamara Comstock (New York: Committee on Research in Dance, 1974), 215, see also 223 (hereafter "The Dance Symbol").

36. Allegra Fuller Snyder, "Level of Events Patterns: A Theoretical Model Applied to the Yaqui Easter Ceremonies," in *The Dance Event: A Complex Phenomenon,* proceedings of the International Council for Traditional Music study group for ethnochoreology, comp. Lisbet Torp (Copenhagen, Denmark: ICTM, 1989) (first version of the paper presented in 1978).

37. Yvonne Daniel, *Rumba: Dance and Social Change in Contemporary Cuba* (Bloomington: Indiana University Press, 1995) (hereafter *Rumba*).

38. Williams, *Ten Lectures*, xi.

39. Drid Williams, "An Exercise in Applied Personal Anthropology," *Dance Research Journal* 11, no. 1 (1976): 16–30.

40. Matteo's full name is Matteo Marcellus Vittucci.

41. Bartenieff introduced this work to the members of the Committee on Research in Dance in the Preliminary Conference on Research in Dance held in Riverdale, New York, on May 26–28, 1967.

42. Alan Lomax, Irmgard Bartenieff, and Forrestine Paulay, "Choreometrics: A Method for the Study of Cross-Cultural Pattern in Film," *CORD Research Annual VI, New Dimensions in Dance Research: Anthropology and Dance—the American Indian*. Proceedings of the Third Conference on Research in Dance, ed. Tamara Comstock (New York: Committee on Research in Dance, 1974), 203. (Originally published in *Sonderdruck aus Research Film* 6 [1969].)

43. Lomax presented the Global Jukebox at the American Anthropological Association meetings in Washington, D.C., in 1990.

44. The following is a Choreometrics observation: "The single most potent observation to be made about movement cross-culturally is whether the trunk is handled as one or several units." Alan Lomax, Irmgard Bartenieff, and Forrestine Paulay, "Dance Style and Culture," in *Folk Song Style and Culture,* ed. Alan Lomax (Washington, D.C.: American Association for the Advancement of Science, 1972), 222–47.

The danger of reductionist/objectivist thinking as demonstrated above is that it removes dance from relationship with context, rendering oversimplified, potentially useless cultural comparisons. However, when tied to a contextual approach, Effort-Shape analysis can yield studies that may contribute to cultural studies of dance (see Ness, *Body, Movement, and Culture;* and Joan D. Frosch, "'. . . And Tell Me America, Where Is Your Dance?':

Examining Body, Effort, Shape and Space in the Diversity Artist Project with the Urban Bush Women" [Certification in Movement Analysis thesis, Laban/Bartenieff School of Movement Studies, New York, 1995], hereafter "And Tell Me America").

45. See Keali'inohomoku, "An Anthropologist Looks at Ballet," and Novack, *Sharing the Dance.*

46. Drewal, "The State of Research," 25.

47. See also Judith Lynne Hanna, *To Dance Is Human: A Theory of Non-Verbal Communication* (Austin: University of Texas Press, 1979); Anya Peterson Royce, *The Anthropology of Dance* (Bloomington: Indiana University Press, 1977); Novack, *Sharing the Dance.*

48. For example, Dissertation Abstracts did not add the word *dance* to its keyword search until 1991.

49. See also Williams, *Ten Lectures,* 127, 136–37; Kaeppler, "Review," 47–48; Keali'inohomoku, "Theory and Methods," 6–7.

50. Keali'inohomoku, "Theory and Methods," 9.

51. Ibid., i.

52. Kaeppler, "Anthropological Perspective," 41.

53. Williams, *Ten Lectures,* 16.

54. Kaeppler, "American Approaches," 12.

55. Ibid., 3.

56. Ness, *Body, Movement, and Culture,* 4.

57. Hultkrantz, cited in Anthony Seeger, "Ethnography of Music," in *Ethnomusicology: An Introduction,* ed. Helen Myers (New York: W. W. Norton, 1992), 88 (hereafter "Ethnography of Music").

58. See James Clifford, *The Predicament of Culture: Twentieth Century Ethnography, Literature, and Arts* (Cambridge: Harvard University Press, 1988); Michael Jackson, *Paths Toward a Clearing: Radical Empiricism and Ethnographic Inquiry* (Indianapolis: Indiana University Press, 1989); George E. Marcus and James Clifford, *Writing Culture: The Poetics and Politics of Ethnography* (Los Angeles: University of California Press, 1986); Paul Stoller, *The Taste of Ethnographic Things: The Senses in Anthropology* (Philadelphia: University of Pennsylvania Press, 1989); et al.

59. James P. Spradley, *Participant Observation* (Fort Worth: Harcourt Brace Jovanovich, 1980), vii (hereafter *Participant Observation*).

60. Seeger, "Ethnography of Music," 88–89.

61. Deidre Sklar, "Invigorating Dance Ethnology," *UCLA Journal of Dance Ethnology* 15 (1991): 4–15, 6 (hereafter "Invigorating Dance Ethnology").

62. Daniel, *Rumba,* inverted "participant observation" to "observing participant" to more accurately reflect her practice of dance ethnography.

63. Ness, *Body, Movement, and Culture,* 12.

64. Sklar, "Invigorating Dance Ethnology," 11.

65. Ibid., 12.

66. Frosch, "Things of Significance," 55.

67. Frosch, "Things of Significance."

68. Carolina E. Robertson and Marcia A. Herndon, personal communication, 1993.

69. George E. Marcus and Michael M. J. Fischer, *Anthropology as Cultural Critique: An Experimental Moment in the Human Sciences* (Chicago: University of Chicago Press, 1986), 159 (hereafter *Anthropology as Cultural Critique*).

70. Loyce Arthur, personal communication, 1995.

71. See Johannes Fabian, *Power and Performance: Ethnographic Explorations Through*

Proverbial Wisdom and Theatre in Shaba, Zaire (Madison: University of Wisconsin Press, 1990).

72. Spradley, *Participant Observation,* 31.

73. Ibid.

74. Keali'inohomoku, "Theory and Methods," 10–11.

75. Novack, *Sharing the Dance,* 17.

76. Ness, personal communication, 1996.

77. Ness, *Body, Movement, and Culture,* 24.

78. Ibid., 232, 233.

79. Novack, *Sharing the Dance,* 17.

80. Hymes, cited in Spradley, *Participant Observation,* 31.

81. Daniel, *Rumba,* 13.

82. Daniel, personal communication, 1996.

83. Daniel, *Rumba,* 13.

84. Ibid.

85. Novack, *Sharing the Dance,* 17.

86. See Ness (*Body, Movement, and Culture,* 16) for other perspectives, such as "passing visitor," "interviewer," "performer," and "temporary resident of the city," that she found "useful to an ethnographer studying choreographic phenomena with a performer's orientation."

87. Gladys Vodi, personal communication, 1993.

88. Brenda Farnell, personal communication, 1991.

89. Drewal, "The State of Research," 50, n. 22. My parenthetical insert.

90. Ness, *Body, Movement, and Culture,* 113.

91. See chapter 10 on Laban Movement Analysis in this volume.

92. John Miller Chernoff, *African Rhythm and African Sensibility: Aesthetics and Social Action in African Musical Idioms* (Chicago: University of Chicago Press, 1979) (hereafter *Rhythm and Sensibility*).

93. Abdulai cited in Chernoff, *Rhythm and Sensibility,* 220.

94. See also Williams, *Ten Lectures,* for a discussion on the study of meaning in movement.

95. John Blacking, ed., *The Anthropology of the Body* (London: Academic Press, 1977), 12.96.

96. Ness, *Body Movement and Culture,* 23.

97. Joan D. Frosch, "Keeping the Poison Out of the Well: Ethical Considerations in the Practice of Dance Ethnography" (paper presented at the 1996 Dance Research Forum of the American Association of Physical Education, Recreation, and Dance, Atlanta).

See also Keali'inohomoku, "Ethical Considerations for Choreographers, Ethnologists, and White Knights," *UCLA Journal of Dance Ethnology* 5 (1981): 10–23.

98. Council of the American Anthropological Association, "Statement on Ethics: Principles of Professional Responsibility," October 1990 (1971).

99. Ibid.

100. Among others, see Ruth Stone, *Let the Inside Be Sweet: Interpretation of the Music Event Among the Kpelle of Liberia* (Bloomington: Indiana University Press, 1982); and Joan Frosch, "*Nutata:* A Ghanaian Community Comes of Age in America" (paper presented at the Congress on Research in Dance special topics conference: "Moving Communities: Dance in Context of Culture and Power in Greater Washington, D.C.," University of Maryland at College Park, 1992).

101. *A Manual for Documentation, Fieldwork and Preservation for Ethnomusicologists*

(Bloomington, Ind.: The Society for Ethnomusicology, 1994). The manual is available directly from SEM, Morrison Hall, Room 005, Indiana University, Bloomington, Ind. 47405.
102. Marcus and Fischer, *Anthropology as Cultural Critique*, 159.

REFERENCES

American Anthropological Association. "Statement on Ethics: Principles of Professional Responsibility." May 1971, amended through October 1990.

Barrère, Dorothy B., Mary Kawena Pukui, and Marion Kelly. *Hula, Historical Perspectives*. Department of Anthropology, Bernice Pauahi Bishop Museum, 1980.

Beckman, Ruth. *Katherine Dunham: A Biography*. New York: Marcel Dekker, 1979.

Birdwhistell, Ray L. *Kinesics and Context: Essays on Body Motion Communication*. Philadelphia: University of Pennsylvania Press, 1970.

Blacking, John, ed. *The Anthropology of the Body*. London: Academic Press, 1977.

Boas, Franziska. *The Function of Dance in Human Society*. Brooklyn: Dance Horizons, 1972.

Briggs, Charles L. *Learning How to Ask: A Sociolinguistic Appraisal of the Role of the Interview in Social Science Research*. New York: Cambridge University Press, 1986.

Chernoff, John Miller. *African Rhythm and African Sensibility: Aesthetics and Social Action in African Musical Idioms*. Chicago: University of Chicago Press, 1979.

Clifford, James. *The Predicament of Culture: Twentieth-Century Ethnography, Literature, and Arts*. Cambridge: Harvard University Press, 1988.

Comstock, Tamara, ed. *CORD Research Annual VI, New Dimensions in Dance Research: Anthropology and Dance—the American Indian*. New York: Committee on Research in Dance, 1974.

Cowan, Jane K. *Dance and the Body Politic in Northern Greece*. Princeton, N.J.: Princeton University Press, 1990.

Daly, Ann. "Unlimited Partnership: Dance and Feminist Analysis." *Dance Research Journal* 23, no. 1 (spring 1991): 2–5.

Daniel, Yvonne. *Rumba: Dance and Social Change in Contemporary Cuba*. Bloomington: Indiana University Press, 1995.

Dell, Cecily. *A Primer for Movement Description*. New York: Dance Notation Bureau, 1970.

Dominy, Jeannine. *Katherine Dunham*. New York: Chelsea House, 1992.

Drewal, Margaret Thompson. "The State of Research on Performance in Africa." *African Studies Review* 34, no. 3 (December 1991): 1–64.

Dunham, Katherine. "Form and Function in Primitive Dance." *Educational Dance* 4, no. 4 (1941): 2–4.

———. *Journey to Accompong*. New York: Henry Holt, 1946.

———. *Las Danzas de Haiti* (monograph). Mexico: *Acta Anthropologica* 2, no. 4 (1947).

———. *Les Danses d'Haiti*. Paris: Fasquelle, 1950.

———. *Island Possessed*. Chicago: University of Chicago Press, 1969.

———. *Dances of Haiti*. Los Angeles: University of California Center for Afro-American Studies, 1983.

Fabian, Johannes. *Power and Performance: Ethnographic Explorations Through Proverbial Wisdom and Theater in Shaba, Zaire.* Madison: University of Wisconsin Press, 1990.

Farnell, Brenda. "Body Movement Notation." In *International Encyclopedia of Communication,* ed. Eric Barnouw, 1:203–209. New York: Oxford University Press, 1989.

Feld, Steven. *Sound and Sentiment: Birds, Weeping, Poetics, and Song in Kaluli Expression.* Philadelphia: University of Pennsylvania Press, 1982.

Foster, Susan Leigh. *Reading Dancing: Bodies and Subjects in Contemporary American Dance.* Berkeley: University of California Press, 1986.

Fox, Richard G. *Recapturing Anthropology: Working in the Present.* Santa Fe: School of American Research Press, 1991.

Frosch, Joan D. "Things of Significance Do Not Vanish: Dance and the Transmission of Culture in a Ghanaian Community." *UCLA Journal of Dance Ethnology* 15 (1991): 54–67.

———. "*Nutata:* A Ghanaian Community Comes of Age in America." Paper presented at Congress on Research in Dance special topics conference: "Moving Communities: Dance in Contexts of Culture and Power in Greater Washington, D.C.," University of Maryland at College Park, 1992.

———. "Recreating Cultural Memory: The Notion of Tradition in Ghanaian-American Performance." *UCLA Journal of Dance Ethnology* 18 (1994): 17–23.

———. "'. . . And Tell Me America, Where Is Your Dance?': Examining Body, Effort, Shape, and Space in the Diversity Artist Project with the Urban Bush Women." Certification in Movement Analysis thesis, Laban/Bartenieff Institute of Movement Studies, New York, 1995.

———. "Keeping the Poison Out of the Well: Ethical Considerations in the Practice of Dance Ethnography." Paper presented at the Dance Research Forum of the American Association of Physical Education, Recreation, and Dance, 1996. Atlanta, Ga.

Geertz, Clifford. *The Interpretation of Cultures.* New York: Basic Books, Inc., 1973.

Georges, Robert A., and Michael O. Jones. *People Studying People: The Human Element in Fieldwork.* Berkeley and Los Angeles: University of California Press, 1980.

Hanna, Judith Lynne. "The Anthropology of the Body." Association of Social Anthropology conference, Belfast report in *Dance Research Journal* 7, no. 2 (1975): 39–43.

———. *To Dance Is Human: A Theory of Non-Verbal Communication.* Austin: University of Texas Press, 1979.

———. *Dance, Sex and Gender: Signs of Identity, Dominance, Defiance and Desire.* Chicago: University of Chicago Press, 1988.

Herndon, Marcia, and Norma McLeod. *Music as Culture.* Pt. Richmond, Calif.: MRI Press, 1990.

Herskovits, Melville J. *The Myth of the Negro Past.* Boston: Beacon Press, (c. 1941) 1958.

Hutchinson, Ann. *Labanotation: The System for Recording and Analyzing Movement.* 3d ed. London: Oxford University Press, 1977.

Jackson, Michael. *Paths Toward a Clearing: Radical Empiricism and Ethnographic Inquiry.* Indianapolis: Indiana University Press, 1989.

Jowitt, Deborah. *Time and the Dancing Image.* New York: William Morrow, 1988.

Kaeppler, Adrienne L. "Method and Theory in Analyzing Dance Structure with an Analysis of Tongan Dance." *Ethnomusicology* 16, no. 2 (1972): 173–217.

———. "Dance in Anthropological Perspective." *Annual Review of Anthropology* 7 (1978): 31–49.

———. "Structured Movement Systems in Tonga." In *Society and the Dance,* ed. Paul Spencer, 92–118. New York: Cambridge University Press, 1985.

———. "Review of *Half a Century of Dance Research* by Gertrude Kurath" (book review). *Dance Research Journal* 20, no. 1 (1988): 47–49.

———. "Dance." In *International Encyclopedia of Communication,* ed. Eric Barnouw, 1:450–54. New York: Oxford University Press, 1989.

———. "American Approaches to the Study of Dance." *1991 Yearbook for Traditional Music* 13:11–21. International Council for Traditional Music, 1991.

Keali'inohomoku, Joann. "An Anthropologist Looks at Ballet as a Form of Ethnic Dance." *Impulse* 20 (1970): 24–33.

———. "Theory and Methods for an Anthropological Study of Dance." Ph.D. diss., Indiana University, 1976a.

———. "A Comparative Study of Dance as a Constellation of Motor Behaviors Among African and United States Negroes." In *Reflections and Perspectives on Two Anthropological Studies of Dance, CORD Dance Research Annual* 7 (1976): 1–179.

———. "Dance Ethnology—the State of the Study." Paper presented to the Society for Ethnomusicology, Baltimore, Md., 1982.

———. "Ethnic Historical Study," in *Dance History Research: Perspectives from Related Arts and Disciplines,* Proceedings of the Second Conference on Research in Dance, ed. Joann W. Keali'nohomoku (1970), 86–97.

———. "Music and Dance of the Hawaiian and Hopi Peoples." In *Becoming Human Through Music: The Wesleyan Symposium on the Perspectives of Social Anthropology in the Teaching and Learning of Music* (Reston, Va.: Music Educators National Conference [Symposium Papers], 1985), 5–22.

———. "Honoring Gertrude Kurath." *UCLA Journal of Dance Ethnology* 10 (1986): 3–6.

———. "Hopi and Hawaiian Responses to Cultural Contact" Paper presented to the Quincentenary Program, Smithsonian Institution, Washington, D.C., 1988.

———. "Variables that Affect Gender Actions and Reactions in Dance Ethnology Fieldwork: A Praxis." *UCLA Journal of Dance Ethnology* 13 (1989): 48–53.

Koskoff, Ellen, ed. *Women and Music in Cross-Cultural Perspective.* Urbana: University of Illinois Press, 1987.

Kurath, Gertrude Prokosch. "Panorama of Dance Ethnology." *Current Anthropology* 1, no. 3 (1960): 223–54.

———. *Half a Century of Dance Research.* Flagstaff: Cross Cultural Dance Resources, 1986.

Lamb, Warren, and Elizabeth Watson. *Body Code: The Meaning in Movement.* London: Routledge Kegan Paul, 1979.

Lomax, Alan, Irmgard Bartenieff, and Forrestine Paulay. "Dance Style and Culture." In *Folk Song Style and Culture,* ed. Alan Lomax, 222–47. Washington, D.C.: American Association for the Advancement of Science, 1968.

Marcus, George E., and James Clifford. *Writing Culture: The Poetics and Politics of Ethnography.* Los Angeles: University of California Press, 1986.

Marcus, George E., and Michael M. J. Fischer. *Anthropology as Cultural Critique: An Experimental Moment in the Human Sciences.* Chicago: University of Chicago Press, 1986.

Merleau-Ponty, Maurice. *Phenomenology of Perception,* trans. C. Smith. London: Routledge Kegan Paul, 1962.

Myers, Helen. *Ethnomusicology: Historical and Regional Studies.* New York: W. W. Norton, 1992.

Ness, Sally Ann. *Body, Movement, and Culture: Kinesthetic and Visual Symbolism in a Philippine Community.* Philadelphia: University of Pennsylvania Press, 1992.

Nketia, J. H. Kwabena. *The Music of Africa.* New York: W. W. Norton, 1974.

Novack, Cynthia J. *Sharing the Dance: Contact Improvisation and American Culture.* Madison: University of Wisconsin Press, 1990.

Peacock, James. *The Anthropological Lens.* New York: Cambridge University Press, 1986.

Royce, Anya Peterson. *The Anthropology of Dance.* Bloomington: Indiana University Press, 1977.

Schechner, Richard. *Between Theater and Anthropology.* Philadelphia: University of Pennsylvania Press, 1985.

Seeger, Anthony. "Ethnography of Music." In *Ethnomusicology: An Introduction,* ed. Helen Myers, 88–109. New York: W. W. Norton, 1992.

Sklar, Deidre. "Invigorating Dance Ethnology." *UCLA Journal of Dance Ethnology* 15 (1991): 4–15.

Snyder, Allegra Fuller. "The Dance Symbol." In *CORD Research Annual VI, New Dimensions in Dance Research: Anthropology and Dance—the American Indian.* Proceedings of the Third Conference on Research in Dance, ed. Tamara Comstock, 213–25. 1972.

Spradley, James P. *The Ethnographic Interview.* Fort Worth: Harcourt Brace Jovanovich College Publishers, 1979.

———. *Participant Observation.* Fort Worth: Harcourt Brace Jovanovich College Publishers, 1980.

Stoller, Paul. *The Taste of Ethnographic Things: The Senses in Anthropology.* Philadelphia: University of Pennsylvania Press, 1989.

Stone, Ruth. *Let the Inside Be Sweet: The Interpretation of Music Event Among the Kpelle of Liberia.* Bloomington: Indiana University Press, 1982.

Thomas, Helen, ed. *Dance, Gender and Culture.* London: Macmillan, 1990.

Whitehead, Tony L., and Mary Ellen Conaway, eds. *Self, Sex, and Gender in Cross-Cultural Fieldwork.* Urbana: University of Illinois Press, 1986.

Williams, Drid. "An Exercise in Applied Personal Anthropology." *Dance Research Journal* 11, no. 1 (1977): 16–30.

———. *Ten Lectures on Theories of the Dance.* Metuchen, N.J.: Scarecrow Press, 1991.

Williams, Drid, and Brenda Farnell. *The Laban Script: A Beginning Text on Movement Writing for Non-dancers.* Canberra: Australian Institute of Aboriginal and Torres Strait Islander Studies, 1990.

PART THREE

RESEARCH TOOLS AND ISSUES

SPECIFIC TO DANCE

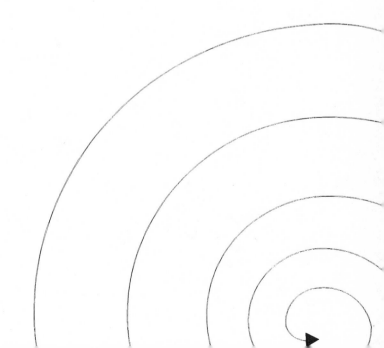

10 EVERY LITTLE MOVEMENT HAS A MEANING ALL ITS OWN

Movement Analysis in Dance Research

Mary Alice Brennan

To STATE THAT HUMAN MOVEMENT is the basis of dance is not a revelation. What is surprising is that its detailed study has not more fully permeated all areas of dance research and that a conceptual framework and systematic approach of movement analysis applicable for inclusion in varied research designs is still not widely accepted. Attention to the analysis of dance movement is not new. For centuries people have given verbal descriptions of steps, drawn pictures or symbols of dance, and eloquently detailed in words the poetry of dance movement. Through these efforts present-day scholars have clues to what dance in the past might have looked liked, how it was performed, and how it derived from or contributed to a particular society or culture. New in recent decades are attempts to impose greater order on the complexities of movement phenomena in order that they can be recorded, preserved, learned, or studied and to edge toward systematic methods of analysis that might be useful beyond a single research question or project.

The Nature of Movement Analysis

What do we mean by movement analysis? Analysis is the examination of a whole to distinguish its component parts. Therefore, in dance research, movement analysis at a basic level is a concern with any aspect of what the human body is doing as it moves or in some instances remains still. It might concern what part or parts of the body are moving, where they are moving, the time the movement takes or how the movement is executed—or it might involve all of these possibilities. These points of inquiry can, of course, refer to any movement—washing our hands, hitting a tennis ball, or talking with a friend—and the more sophisticated systems of analysis can be applied to forms of movement other than dance. A movement might be as subtle as exhaling a breath or as obvious as stamping the foot.

What is initially important for useful analysis in any of these or other movement activities is to know precisely what is happening. Exhaling the breath can be done in any number of ways. It can take a short or long time, the torso can have various shapes and configurations, and adjacent body parts may move as well. In stamping the foot the leg may be raised just a little way off the ground or it may be brought up high and close to the body, the torso may be bent over to impart more force or remain straight, and the foot may strike with minimum energy or with great vigor. In each of these examples the reader has a general idea of an action based on movement terms that are part of a common vocabulary, but too much information is missing to know precisely what occurred. Also absent in these examples is the context of the movement. Was the breath exhalation a sigh of resignation or an attempt to blow out a candle? Is the stamping foot part of an angry tantrum or a movement in a folk dance? Movement description, as the first level of analysis, "permits a *synthesis* of the results of the detailed observation with contextual knowledge, which then furthers the process of *interpreting* and *evaluating* the dance."[1] What should be understood is that movement analysis as a methodology is not complete until it is integrated into the larger focus of the study. It is at this point that it acquires meaning in scholarly inquiry.

The approach to a method of movement analysis as well as the subsequent steps in the process are dependent upon the broader focus of the research, which includes the underlying theory or question, the research design, the methodological strategies employed, and the background and expertise of the researcher. There is no one method of movement analysis that fits every study, and given the diversity of dance perhaps that is well and good. As research in dance develops, new approaches will be sought to meet contemporary needs and the enhanced skills of dance scholars. But concurrent with openness to new methods there is also a search for analytic techniques in movement, which can be shared among groups of scholars, so they might build on previous research rather than each inventing a separate system, which serves little heuristic function.

Systems of Movement Analysis

Methods of movement analysis used in dance research fall into three general categories: (1) word descriptions, (2) single-use systems, and (3) complex analytic systems accepted by certain researchers in the field. In word descriptions commonly understood terms are used to depict movement with the goal to give a sense of the action within a broader treatment of dance movement without invoking a specialized or technical vocabulary. The author does not attempt to create new terms or specific jargon or develop a unique system of explanation. The movement description is often interwoven with commentary on other aspects of the dance event or activities. Word descriptions of dance movement abound in the literature and are frequently, but not exclusively, found in anthropological, ethnographic, historical, and philosophical dance research. The descriptive language choices of an investigator reflect the needs of the study, and in many instances a more detailed movement analysis is unnecessary or inappropriate.

In the single-use category an investigator creates a unique method of classifying and analyzing movement to fit the research design. This may include using a mixture of approaches and borrowing features of another system. Unique approaches to movement analysis devised by a researcher to fit the particular data of interest and their integration within the broader context of a study may reflect a highly sophisticated framework but may only be used by the creator for his or her own projects. Occasionally other researchers may adopt someone's analytic system if it fits a research need, but usually its use stays with the originator.

The third grouping includes analytic systems, based on elaborate conceptual frameworks using words, signs, or symbols[2] to designate aspects of human movement, that have gained some acceptance among a group of scholars. Each system has a generally agreed upon word vocabulary and taxonomy of signs. Laban Movement Analysis systems, which include Labanotation or Kinetography Laban,[3] and Laban Movement Analysis, Benesh Notation, and Eshkol-Wachmann Notation, are the frameworks most commonly found in research. For the purpose of this chapter the focus is on the Laban-derived approaches to analysis since these are the ones most widely used in the United States and, in the case of Labanotation, also in Europe. Benesh Notation, developed in England by Rudolf and Joan Benesh in the 1950s, is a system of graphic signs representing key points of the human body on a horizontal staff matrix. It is used primarily in Great Britain and particularly for the recording of ballet movement, although it has been applied in other areas such as anthropology and medical research.[4] Eshkol-Wachmann Movement Notation, created in Israel by Noa Eshkol and Abraham Wachmann in the 1950s, uses numbers and signs to depict the rotary movement possible at the body joints and subsequent changes in the body's configuration.[5] It has found the most acceptance and use in Israel. Both of these latter systems have been developed to a high degree of sophistication and may be useful to investigators because of a particular research focus. Ann Hutchinson Guest's excellent book *Dance Notation*[6] discusses these and other systems, provides criteria for evaluating a notation system, and compares the major approaches. It should be noted that the above-mentioned notation systems are also applied in other movement contexts besides dance.

> In the broadest sense Laban Movement Analysis refers to any and all concepts for describing movement found in the formal systems developed by Rudolf Laban and his students. Technically, this includes the terms and principles of Labanotation or Kinetography Laban with its ingenious ways for describing weight placement, level, spatial path, duration, grouping patterns to name a few major categories of this movement notation. It also includes the terms and concepts for analyzing movement qualities and dynamics which Laban first called "antrieb" or "effort" and which many years later evolved into "Effort-Shape Analysis."
>
> In practice, those who call themselves Laban Movement Analysts and Certified Movement Analysts (CMAs) concentrate primarily on the qualitative aspects of movement: dynamics of space, force, time, and flow, and qualitative distinctions as to how the mover projects into space from shapeless variations toward and away from the body to elaborate three-dimensional sculpting of the body into space.[7]

More specifically, Laban Movement Analysis (LMA), also known as Labananalysis, includes the concepts formerly known as "Effort-Shape" and further embraces Laban's Space Harmony or Choreutics, the study of the relationships between the body and its spatial environment, and Bartenieff Fundamentals, the application of movement principles to achieve efficient and integrated movement.[8] Thus, for this chapter *Laban Systems of Movement Analysis* refers to all Laban-derived work, with Labanotation and Laban Movement Analysis (LMA) and its subareas as the main categories within that rubric.

Labanotation

Guest defines dance notation as "the translation of four dimensional movements (time being the fourth dimension) into signs written on two dimensional paper. (Note: a fifth 'dimension'—dynamics—should also be considered as an integral part, though usually it is not.)"[9] In her research on notation, Guest discloses the extensive use of signs and symbols over the ages to record dance movement and chronicles the introduction of eighty-six different movement notation systems since the beginnings in the fifteenth century, an amazing number considering it is only in recent decades that dances have notation scores that can be read to reproduce dance movement with great accuracy. Of these, Labanotation has met with the most acceptance in dance research studies in the English language that involve detailed description and examination of the movement components of the dance. It is the only notation system in which the four factors of direction (shape), level (shading), timing (length), and body part (placement on the staff) are combined in one symbol.[10] A strength of this system is its focus on the "flow of movement rather than a series of positions present in a movement sequence. This allows Labanotation to render a more naturalistic account of dance than other notation forms."[11]

The importance of Labanotation as a comprehensive contemporary movement/dance notation system in wide use for dance research is due in no small part to the existence of the Dance Notation Bureau in New York, a teaching facility and overseer and repository for dance notation scores in the United States, and to notation centers in France and the United Kingdom. Its importance is also due to the biennial conferences of the International Council of Kinetography Laban, an organization that "serves as the decision-making body with regard to standard usage and the spelling out of movements by means of signs of the system; promotes research into matters of notation which are likely to increase the efficiency and international usage of the system; and disseminates information about the Laban systems to all interested persons."[12] These organizations serve to insure accuracy and consistency in recording procedures, and they promote the continued growth and development of the system, a feature that is necessary if a mode of analysis is to have any widespread and ongoing use.

Labanotation lends itself to a variety of dance research purposes such as the preservation and reconstruction of dances, discovery of underlying movement and choreographic structures, documentation of selected aspects of dance movement in cultural, behavioral, and other studies, and comparative research in these areas. Its strengths lie in its comprehensiveness, scientific soundness in adherence to facts of anatomy and laws of physics, versatility, and its universality and flexibility for wide application in movement.[13] The organizational structures cited above guarantee continued uniformity, evaluation, and growth and enhance its prospects for wider use and acceptance. A factor that hampers such use is the extensive training required to become a professional notator. Although more and more dancers study Labanotation and acquire some facility with its use, dance researchers may not have sufficient training and skill to effectively notate the movement they wish to study. Another concern of scholars doing fieldwork is the difficulty in recording the movement with complex notation when seeing a dance for the first time.[14] The use of film and videotape somewhat alleviates this problem, especially with the advent of the handheld video recorder and its ability to clearly record events even in low light. Most researchers of dance movement now use videotape, often in conjunction with notation, where they can refine the data script at a later time. The tedious process of manually writing the symbols is facilitated with computer programs such as *Labanwriter,* a software program developed at Ohio State University to create the graphic symbols of Labanotation. Starting with the rehearsal of a new dance, a notator with computer software can immediately enter notes and continually update the score as the choreography is completed.[15]

Even though Labanotation is extremely detailed and so highly evaluated on criteria for a good system, there are still concerns surrounding its use or the use of other recording systems. What version of a dance is to be notated? What aspects of it should be recorded if the intent is not to repeat it exactly or if it contains improvisation?[16] Does the notator capture the movement intention? What details of the movement are to be included or omitted?[17] Does learning a particular system of notation bias and direct perception?[18] All of these are ongoing concerns and still debated within the field. Each researcher choosing to use a notation system will have to confront some of these questions.

Laban Movement Analysis

While Labanotation primarily records the spatial and temporal aspects of movement—the what, where, and when—Laban Movement Analysis (LMA) provides a vocabulary for describing, in particular, the qualitative features of movement; that is, "how" movement is executed. Laban's concept of effort evolved during the Second World War years as he observed industrial workers and developed a unique method to describe their movement patterns. Effort is designated through four factors, with each having two extremes: flow, that is free or bound, weight that is light or strong, time that is sudden or sustained, and space that is direct or indirect. Effort states are combinations of two effort elements, and effort drives contain three elements. Shape, a concept conceived by Warren Lamb during his work with Laban in the 1950s, refers to the manner in which the body changes its form to adapt to its spatial environment.[19] The predominant concepts of the shape category are shape flow, shaping, and directional movements. Preceding his work with effort, Laban devised a theory of how the body creates and relates to pathways in space called Choreutics or Space Harmony.[20] This aspect of the Laban framework "deals with such concepts as spatial designs, the relationship between the limbs and torso in moving, and movement scales built on linear dimensions, planes or three dimensional forms."[21]

Irmgard Bartenieff, a student of Laban's, a dancer, and a physical therapist, applied his theories to the more physiological components of movement and developed an approach that emphasized the use of movement concepts such as movement initiation, spatial intent, and kinesthetic awareness. Bartenieff's work integrated the areas of body, space, effort, and shape into the system known as Laban Movement Analysis. In 1978 she founded what is now called the Laban—Bartenieff Institute of Movement Studies in New York City, which is dedicated to training professionals in the analysis system and furthering its development and application. LMA concepts are used in a variety of contexts, and like Labanotation, the use of this system also requires extensive training.

Using a dance from the repertoire of the Indian dance form of *Mōhiniyāttam* as a focus of study, Bartenieff and her colleagues proposed methodologies for utilizing movement analysis in dance research. As an exploratory study the results provided valuable insights on movement observation techniques, the identification of the core characteristics of a dance, a hierarchy of classification related to choreographic form, the process of data collection, reliability in scoring, and the development of an integrated choreographic score comprising Labanotation, Effort-Shape notation, and Space Harmony notation. They also identified areas of concern pertinent to future research projects utilizing in-depth movement analysis.[22]

Examples of movement analysis applied in specific areas of dance research are given in the following sections. Several general categories of research are created here to focus the discussion, but movement analysis is and can be used in many and diverse ways in dance research. The literature in the subareas below, which include some form of movement analysis as part of the methodology, is extensive and the examples cited here are only meant to provide a overview of where movement analysis is employed and how it is approached. The intention is to illustrate the variety of projects that use some method of movement analysis in the research design.

Cultural Studies

There are numerous examples of scholars in anthropology and dance ethnography who use movement analysis to further their understanding of dance in human cultures. These specializations are also promising areas for expanded use of cross-cultural analysis as we increasingly become part of a global community and seek to understand other societies and cultures through their arts and movement activities. For some scholars the thrust of their research is on what dance says about the society, while others may focus more on the content of the dances themselves.

Kaeppler's pioneer work not only brings an anthropologist's perspective to the study of dance but also illustrates her own use of different movement analysis techniques.[23] Borrowing from structural linguistics in her early study on the structure of Tongan dance she proposed *kinemes* and *morphokines* as the movement equivalents of the linguist's terms of *phonemes* and *morphemes* and devised a multilayered system of analysis to search for what the Tongans considered significant units of movement. The kinemes or significant movements and positions are classified by body part and numbered, with selected positions illustrated in drawings. The morphokines, or meaningful movement units made up of certain kinemes, are also systematically classified and detailed in word descriptions that mix anatomical terms (flex, rotate, extend) and terms of everyday usage (bend, twist). This mixture of terms presents some inconsistency in that scientific terms for joint actions are used sometimes but not always, and it points out the difficulty and imprecision of using words to communicate the movement to the reader who may not be familiar with a specific vocabulary.

Twenty years later, Kaeppler's refinement of analysis techniques is evident in her investigation of Hula Pahu, Hawaiian Drum Dances.[24] In the movement analysis portions of a comprehensive documentation,

> attention progresses from individual motifs to entrance and exit sequences, and finally culminates in a unit-by-unit description of entire dances, all of which are supported by Labanotation scores (notated by Judy Van Zile and certified by the Dance Notation Bureau).
>
> Even readers unfamiliar with Labanotation can appreciate qualitative differences between performers in different traditions of *hula pahu* by simply putting two versions of the same motif or sequence side-by-side. The notation and the consistency in vocabulary it engenders propels movement analysis to a further horizon than is commonly encountered in cultural studies of dance. Although the Labanotation does not alleviate the need for lengthy verbal descriptions, the sheer quantity of it in this monograph does constitute fuel for the fires of advocacy for dance literacy.[25]

The analysis of movement is a major component in the research of other dance anthropologists. Also using linguistic analogies, Drid Williams proposed a theory of human action with an emphasis on the "semasiological" or expressive body. Her theory is based on "studies of dance movement which are linguistically tied, mathematically structured and empirically based" and assumes that dance, as other human interactions, is a structured system of meaning. In discussing her theory she uses samples of Labanotation as part of the explication.[26] In her comparative study of motor behavior among Africans and African Americans, Joann Keali'inohomoku uses a notation system devised by dance ethnologist Gertrude Kurath, who in turn borrows certain symbols from Labanotation. Detailed charts of symbols accompanied by word descriptions and lists of typical characteristics are drawn from Keali'inohomoku's field observations and serve as the basis for analysis and comparison. The author notes she regards her use of Kurath's "glyph" writing as more practical than Labanotation for readers who are nondancers; it was also quicker to use and was readable after the passage of time. She resisted translating her symbology into Labanotation since her goal was not reconstruction.[27]

Jane Cowan,[28] in her study of Greek dance, in particular its gender relations, weaves her verbal descriptions of dance movement into a wider frame of hermeneutic text. Her evocative use of language contributes a sense of the spirit of dance patterns in the social context of the event rather than the specifics of the movement. Cowan's explanation of her approach to movement description may well reflect the opinion of other researchers who choose not to employ specialized movement analysis systems such as notation.

> The descriptions I give about each dance are oriented toward the goal of providing sufficient information on the forms and connotations of the dances so that their (sometimes renegotiated) meanings in performance can be understood. Detailed descriptions or analysis of steps, body movements, or the structural aspects of individual dances are, for the most part, not directly relevant to the basic questions explored here.[29]

For researchers who utilize word descriptions, the following comments by Ness may be instructive.

> There are no easy solutions to the problem of representing choreographic phenomena legitimately and without distortion in linguistic textual form. . . . There is no escape from the historical and cultural baggage that inevitably accompanies a linguistic representation of the bodily experiences of another culture. There can be no absolutely objective and completely unproblematic description of an "other" culture's dances. . . . a linguistic account of choreographic experiences . . . must use the full resources of the language conscientiously and creatively in order to represent these experiences as vividly and accurately as the language will allow. Ideally, the very act of careful descriptive interpretation, when successful, can serve to override whatever negative cultural biases might be at work, inhibiting the reader's interpretative process. Linguistic systems and the ideological frameworks they include must be recognized as deeply compromised instruments of communication, insofar as the field of cross-cultural dance research is concerned. However, they remain widely accessible modes of representation and analysis that the discipline cannot yet do without.[30]

Other cultural studies make use of more formalized notation systems and create detailed scores of all or parts of the dance with accompanying word descriptions. Judy Van Zile's exploration of the origins and significance of Japanese Bon dances in Hawaii encouraged readers to experience Bon dancing, and to facilitate this participation she provided three types of description: "verbal instructions that should be easy for the layman to follow; line drawings to aid in clarifying key positions and Labanotation scores for the movement specialist."[31] To better arrive at the dynamics of Ghanaian dance, Odette Blum[32] experimented with adding phrasing signs to Labanotation and effort scores of basic motifs of three religious dances of the Ga people. With this more complete record she identified the movement qualities and the complex phrasing that make up the dynamic component of the dance segments.

In a number of cultural studies the concern is not with recording every detail that might be needed for reconstruction but with other issues that can be clarified using certain aspects of the Laban-related systems in the movement analysis. In her study as a participant-observer of the *sinulog* dances in the Philippines, Sally Ann Ness used selected LMA concepts within her detailed word descriptions, discussion, and interpretation of the dance activities in an "attempt to return bodily experience *as a form of consciousness and understanding* to a central place within the discipline of ethnographic inquiry."[33] Salient characteristics of certain ritual performances were "initiation patterning," where at times there was "core" or center body initiation and in other instances "distal" or ends of the body initiation, and "a spatial constellation, or tension, employed to integrate the gestural and postural statements of the performance."[34] These concepts come from the LMA discussions of body and space, and the terminology is appropriate to identify these discoveries even though LMA is not an obvious focus of analysis. Rather, LMA terminology is dispersed throughout the book in a logical and natural manner that is meaningful to readers unaccustomed to movement language. This process exemplifies Ness's ideas, quoted earlier, to make full and creative use of whatever is available in the language.

Choreography

Movement analysis techniques have proven invaluable in recording dance for preservation and reconstruction and illuminating compositional techniques. The development of sophisticated notation systems in the last half-century has meant that dances that would be lost after performance, or had limited continuity in someone's memory, can be precisely recorded and, like music, be read and restaged again. Through these scores and analyses scholars have access to dances to build a literature of and about them.

Such reconstruction of choreography may be particularly difficult when the original dance was created years ago and the extant materials are unclear or incomplete. From 1987 to 1989 Ann Hutchinson Guest and Claudia Jeschke under-took a daunting task to revive Vaslav Nijinsky's *L'Après-midi d'un faune.* Using Nijinsky's personal movement notation, photographs, notes, and materials sup-plied by his family, they deciphered his incomplete movement codes and trans-lated them into Labanotation. The final result was a revival of the original version of the dance by students at the Juilliard School who learned their parts solely from the score.[35] In a similar manner, Knud Jürgensen worked from an old score, the personal notes of the choreographer on the sheet music, research on the au-thentic Polish Mazur and Krakowiak dances, and accounts of the original perfor-mance to revive Bournonville's character dance *La Cracovienne* created for Fanny Elssler in 1839. It too was restaged for a contemporary audience and translated into Labanotation. The latter score is used to share with readers the main steps of the dance.[36] This process demonstrates how diverse resources, including a chore-ographer's personal notation system, can be used together to make a dance be-lieved to be lost to history come back to life.

Examination of a detailed dance score can reveal complexities in the structure of a dance or in the choreographic process that would remain hidden if the dance was viewed only in live performance or on film or videotape. A score on paper or computer allows unlimited study not bound by a linear time line, as movement appears and disappears in performance and there is no need to continually rewind to catch a movement. Using a Labanotation and effort notation score of Anna Sokolow's *Rooms* as a primary resource, Robyn Bissel illustrated how "the quality and effort motivating the movement were paramount to her purpose" and re-vealed insights into Sokolow's aesthetic.[37] Parallels were drawn between the chore-ographic styles of George Balanchine and Antony Tudor in Muriel Topaz's analysis of common steps found in both of their dances. From her comparison of Laban-otated scores emerged the idiosyncratic manner in which each choreographer treated elements "such as use of rhythm, gestures, repetition, context, complexity and the handling of groups" and which serve to clearly identify the creator of the dance.[38] In studying the relationship between the musical structures of Igor Stravinsky's music and the choreographic structures in *Agon,* the dance George Balanchine created to that music, Stephanie Jordan traces the interplay between the two and uses samples of Labanotated movements juxtaposed with the music score to show how, through the manipulation of the rhythmic elements in par-ticular, "the music and dance are in dialogue in a dynamic relationship."[39]

Dance scholarship in movement analysis is still in a novice stage in compari-son to other arts that have an extensive literature analyzing major works or the oeuvres of key artists. Only gradually are we moving beyond single studies on many topics to an accumulation of research on one topic that has been studied in many ways and revealed in greater depth. The initial single study is the necessary base for further development on a topic, but potential researchers should consider how to build on work already done. Sheila Marion's[40] study of four previous analyses of Doris Humphrey's dance *Water Study* exemplifies this second level of movement analysis, wherein past analytic research is synthesized to gain further insights on a dance. The study by Martha Ann Davis and Claire Schmais[41] focuses on the significant movement variables of *Water Study* and their relation to phrasing and compositional progression. Ann Rodiger[42] proposes identifying the important parameters that change during the dance and creating a visual graphing of these to show the dynamic shape of the piece. Marcia Siegel and Deborah Jowitt[43] in their separate studies contextualize the work, offering historical explanations for its form as well as its significance. In addition, Siegel describes the dance in detail, dissecting in the process its components, structure, and impact. These scholars, including Marion, are further related through their background in and use of aspects of the Laban framework and Marion, in her analysis, expands on the way concepts in the framework are realized in the dance and revealed by the different analyses.[44]

Movement Style

A small but developing area of research interest using movement analysis as a primary methodology is the study of movement style. Style here means the predominant, distinctive, and replicated movement features that characterize a person, a choreographer's work, or a dance form. A broader and comprehensive consideration of style in dance will attend to such issues as expression and context but in the following studies attention is on the examination of movement. If the subjects are choreographers these characteristics presumably are reflected in the works they create and contribute to the aesthetic and artistic merit of the dances.

Billie Lepczyk[45] chose to analyze three of Twyla Tharp's dances created between 1973 and 1976, *Deuce Coupe, As Time Goes By,* and *Push Comes to Shove,* to determine what movement qualities characterize her choreography. The investigator viewed each dance a minimum of three times in live performance and also extensively reviewed the videotape of *Push Comes to Shove.* Using the effort-shape concepts of LMA, she concluded that shape flow and free flow effort with changes in time are baseline qualities in Tharp's movement style. These are especially reflected in the growing and shrinking shape changes in the torso and limbs and through her use of effort states, the combination of two effort elements, which merge free flow and variations in quick or sustained time effort. Another study by the same author describes in the language of Laban Movement Analysis the dynamics and spatial orientation as well as the innovative movement patterns of the pioneer dancer and choreographer Martha Graham.[46]

The search for movement style characteristics in specific dances or dance forms is also a research direction with varied choices of analytic procedures. In studying the role of certain space elements in the style of the upper body movement in classical ballet technique, Lepczyk turned to Laban's *choreutics* or space concepts. Selected ballet steps were analyzed in terms of spatial pulls or tension, dimensional and planal tendencies, and relationship to crystalline forms. She found that the basic *port de bras* or carriage of the arms occurred within the form of the octahedron, that the movements of *epaulement, croise,* and *efface* create diagonal tension, and that *epaulement,* the oblique angle positioning of the head and shoulders in relation to the legs, creates various spatial tensions, including octahedral, planal, diagonal, and cubic.[47]

Labanotated examples support Svea Becker's[48] contention that fall and recovery, use of body weight, suspension, oppositional motion, successional movement, and body part motivation are key movement qualities in the technique and dances of Doris Humphrey and Charles Weidman. Contending that Labanotation alone could not capture certain expressive and stylistic features of a dance, Elizabeth Kagan[49] added effort-shape analysis to compare Paul Taylor's *Three Epitaphs* and Doris Humphrey's *Water Study.* Selecting characteristic motif phrases from each dance, she found that breath was a shared expressive element in both dances but that Taylor's dance found dynamic stress on the exhalation and collapse while Humphrey's expressiveness was on the inhalation and rebound. Suzanne Youngerman[50] also chose LMA to analyze the style and imagery of Humphrey's dance *The Shakers.* Her analysis reveals how the steps and movement patterns and especially the dynamics created through effort and shape combinations embody aspects of the culture of the religious sect represented in the dance. Jill Gellerman[51] used Labanotation and LMA as tools to identify the core movement characteristics of the Hasidic Orthodox Jewish culture and to compare the stylistic differences of the women in the dances of three Hasidic communities in New York. The similarities and differences she found provided clues to the expressive behavior, religious convictions, and view of the world of each of the groups.

Behavioral Studies

Research in dance/movement therapy frequently uses movement analysis to develop diagnostic and therapeutic procedures and to assess changes in movement behavior. The movement variables of quickness and strength chosen from LMA and the traits of unexpected transition and intensity devised by Linda Goodman[52] were used to determine movement characteristics of hyperactive children as compared to their normal peers. Observations were taken from videotapes of forty-four hyperactive and thirty-three normal boys playing a board game. Results showed hyperactive children to exhibit more strength, intensity, and unexpected transition than the comparison group. Modestly strong correlations were also found between the movement variables and a standard measure of hyperactivity, fostering speculation that these characteristics might compose a hyperactive movement style. Multiple personality disorder as displayed by a single subject was studied by Kluft, Poteat, and Kluft.[53] Nine personalities of the subject were observed on videotape and rated on three parameters: predominant body parts, tension-flow rhythms, and effort qualities. Each personality was found to have a distinctive movement pattern, suggesting this was a fruitful area for future research.

Movement analysis also provides insight into the role movement plays in the wider perspective of human behavior. Martha Davis, Shirley Weitz, and Joseph Culkin[54] examined sex role differences in twenty-two male and twenty-two female subjects videotaped in informal conversation who were rated by trained movement analysts using Laban-based instruments with twenty-six variables. Using the statistical techniques of factor analysis to sort out key factors, and stepwise multiple regression to relate these factors to observations of personality traits judged by naive observers, they found the most prominent variables for each sex to be openness for females and dominance for males. These findings support previous research findings on sex differences in movement patterns. A multifaceted research design was employed by Karen Bond[55] to study personal style as a mediator of engagement in dance in an educational setting. The subjects were six nonverbal children with dual sensory impairments. Effort and spatial elements from LMA were combined with other variables to determine personal style from observation of videotaped dance and play sessions and supplementary data. The children were found to be physically expressive with individually distinctive movement characteristics.

Derivative systems from the Laban framework, although used primarily for nondance movement analysis, are worthy of mention since they can inform researchers in dance of potentially useful methods and approaches to analysis. The Kestenberg Movement Profile, developed by psychoanalyst Judith Kestenberg, is a Laban-derived, developmentally based system of movement description that can be applied to movement across the entire developmental life span. It comprises a conceptual framework and a complex cataloguing system that distinguishes fifty-eight distinct movement patterns, with the concepts of tension-flow, effort,

and shaping as key parameters in the system. It has found application in dance/
movement therapy[56] and it has potential use in cross-cultural research studies.[57]
Action Profiling, developed by Warren Lamb, a student and colleague of Rudolf
Laban, expands on the use of effort and shape qualities to evaluate the decision-
making style of individuals as they move during interviews with the profiler.[58] It
has particular application in assessing the action motivation of business execu-
tives and managers.[59] In Movement Signature Analysis, selected samples of filmed
or videotaped movement of well-known figures in public speaking situations are
examined to determine their distinctive movement characteristics. Interpretations of the inventory data "draw on aspects of the movement having a symbolic
or metaphoric character but which are hypothesized here to literally and intrinsically relate to broader aspects of personality and coping style."[60]

Data Collection

The manner of movement data collection varies in relation to the purpose of the
research, the theory underlying it, the location of the dance activity, the time al-
lotted, and the background and skill of the researchers. Since movement analysis
is usually used within the broader context of a larger research goal rather than as
an end in itself, the investigator seeks as many additional resources as possible for
information about the movement and its context. This might include historical
documents and materials, interviews, films, audio or videotapes, notes, diaries,
movement scores, and personal movement experience. In cultural studies the investigator often becomes a participant and observer, spending time within the
culture, learning the dances and possibly the music, dancing with the people, and
gathering information from any source that will inform the purpose of the study.
A long period of such assimilation provides the opportunity for the researcher to
become more kinesthetically perceptive to nuances of the movement and how
they might "feel" and what they might mean to the dancers of the culture.

Video recording has become the major electronic tool for capturing movement images and currently is at least a partial source for most of the dance movement data. It has largely replaced film because of ease of use, clarity of image,
lower cost both for equipment and processing, use in still frame and slow motion, and ease with which it can be edited. Small, battery-operated, handheld
video recorders using miniature tape cassettes can be taken anywhere. With all its
advantages videotape has its drawbacks. It records three-dimensional movement
onto a two-dimensional screen, which means other views of the movement are
lost. In taping a group the movements of everyone may not be seen because they

are blocked or out of range. Video also distorts movement to some degree so that it might not provide a true representation of the movement and, in particular, of the dynamic qualities present in the live performance. Care must be taken in planning the use of film or video to ensure that light levels are adequate, camera angles are appropriate, and the background, if it can be arranged, allows the movement to stand out. Despite these concerns the use of video plays a major role in collecting movement data and will continue to do so.

Trained notators try to capture the movement data from live performance when possible but they often rely on film or videotape and other pertinent materials to supplement their observations. Prior to the last decade most recording of movement data for analysis, even from videotape, was done with paper and pencil. The introduction of the computer now enables researchers to immediately create a Labanotation score or to electronically code and process movement data. The potential this has for dance research is just beginning to be investigated. Software programs can be developed that will search the electronic data for the units or structures of interest—certain movement patterns or phrases, movement repetitions, or relationships between movement and music elements, to name just a few of the possibilities. Brennan et al.,[61] for example, developed a methodology for computer coding dance movement data using LMA concepts. By electronically searching the codes, occurrences of effort states and drives and other movement element combinations can be discovered. This approach is used to identify the movement style characteristics of *bharatanatyam* Indian classical dance.[62]

Computers also permit the creation of large databases of information about movement. Lisbet Torp[63] indexed and encoded information about 1,300 European chain and round dances still existing in living tradition and performed a structural analysis of the rhythmic, spatial, and kinetic characteristics of the dances. Once significant elements were identified, further work was done to establish main and sub categories, the patterns of which serve as theoretical models of systematization. As this demonstrates, databases could provide opportunities for comparative research in movement analysis, especially in cross-cultural studies and collaborative work. However, such a use speaks to the need for a generally accepted system of analysis to allow an accumulation of similar data by different researchers. If, for example, the Laban Movement Analysis systems were used, whole or in part, by investigators of dances of a particular culture or of a certain choreographer, and the data each collected were entered into a database accessible through the Internet to researchers around the world, imagine how much could be learned and shared and the depth of inquiry that would be possible. Technology now permits notation scores, videotape movement, clips, and text to be sent to other scholars on the Internet. It just remains for us to do it.

Reliability and Validity

The various permutations found in the Laban Movement Analysis systems allow for application in a wide variety of behavioral research studies, not only in dance but also in other disciplines concerned with nonverbal communication or other motor behavior. Most often the goal is not a complete recording of all the movement but an interest in specific aspects such as effort qualities or how the body moves in space. One limitation to greater use is the lack of rigorous study of observer agreement, that is, the reliability, within acceptable limits of error, that two or more trained persons would agree on what they observed. Procedures for evaluating observer agreement are routinely included in science and social science research, and if empirical data are to be used with confidence and accepted in a larger research community it is essential that dance researchers address this issue as they plan projects involving movement analysis.

A few investigators have specifically studied observer reliability assessment in movement analysis and established a discourse on the subject.[64] In a project sponsored by the Laban/Bartenieff Institute of Movement Studies, Martha Davis enlisted the aid of thirty-one certified movement analysts for pilot work coding movement observations on check sheets from videotaped dance segments. This led to the subsequent development of computer software for coding movement variables and its use with teams of three observers assessing one to two of the following components: posture-gesture merger, shaping, strong and light effort, sudden and sustained effort, direct and indirect effort, and bound and free-flow effort. Statistical assessment of the extent of agreement, determined by using both Pearson's and Cohen's kappa reliability coefficients, exhibited a range of reliability results, with some variables reaching an acceptable level of agreement and some not meeting the criterion. A valuable aspect of this study was the discussion of reliability issues such as training of observers, precision and clarity of operational definitions, criteria for agreement, nature of the movement, quality and quantity of observation practice, intra-rater agreement, stability of agreement over time, statistical evaluation techniques, conditions for observing and recording, and the quality of videotape or film and visibility in a live event.

Reliability evaluation has gained support among researchers using Laban-derived systems for nondance movement analysis. Adapting LMA elements and other variables identified in nonverbal communication research, Martha Davis devised the Davis Nonverbal Communication System and used it to code and analyze movement behavior in psychotherapy sessions. The resultant reliability coefficients demonstrated that coding based on LMA variables can be reliable.[65] The Kestenberg Movement Profile mentioned above produced adequate levels of observer reliability for eight of nine subsystems in a two-observer film study of the interactions between mothers and their infants. Although the levels were modest the results were encouraging, given the complexity of the coding system and the subtleties of the movement qualities and rhythms assessed.[66] Using multiple profiles of posture-gesture mergers of twenty-four individuals collected in Action Profiling interviews, Deborah Winters[67] was able to check the consistency among judges' scores, some taken up to seven and one-half years apart. Pearson r coefficients were high, ranging from .735 to .973, with an average of .872 across all conditions. Further comparisons showed that high levels of agreement persisted regardless of the subjects' knowledge of Action Profiling. Although these projects and approaches are not directly concerned with dance movement they do use movement elements important in dance research and serve to point us toward the scientific procedures dance researchers must adopt to attain credibility among other disciplines. Evidence of observer reliability in our movement analysis systems might also encourage other disciplines involving movement behavior to use these tools rather than inventing their own.

The question of validity, the accuracy with which evaluation devices reflect the concepts they purport to measure, is barely touched upon in dance movement analysis, and it is an area that needs further study and consideration in planning research projects. Penny Bernstein and Enzo Cafarelli[68] used electromyography (EMG) to validate the LMA effort factors in relation to their physiological base. EMG tracings from the biceps and triceps arm muscles were analyzed for the elements of time, force, space, and tension flow and compared to trained judges' ratings of effort components from films taken of the movements. Validity was established in that the judges identified the same effort factors found by the EMG. Winter used the Myers-Briggs Inventory, a measure of preferences for activities, to provide concurrent validity for 200 Action Profiling scores. Statistical analyses supported the hypotheses that postulated a relationship between the two types of scores. This and three other studies reported by Winter "support the validity of the AP scores as a reflection of ongoing cognitive style."[69] Both of the above studies are examples of the kind of work needed to be done as movement analysis in dance seeks to establish a place with analytic methods in other research fields.

Advanced Technologies

While computers are facilitating the collection of movement data by electronically processing notation signs and coding information, they are also used in more imaginative ways that point toward a future of high-tech movement analysis. Leslie Bishko[70] considers movement to be the fundamental expressive element in computer animation but finds that it is often more mechanical and less engaging than the traditional frame-by-frame animation done by hand. To make the animation more aesthetically expressive, she is exploring methods of developing computer animation techniques that allow better emulation of such dynamic movement qualities as weight, time, space, flow, and shaping. These qualities may apply to nonhuman as well as human representational animation figures. *Life Forms,* a computer-choreography tool, allows one to create human movements on a three-dimensional screen figure that can be viewed from all sides. These can be edited, stored, and combined with other composed figures to illustrate how dance movement might look before it is tried by a human dancer. While time is needed for training on the software, *Life Forms* and developments like it have the potential to make us rethink methods of movement analysis. It could be possible that "notating," "recording," or "coding" dance movements will mean to store them as computer figures that can be played back on the screen rather than using visual signs. With multimedia software, these computer images could be combined with text, sound, and video images and immediately made accessible to scholars through computer networks.[71] As technology evolves it must be kept in mind that it provides a tool: the movement analyst must still provide the theory.

Does each little movement have a meaning all its own? Yes, it does, but the meaning can only be understood in context. The significance of a movement lies in what is done, who does it, where and when it is done, and why. Movement analysis, however it is approached, plays a major role in answering these questions. As technology advances at a pace we can hardly grasp and we use the word *world* to refer to our community, our need grows for understanding how dance and movement help define us as individuals and groups and also unite us as humans. Our ability to express ourselves in movement is something we all share. As yet, we still know very little about how we go about that. A challenge for dance research is to find out—and the pursuit starts with the movement itself.

Study Questions

1. Name the main categories of methods of movement analysis, and for each of the categories cite one or more examples discussed in this chapter.

2. Discuss the differences between Labanotation and Laban Movement Analysis (LMA). Pose a dance research question that could be studied by using each of these methods of analysis and discuss how you would use the method in your inquiry.

3. How might technology expand and provide more in-depth study in the use of movement analysis in dance research? Select a research question of your own that can be approached through movement analysis and discuss ways in which technology might assist you in answering it.

NOTES

"Every Little Movement" is a song with music by Karl Hoschna and lyrics by Otto Hauerbach, published by M. Witmark and Sons in 1910.

1. Jane Adshead, ed., *Dance Analysis: Theory and Practice* (London: Dance Books Ltd., 1988).

2. The terms *symbol* and *sign* are often used interchangeably in the dance literature and this is how they are used here. It is acknowledged that these words may not be considered synonymous by all readers and in all contexts.

3. Laban's notation system is known as Kinetography Laban in Europe and as Labanotation in the United States.

4. Julia McGuinness-Scott, *Movement Study and Benesh Movement Notation: An Introduction to Applications in Dance, Medicine, Anthropology, and Other Studies* (New York: Oxford University Press, 1985).

5. Noa Eshkol and Abraham Wachmann, *Movement Notation* (London: Weidenfeld and Nicolson, 1958).

6. Ann Hutchinson Guest, *Dance Notation: The Process of Recording Movement on Paper* (New York: Dance Horizons, 1984).

7. Martha Davis, "Between Glassy Eyes and Sweaty Palms," *Movement Studies* 2 (1987): 1.

8. Suzanne Youngerman, "Movement Notation Systems as Conceptual Frameworks: The Laban System," in *Illuminating Dance: Philosophical Explorations,* ed. Maxine Sheets-Johnstone (Cranbury, N.J.: Associated Presses, 1984), 101–23.

9. Guest, *Dance Notation,* xiv.

10. Ibid., 84.

11. Jill Beck, "Systems of Dance/Movement Notation," in *Theatrical Dance: A Bibliographical Anthology,* ed. Bob Fleshman (Metuchnin, N.J.: Scarecrow Press, 1986), 92.

12. Sharon Rowe, Lucy Venable, and Judy Van Zile, "Index of Technical Matters and Technical and Non-technical Papers from the Biennial Conferences of the International Council of Kinetography Laban" (Columbus, Ohio: International Council of Kinetography Laban Publications, 1993), 60.

13. Guest, *Dance Notation,* 189.

14. Anya Peterson Royce, *The Anthropology of Dance* (Bloomington: Indiana University Press, 1977).

15. Lucy Venable and Scott Sutherland, "Labanwriter 2.2 Workshop: Abstract," in *Dance and Technology Moving Toward the Future,* ed. A. William Smith (Westerville, Ohio: Fullhouse Publishing, 1992), 59–60; János Fügedi, "Dance Notation and Computers," *1991 Yearbook for Traditional Music,* ed. Deiter Christensen, Anca Giurchesu, and Adrienne Kaeppler (New York: International Council for Traditional Music, 1991), 23:101–11.

16. Judy Van Zile, "Seeking Notation Solutions," *Dance Research Journal* 14, nos. 1 and 2 (1981–1982): 53–54.

17. Judith Chazin-Bennahum, "Hong Kong International Conference," *Dance Chronicle* 13, no. 3 (1990–91): 393–400.

18. Dawn Lille Horwitz, "Philosophical Issues Related to Notation and Reconstruction," *Choreography and Dance* 1 (1988): 37–53.

19. Susan M. Lovell, "An Interview with Warren Lamb," *American Journal of Dance Therapy* 15, no. 1 (spring/summer 1993): 19–34.

20. Rudolf Laban, *The Language of Movement* (Boston: Plays, Inc., 1966).

21. Youngerman, "Movement Notation Systems," 108.

22. Irmgard Bartenieff, Peggy Hackney, Betty True Jones, Judy Van Zile, and Carl Wolz, "The Potential of Movement Analysis as a Research Tool: A Preliminary Analysis," *Dance Research Journal* 16, no. 1 (1984): 3–26.

23. Adrienne L. Kaeppler, "Method and Theory in Analyzing Dance Structure with an Analysis of Tongan Dance," *Ethnomusicology* 16, no. 2 (1972): 173–217.

24. Adrienne Kaeppler, *Ha'a and Hula Pahu: Sacred Movements,* vol. 1 of *Hula Pahu: Hawaiian Drum Dances,* 2 vols. (Honolulu: Bishop Museum Press, 1992).

25. Amy Ku'uleialoha Stillman, "Review of *Hula Pahu: Hawaiian Drum Dances* [2 vols]. I. *Ha'a and Hula Pahu: Sacred Movements,* by Adrienne Kaeppler. II. *The Pahu Sounds of Power,* by Elizabeth Tatar." *1991 Yearbook for Traditional Music,* ed. Deiter Christensen, Anca Giurchesu, and Adrienne Kaeppler (New York: International Council for Traditional Music, 1991), 23:135.

26. Drid Williams, "The Human Action Sign and Semasiology," in *Dance Research Collage, CORD Dance Research Annual X,* ed. Patricia A. Rowe and Ernestine Strodelle (New York: Congress on Research in Dance, 1979), 39.

27. Joann Keali'inohomoku, "Theory and Methods for an Anthropological Study of Dance" (Ph.D. dissertation, Indiana University, 1976).

28. Jane Cowan, *Dance and the Body Politic in Northern Greece* (Princeton, N.J.: Princeton University Press, 1990).

29. Ibid., 18.

30. Sally Ann Ness, *Body, Movement and Culture: Kinesthetic and Visual Symbolism in a Philippine Community* (Philadelphia: University of Pennsylvania Press, 1992), 238.

31. Judy Van Zile, *The Japanese Bon Dance in Hawaii* (Honolulu: Press Pacifica, 1982), 32.

32. Odette Blum, "An Initial Investigation into Ghanian Dance in Order to Ascertain Aspects of Style by the Analysis and Notation of the Dynamic Phrase," in *A Spectrum of World Dance, CORD Dance Research Annual XVI,* ed. Lynn Ager Wallen and Joan Acocella (New York: Congress on Research in Dance, 1987), 52–67.

33. Ness, *Body, Movement and Culture,* 239.

34. Ibid., 119.

35. Jill Beck, ed., *A Revival of Nijinsky's Original L'Après-midi d'un faune,* vol. 1, part 3 of *Choreography and Dance* (New York: Harwood Academic Publishers, 1991).

36. Knud Arne Jürgensen, "Reconstruction of *La Cracovienne,*" *Dance Chronicle* 6, no. 3 (1983): 228–47.

37. Robyn Bissell, "Rooms: An Analysis," *Dance Notation Journal* 1, no. 1 (January 1983): 19.

38. Muriel Topaz, "Specifics of Style in the Works of Balanchine and Tudor," *Choreography and Dance* 1 (1988): 32.

39. Stephanie Jordan, "Agon: A Musical/Choreographic Analysis," *Dance Research Journal* 25, no. 2 (fall 1993): 1–12.

40. Sheila Marion, "Studying *Water Study,*" *Dance Research Journal* 24, no. 1 (spring 1992).

41. Martha Ann Davis and Claire Schmais, "An Analysis of the Style and Composition of 'Water Study,'" in *Research in Dance: Problems and Possibilities, CORD Dance Research Annual 1* (New York: Congress on Research in Dance, 1967).

42. Ann Rodiger, "Dance Graph Analysis," *Dance Notation Journal* 1, no. 2 (fall 1984): 21–29.

43. Marcia B. Siegel, *The Shapes of Change* (Berkeley: University of California Press, 1985); Deborah Jowitt, *Time and the Dancing Image* (New York: William Morrow, 1988).

44. Marion 1992, 1.

45. Billie Lepczyk, "Twyla Tharp's Movement Style Viewed Through Laban Analysis," in *Educating the Dancer and Scholar for the 21st Century, Conference on Research in Dance* (Seattle: Congress on Research in Dance, 1986), 39–44.

46. Billie Lepczyk, *Martha Graham's Movement Invention Viewed Through Laban Analysis*. Vol. 1 of *Dance Current Selected Research,* ed. Lynnette Y. Overby and James H. Humphrey. (New York: AMS Press, 1989), 45–46.

47. Billie Lepczyk, "An Analysis of the Pathways Defined in the Ballet Barre Through Choreutics," in *International Council of Kinetography Laban Fifteenth Biennial Conference* (Namur, Belgium: ICKL, 1987), 115–29.

48. Svea Becker, "A Reaffirmation of the Humphrey-Weidman Quality," *Dance Notation Journal* 1, no. 1 (January 1983): 3–12.

49. Elizabeth Kagan, "Towards the Analysis of a Score," in *Essays in Dance Research from the Fifth CORD Conference, Dance Research Annual IX,* ed. Dianne L. Woodruff (New York: Congress on Research in Dance, 1978), 75–92.

50. Suzanne Youngerman, "The Translation of a Culture into Choreography," in *Essays in Dance Research from the Fifth CORD Conference, Dance Research Annual IX,* ed. Dianne L. Woodruff (New York: Congress on Research in Dance, 1978), 93–110.

51. Jill Gellerman, "The Mayim Pattern as an Indicator of Cultural Attitudes in Three American Hasidic Communities," in *Essays in Dance Research from the Fifth CORD Conference, Dance Research Annual IX,* ed. Dianne L. Woodruff (New York: Congress on Research in Dance, 1978), 111–44.

52. Linda Goodman, "Movement Behavior of Hyperactive Children: A Qualitative Analysis," *American Journal of Dance Therapy* 13, no. 1 (spring/summer 1991), 19–31.

53. Estelle Kluft, Janis Poteat, and Richard P. Kluft, "Movement Observations in Multiple Personality Disorder: A Preliminary Report," *American Journal of Dance Therapy* 9 (1986): 31–46.

54. Martha Davis, Shirley Weitz, and Joseph Culkin, "Sex Differences in Movement Style: A Multivariate Analysis of Naive and Laban Based Ratings," *American Journal of Dance Therapy* 3, no. 2 (1980): 4–11.

55. Karen Bond, "Personal Style as a Mediator of Engagement in Dance: Watching Terpsichore Rise," *Dance Research Journal* 26, no. 1 (spring 1994): 15–26.

56. Penny Lewis and Susan Loman, eds., *The Kestenberg Movement Profile: Its Past, Present Applications and Future Directions* (Keene, N.H.: Antioch New England Graduate School, 1990).

57. Janet Kestenberg Amighi, "The Application of the KMP Cross-Culturally," in *The Kestenberg Movement Profile: Its Past, Present Applications and Future Directions,* ed. Penny Lewis and Susan Loman (Keene, N.H.: Antioch New England Graduate School, 1990), 114–25.

58. Action Profiling was developed by Warren Lamb and furthered by Pamela Ramsden. Because of differences in approach, Lamb and some of his colleagues now continue their work under the designation Movement Pattern Analysis while other specialists retain the Action Profiling name.

59. Warren Lamb and Elizabeth Watson, *Body Code: The Meaning of Movement* (London: Routledge Kegan Paul, 1979).

60. Martha Davis and Dianne Dulicai, "Hitler's Movement Signature," *The Drama Review* 36, no. 2 (summer 1992): 158.

61. M. A. Brennan et al., "A Computerized Methodology for Determining the Movement Profile of a Dancer Using Laban Movement Analysis," in *Dance Technology Research and Development,* ed. Judith Gray (Reston, Va.: American Alliance for Health, Physical Education, Recreation and Dance Publications, 1989), 93–101.

62. Mary A. Brennan and Parul Shah, "The Analysis of an Adavu in Bharatanatyam," *Movement Studies* 1 (fall 1992): 1–3.

63. Lisbet Torp, "European Chain and Round Dances," *Dance Studies* 10 (1986): 13–48.

64. Davis, "Between Glassy Eyes and Sweaty Palms."

65. Martha Davis and Dean Hadiks, "The Davis Nonverbal States Scales for Psychotherapy Research: Reliability of LMA-Based Coding," *Movement Studies* 2 (1987): 29–34.

66. K. Mark Sossin, "Reliability of the Kestenberg Movement Profile," *Movement Studies* 2 (1987): 23–28.

67. Deborah Du Nann Winter, "Field Studies of Action Profiling Reliability," *Movement Studies* 2 (1987): 21–22.

68. Penny Bernstein and Enzo Cafarelli, "An Electromyographical Validation of the Effort System of Notation," *American Dance Therapy Association Monograph* 2 (1972): 78–94.

69. Deborah Du Nann Winter, "Body Movement and Cognitive Style: Validation of Action Profiling," in *The Body-Mind Connection in Human Movement Analysis,* ed. Susan Loman (Keene, N.H.: Antioch New England Graduate School, 1992), 193.

70. Leslie Bishko, "Expressive Technology: The Tool as Metaphor as Aesthetic Sensibility," *Animation Journal* (fall 1994): 74–91.

71. Lisa C. Arkin, "Dancing Data: The Implications of Hypermedia in Dance Ethnology," in *Retooling the Discipline: Research and Teaching Strategies for the 21st Century,* ed. Linda J. Tomko (Provo: Brigham Young University, Society of Dance History Scholars, 1994), 299–302.

REFERENCES

Adshead, Jane, ed. *Dance Analysis: Theory and Practice.* London: Dance Books Ltd., 1988.

Amighi, Janet Kestenberg. "The Application of the KMP Cross-culturally." In *The Kestenberg Movement Profile: Its Past, Present Applications and Future Directions,* ed. Penny Lewis and Susan Loman, 114–25. Keene, N.H.: Antioch New England Graduate School, 1990.

Arkin, Lisa C. "Dancing Data: The Implications of Hypermedia in Dance Ethnology." In *Retooling the Discipline: Research and Teaching Strategies for the 21st Century,* ed. Linda J. Tomko, 299–302. Provo: Brigham Young University, Society of Dance History Scholars, 1994.

Bartenieff, Irmgard, with Dori Lewis. *Body Movement: Coping with the Environment.* New York: Gordon and Breach Science Publishers, 1980.

Bartenieff, Irmgard, Peggy Hackney, Betty True Jones, Judy Van Zile, and Carl Wolz. "The Potential of Movement Analysis as a Research Tool: A Preliminary Analysis." *Dance Research Journal* 16, no. 1 (1984): 3–26.

Beck, Jill. "Systems of Dance/Movement Notation." In *Theatrical Dance: A Bibliographical Anthology,* ed. Bob Fleshman, 89–99. Metuchnin, N.J.: Scarecrow Press, 1986.

—, ed. *A Revival of Nijinsky's Original L'Après-midi d'un faune.* Vol. 1, part 3 of *Choreography and Dance.* New York: Harwood Academic Publishers, 1991.

Bernstein, Penny, and Enzo Cafarelli. "An Electromyographical Validation of the Effort System of Notation." *American Dance Therapy Association Monograph* 2 (1972): 78–94.

Bishko, Leslie. "Expressive Technology: The Tool as Metaphor as Aesthetic Sensibility." *Animation Journal* (fall 1994): 74–91.

Bissell, Robyn. "Rooms: An Analysis." *Dance Notation Journal* 1 (1 January 1983): 18–34.

Blum, Odette. "An Initial Investigation into Ghanian Dance in Order to Ascertain Aspects of Style by the Analysis and Notation of the Dynamic Phrase." In *A Spectrum of World Dance, CORD Dance Research Annual XVI,* ed. Lynn Ager Wallen and Joan Acocella, 52–67. New York: Congress on Research in Dance, 1987.

Bond, Karen. "Personal Style as a Mediator of Engagement in Dance: Watching Terpsichore Rise." *Dance Research Journal* 26, no. 1 (spring 1994): 15–26.

Brennan, Mary A., and Parul Shah. "The Analysis of an Adavu in Bharatanatyam." *Movement Studies* 1 (fall 1992): 1–5.

Brennan, M. A., G. R. Stephenson, M. A. Brehm, and M. C. Deicher. "A Computerized Methodology for Determining the Movement Profile of a Dancer Using Laban Movement Analysis." In *Dance Technology Research and Development,* ed. Judith Gray, 93–101. Reston, Va.: American Alliance for Health, Physical Education, Recreation and Dance Publications, 1989.

Chazin-Bennahum, Judith. "Hong Kong International Conference." *Dance Chronicle* 13, no. 3 (1990–91): 393–400.

Cowan, Jane. *Dance and the Body Politic in Northern Greece.* Princeton, N.J.: Princeton University Press, 1990.

Davis, Martha. "Between Glassy Eyes and Sweaty Palms." *Movement Studies* 2 (1987): 1–2.

Davis, Martha, and Dianne Dulicai. "Hitler's Movement Signature." *Drama Review* 36, no. 2 (summer 1992): 152–72.

Davis, Martha, and Dean Hadiks. "The Davis Nonverbal States Scales for Psychotherapy Research: Reliability of LMA-Based Coding." *Movement Studies* 2 (1987): 29–34.

Davis, Martha, and Claire Schmais. "An Analysis of the Style and Composition of 'Water Study.'" In *Research in Dance: Problems and Possibilities, CORD Dance Research Annual 1,* ed. Richard Bull. New York: Congress on Research in Dance, 1967, 105–13.

Davis, Martha, Shirley Weitz, and Joseph Culkin. "Sex Differences in Movement Style: A Multivariate Analysis of Naive and Laban Based Ratings." *American Journal of Dance Therapy* 3, no. 2 (1980): 4–11.

Eshkol, Noa, and Abraham Wachmann. *Movement Notation.* London: Weidenfeld and Nicolson, 1958.

Fügedi, János. "Dance Notation and Computers." In *1991 Yearbook for Traditional Music,* ed. Deiter Christensen, Anca Giurchesu, and Adrienne Kaeppler, 23:101–11. New York: International Council for Traditional Music, 1991.

Gellerman, Jill. "The Mayim Pattern as an Indicator of Cultural Attitudes in Three American Hasidic Communities." In *Essays in Dance Research from the Fifth CORD Conference, Dance Research Annual IX,* ed. Dianne L. Woodruff, 111–44. New York: Congress on Research in Dance, 1978.

Goodman, Linda. "Movement Behavior of Hyperactive Children: A Qualitative Analysis." *American Journal of Dance Therapy* 13, no. 1 (spring/summer 1991): 19–31.

Guest, Ann Hutchinson. *Dance Notation: The Process of Recording Movement on Paper.* New York: Dance Horizons, 1984.

Horwitz, Dawn Lille. "Philosophical Issues Related to Notation and Reconstruction." *Choreography and Dance* 1 (1988): 37–53.

Jordan, Stephanie. "Agon: A Musical/Choreographic Analysis." *Dance Research Journal* 25, no. 2 (fall 1993): 1–12.

Jowitt, Deborah. *Time and the Dancing Image.* New York: William Morrow, 1988.

Jürgensen, Knud Arne. "Reconstruction of *La Cracovienne*." *Dance Chronicle* 6, no. 3 (1983): 228–47.

Kaeppler, Adrienne L. "Method and Theory in Analyzing Dance Structure with an Analysis of Tongan Dance." *Ethnomusicology* 16, no. 2 (1972): 173–217.

———. *Ha'a and Hula Pahu: Sacred Movements.* Vol. 1 of *Hula Pahu: Hawaiian Drum Dances.* Honolulu: Bishop Museum Press, 1992.

Kagan, Elizabeth. "Towards the Analysis of a Score." In *Essays in Dance Research from the Fifth CORD Conference, Dance Research Annual IX,* ed. Dianne L. Woodruff, 75–92. New York: Congress on Research in Dance, 1978.

Keali'inohomoku, Joann W. "A Comparative Study of Dance as a Constellation of Motor Behaviors Among African and United States Negroes." In *Reflections and Perspectives on Two Anthropological Studies of Dance, CORD Dance Research Annual VII,* ed. Adrienne L. Kaeppler, 15–187. New York: Congress on Research in Dance, 1976.

Kluft, Estelle, Janis Poteat, and Richard P. Kluft. "Movement Observations in Multiple Personality Disorder: A Preliminary Report." *American Journal of Dance Therapy* 9 (1986): 31–46.

Laban, Rudolf. *The Language of Movement.* Boston: Plays, Inc., 1966.

Lamb, Warren, and Elizabeth Watson. *Body Code: The Meaning of Movement.* London: Routledge Kegan Paul, 1979.

Lepczyk, Billie. "Twyla Tharp's Movement Style Viewed Through Laban Analysis." In *Educating the Dancer and Scholar for the 21st Century, Conference on Research in Dance,* 39–44. Seattle: Conference on Research in Dance, 1986.

———. "An Analysis of the Pathways Defined in the Ballet Barre Through Choreutics." In *International Council of Kinetography Proceedings of the Laban Fifteenth Biennial Conference,* 115–29. Namur, Belgium: ICKL, 1987.

———, ed. *Martha Graham's Movement Invention Viewed Through Laban Analysis.* Vol. 1 of *Dance Current Selected Research,* ed. Lynnette Y. Overby and James H. Humphrey. New York: AMS Press, 1989.

Lewis, Penny, and Susan Loman, eds. *The Kestenberg Movement Profile: Its Past, Present Applications and Future Directions.* Keene, N.H.: Antioch New England Graduate School, 1990.

Lovell, Susan M. "An Interview with Warren Lamb." *American Journal of Dance Therapy* 15, no. 1 (spring/summer 1993): 19–34.

Marion, Sheila. "Studying Water Study." *Dance Research Journal* 24, no. 1 (spring 1992): 1–12.

McGuinness-Scott, Julia. *Movement Study and Benesh Movement Notation: An Introduc-*

tion to Applications in Dance, Medicine, Anthropology, and Other Studies. London: Oxford University Press, 1983.

Ness, Sally Ann. *Body, Movement and Culture: Kinesthetic and Visual Symbolism in a Philippine Community.* Philadelphia: University of Pennsylvania Press, 1992.

Rodiger, Ann. "Dance Graph Analysis." *Dance Notation Journal* 1, no. 2 (fall 1984): 21–29.

Rowe, Sharon, Lucy Venable, and Judy Van Zile. "Index of Technical Matters and Technical and Non-technical Papers from the Biennial Conferences of the International Council of Kinetography Laban." Columbus, Ohio: International Council of Kinetography Laban Publications, 1993.

Royce, Anya Peterson. *The Anthropology of Dance.* Bloomington: Indiana University Press, 1977.

Shiphorst, Thecla. "Life Forms: Design Tools for Choreography." In *Dance and Technology I,* ed. A. William Smith, 46–59. Madison, Wis.: Fullhouse Publishing, 1994.

Siegel, Marcia B. *The Shapes of Change.* Berkeley: University of California Press, 1985.

Sossin, K. Mark. "Reliability of the Kestenberg Movement Profile." *Movement Studies* 2 (1987): 23–34.

Topaz, Muriel. "Specifics of Style in the Works of Balanchine and Tudor." *Choreography and Dance* 1 (1988): 1–36.

Van Zile, Judy. "Seeking Notation Solutions." *Dance Research Journal* 14, nos. 1 and 2 (1981–1982): 53–54.

———. *The Japanese Bon Dance in Hawaii.* Honolulu: Press Pacifica, 1982.

———. "What Is the Dance? Implications for Dance Notation." *Dance Research Journal* 17, no. 2 (fall 1985/spring 1986): 41–47.

Venable, Lucy, and Scott Sutherland. "Labanwriter 2.2 Workshop: Abstract." In *Dance and Technology Moving Toward the Future,* ed. A. William Smith, 59–60. Westerville, Ohio: Fullhouse Publishing, 1992.

Williams, Drid. "The Human Action Sign and Semasiology." In *Dance Research Collage, CORD Dance Research Annual X,* ed. Patricia A. Rowe and Ernestine Strodelle, 39–64. New York: Congress on Research in Dance, 1979.

Winter, Deborah Du Nann. "Field Studies of Action Profiling Reliability." *Movement Studies* 2 (1987): 21–22.

———."Body Movement and Cognitive Style: Validation of Action Profiling." In *The Body-Mind Connection in Human Movement Analysis,* ed. Susan Loman, 153–201. Keene, N.H.: Antioch New England Graduate School, 1992.

Youngerman, Suzanne. "The Translation of a Culture into Choreography." In *Essays in Dance Research from the Fifth CORD Conference, Dance Research Annual IX,* ed. Dianne L. Woodruff, 93–110. New York: Congress on Research in Dance, 1978.

———. "Movement Notation Systems as Conceptual Frameworks: The Laban System." In *Illuminating Dance: Philosophical Explorations,* ed. Maxine Sheets-Johnstone, 101–23. Cranbury, N.J.: Associated Presses, 1984.

❚ ENGENDERING DANCE

Feminist Inquiry and Dance Research

Jane C. Desmond

In its broadest contours, feminist scholarship investigates the historical constitution of gender as a category of social differentiation and analyzes the effects of this epistemological divide in all realms of human endeavor including economics, the arts, public institutions, popular culture, and the daily experiences of individuals and groups. It also investigates how ideologies of gender difference operate to naturalize such concepts and their material effects so that they appear normal and inevitable.

Gender systems are always political in the most fundamental sense of articulating a division of power. They operate in complex and often contradictory ways and intersect with other categories of social differentiation such as race, class, ethnicity, age, national origin, and so on. These categories too are produced in and through history—that is, they come into being at certain historical moments, and their meanings change over time. These categories and their intersection with concepts of gender are of vital importance in shaping the social and material circumstances of individuals and groups.

Feminist scholarship is, then, not just about women, it is about the historical constitution of the category *women* and the mobilization of this category in generating meaning. Since this category is always produced relationally and usually hierarchically vis-à-vis that of *men*, it includes the study of those constructions and their effects as well. The anchorage of a binary gender system (the categories *men* and *women*) on a biological divide constituted as "male" and "female" powerfully naturalizes this conceptual system and facilitates its discursive power.[1]

Feminist scholar Teresa de Lauretis develops this idea when she argues that

> we need a notion of gender that is not so bound up with sexual difference as to be virtually coterminous with it. . . . The cultural conceptions of male and female as two complementary yet mutually exclusive categories into which all human beings are placed constitute within each culture a gender system, a symbolic system or system of meanings, that correlates sex to cultural contents according to social values and hierarchies. . . . The construction of gender is both the product and the process of its representation.[2]

Dance, as a symbolic system of meanings based on bodily display, offers a particularly rich arena of investigation for feminist scholars. This chapter sketches broadly several contours of feminist scholarship as it has developed in the United States in the last two decades and considers the implications of that scholarship for dance research.

Modes of Feminist Inquiry

Just as there are multiple feminisms,[3] there are numerous feminist approaches to research and analysis. All these approaches value investigating the variable construction of the category *woman* and the variety of lived experiences shaped by such ideologies. Growing from the second wave of feminism in the 1960s and 1970s, contemporary feminist scholarship developed from and remains implicitly related to an activist agenda, one that seeks to improve women's lives by unsettling the status quo in any number of ways. These ways include producing more information about women's lives, unearthing the historical roots of current systems of inequalities, and articulating and challenging those inequalities or subjugations wherever they may be found.

One arena of feminist scholarship has proceeded from a recognition of the historical subordination of women and endeavored to recover the undocumented history of *women* as a social class in a variety of times and places. This recovery approach to history has resulted in a profusion of texts, especially in the last twenty-five years. These bring to light the wide range of women's activities, making the invisibility of women as social agents in traditional histories (of the state, of labor, of political science) visible. This approach values as "history" realms of action heretofore devalued in the great-men, great-deeds, great events scenarios of history. Embroidery becomes included in the category *art,* for instance, and women's personal letters are brought into canonical studies of *literature* devoted to time periods when few women published or were allowed to publish books. The goal of much of this work has been to present a "more complete" version of history. Such a move has its corollaries in the writings of working-class histories and the histories of other socially subordinated groups such as African Americans and Native Americans.

Despite its demonstrated usefulness, the limitation of this approach, as Joan Scott has argued so eloquently in her book *Gender and the Politics of History*,[4] is that it often leaves preexisting categories of analysis intact and unexamined (*labor* history, for example, and *men* and *women*). More recent work takes as its point of analysis the historical constitution of gender as a category itself. This is especially true for work across a number of disciplines influenced by varieties of poststructural thought. Such work presumes that gender is one of the most important categories of social differentiation, and that as a social construction it must be continually asserted and reproduced, thus always subject to contestation, realignment, and negotiation. As a process of social demarcation, it is historical and simultaneously plays a constitutive role in social history. Such practices are played out in nearly every aspect of daily life and in various discursive fields and institutional structures such as literature, industry, popular culture, and scholarship. It is this process of engendering and its effects (social, psychological, material) that constitute the subject of feminist inquiry.

All feminist scholars share some sense of an activist intervention in the production of knowledge, not merely its reproduction.[5] Within this broadly shared agenda, however, the varieties of viewpoints, political stakes, and social situations inhabited by feminist critics mean that debate is fierce and fecund. Feminist scholars inhabit a wide spectrum of radical, liberal, or materialist beliefs. They differ in how they address the intersection of gender with other categories of social classification, such as sexuality, race, or class.

Within the last twenty-five years, U.S. feminist scholarship has increasingly confronted the difficulties inherent in theorizing the full complexities of social relations. Social categories are always relational, and only rarely do they operate in isolation from one another. Thus, the constitution of a social class of *women* is not only created and activated in relation to the category *men* but is differentially refracted with other categories like class, age, race, and nationality. Increasingly it is the challenges of this complexity that have shaped feminist scholarship.

In the late 1960s and 1970s, U.S. feminist scholarship built on earlier waves of feminist thought and action but was most indebted to the political activism of the women's movement of the time, and to the civil rights movement.[6] The 1974 English translation of Simone de Beauvoir's *The Second Sex*, originally written in French in 1949, gave a new generation of feminist scholars access to her path-breaking work. Her assertion that "One is not born a woman, one becomes a woman" ushered in a new era of scholarship that investigated the social formulation of the category of *woman*. In France, feminist theorists like Cixous, Irigaray, and Kristeva developed a line of inquiry tied to issues of female embodiment. Some U.S. critics have adopted this work, as well as the strain of psychoanalysis based on Jacques Lacan's reworking of Freud. Others have muted a phenomenological emphasis on the body to concentrate on how meanings and hierarchies are socially constituted through representation.[7] Influential 1970s works in this vein by U.S. scholars, like Kate Millet's *Sexual Politics* and key articles by Elaine Showalter and Annette Kolodney, discussed *woman* as a relatively universal category in relation to literature and art.

These universalizing assumptions of U.S. white middle-class liberal feminism have been critiqued on a number of grounds since then. Feminists like bell hooks *(Yearning: Race, Gender, and Cultural Politics)*, Gloria Anzaldua *(Borderlands/La Frontera: The New Mestiza)*, Patricia Hill Collins *(Black Feminist Thought: Knowledge, Consciousness, and the Politics of Empowerment)*, and Chela Sandoval ("U.S. Third World Feminism: The Theory and Method of Oppositional Consciousness in the Postmodern World") have pointed out the salience of race and racializing practices. Lesbian feminists like Adrienne Rich, in her groundbreaking article, "Compulsory Heterosexuality and Lesbian Existence," and Gayle Rubin ("The Traffic in Women: Notes on the Political Economy of Sex") have made similar critiques regarding the presumption of heterosexuality. Feminists outside of the European/U.S. axis, such as Chandra Mohanty ("Under Western Eyes") and Gayatri Spivak *(In Other Worlds),* have pointed out that analyses of gender oppression do not translate unproblematically from one national or regional position to another but must be worked through with historical, political, and geographical specificity. These enormously empowering debates and critiques, while seeming to threaten in the short run the broad alliances necessary for political action, will in the long run reveal more truly the complexity of gender as an ideological formation. Any feminist analysis needs to be alert to these conditions of specificity and historicity.[8]

The wide range of positions in feminist scholarship is complemented by a wide range of scholarly methodologies. Feminist scholars can use many methodological approaches, fine-tuning them at three levels to address feminist issues: (1) at the level of the formation of the questions/hypothesis to be investigated, (2) in the interpretation of the data gathered, and (3) in determining what "counts" as data.[9] Textual analysis, ethnography, social science perspectives, phenomenological approaches, archival research, oral history interviews—all these and other methods as well can yield useful information.

Feminist Inquiry in Dance

Feminist inquiry in dance scholarship can ask: in what ways are dance practices gendered, and in what ways do dance practices (and the shifting constitution of *dance* as an epistemological category) historically construct gendered categories of meaning and valuation?

The questions that arise from such a starting point are huge and require attention to the ways in which dance is historically separated out from or linked to other forms of social practice, and to the ways in which the public display of the dancing body engenders and is engendered in its meanings. How, when, where, and why do (which) people dance, and to what effect? Historically shifting boundaries between what is denoted as *dance* and nondance, among genres of *dance* activities (social dance, theatrical dance), and among values attached to these practices, all provide clues to gendered constructions of populations, actions, and meanings. The case of classical ballet can provide a starting point for considering some of these questions.

As Ann Daly has noted in her brief but pungent essay, "Classical Ballet: A Discourse of Difference,"

> ballet discourse as a whole . . . is inextricably rooted in the notion of "inborn" or "natural" gender differences. Across the centuries, these differences have been an unabashed hallmark of classical ballet at every level: costuming, body image, movement vocabulary, training, technique, narrative, and especially the pas de deux structure. Like a thicket grown fat around a fencepost, discourse has entwined itself with stage practice in inscribing gender difference as an aesthetic virtue.[10]

Feminist analyses of various ballets, or of the history of ballet, can start to untangle that thicket of meanings, asking specifically how gender operates in each of the levels that Daly notes, such as the division of movement vocabularies into "male" and "female" steps and performance styles, how costuming has changed in its differential delineations of male and female bodies, how dance training regimes have historically produced specific "technologies of the body," and so forth.[11]

We can then theorize about how these specific "technologies of gender"[12] are bundled into aesthetic discourse and weighted with specific values, marked as "good," or "beautiful," or "timeless." We can ask too how these aesthetic systems fundamentally rely on gendered oppositions for their production of pleasure, and how specific audiences, shaped but not determined by class, race, national origin, region, and so on, have reacted to those proffered pleasures in various times and places.

Evan Alderson takes just such an approach in his article "Ballet as Ideology: *Giselle*, Act II," when he considers the contemporary appeal of *Giselle*, and his own fascination with the "unity of longing, purity, beauty, and death which the second act proposes." Noting that "ideology is presented in and through aesthetics, not apart from it," Alderson charts the complex relationships between a Romantic ideal of ethereal disembodiment and self-sacrifice, and the contemporary glamour ideal which, when taken to extremes, can express itself most tragically in anorexia. Alderson reminds us that "our assent to this beauty entails a further assent to a network of social ideas" and helps to situate us within the broader social order.[13]

Social Practices/Social Production

Once we shift our attention from a concept of dance as a collection of products, to a social practice of production, consumption, and the generation of meaning in a complex and related field of practices, our concept of "data" expands, as do the questions we derive from it. The works of Pierre Bourdieu and Michel Foucault among others are particularly useful here. Foucault emphasizes the ways in which power and knowledge are intertwined. As Wendy Hollway puts it: "He stresses the mutually constitutive relation between power and knowledge: how each constitutes the other to produce the truths of a particular epoch."[14] To do so, Foucault traces the historical development of particular discourses (on topics such as "sexuality," or "criminality,") and the social, political, and material structures and practices that they produce and are produced by.[15] Feminist critics like Hollway have criticized Foucault's work on the social construction of sexuality for its failure to adequately account for gender relations in these analyses, but they have been able to build on his work in ways that do. Hollway does so, for instance, by concentrating on heterosexual relations as "the primary site where gender difference is reproduced."[16]

Sociologist Pierre Bourdieu similarly develops ways of theorizing how people are situated as social subjects. In his book *Distinctions: A Social Critique of the Judgement of Taste*,[17] for example, he analyzes the ways in which our relations to cultural practices are learned both implicitly and explicitly (at home and at school), resulting in class-linked attitudes toward things like museums, the arts, and so on. "Taste," or our preferences in all things from food to fashion to art, is a process of classification, he argues, and one that simultaneously classifies both us and that which we prefer. As such, it both marks and organizes us into groups that share social values and knowledges, helping to situate us in structured social relations. We may inhabit several groups at once, even when the attached systems of power and prestige conflict.

Consider, for example, the multiple positionings inhabited by a contemporary freelance Caucasian choreographer working in the downtown New York art scene and coming from a working-class background. She may be high in social prestige, what Bourdieu terms "cultural capital," based on her knowledge of the arts, but low in economic capital, based on her limited income as an artist. Racially she is associated with the hegemonic group and presumably reaps the privileges of being part of the "unmarked" category. However, her gender may at times position her as a second-class citizen, and she may remain caught somewhat in between the upper-middle-class milieu of the experimental art scene and her own upbringing in a working-class community where mainstream arts and popular culture, not avant-garde explorations, may have been part of her daily life. Similar complexities shape our agency as viewers in the theater or as social dancers in a dance club. Bourdieu's models provide a way to think through the complexities of social structures and our ways of inhabiting and negotiating them. Drawing on works by scholars such as these can help frame our thinking about dance as both a cultural practice and a series of cultural products.

For example, in considering a specific performance of a ballet from this expanded perspective of cultural practice, we can ask a number of questions. Who went, why did they go, and what exactly did they see? How were the bodies staged? How much did it cost and who could afford it? How did audience members respond? What meanings were attached to the practice of spectatorship? To being a worker in the theater (for men and for women)? What other social, labor, or aesthetic practices did such entertainments resemble? From what were they perceived to be markedly different? Why? What values were attached to the practice, and how were they articulated in public discourse surrounding the event? In what ways did gender contribute to the construction of meaning in all of the above questions?

I use ballet as an example here because it is a genre so well-known to most U.S. dance scholars and among our most highly codified and historically documented forms.[18] However, investigations can engage any form of dance practice, such as social dance, liturgical dance, danced rituals, and so forth, as dance scholars like Sally Ness, Cynthia Novack, and Katrina Hazzard-Gordon have demonstrated.[19]

What we can count as "data" (meaningful information for analysis) can be very widely construed. Taking the example of *Giselle* once again, we might consider costume, choreography, audience reception, narrative, the labor history of dancers, theater architecture, conventions of audience behavior, wider discourses of meaning (such as the Romantic ideal of transcendent diaphanous beauty), and the social relations based on gender and class between male audience members and female employees (ballerinas), as well as the social parameters of single working women at the time of the ballet's performance.

We can look beyond issues of choreographic construction to those of audience reception as recorded in public and private records like reviews, personal letters, and diaries. We can consider employment records, historical legal statutes regarding prostitution, labor conditions for working women as ballerinas, the variable responses of male and female audience members, and the class-specific meanings attached to going to the ballet at particular historical junctures. Archival research, legal research, aesthetic history, biography, economic records, architectural designs—all these and more can provide evidence for our investigations. Further, we can chart these changes comparatively over time.

As is evident from the discussion above, a key challenge for feminist theorists is to link analyses of ideological production (the meanings attached to gender constructions and their representations) with specific social practices, public discourse, institutional structures, and material conditions. I use the term *ideological* here and throughout this chapter not in the traditional Marxist sense of false understanding or "false consciousness," as opposed to the "scientific" revelation of the perception of the class system, but in the more extended sense developed by Antonio Gramsci, Louis Althusser, and others.

Ideological formations are intensely naturalized belief systems ("common sense") that position individuals as social subjects. Ideologies frame what is perceived as "right," "good," "true," and "valuable" as well as the standards used to make such determinations. As such, they can shape our actions but do not fully determine them. No ideologies are completely hegemonic; social subjects retain agency. But as Gramsci states, dominant ideologies frame "a conception of the world [that] . . . is implicitly manifest in art, in law, in economic activity and in all manifestations of individual and collective life."[20]

Although Marx saw class structure as the most important social structure, and economics as the determining cause, Althusser elaborated on these theories. Rejecting a strict base-superstructure model, he emphasized the importance of institutions like the schools, the arts, religion, and the media, which he termed the "ideological state apparatuses," in promulgating the ideologies of those in power.[21]

While several scholars have criticized Marxism for its ultimate subordination of gender to class and its incapacity to account for racial oppression, the expanded formulation of concepts of ideology that Gramsci and Althusser provide are very useful. They can provide a framework for uncovering the naturalization of arbitrary social structures, including gender and race, and of situating the arts alongside other major social institutions as powerful sites of ideological production. Both of these moves are of great importance for feminist critics working in dance scholarship.

The sweeping influence of poststructuralist thought through the humanities, more latterly through portions of the social sciences, and even into the sciences, has revealed the perspectival nature of all knowledge (no knowledge is disinterested) and has thrown into relief the historicity of disciplinary modes of knowledge and of knowledge production. Feminist scholarship has been among the most powerful critiques of the presumption of value-free knowledge. The resultant destabilization of canons, fields, disciplines, and their attached methodologies facilitates the interdisciplinary or antidisciplinary critique that feminist scholarship can provide, as Chris Weedon makes clear in her *Feminist Practices and Poststructural Theory*.[22]

We can now ask questions about dance history that were usually confined to other spheres, like labor history, political science, literature, economics, and philosophy. And we can now integrate work on dance history into any of these other spheres. Working from a concept of the social production of art, aesthetic history becomes one history among many interconnected histories.[23] Several dance scholars like Susan Manning, Amy Koritz, Brenda Dixon-Gottschild, Ann Daly, and myself are now combining feminist perspectives with these larger frameworks to investigate such issues as dance and national identity.[24]

Interdisciplinary Feminist Analysis

Among these interconnected histories with which dance history participates is the social history of the body, the most powerful naturalizing trope of gender ideologies. In dance practices and dance "products" (specific choreographies, styles, modes of social dance, and so on) we can see the staging of gender. Gender categories, as Judith Butler has argued recently, depend upon the constant reiteration of gendered behavior.[25] These "performances" of gender are learned and reproduced. The required reproduction makes possible the potential disruption of gender systems through "misperformances" or realigned components.

It is important to note that Butler is not using the concept of "performance" in the sense of artifice, as if one could suddenly just stop performing gender or could switch genders by switching performative scripts, although some scholars have adopted her work in that way.[26] Rather, she points to the powerful function of bodily enactment in the production and maintenance of ideologies of gendered subjects. These learned (and historically and geopolitically specific) systems of deportment, gesture, posture, ways of moving through space, speech patterns, facial expressions, dress, and so forth are deployed, minute to minute and day to day, usually without conscious awareness due to their naturalization. "Performativity" is a concept that includes all of these enactments.[27]

Theatrical dance forms provide an opportunity to analyze related systems of gender performativity mediated through the conventions of historical dance forms, styles, and techniques. These historical conventions crystallize, exaggerate, diffuse, abstract, and otherwise intensify the enactment of the gender system as it operates in nontheatrical, everyday arenas (which are nonetheless highly codified). Specific dance training techniques, as "technologies of the body," can provide explicit instruction in stylized renditions of social embodiment, as dance scholars like Susan Foster and Mark Franko have shown.[28]

Theatrical practice, seen as a space and time set apart from daily action, also provides a potentially utopian arena for the contestation and reimagining of nonnormative renditions of bodily identity.[29] Isadora Duncan, Senta Driver, and Elizabeth Streb have staged new visions of female embodiment, for example. The meanings that can potentially be generated in such a space are always relationally produced, however, and the utopian potential of theater is counterbalanced by its social designation as the "not-real." Other dance practices, such as social dancing, can offer similar prohibitions and possibilities for related reasons.

That the primary material in dance is the dancing body, most often a mute body, and most often (at least in U.S. theatrical dance) a female body, means that theories of visual representation and kinesthetic interpretation are extremely useful for feminist scholars of dance. To date, dance scholarship has drawn most heavily on film theory, especially that imported via theater studies. Laura Mulvey's initial formulation of the social structure of looking as "the male gaze" (men look, women are to-be-looked-at) continues to fuel discussion and analyses more than twenty years after the publication of her groundbreaking psychoanalytical essay on how cinema produces pleasure and genders spectatorship.[30] The "male gaze" concept is now more fully elaborated to attempt to account for female spectatorship, cross-gender identification, and gay and lesbian spectatorship. Concepts of spectatorship and pleasure are central ones for dance scholars, and many writers are now drawing on these debates as they have developed in film studies and the visual arts.[31]

After the initial excitement of adopting this theoretical "tool" as a way of thinking about dance performances, scholars like Susan Manning, Ann Daly, and others are now focusing on modifying and extending theories of spectatorship to account for the kinesthetic power of dance and the live presence of the dancer.[32] In this way dance scholarship not only draws on feminist theories from other disciplines but contributes to the development of new theoretical paradigms, paradigms for the analysis of movement and bodily display that can have important implications beyond the dance field. Similar exchanges are underway in literary theory as dance scholars consider narrative as a component of dance history and literary specialists consider movement and the invocation of bodily presence in verbal texts.[33]

Feminist dance scholars can expand their intellectual "interlocutors" even further, engaging with new feminist scholarship in anthropology, the history of science, communication studies, psychology, exercise physiology, leisure studies, ethnic studies, postcolonial studies, and art history, among others. In each of these areas dance scholars will find new feminist perspectives, specific "technologies of the body," and ongoing research that may have relevance. Anthropologist Anna Aalten, for example, is studying contemporary ballet dancers and their "female" body image, diet, and training regimes in the Netherlands.[34] Dance studies may in turn offer a unique perspective of bodily semiotics and specialized analytical tools, such as movement analysis, to these fields.

Sexuality Studies: A Deafening Silence in Dance Scholarship

Outstanding among these "interlocutory fields" is the newly exploding category of gay and lesbian scholarship. With only a few exceptions we, as dance scholars, have not begun to engage seriously with this new scholarship.[35] This lack is all the more striking when we consider the rapid growth of feminist dance criticism in the last ten years or so. What do we have to gain by joining these debates, and what particular insights might dance provide? What special analytical techniques might studies of dance and sexuality demand, or offer?

Dance provides an unmined wealth of information regarding sexuality for some of the same reasons that it is a prime site of gender analysis. It is dependent on bodily display and bodies are the naturalizing anchors for systems of gender. A gendered body is often perceived as a sexualized body. It is important to disarticulate the triumvirate of sexual differentiation (biological sex), gendered positioning, and presumed sexuality. Although perhaps more difficult for us to recognize, sexuality is, like gender, a historically developed and developing system of social categorization that was not always as it is now and is not always the same in every location, as scholars like Adrienne Rich, Serena Nanda, and David Greenberg have amply demonstrated.[36] Since the nineteenth century, sexuality has functioned as a marker of social categorization of people on the basis of presumed desire and its relation to biological difference.[37] This relationship between biology and body parts is one of the defining tenets of popular belief about homosexuality. Females are presumed to be *women* and to be heterosexual, males to be *men* and heterosexual as well. Or, they may "be" the "opposite," that is, homosexual, or more recently in public discourse, "bisexual," which retains the binary division while coupling it. The foundational effect of the binary *male/female* biological divide remains intact and gives meaning to these other categories. As dance scholars we can begin to unpack this linkage. Just as we might investigate the staging of gender, so too can we analyze the staging of implicit and explicit desire.

That we have not done so is, I think, not only a mark of the come-lately status of dance scholarship, but a consequence of the "spectre" of homosexuality that has for so many years hung over the U.S. dance profession, painting dancing men as "effeminate," as gays. Female performers, already being feminized through their bodily display, escape the label. The significant presence of gay men in dance, and in the art world generally, is both one of the reasons for this silence and its contradiction.

While some scholars might see sexuality as a tangential, add-on category for analysis, a consideration of dance histories in the United States reveals that the "spectre" of homosexuality has profoundly shaped the development of both popular and theatrical dance forms, and their critical and audience reception. Do we really understand the rise of the female ballerina to prominence since the Romantic era? How do we account for the emphasis on "athleticism" in male stars like Baryshnikov, or the jaunty maleness of the sailors in Jerome Robbins's *Fancy Free*, or of the cowboys in de Mille's *Rodeo*? Why are eighth-grade boys more likely to be found at the punch bowl than out on the floor at the local teen dance? What was/is allowable on the stage, in print, in dance clubs, and in choreography is shaped by the invisible contours of the walls of homophobia in this country. It is a powerful structuring absence in dance history.

Writing a history of this absence will entail careful consideration of the particularities of U.S. history as well. This patina of male homosexuality extends to all arts and is in part a result of the postcolonial United States vis-à-vis Europe. Early national ideologies situated the democratic United States in opposition to the aristocratic nations of Europe. The elite arts (and artists) were associated with those aristocracies. Hence, the ideal U.S. citizen (white and male at the time) was *not* an artist. And vice versa; artists were associated with the not-male, the feminine. Women however were already too "feminized" to easily claim the agency associated with being an artist. When they did, they had to carefully contend with the threat of public sexualization when putting their bodies on display.[38] The potential sexualization of the male body on ("passive") display and hence its associated "femininity" combine with nationalist ideologies of populism to produce a particular formulation of the arts in the United States, a formulation subtly rooted in fears of homosexuality. Recent attacks on the National Endowment of the Arts, spearheaded by Senator Jesse Helms's denouncement of homoerotic imagery, makes clear that issues of national identity, sexuality, and artistry remain tightly entwined and potentially explosive today.[39]

New dance critics can begin to unveil the structuring absence of homophobia and its formative effects. They can analyze the ways in which this powerful fear has framed the status of dance as a profession and shaped what is said and thought about dancers, and how the display of dancing bodies, in both social and theatrical forms, is affected by the linkage of public bodily display with feminization, except when underwritten by aggression, as in the sports arena. New critics can specify the intersection of homophobia with gender, region, race, and class and reveal its profound influence in shaping the contours of dance practice and dance history in the United States. Critics can also actively chart the flow of "queer" dance and movement styles out of subcultural spaces and into nongay styles in popular culture and on the stage. (Vogueing is a recent example, gone mainstream and crossing racial and class lines through Madonna's restaging on MTV.)

The borders of hegemonic masculinity and femininity are patrolled at the site of homosexuality. But these borders are never perfectly patrolled; they are relatively permeable depending on time and place. The boundary zones are sometimes the most illuminating because their continual redrawing clarifies what is at stake in their maintenance. We can consider what the historical parameters have been in certain times and places for male bodily display. Expressivity versus athleticism, and passivity versus activity are two of the dimensions at play, as film scholars have noted in their discussions of the contradictions that arise in a spectatorial apparatus that positions woman as "to-be-looked-at," as fetish or spectacle, and man as active agent.[40] The current popularity of male hip-hop–style dancing, for example, with strong, aggressive, athletic movements, fetishizes maleness as physical power and not passive spectacle to be visually consumed.

Staging Desire

Most contemporary theatrical dance performance in the United States presents spectators with bodies that can be read as biologically "male" or "female."[41] That is, most of us recognize specific dancers on the stage as male or female. Conventions for what are "appropriate" or aesthetically pleasing bodies shift historically, the current trend for example inflected by the popularity of fitness and a streamlined athleticism for women. Movement vocabularies and choreographic conventions (such as who partners whom and how) may be coded as masculine or feminine, or "neutral" (hence marked by its "unmarked" status). These conventions too change over time and may be actively reconfigured, as in the work of the

Canadian group La La La Human Steps. But within these conventions, the inter-relational aspects of the staging, from body angle to eye contact, may imply vari-ous trajectories of desire. Costuming, makeup, sound scoring, lighting, and any spoken texts may also imply a gendered or sexuality-inflected frame that shapes meaning for spectators. Similarly, spectators' own experiences, knowledge of aes-thetic conventions, and beliefs provide the ground for meaning-making.

The relationship among these various semiotic systems, of reading biological sex, of reading choreographic and staging conventions, of framing social intelli-gibility, may be complex. They may line up in conventional ways, with "female" dancers dancing "female" movement vocabularies in narratives of romantic het-erosexual love, for example, thus replicating hegemonic ideologies. Or they may slip, interrupt one another, challenge previous perceptions, or simply be per-ceived by some as unintelligible. When Mark Morris "redid" the *Nutcracker* in his (1992 U.S. premiere) version of *The Hard Nut* at the Brooklyn Academy of Music, a great deal of the audience's pleasure, indicated by laughter and spontaneous ap-plause, depended on knowing certain conventions and seeing them blasted or given a new spin. The staging of sexuality, always central to the *Nutcracker* which is poised around fantasies of adolescence, received a new rendition when Morris cast and rechoreographed the ballet.

Critic Gay Morris recounts some of the results of the new staging in the first act:

> The situation then is this: Mrs. Stahlbaum, played by a man, is attracted to Drosselmeyer who is played by a man. When Mr. Stahlbaum, played by a man, staunchly defends Mrs. Stahlbaum's honor in the face of Drosselmeyer's lascivi-ous kiss to her bosom, there is gender trouble a plenty. Later in the evening Mrs. Stahlbaum touches the housekeeper [played by a man in drag in a campy style] on the shoulder and gives her a provocative look. Could there be something going on between these two, and if there is, is it between the men who are play-ing women or between the women characters? If Mrs. Stahlbaum is engaged in a flirtation with the housekeeper, as their glances suggest, desire is shown to be not only unrelated to gender but to be a changeable thing within a single individual. [Mark] Morris here presents gender as a field rather than a spectrum along which individuals are permanently placed. In Morris's gender field not only do people's desires not necessarily match what is claimed to be their "natural" gen-der, but that desire is dynamic and shifting.[42]

Mark Morris uses more than cross-gender casting and suggestive looks to un-settle the traditional *Nutcracker*. For example, the Snowflake Waltz, usually per-formed by a female corps de ballet on point, is performed by men and women in identical costumes, executing the same steps. Half the dancers (both men and women) are on point, the rest are barefoot. Cropped tops and icy caps hide hair but reveal midriffs. Gay Morris asserts that this casting "undermines identity even more than an all-male corps de ballet would, because it makes the viewer less certain of defining the dancers in terms of binary gender" (p. 242).

But it is Mark Morris's revision of the duet usually danced by the Snow King and Queen that is perhaps the most startling moment in the ballet. Staging this as a duet for Drosselmeyer and his nephew, he utilizes many of the balletic conventions of the nineteenth-century pas de deux, a heterosexual love duet in which the male supports, lifts, and displays the female with courtly affection. The older, taller Drosselmeyer guides and supports the younger smaller man, framing his body with his own in parallel arabesques and gently embracing him with an arm encircling his chest as they dance together. The soaring arc of the Tchaikovsky score underscores an emotional subtext. As Gay Morris notes, many critics interpreted this as a dance of homosexual passion, but the choreographer denied that intent, saying that the uncle is instructing the young man in the skills for heterosexual wooing that he might need later in life. And many of the same movements do recur in the grand pas de deux between Young Drosselmeyer and Marie in the second act, where Mark Morris uses the heterosexual conventions of the ballet (p. 241, 243).

That the critics "got it wrong," that is, interpreted the scene between the two men differently than the choreographer's stated intent, is telling. It indicates that at least some "homosexual readings" of the duet did occur, and in so doing, they necessarily inflected some audience members' perceptions of the rest of the ballet as well. The heterosexual duet that echoes it later is equally unsettled, now somewhat inflected with the desiring trace of homosexuality. We might even assume that subsequent traditional stagings of the perennial *Nutcracker* will be viewed through a frame of aesthetic experience that now includes that remembered trace.

The careful and at times overly compensatory staging of the heterosexual male in theatrical dance is here complemented with one of the few highly visible instances of a male duet interpreted, at least by some, as a representation of homosexuality. Given the past, how can we account for the dramatic current popularity of several choreographers who may at times stage overtly homosexual representations or at least blatantly trip up traditional expectations of heterosexuality, such as Bill T. Jones, Joe Goode, and Michael Clark, and to some extent Steven Petronio? Johanna Boyce's piece *Ties That Bind 2* (1985), although less well-known, also breaks new ground in its overt representation of a lesbian relationship.

One of the goals of new dance criticism might be to account for the popularity of these choreographies. What enabling conditions now exist in public discourse that can result in Bill T. Jones's portrait on the cover of *Time* magazine in the winter of 1994 following the U.S. premiere of his new work *Still/Here?* And why do nonnormative representations of female sexuality remain relatively less visible in the dance world? To begin to sketch answers to these questions regarding Jones, we must trace the historically shifting contours of art reception, economics, racial politics, the gay liberation movement, and discourses about AIDS in the United States.[43]

As a focal point for this discussion, I have chosen work by Mark Morris that makes the staging of gender and sexuality central to its choreography. But it is important to stress that the staging of sexuality occurs in most dance forms and social dance practices in the United States, past and present. What's different about work like Morris's is just that he challenges and makes explicit that which is usually either implicit, or so naturalized it is regarded as an integral part of the aesthetic, like the romantic, stereotypic heterosexuality of the classical pas de deux form.

Sexuality studies prompt us to ask new questions about dance. How does bodily movement signify sexual desire, and what is the relationship of such desire to gendered positionings? How are our perceptions of those engendered sexualities related to social and material practices? These new questions can further illuminate feminist inquiry of dance, unsettling presumed linkages between biological sex, sexuality, and gender. In turn, we can contribute to feminist scholarship by revealing the intimate links between the construction of desire, kinesthetics, and social power.[44]

NOTES

1. See Anne Fausto-Sterling, "The Five Sexes: Why Male and Female Are Not Enough," *The Sciences* 33, no. 2 (March/April 1993): 20–25, for a discussion of the range of human biological "sexes" masked by the binary division.

2. Teresa de Lauretis, *Technologies of Gender: Essays on Theory, Film, and Fiction* (Bloomington: Indiana University Press, 1987): 2, 5.

3. See Jill Dolan, *The Feminist Spectator as Critic* (Ann Arbor: UMI Research Press, 1988), for a discussion of contemporary U.S. feminisms in "liberal," "cultural or radical," and "materialist" modes. See Toril Moi, *Sexual/Textual Politics: Feminist Literary Theory* (New York: Methuen, 1985), for a summary of Anglo-American and French feminist theories. See *This Bridge Called My Back: Writings by Radical Women of Color*, 2d ed., ed. Cherríe Moraga and Gloria Anzaldua (New York: Kitchen Table: Women of Color Press, 1983), for an introduction to feminist theory by women of color. See also works by Collins and hooks, cited below. Additional suggestions are found in the references, below.

4. Joan Wallach Scott, *Gender and the Politics of History* (New York: Columbia University Press, 1988), especially chaps. 1 and 2.

5. For suggested readings, see the references, below.

6. For an excellent discussion of the history of U.S. feminism and its relation to particular theoretical formulations since the late 1960s, see Katie King, *Theory in Its Feminist*

Travels: Conversations in U.S. Women's Movements (Bloomington: Indiana University Press, 1994).

7. For a good introduction to work by French feminists, see *New French Feminisms: An Anthology*, ed. Elaine Marks and Isabelle de Courtivron (New York: Schocken Books, 1981). For a contemporary phenomenological approach that critiques and extends some of that work in an unusual way, see Maxine Sheets-Johnstone, *The Roots of Power: Animate Form and Gendered Bodies* (Chicago: Open Court, 1994). For a good example of contemporary dance scholarship drawing on the French theorists, see Ann Cooper Albright, "Incalculable Choreographies: The Dance Practice of Marie Chouinard," in *Bodies of the Text: Dance as Theory, Literature as Dance*, ed. Ellen Goellner and Jacqueline Shea Murphys (New Brunswick: Rutgers University Press, 1995), 157–82.

8. See Simone de Beauvoir, *The Second Sex*, trans. E. M. Parshley (New York: Vintage, 1973); Kate Millet, *Sexual Politics* (London: Virago, 1977), originally published in 1969; Elaine Showalter, "Towards a Feminist Poetics," in *Women Writing and Writing About Women*, ed. Mary Jacobus (London: Croom Helm, 1979), 22–41; and Showalter, "Feminist Criticism in the Wilderness," *Critical Inquiry* 8, no. 1 (1981): 179–205; Gayatri Spivak, *In Other Worlds: Essays in Cultural Politics* (New York: Methuen, 1987); Patricia Hill Collins, *Black Feminist Thought: Knowledge, Consciousness, and the Politics of Empowerment* (Boston: Unwin Hyman, 1990); Gloria Anzaldua, *Borderlands/La Frontera: The New Mestiza* (San Francisco: Aunt Lute Books, 1987); bell hooks, *Yearning: Race, Gender, and Cultural Politics* (Boston: South End Press, 1990), and *Ain't I a Woman: Black Women and Feminism* (Boston: South End Press, 1981); Chandra Mohanty, "Under Western Eyes: Feminist Scholarship and Colonial Discourses," *Feminist Review* 30 (autumn 1988): 65–88; Chela Sandoval, "U.S. Third World Feminism: The Theory and Method of Oppositional Consciousness in the Postmodern World," *Genders* 10 (spring 1991): 1–24; Gayle Rubin, "The Traffic in Women: Notes on the 'Political Economy' of Sex," in *Toward an Anthropology of Women*, ed. Rayna Reiter (New York: Monthly Review Press, 1975), 157–210; and Adrienne Rich, "Compulsory Heterosexuality and Lesbian Existence," in *Powers of Desire: The Politics of Sexuality*, ed. Ann Snitow, Christine Stansell, and Sharon Thompson (New York: Monthly Review Press, 1983), 177–205. For a thoughtful discussion of feminist debates since the 1970s, see King, *Theory in Its Feminist Travels*.

9. Ann Daly makes a similar point in her article, "Unlimited Partnership: Dance and Feminist Analysis," *Dance Research Journal* 23, no. 1 (spring 1991): 2–5. As she notes on page 2: "Rather than being defined by any particular methodology, feminist analysis is distinguished by its point of view."

10. Ann Daly, "Classical Ballet: A Discourse of Difference," *Women and Performance: A Journal of Feminist Theory* 3, no. 2 (1987–1988): 58.

11. Susan Foster develops this last point in her article "Dancing Bodies," *Zone 6: Incorporations*, ed. Jonathan Crary and Sanford Kwinter (New York: Zone Books, 1992), 480–95, reprinted in Jane Desmond, ed., *Meaning in Motion: New Cultural Studies of Dance* (Durham: Duke University Press, 1997).

12. The phrase is Teresa de Lauretis's, from her book, *Technologies of Gender: Essays on Theory, Film, and Fiction* (Bloomington: Indiana University Press, 1987).

13. Evan Alderson, "Ballet as Ideology: *Giselle*, Act II," *Dance Chronicle* 10, no. 3 (1987): 293–301. Reprinted in Jane Desmond, ed., *Meaning in Motion: New Cultural Studies of Dance* (1997). See also Ramsay Burt, *The Male Dancer* (London and New York: Routledge, 1996); and Susan Foster, "The Ballerina's Phallic Pointe," in *Corporealities: Dancing Knowledge, Culture, and Power*, ed. Foster (London and New York: Routledge, 1996), 1–24.

14. Wendy Hollway, quoted in Teresa de Lauretis, *Technologies of Gender*.

15. See Michel Foucault, *The History of Sexuality, Vol. I.: An Introduction* (New York: Vintage Books, 1980); and *Discipline and Punish: The Birth of the Prison* (New York: Pantheon, 1977), for example.

16. Hollway quoted in de Lauretis, *Technologies of Gender*, 15.

17. Pierre Bourdieu, *Distinction: A Social Critique of the Judgement of Taste* (Cambridge: Harvard University Press, 1984).

18. This form, like any other, is subject to historical change. Contemporary "ballet" and "modern dance," for instance, are often blurred at many levels, including choreographic conventions, movement vocabularies, training techniques, and professional employment.

19. See, for example, Sally Ness, *Body, Movement, and Culture: Kinesthetic and Visual Symbolism in a Philippine Community* (Philadelphia: University of Pennsylvania Press, 1992); Cynthia Novack, *Sharing the Dance: Contact Improvisation and American Culture* (Madison: University of Wisconsin Press, 1990); and Katrina Hazzard-Gordon, *Jookin': The Rise and Fall of Social Dance Formations in African-American Culture* (Philadelphia: Temple University Press, 1990). Each of these authors includes perspectives on gender in her work, although that dimension is not always foregrounded.

20. Antonio Gramsci quoted in Stuart Hall, "The Toad in the Garden: Thatcherism Among the Theorists," in *Marxism and the Interpretation of Culture*, ed. Cary Nelson and Lawrence Grossberg (Urbana: University of Illinois Press, 1988), 55.

21. Louis Althusser, "Ideology and Ideological State Apparatuses," in his *Lenin and Philosophy* (London: New Left Books, 1971), 127–86.

22. For an excellent introduction, see Chris Weedon, *Feminist Practice and Poststructuralist Theory* (London: Basil Blackwell, 1987). For a discussion of dance history in relation to the shifting borders of disciplinarity, see Janet Adshead-Lansdale, "Border Tensions in the Discipline of Dance History," in *Retooling the Discipline: Research and Teaching Strategies for the 21st Century*, ed. Linda J. Tomko (Provo: Brigham Young University, Society of Dance History Scholars, 1994), 13–25. *Proceedings: Society of Dance History Scholars*, 1994 annual meeting, Provo, Utah.

23. See Janet Wolff, *The Social Production of Art* (New York: New York University Press, 1981).

24. See Susan Manning, *Ecstasy and the Demon: Feminism and Nationalism in the Dances of Mary Wigman* (Berkeley: University of California Press, 1993); Amy Koritz, "Dancing the Orient for England: Maud Allan's *The Vision of Salome*," *Theatre Journal* 46, no. 1 (March 1994): 63–78; Brenda Dixon-Gottschild, "Some Thoughts on Choreographing History," in *Meaning in Motion: New Cultural Studies of Dance*, ed. Jane Desmond (Durham: Duke University Press, 1997), 7–178; Ann Daly, *Done into Dance: Isadora Duncan in America* (Bloomington: Indiana University Press, 1995); and Jane Desmond, "Dancing Out the Difference: Cultural Imperialism and Ruth St. Denis' 'Radha' of 1906," *Signs: Journal of Women in Culture and Society* 17, no. 1 (autumn 1991): 28–49.

25. Judith Butler, *Gender Trouble: Feminism and the Subversion of Identity* (New York: Routledge, 1990); and her "Performative Acts and Gender Constitution: An Essay in Phenomenology and Feminist Theory," in *Performing Feminisms: Feminist Critical Theory and Theater*, ed. Sue-Ellen Case (Baltimore: Johns Hopkins University Press, 1990), 270–82.

26. Butler clarifies what she perceives as this misreading in her article "Critically Queer," *GLQ: A Journal of Lesbian and Gay Studies* 1, no. 1 (1993): 17–32. See also her *Bodies that Matter: On the Discursive Limits of "Sex"* (New York: Routledge, 1993).

27. Originally drawn from J. L. Austin's concept of speech acts, *performative* and *performativity* are references in literary theory, feminist theory, and in performance studies increasingly used to denote the wider range of bodily enactment. These enactments are

not random or individual; rather, they belong to semiotic systems through which their meanings emerge. A related distinction is that made in linguistics between *langue* and *parole*, language as a system versus specific acts of language usage.

28. See Foster, "Dancing Bodies," cited above, and Mark Franko, *Dance as Text: Ideologies of the Baroque Body* (New York: Cambridge University Press, 1993).

29. Janet Wolff makes this point in the last chapter of her book, "Reinstating Corporeality: Feminism and Body Politics," in her *Feminine Sentences: Essays on Women and Culture* (Berkeley: University of California Press, 1990), 120–41, also reprinted in *Meaning in Motion*, ed. Jane Desmond.

30. Laura Mulvey, "Visual Pleasure and Narrative Cinema," *Screen* no. 3 (autumn 1975): 6–18.

31. In film and media studies see, for example, E. Ann Kaplan, "Is the Gaze Male?" in her *Women and Film: Both Sides of the Camera* (New York: Methuen, 1983), 23–35; Mary Ann Doane, "Film and the Masquerade—Theorizing the Female Spectator," *Screen* 23, nos. 3–4 (September/October 1982): 74–88; and her "Masquerade Reconsidered: Further Thoughts on the Female Spectator," *Discourse* 11, no. 1 (1988/1989): 42–54; and Mulvey's own extension of her original idea in "On Duel in the Sun," *Framework* no. 15 (1981): 12–15; Linda Williams, "When the Woman Looks," in *Re-Vision: Essays in Feminist Film Criticism,* ed. Mary Ann Doane, Patricia Mellencamp, and Linda Williams (Frederick, Md.: University Publications of America, 1984), 83–99. See also Lorraine Gamman and Margaret Marshment, eds., *The Female Gaze: Women as Viewers of Popular Culture* (Seattle: The Real Comet Press, 1990).

32. See Susan Manning, "The Female Dancer and the Male Gaze: Feminist Critiques of Early Modern Dance," in *Meaning in Motion: New Cultural Studies of Dance,* ed. Jane Desmond (Durham: Duke University Press, 1997), 153–56; and Ann Daly, "Dance History and Feminist Theory: Reconsidering Isadora Duncan and the Male Gaze," in *Gender in Performance,* ed. Laurence Senelick (Hanover, N.H.: University Press of New England), 239–59.

33. See, for example, Jacqueline Shea Murphy, ed., *Bodies of the Text* (New Brunswick, N.J.: Rutgers University Press, 1995); and Amy Koritz, *The Dancer from the Dance: Literature, Dance and Gender in Early Twentieth Century British Culture* (Ann Arbor: University of Michigan Press, 1995).

34. Anna Aalten, "Femininity and the Body: Female Ballet Dancers in the Netherlands," paper delivered at the 1994 annual conference of the Congress on Research in Dance, Denton, Texas.

35. See Carol Martin's introduction and the roundtable discussion in Johanna Boyce, Ann Daly, Bill T. Jones, and Carol Martin, "Movement and Gender: A Roundtable Discussion," *The Drama Review* (*TDR*) 32, no. 4, T-120 (winter 1988): 82–101. See also Bud Coleman, "Ballerinos en Pointe—Les Ballets Trockadero de Monte Carol," paper delivered at the 1994 annual conference of the Congress on Research in Dance, Denton, Texas. The new collection *Bodies of the Text: Dance as Theory, Literature as Dance*, edited by Ellen W. Goellner and Jacqueline Shea Murphy (New Brunswick: Rutgers University Press, 1995), contains several articles that discuss issues of sexuality in live dance or in dance on film. One hopes that the collection of these articles in one volume will give a sense of presence to sexuality studies in dance scholarship and will stimulate further work in that area. See Jacqueline Shea Murphy's "Unrest and Uncle Tom: Bill T. Jones/Arnie Zane Dance Company's *Last Supper at Uncle Tom's Cabin/The Promised Land*," Michael Moon's "Flaming Closets," and Gaylyn Studlar's "Douglass Fairbanks: Thief of the Ballet Russes," in that volume.

36. Adrienne Rich, "Compulsory Heterosexuality," cited above; Serena Nanda, "Hijras as Neither Man Nor Woman," in *The Lesbian and Gay Studies Reader*, ed. Henry Abelove, Michele Aina Barale, and David M. Halperin (New York: Routledge, 1993), 542–53; David F. Greenberg, *The Construction of Homosexuality* (Chicago: University of Chicago Press, 1988).

37. This is the case for Europe and North and South America generally, but not for all communities therein. By *sexuality* in this context, I mean a division into categories of homosexuality and heterosexuality. As Greenberg and others have shown, it was only in the nineteenth century that these terms crystallized as denoting categories of people rather than categories of sexual acts.

38. See my discussion of Ruth St. Denis's sublimation of sensuality into spirituality in her framing of her work in my "Dancing Out the Difference," cited above.

39. See Richard Bolton, ed., *Culture Wars: Documents from the Recent Controversies in the Arts* (New York: New Press, 1992).

40. See Mulvey, "Visual Pleasure and Narrative Cinema," cited above. Just as the limitations of the "male gaze" theory have prompted a reworking of ideas of female spectatorship, so too have the complexities of cross-gender identifications and of gay male (and lesbian) spectatorship. See Richard Dyer, "Don't Look Now: The Instabilities of the Male Pin-Up," in his *Only Entertainment* (New York: Routledge, 1992), 103–20.

41. Some of Nikolais's work is an exception. There are also cases where, due to particularities of body size and shape, as well as costuming, this may not always be apparent.

42. Gay Morris, "Subversive Strategies in *The Hard Nut*," in *Retooling the Discipline: Research and Teaching Strategies for the 21st Century*, ed. Linda J. Tomko (Provo: Brigham Young University, Society of Dance History Scholars, 1994), 237–44.

43. For an ambitious attempt to read Jones's work in the widest possible parameters of cultural politics, see Randy Martin, "Overreading 'The Promised Land': Toward a Narrative of Context in Dance," unpublished manuscript.

44. I develop these issues further in my article, "Embodying Difference: Issues in Dance and Cultural Studies," *Cultural Critique* 26 (winter 1993–1994): 33–64.

REFERENCES

The following works are recommended, but there are many, many others that could have been included. Check bibliographies in these books for further leads.

Suggested Topics

Researchers may find it helpful to read each of the four sections in this reference list in relation to or against one another to find their areas of overlap, disjuncture, and distinctiveness.

For example, analyze the current state of work in feminist dance history and criticism in relation to the suggested readings in feminist theory and sexuality studies. Which debates, strains of thought, and theoretical formulations have emerged most visibly so far in feminist dance writings? In charting these debates, consider which aspects of dance feminist scholars have focused on: individual dance works or choreographers, our historiographic practices, dance institutions and training regimes, the categories of theatrical, popular, ritual, or social dancing? Dance as a profession? Dance as a cultural practice? The relationship between scholarship and pedagogy—how and what we teach about dance?

How does the work of feminist dance scholars relate to dominant issues or formulations in non-dance-oriented feminist scholarship? What further issues for investigation arise when we bring dance and feminism together?

Special concerns pertain when analyzing dance as an embodied social practice. How, for instance, is a complex semiological system (a system of signs) based on motion, rather than static display, to be theorized? How does the physical presence of the live body (as performer or participant) shape our analyses of dance? Dance is different from related representational systems based on visual display, like film with its celluloid bodies, or like many forms of theater with a narrative base. How can the specific concerns of dance open up new questions for feminist theorizing in general, or for sexuality studies?

Keep in mind that other modes of analyses referred to in this essay may also have particular relevance for future work in dance, such as Marxist analyses that foreground issues of class, and postcolonial studies that attempt to account for legacies of particular national histories of domination and resistance. In turn, dance studies may also contribute new ideas to those arenas, revealing ways in which class and national identity are represented in formalized systems of embodiment. (I develop these issues further in my article, "Embodying Difference: Issues in Dance and Cultural Studies," *Cultural Critique* 26 [winter 1993–1994]: 33–64.) Feminist analysis of dance requires a broadly interdisciplinary approach because systems of gender constitution and the ideologies that support them inflect all social formations.

I. Selected Works in Feminist Theory and History

Anzaldua, Gloria. *Borderlands/La Frontera: The New Mestiza*. San Francisco: Aunt Lute Books, 1987.

Bordo, Susan. *Unbearable Weight: Feminism, Western Culture, and the Body*. Berkeley: University of California Press, 1993.

Butler, Judith. *Gender Trouble: Feminism and the Subversion of Identity*. New York: Routledge, 1990.

———. *Bodies that Matter: On the Discursive Limits of "Sex."* New York: Routledge, 1993.

Case, Sue-Ellen, ed. *Performing Feminisms*. Baltimore: Johns Hopkins University Press, 1991.

Collins, Patricia Hill. *Black Feminist Thought: Knowledge, Consciousness, and the Politics of Empowerment*. Boston: Unwin Hyman, 1990.

Cott, Nancy F. *The Grounding of Modern Feminism*. New Haven: Yale University Press, 1987.

de Lauretis, Teresa. *Technologies of Gender: Essays on Theory, Film, and Fiction*. Bloomington: Indiana University Press, 1987.

Diamond, Irene, and Lee Quinby. *Feminism and Foucault: Reflections on Resistance*. Boston: Northeastern University Press, 1988.

Dolan, Jill. *The Feminist Spectator as Critic*. Durham: Duke University Press, 1988.

hooks, bell. *Ain't I a Woman: Black Women and Feminism*. Boston: South End Press, 1981.

———. *Black Looks: Race and Representation*. Boston: South End Press, 1992.

———. *Yearning: Race, Gender, and Cultural Politics*. Boston: South End Press, 1990.

Hull, Gloria T., Patricia Bell Scott, and Barbara Smith, eds. *All the Women Are White, All the Blacks Are Men, But Some of Us Are Brave: Black Women's Studies*. New York: Feminist Press, 1982.

Jaggar, Alison M., and Susan R. Bordo, eds. *Gender/Body/Knowledge: Feminist Reconstructions of Being and Knowing.* New Brunswick: Rutgers University Press, 1989.

Kerber, Linda, Alice Kessler-Harris, and Kathryn Kish Sklar, eds. *U.S. History as Women's History: New Feminist Essays.* Chapel Hill: University of North Carolina Press, 1995.

Marks, Elaine, and Isabelle de Courtivron. *New French Feminisms: An Anthology.* New York: Schocken Books, 1981.

Minh-ha, Trinh T. *Woman, Native, Other: Writing Postcoloniality and Feminism.* Bloomington: Indiana University Press, 1989.

Mohanty, Chandra. "Under Western Eyes: Feminist Scholarship and Colonial Discourses." *Feminist Review* 30 (autumn 1988): 65–88.

Moi, Toril. *Sexual/Textual Politics: Feminist Literary Theory.* New York: Methuen, 1985.

Moi, Toril, and Janice Radway, eds. *Materialist Feminism.* Special issue, *South Atlantic Quarterly* 93, no. 4 (fall 1994).

Moraga, Cherrie, and Gloria Anzaldua, eds. *This Bridge Called My Back: Writings by Radial Women of Color.* 2d ed. New York: Kitchen Table: Women of Color Press, 1983.

Narayan, Uma. "The Project of Feminist Epistemology: Perspectives from a Nonwestern Feminist." In *Gender/Body/Knowledge: Feminist Reconstructions of Being and Knowing,* ed. Alison Jaggar and Susan Bordo, 256–72. New Brunswick: Rutgers University Press, 1989.

Pharr, Suzanne. *Homophobia: A Weapon of Sexism.* Inverness, Calif.: Chardon Press, 1988.

Reinharz, Shulamit. *Feminist Methods in Social Research.* New York: Oxford University Press, 1992.

Riley, Denise. *"Am I That Name?": Feminism and the Category of "Women" in History.* London: Macmillan, 1988.

Rubin, Gayle. "The Traffic in Women: Notes on the 'Political Economy' of Sex." In *Toward an Anthropology of Women,* ed. Rayna Reiter, 157–210. New York: Monthly Review Press, 1975.

Sandoval, Chela. "U.S. Third World Feminism: The Theory and Method of Oppositional Consciousness in the Postmodern World." *Genders* 10 (spring 1991): 1–24.

Scott, Joan Wallach. *Gender and the Politics of History.* New York: Columbia University Press, 1988.

Senelick, Lawrence. *Gender and Performance: The Presentation of Difference in the Performing Arts.* Hanover, N.H.: University Press of New England, 1992.

Showalter, Elaine, ed. *The New Feminist Criticism: Essays on Women, Literature, and Theory.* New York: Pantheon Books, 1985.

Snitow, Ann, et al. *Powers of Desire: The Politics of Sexuality.* New York: Monthly Review Press, 1983.

Tong, Rosemarie. *Feminist Thought: A Comprehensive Introduction.* Boulder, Colo.: Westview, 1989.

Weedon, Chris. *Feminist Practice and Post–Structuralist Theory.* London: Basil Blackwell, 1987.

Wolff, Janet. *Feminine Sentences.* Berkeley and Los Angeles: University of California Press, 1990.

II. Selected Works in Dance and Gender

Adair, Christy. *Women and Dance: Sylphs and Sirens*. New York: New York University Press, 1992.

Albright, Ann Cooper. "Mining the Dancefield: Feminist Theory and Contemporary Dance." *Dissertation Abstracts International* 52 (1991): 0718A.

———. "Auto–Body Stories: Blondell Cummings and Autobiography in Dance." In *Meaning in Motion: New Cultural Studies of Dance,* ed. Jane Desmond, 179–206. Durham: Duke University Press, 1997.

Alderson, Evan. "Ballet as Ideology: *Giselle,* Act II." *Dance Chronicle* 10, no. 3 (1987): 290–304.

Allen, Robert. *Horrible Prettiness: Burlesque and American Culture*. Chapel Hill: University of North Carolina Press, 1991.

Burt, Ramsay. *The Male Dancer*. London and New York: Routledge, 1996.

Daly, Ann. "Classical Ballet: A Discourse of Difference." *Women and Performance: A Journal of Feminist Theory* 3, no. 2 (1987–1988): 57–66.

———. "Dance History and Feminist Theory: Reconsidering Isadora Duncan and the Male Gaze." In *Gender and Performance: The Presentation of Difference in the Performing Arts,* ed. Laurence Senelick, 239–59. Hanover, N.H.: University Press of New England, 1992.

———. *Done into Dance: Isadora Duncan in America*. Bloomington: Indiana University Press, 1995.

Desmond, Jane. "Dancing Out the Difference: Cultural Imperialism and Ruth St. Denis' 'Radha' of 1906." *Signs: Journal of Women in Culture and Society* 17, no. 1 (autumn 1991): 28–49.

Foster, Susan. *Reading Dancing: Bodies and Subjects in Contemporary American Dance*. Berkeley: University of California Press, 1986.

———. "Dancing Bodies." In *Zone 6: Incorporations,* ed. Jonathan Crary and Sanford Kwinter, 480–95. New York: Zone Books, 1992.

———. "The Ballerina's Phallic Pointe." In *Corporealities: Dancing Knowledge, Culture and Power,* ed. Foster, 1–24. New York: Routledge, 1996.

Franko, Mark. "Double Bodies: Androgyny and Power in the Performances of Louis XIV." *The Drama Review* 38, no. 4, T-144 (winter 1944): 71–82.

Garafola, Lynn. "The Travesty Dancer in Nineteenth Century Ballet." *Dance Research Journal* 17, no. 2, and 18, no. 1 (fall 1985/spring 1986): 35–40.

Goldberg, Marianne, ed. *The Body as Discourse*. Special issue of *Women and Performance: A Journal of Feminist Theory* 3, no. 4 (1987–1988).

Hanna, Judith Lynne. *Dance, Sex, and Gender: Signs of Identity, Dominance, Defiance, and Desire*. Chicago: University of Chicago Press, 1988.

Koritz, Amy. *The Dancer from the Dance: Literature, Dance and Gender in Early Twentieth Century British Culture*. Ann Arbor: University of Michigan Press, 1995.

Manning, Susan. *Ecstasy and the Demon: Feminism and Nationalism in the Dances of Mary Wigman*. Berkeley: University of California Press, 1993.

———. "The Female Dancer and the Male Gaze." In *Meaning in Motion: New Cultural Studies of Dance,* ed. Jane Desmond, 153–56. Durham: Duke University Press, 1997.

Martin, Carol. *Dance Marathons: Performing American Culture of the 1920's and 1930's*. Jackson: University of Mississippi Press, 1994.

Morris, Gay. "Subversive Strategies in *The Hard Nut*." In *Retooling the Discipline: Research and Teaching Strategies for the 21st Century*, ed. Linda J. Tomko, 237–44. Provo: Brigham Young University, Society of Dance History Scholars, 1994.

Ness, Sally. *Body, Movement, and Culture: Kinesthetic and Visual Symbolism in a Philippine Community*. Philadelphia: University of Pennsylvania Press, 1992.

Novak, Cynthia. *Sharing the Dance: Contact Improvisation and American Culture*. Madison: University of Wisconsin Press, 1990.

III. Edited Collections

A number of recent edited collections contain relevant articles that engage issues of feminist theory.

Albright, Ann Cooper. *Choreographing Difference: The Body and Identity in Contemporary Dance*. Hanover: University Press of New England, 1997.

Desmond, Jane, ed. *Meaning in Motion: New Cultural Studies of Dance*. Durham: Duke University Press, 1997.

Foster, Susan Leigh, ed. *Corporealities: Dancing Knowledge, Culture and Power*. New York: Routledge, 1996.

Goellner, Ellen W., and Jacqueline Shea Murphy, eds. *Bodies of the Text: Dance as Theory, Literature as Dance*. New Brunswick: Rutgers University Press, 1995.

Morris, Gay, ed. *Moving Words: Re-writing Dance*. London and New York: Routledge, 1996.

IV. Selected Works in Sexuality Studies

Abelove, Henry, Michele Aina Barale, and David M. Halperin, eds. *The Lesbian and Gay Studies Reader*. New York: Routledge, 1993.

Case, Sue-Ellen. "Towards a Butch-Femme Aesthetic." In *Making a Spectacle: Feminist Essays on Contemporary Women's Theatre*, ed. Lynda Hart, 282–99. Ann Arbor: University of Michigan Press, 1992.

———. *The Domain Matrix*. Bloomington: Indiana University Press, 1997.

D'Emilio, John. *Sexual Politics, Sexual Communities: The Making of a Homosexual Minority in the United States, 1940–1970*. Chicago: University of Chicago Press, 1983.

Evans, David. *Sexual Citizenship: The Material Construction of Sexualities*. New York: Routledge, 1993.

Foucault, Michel. *The History of Sexuality. Vol. I: An Introduction*. New York: Vintage Books, 1980.

Fuss, Diana, ed. *Inside/Out: Lesbian Theories/Gay Theories*. New York: Routledge, 1991.

Greenberg, David. *The Construction of Homosexuality*. Chicago: University of Chicago Press, 1988.

Jagose, Annamarie. *Lesbian Utopics*. New York: Routledge, 1994.

———. *Queer Theory: An Introduction*. New York: New York University Press, 1996.

Meyer, Moe, ed. *The Politics and Poetics of Camp*. New York: Routledge, 1994.

Rich, Adrienne. "Compulsory Heterosexuality and Lesbian Existence." In *Powers of Desire: The Politics of Sexuality,* ed. Ann Snitow, Christine Stansell, and Sharon Thompson, 177–205. New York: Monthly Review Press, 1983.

Sedgewick, Eve. *Epistemology of the Closet*. Berkeley: University of California Press, 1990.

12 CULTURAL DIVERSITY AND DANCE HISTORY RESEARCH

John O. Perpener III

DANCE HISTORY, like other academic disciplines, is influenced by contemporary trends in education and the new directions in scholarship that those trends produce. For more than a decade, the reassessment of research goals has been influenced by issues of multiculturalism and diversity in American education. As university curricula continue to be restructured in acknowledgment of the diverse roots of America's intellectual and cultural heritage, scholars from various disciplines are searching for ways to include traditionally disenfranchised voices in their discourses. Such developments have increasingly influenced dance history scholars to recognize that diverse and historically marginalized groups have made profound contributions to American art and culture. As a result of these realizations, more and more researchers have begun to broaden the scope of their work and examine their methodologies because traditional approaches have not developed perspectives on American dance that comprehensively include matters of gender, race, ethnicity, and sexual preference.

This chapter discusses some of the problems encountered in developing research methodologies in areas that have not been traditionally included within the scope of dance history scholarship. In the broadest purview of dance history, it is possible to find many omissions from studies of particular periods, but the following discussion is primarily concerned with areas that have been neglected within the history of twentieth-century theatrical concert dance. The early history of African American concert dance is only one example of this type of omission, but here it is used to illustrate problems that are common to researchers who explore similar areas. By looking at the specific concerns of historians involved in African American dance, it is hoped that this chapter will contribute to the formulation of methodologies that can be applied to other research areas where issues of cultural diversity play an important role.

An important aspect of developing more inclusive approaches to the historiography of dance is the recognition and examination of some key issues that are imbedded in these efforts. In the essay "Diversity and Multicultural Concerns," dance educator Nancy Smith-Fichter conducts such an examination as she discusses several broad strategies for the general restructuring of dance curricula. She begins by pointing out the pros and cons of two of the most prominent strategies that have been used in such attempts. The first approach, a multicultural one, can ideally establish "the productive coexistence of autonomous unique cultural entities within curricular programs"; while the second, an intercultural approach, can result in "the integration of . . . diverse cultural entities into a whole."[1]

One of her major concerns, however, is that both of these approaches, when taken to the extreme, have inherent drawbacks. Multiculturalism can lead to patterns of alienation and curricular apartheid that do not truly solve the problems of exclusion. Interculturalism, on the other hand, can lead to a kind of homogenization that can destroy the sense of identity being striven for by the very groups that are seeking recognition. "Is the melting pot idea," she asks, "not just a tired and irrelevant cliché but also a denigrating threat? Is melting pot really meltdown—a subsuming of racial, ethnic, and gender identities within an established, ensconced, historically tenured pattern of American higher education?"[2]

The nature of her questions underscores a point that is hard to ignore in the examination undertaken here: Attempts to establish more diverse perspectives on the study of dance can lead into territories that are rife with political issues. Confronting these issues brings up additional questions that seem to become exponentially complex as one proceeds. To what extent should educators, artists, and scholars become concerned with matters that involve empowering particular groups? To what extent should their intellectual and artistic pursuits advocate and facilitate a particular vision of society? These are questions that are not new to our age of multicultural emphases. Others have answered them before, and it is the nature of those answers that necessitates developing strategies for recounting the histories that have been overlooked.

The questions asked above are also relevant to this discussion because they begin to reveal how art and culture, like other areas of human interaction, can serve as an arena where power struggles over group recognition, representation, and identity take place. In more traditional approaches to dance history research, these types of issues are often sublimated or overlooked altogether, but when researchers see that they are dealing with areas where such issues are clearly apparent, it is efficacious to face them in a straightforward manner and proceed to establish a perspective on dance in relationship to the broader contexts that shape it.

Historians who research the dance history of marginalized groups will discover that there are a number of other concerns that shape their modes of engagement in their work. When researching the history of African American dance, for example, one finds that there are complex relationships between the dance aesthetics of African American artists and the aesthetics of the mainstream. It will become apparent that art within and outside of the mainstream is connected in an ironically symbiotic and mutually defining relationship. Researchers who strive to develop approaches to historical subject matter where these types of complex relationships exist will find that they are confronted with issues that take them beyond the customary boundaries of the discipline.

As suggested above, when dance historians begin to examine the dynamics that exist between mainstream American dance traditions and those traditions that have existed beside and in synthesis with them, they will be drawn further and further into politically sensitive territory; and, as Smith-Fichter points out, there is always the danger of political polemics overpowering the subject matter of dance. In order to guard against this, she suggests a balanced approach that mediates political issues by focusing upon specific artistic traditions within an inclusive context that acknowledges the diverse groups whose contributions have enriched those traditions. "We don't," she says, "need to dilute or distort dance to do this; we desperately need to deepen and enhance the context—a multicultural one—in which it functions."[3]

Such a call for balance, as it relates to dance history research, suggests a methodology that synthesizes a wide array of historical, aesthetic, social, and political information that builds toward new and more inclusive bodies of knowledge. I further suggest that researchers who are attempting to recover the history of dance in areas that have been, for the most part, excluded from prior investigations should go a step further. While maintaining a balance that guards against dance becoming a mere exemplar of underlying social or political situations, they might strongly position themselves as proponents of change whose work is to create a more accurate and representative record of America's cultural and artistic heritage.

In the research areas I am concerned with here—the dance history of America's minority groups—the proposed approach seems even more efficacious when one considers the different levels of engagement at which a historian's work is affected by sociopolitical factors. For example, the job of retrieving the stories of those artists whose work has barely been chronicled would not exist were it not for the social and political forces that affect the documentation of art. The unique configuration of the artistic elements being investigated—choreographic works, dance techniques and styles, and approaches to performance—is strongly influenced by social and political forces, as are the lives of the artists who created them. In addition, many of the resources that the dance historian draws upon have also been thoroughly shaped by broader sociopolitical contexts. At all levels of engagement with their subject matter, researchers are faced with concerns that require alternative ways of looking at dance in relationship to its multifaceted surroundings.

These complex ways in which political and social factors are related to the creation, analysis, and historiography of art are examined by philosopher and theologian Cornell West in his collection of essays, *Keeping Faith*. He opens his discussion by pointing out a change taking place in the sensibilities of individuals he refers to as the "new cultural workers." He distinguishes them as artists and critics, but he uses the terms broadly to include a diverse grouping of men and women who are involved in creating, chronicling, and commenting on art and culture. It is exactly their inability to be easily categorized that makes them unique. These cultural workers, whose objective is to create more inclusive perspectives on art and culture, cross the boundaries that traditionally separate disciplines in academic and cultural institutions. They are individuals characterized by appetites for wide-ranging intellectual consciousness, and they reconceive of their role in society by actively engaging in what he calls the "new politics of difference." He describes the situation as follows: "Distinctive features of the new cultural politics of difference are to trash the monolithic and homogenous in the name of diversity, multiplicity and heterogeneity; to reject the abstract, general and universal in light of the concrete, specific and particular; and to historicize, contextualize and pluralize by high-lighting the contingent, provisional, variable, tentative, shifting and changing." These tendencies, he concedes, are not new in the history of art and criticism, but what is new about today's cultural politics of difference is the extent to which emphasis is placed upon confronting issues such as "exterminism, empire, class, race, gender, sexual orientation, age, nation, nature, and region."[4]

To establish a perspective on the role of artists and critics in contemporary society, West traces a historical continuum that has brought us to our present moment of conflict in cultural politics. Within this continuum, he highlights three important periods that have shaped the antagonistic relationships between Western and non-Western cultures—the centuries-long age of European expansionism and imperialism, the emergence of the United States as *the* world power, and the decolonization of the Third World. He notes that the last of these historical coordinates has had continuing ramifications in America as it has fueled the Civil Rights and Black Power movements and contributed to other major changes in our society. "The inclusion of African Americans, Latino/a Americans, Asian Americans, Native Americans and American women into the culture of critical discourse yielded intense intellectual polemics and inescapable ideological polarization that focused on the exclusions, silences and blindnesses of male, WASP, cultural homogeneity."[5]

These references to West's discussion of contemporary cultural politics do not begin to do justice to his insightful analysis of the situation. But this brief look at his ideas is relevant to developing dance history methodologies in that it reveals how deeply artists, critics, and historians may dig into the contiguous contexts of art in order to understand its multidimensionality. For West's cultural worker, this broad approach is implemented with important objectives in mind: to project "alternative visions, analyses and actions that proceed from particularities and arrive at moral and political connectedness."[6]

There are similarities between these objectives and those of the dance historian described above who becomes a proponent of change, but West's concept goes a step further in that it affirms a position of partisan political activism. Whether or not adopting such a position moves a researcher too far afield from the traditional territory of dance history is a point that can obviously lead to controversy and debate. But by looking at some of the fundamental concerns of a dance historian, we may come closer to understanding whether or not there are boundaries of the discipline that should not be crossed; and we may even gain insight into an equally important point—the possibility that the boundaries of the discipline can shift under different circumstances.

In discussing the purview of the field, dance historian and theorist June Layson reminds us that the discipline makes a contribution to the general study of dance in that it "reveals a highly complex human activity serving many purposes and developing a multiplicity of types which proliferate, prosper, decline and otherwise change through time."[7] Sorting through these diverse aspects of dance, the dance historian, like historians in general, attempts to chronicle and interpret thematic developments, trace the configuration of continuity and change through time, and engage in selective processes that determine which concerns are central and important and which are trivial and peripheral to the work at hand.[8]

Layson continues her discussion by outlining three important areas in which dance historians' selective processes affect the nature and scope of their work. First, a time span must be decided to determine the compass of a study. Second, a historian's approach is shaped by the function of the dance being investigated. Is it primarily religious, recreational, or theatrical, or does it serve some other function? Within these larger categories, dance can be further categorized by genres, styles, and geographic provenances. It is, however, the third area of selectivity —deciding to what extent contextual material should be used—that is of most concern to this discussion.

Layson points out that various contexts are a vital means of understanding dance, but she also feels that the examination of contexts has often been dealt with in a perfunctory manner. Without this important element, studies can be seriously flawed. On the other hand, it can be equally disadvantageous to give inordinate attention to contextual matters. Except in those instances when a researcher feels justified in moving toward one extreme or the other, the solution is, once again, to find a balanced approach.[9]

At the risk of relegating the dance histories of marginalized groups to a methodological ghetto, I am suggesting that they belong to those exceptional instances when a researcher should place a great deal of emphasis upon wide-ranging contextual matters. In these instances, this approach is the most efficacious one because the dynamics that have affected the historical development of dance are so closely knitted to sociopolitical factors such as racism and matters of ethnic identity that failing to explore broader contexts would diminish our understanding and appreciation of our central focus, the dance itself.

By taking Layson's schematic for the fundamental concerns of a dance historian and applying it to the research areas we are concerned with, we come closer to articulating a methodological approach that addresses our particular needs. In chronicling and interpreting the dance history of marginalized groups, the researcher's selective processes necessitate tracing the *thematic developments* of the dance subject matter as it is related to a number of contextual matters (aesthetic, social, political, and so on) and holistically examining the entire complex of elements as it reveals *the character of continuity* and *the nature of change through time*.

Although a number of dance historians today have moved closer to this type of contextually inclusive and holistic investigation, earlier studies of theatrical concert dance have often been written from perspectives that focus almost exclusively upon aesthetic contexts. These studies tend to view dance as a circumspect reflection of particular aesthetic ideals, as an isolated phenomenon that is not connected to the social and political contexts that surround it. To suggest that the researcher should move beyond this type of one-dimensional approach does not deny the importance of stressing aesthetic matters. In studying the history of dance as a theater art, it is clear that a major aspect of our work is to understand how various artistic trends and forces have led to the development of unique dance expressions. But it is important for us to look closely at methods that veer too far in this direction—especially in terms of the historical precedents they have set—because they contain clues concerning how and why the dance histories of marginalized groups have gone unrecorded in the first place.

In much of the criticism and history of twentieth-century European American theatrical dance, the first criterion that has traditionally determined which artists and works are worthy of serious consideration or not is the degree to which they meet the established aesthetic standards in one of two dance genres —ballet or modern dance. Within these categories, further distinctions are made to single out artists and works of the highest merit. These, in turn, serve as yardsticks by which other works are measured as being of enduring and universal value.

For a number of reasons, there are types of theatrical dance that are not considered for any of these distinctions. Popular entertainment forms are categorically denied, because of distinctions between "high" art and "low" art. Some dance is not acceptable because of its innovative departure from mainstream aesthetics; or, as in the case of African American dance, it is not acceptable because of the entrenched racial biases that affect the ways in which it is perceived. In the latter example, and others like it, certain artistic expressions are pushed to the margins of serious consideration because of obviously nonaesthetic matters. In many such instances, these types of exclusions have more to do with maintaining an aesthetic status quo that is tied to political and social objectives than they have to do with matters that are purely aesthetic.

Setting the boundaries of genres, establishing artistic standards, and building hierarchical classifications and canons are not processes that are as pristinely objective as the cultural arbiters of high art would have one believe. At their most subjective, these processes can be little more than the labeling of art with appellations such as "beautiful," "significant," "universal," or "refined." Much of the powerful influence of elevated forms of art can be attributed to the fact that a specific—and a powerful—group of people has agreed upon and perpetuated the idea that select forms of art deserve a position of prominence.

It has already been noted how dance can be examined as a solely aesthetic phenomenon. This approach, which gives little or no attention to social and political factors, has often been used in chronicling the history of high art forms, and it has resulted in studies that create and perpetuate the impression that these forms have always existed in a rarefied atmosphere, unaffected by more mundane matters such as group conflicts and power struggles.

Ballet, for example, born out of sixteenth- and seventeenth-century European aristocratic traditions, is characterized by its movement metaphors that have become symbols of classical purity and ideal beauty. In this respect, it shares in an aesthetic mystique of elegance and refinement associated with particular times and places. But one will be hard-pressed to find studies of ballet that examine the early development of the art form and its symbolism in relationship to the centuries-long imperial expansionism and colonial domination that characterized European contacts with non-Western people. These less salutary aspects of European history are part of the same cultural/political/economic complex that inspired, financed, and in other ways enabled the development of European imperial art. Deeper examinations of these contexts could reveal interesting and important details concerning the relationships between dance and cultural imperialism.

As pointed out above, a likely criticism of studies that probe deeply into non-aesthetic contexts is that dance historians can stray too far from their central subject matter and be distracted by concerns that would more appropriately be handled by scholars in the social sciences or other disciplines. This criticism may be valid in some instances, but I believe that the possibility of becoming sidetracked by the "outlying" areas of dance history, where disciplinary boundaries begin to blur, is a risk worth taking. In the areas of research discussed here, working through such problems proves to be valuable because it contributes to understanding why certain aspects of dance have been so consistently overlooked and why there has been a mystical silence drawn around some contexts and not others. Such understandings can lead to provisional steps that begin to increase researchers' capabilities of studying dance from multidimensional perspectives.

One of the things that should be examined in histories of dance in which certain sociopolitical contexts have been overlooked is the possibility that the revelations that lie within those contexts might threaten the elevated position of privileged art forms. In the example just cited, classical ballet, such investigations could expose the sociopolitical underpinnings of an art form that has gained its hierarchical status, in large part, because it is historically rooted in empires that achieved their cultural dominance and built their images of superiority upon the subjugation and denigration of non-European people (as well as European people of lower classes). By taking an unflinching look at these underlying—and politically loaded—historical factors as they relate to the creation of dance, one can begin to demystify the aura of innate superiority that surrounds European high art forms and forms such as modern dance that have been derived from them; and one can begin to correct the misconception that this art is, for the most part, detached from social and political concerns.

The relationships between dominant empires, the art and culture of subjugated people, and the establishment of aesthetic hierarchies are analyzed by philosopher Francis Sparshott in his essay, "How Can I Know What Dancing Is?" Empires, he states, are groupings of societies and cultures forming a heterogeneous domain held together by the strength of an imperial power. The central authority imposes its concepts of art and culture upon the subordinate people. Under these circumstances, the cultural and artistic expressions of those who are ruled may continue to exist, but they are labeled with new referents by those who rule. For example, dances other than those of the dominant culture may be redefined as "'folk dance' or 'ethnic dance,' as provincial or social or in some other downgrading terms masquerading as classifications."[10] The organizing concepts of imperial systems accommodate the art and culture of the subordinate groups by categorizing them as being variant or deviant. This is one of several prearranged strategies for asserting and justifying the cultural hegemony of the dominant society. As Sparshott succinctly puts it, "Empires are not innocent."[11]

In Sparshott's analysis of the power relationships that facilitate the imposition of one group's cultural values upon a subordinate group, we can see dynamics that have historically shaped the creation, criticism, and documentation of art in situations where Western and non-Western cultures have come into contact. (Or, as in our primary example, where a minority group resides within the cultural dominance of a majority culture.) His discussion also brings into focus one of the conceptual frameworks that supports many of these sociocultural operations —the use of dichotomies in which one side of the construct is positively conceived at the expense of and denigration of the other side. This idea is implicit in the development of cultural and artistic hierarchies, and it results in divisive systems that are used to maintain the power of dominant groups. In this sense, these are concepts that are socially constructed.

When, for example, the dichotomy *black/white* is used to signify racial classification, it often includes the implied meaning of *inferior/superior* that has been historically associated with it. Subordinate groups play no direct role in the construction of these dichotomies or in the determination of their meanings. Those operations are totally in the control of the dominant group. However, in their relatively powerless position, subordinate groups do exert some influence upon the situation in that it is their presence (and the mainstream representations of their presence) that the dominant group uses, to a large extent, to build its identity upon. It is again Cornell West who illuminates the way to understanding these ironic racial dualities. He points out the need to "examine and explain the historically specific ways in which 'whiteness' is a politically constructed category parasitic on 'blackness,' and thereby to conceive of the profoundly hybrid character of what we mean by 'race,' 'ethnicity,' and 'nationality.'"[12]

To doubly insure the hegemony of European American art, an additional strategy of cultural arbiters has been to weld racial dichotomies and aesthetic dichotomies (such as *beautiful/not beautiful, high art/low art,* etc.), with all of their implied meanings of inferiority and superiority, into one seamless concept. This has resulted in the creation and perpetuation of negative images of nonwhite people, their cultures, and their art. West refers to this tactic as the "widespread, modern, European denial of the intelligence, ability, beauty and character of people of color."[13] He goes on to examine some of the ways that African Americans have responded to these debilitating circumstances, and he points out that African American artists have often used their art to cope with living in a racist society.

During the primary period discussed here, the early years of African American concert dance, artists were extremely concerned with gaining control of representation, engaging in the reconstruction of identities, and recasting images of their people. They were active during a time that was rife with political and social dynamics that resulted in the marginalization of non-Western art.

In the early decades of the twentieth century, African American dancers were faced with derogatory racial imagery of their people at every turn. From the gross caricatures of commercial advertisements to the images of blacks as "shuffling darkies" that were promoted in popular entertainment, racial denigration was an accepted part of mainstream American culture. Beginning in the late 1920s, a small group of dancers began attempting to change these images by turning away from popular entertainment genres of dance (for example, tap, jazz, and eccentric dance) to explore America's newly developing concert dance field.

In their efforts to create more positive representations of their people, one of their main tactics was to draw upon elements from different cultures—African American, European American, West Indian, and African—to capture the complex beauty of their cultural heritage. The earliest African American artists who began to make inroads in the field of theatrical concert dance, Edna Guy and Hemsley Winfield, began to create works that reflected their limited training in European American dance forms, their distillation of African American vernacular cultural elements, and their impressionist interpretations of African dance.

Katherine Dunham, who began to attract critical attention in the 1930s, also based her choreography upon Western and non-Western elements. Her approach differed, however, in the respect that the non-Western aspects of her work were thoroughly informed by the anthropological research that she conducted in the West Indies. During the 1940s her dance was called a "combination of classical ballet with Central European, Caribbean and African elements."[14] Dunham and her contemporaries created art that was a synthesis of different cultural expressions. In their attempts to be accepted as serious artists they were breaking new ground in African American culture and in American culture as a whole. These types of cultural practices, as West puts it, consist of the "selective appropriation, incorporation and rearticulation of European ideologies, cultures and institutions alongside an African heritage."[15]

Although African American artists' approaches often differed considerably from those of mainstream concert dancers of the time, their work was related to contemporary dance experimentation in that they brought innovative new ideas to the concert stage; and, although they were constantly challenged in ways that their white contemporaries were not, they too expanded the boundaries of what constituted the serious genres of dance.

In many respects, these artists existed between two worlds—the African American community and the mainstream American community. The boundaries that separated the two worlds were determined by historically entrenched racial concepts that affected the artists' creative efforts in numerous ways. When, for example, they turned to the white community to gain access to training and performance opportunities, their efforts were often thwarted. On the other hand, race-based thinking within the African American community influenced artists to adopt ideas that encouraged them to channel most of their creative energy into projects that could contribute toward bettering the lot of their people. As a researcher probes the complexity of the ways that racial proscriptions affected these artists' personal and professional lives, it becomes clear that historical research in these areas calls for a methodology that weaves a historical narrative based upon the examination of numerous contextual threads.

The importance of such an approach becomes further apparent when one examines the ways in which the art of marginalized groups was critically received during its own time. In this respect, critical literature provides a wealth of information that not only reflects contemporary appraisals of choreographic works but that can also reflect the biases and preconceptions that lie just beneath the surface of commentary on art. In the criticism of African American artists during the 1930s and 1940s, we find, for example, that most writers refused to discuss emerging black artists from the same point of view that they used for white artists. When discussing the former, they trotted out new "theories" and dredged up old stereotypes; they recurrently referred to ideas that addressed the "problems" related to African American dancers.

One of the most recurrent of these ideas was that of the African American dancer as a "natural" performer whose work sprang from atavistic impulses that resulted in the kind of effortless, unconscious expression that was to be expected of all black people. From this perspective, the work of black artists—unlike that of white artists—did not need to be viewed as reflecting dedicated attention to technical training and artistic refinement. By framing artists' work as unadulterated racial expression, critics could in effect exclude them from the serious genres of contemporary concert dance.

Critics found other types of inventive strategies to separate black artists from mainstream traditions. John Martin, dance critic for the *New York Times,* promoted the idea that black dancers were cultural interlopers and implied that they were ill-prepared to engage in European American dance genres because the cultures in which these forms originated were foreign to them. He often chastised artists for dabbling in the "alien techniques" of ballet, for example. The tenacity of this particular idea is indicated by the fact that he began using it during the 1920s, and in 1963 he was still contending that the wholly European outlook, history, and technical theory of classical ballet were alien to African American dancers because of matters of culture, temperament, and anatomy.[16]

Ideas such as these appeared in critical writing so often that they assumed an aura of verity and authority when, in fact, they were specious constructs that perpetuated images of black people as being inherently inferior. The tactical use of these racist ideas disguised as aesthetic theories served the same purpose as other methods that were used to relegate black people to the bottom rungs of America's social, political, and economic life. In these instances, we can see the symbiotic relationship that existed between artistic commentary and the political motive of maintaining a particular social structure. In a sense, artists and critics engaged in an ongoing agon in which one group used their creative talents to improve the image of their race while the other group used their commentary to keep the first in their predesignated place in society.

At this point, it is worth repeating that an approach to dance history that closely analyzes the types of complex factors cited above does not necessarily discount the examination of dance as being the expression of individually unique artists who are creating in specific styles and techniques that reflect particular aesthetics. But when historians began to fully understand the extent to which racial and other types of proscriptions have shaped mainstream European American dance traditions and the traditions that have existed beside and in synthesis with them, the need for an approach that weds the examination of aesthetic influences to a concomitant examination of sociopolitical factors becomes increasingly clear.

In the examples of African American dance history that have been cited above, these connections point toward the realization that one of the central thematic developments that determines the "character of continuity and the nature of change through time"—to use Layson's words again—is the way in which racial proscriptions dominated many aspects of the artists' creative efforts and ultimately affected their work. This realization suggests a methodology in which the historian's selective process includes a concerted effort to analyze the effects that factors such as racism have had upon the creation of art in American society.

An excellent example of this type of approach may be found in the work of Joyce Aschenbrenner, an anthropologist, dance historian, and social activist, who began to unravel the complexity of African American dance history in her 1981 study of the career of Katherine Dunham. Early in her discussion, she makes it unequivocally clear that the area she in researching is strongly connected to contexts in which group dynamics and social interactions are of primary importance. Borrowing a paradigm—a "conflict model"—from the discipline of anthropology, she focuses upon "the social and political contexts of cultural expression, i.e., identification of the involved groups, the history of their interactions and the goals generated (directly or indirectly) by those interactions."[17]

From a baseline that identifies African Americans as a historically oppressed group that has been controlled by the institutions of a politically dominant group, she begins to analyze the various ways in which the work of black artists has been affected by racist and powerful interests in American society.[18] In regard to matters of economics, for example, she shows how the artistic expressions of African American artists have been dealt with in an extremely duplicitous manner. On the one hand, their innovative dance forms have been consistently demeaned by critics; and, on the other hand, these same forms have been shamelessly appropriated for the economic gain of others. From mid-nineteenth-century minstrelsy through early twentieth-century Broadway shows that featured the uncredited work of black dancers and choreographers, to Katherine Dunham's early revues that inspired reels of Hollywood exotica, Aschenbrenner surveys the history of African American dance in a society that has always seemed to thrive upon and profit from the very cultural elements that it casts a disdainful eye upon.

Against this historical background that details the ways in which African American art is sometimes dismissed, sometimes appropriated, but always dealt with in a way that satisfies mainstream interests, Aschenbrenner paints a picture of Katherine Dunham's career that highlights numerous instances where racist preconceptions and conflicting views of art and culture led to misunderstandings of her work. For example, the sensuality of her performances was often frowned upon because critics and audiences did not realize that her material was drawn from cultures where sexual imagery had positive, religious associations. Her dancers' artistry was dismissed because of the stigma of the "natural" performer, mentioned above. She was caught in a double bind in which her work was criticized for incorporating European American dance elements, and at the same time, it was dismissed because of its ethnic roots.[19]

Another aspect of Aschenbrenner's work that makes it noteworthy for this discussion is the position that she takes in relation to her subject matter. She does not attempt to maintain an ideally "objective" point of view. Instead, she takes what she describes as a position of "advocacy," acknowledging her subjective involvement in her research material. She achieves a certain degree of impartiality, however, by tempering her approach with a "'perspectivism' that recognizes the existence of more than one complementary (and not exclusionary) viewpoint."[20]

In this respect—and in others—we can see that Aschenbrenner bears a kinship to West's cultural worker "who stays attuned to the best of what the mainstream has to offer—its paradigms, viewpoints and methods—yet maintains a grounding in affirming and enabling subcultures of criticism.[21]

A comparison between West's cultural worker and Aschenbrenner appears to become strained, however, when we note that she is a white scholar, while West's cultural workers—as he describes them in much of his discussion—are artists and critics of color. But what, for some, might appear to be a problem in the comparison being made here does not remain so for long. In a gesture of inclusiveness that proves racial divisiveness to be inimical to the work that needs to be done, West tells us that what is ultimately needed is a broad coalition of diverse individuals who use their work to enable marginalized people to overcome the cultural degradation, political oppression, and economic exploitation they have endured.[22] In this respect, the work of Joyce Aschenbrenner places her clearly within this camp.

Realignment is a major theme in West's project. He speaks of individuals who realign themselves for the purpose of establishing connections across customary divisions of gender, race, age, and sexual orientation, who realign themselves in order to cross the traditional boundaries of their disciplines. In their reconfiguration of disciplines, these individuals—like the dance historian discussed above—synthesize a wide spectrum of knowledge in an effort to create new insights into art and culture. As pointed out earlier, such efforts are timely because of the omissions that are apparent in dance history as well as other disciplines.

Turning once more to June Layson's discussion, we see that she identifies a number of additional reasons why establishing innovative approaches to dance history is a timely undertaking. As an academic discipline, the field is ready for change because it has begun to move beyond the basic documentation and chronicling that was the major concern of its early years. Since considerable progress has been made in that direction, scholars are at a juncture where they can begin to pursue other goals such as the exploration of different methodologies and the incorporation of new theoretical models. In addition, because the discipline is still relatively young, it can be uniquely accommodating. "It can, unlike the longer-established general history discipline, respond, adapt to and even embrace radical modes of thought in an immediate manner."[23]

In her examination of newer theoretical models that might influence research methodologies, Layson briefly discusses some primary ways in which postmodern approaches to history differ considerably from traditional ones. These modes of thought abandon linear concepts of time, they distrust hierarchical structures and classifications, and they examine contexts holistically without prioritizing certain ones.[24] The striking similarities between these approaches and those I have been projecting indicate the value that the evolving methodology discussed here may hold for the field in general.

Research in the dance histories of marginalized groups is also at a point where it can incorporate newer theoretical models, but it is in that receptive position for different reasons. Its openness to new ideas is not based on the fact that a substantial amount of its foundational documentation has been completed. On the contrary, there is still a tremendous amount of work that needs to be done in that respect. The flexibility of its options is due, in large part, to the fact that so little prior work has been done, and there are few precedents and preconceptions to inhibit the development of innovative research strategies.

In the same way that general dance history is in a position to be more accommodating to new approaches than longer-established historical disciplines, the marginalized areas of dance history—because they are in an early stage of development—are capable of being even more accommodating to new approaches. These research areas have a special capacity for engendering new ways of looking at dance because of the groundbreaking nature of the researcher's work; and innovative thinking is imperative because of the contextual complexity that is a part of the dance subject matter being investigated. In all of this lies the potential for research that can provide new models for the discipline.

In addition to the impact of the pioneering nature of their work, there is another important factor that ultimately affects researchers and leads them toward nontraditional, alternative approaches to their work. This has to do with the realization that developing strategies to include the dance histories of marginalized groups within the flow of mainstream chronicles can be a self-defeating undertaking if that is the sole purpose of one's work.

The body of knowledge into which inclusion is being sought supports the same hierarchical cultural system that denigrates the very cultural expressions one is seeking to substantiate. To attempt to prove that the dance of marginalized groups is worthy of being a part of the canons that have historically highlighted positive European cultural values against a negative background of non-European cultures affirms the superiority of the former and inferiority of the latter.

This quandary shines a new light on our discussion above of intraculturalism in which disenfranchised groups were shown to be at risk of losing their identity in homogenizing efforts of inclusion. Not only does such a situation threaten a loss of identity, but it also threatens a kind of ultimate psychic defeat in which one admits that one's future lies in a direction that is inscribed with images of one's own inferiority.

Solving this quandary does not entail discarding everything that has gone before in a flurry of mindless revisionism; but it does mean at least three things: (1) meticulously reappraising cultural records in light of new sensibilities, (2) ferreting out the stories that have gone unchronicled, and (3) building a body of knowledge that reflects a new sense of inclusiveness. With these goals in mind, we may view dance history as a constantly evolving discipline, and we may accept the idea that our work—like other human endeavors—cannot be neatly limited by a set of comfortable parameters.

Study Questions

1. The preceding discussion has concentrated primarily on African American dance. What are some other examples of artists from minority groups who have contributed to American and European dance traditions? In what ways do these artists' works reveal similarly complex issues?

2. In the examples you have noted for question 1, can you find unique ways in which the aesthetics of minority artists have relationships to mainstream aesthetics?

3. What are some of the pros and cons of involving dance research in the empowerment of particular groups?

4. Do you feel that there are areas of dance history research in which it is inappropriate to examine sociopolitical contexts to the extent that we have been suggesting?

5. What are some of the ways an individual researcher can begin to develop interdisciplinary approaches to the study of dance history?

6. Many artists (including those belonging to minority groups) do not make intentional references to social and political matters. To what extent should a researcher investigate issues that are not an intended part of an artist's work?

NOTES

1. Nancy Smith Fichter, "Diversity and Multicultural Concerns: Their Impact on the Preparation of Dance Professions" (paper presented at the National Association of Schools of Dance [NASD] annual meeting, 1992), 2.

2. Ibid., 3.

3. Ibid., 9.

4. Cornell West, *Keeping Faith: Philosophy and Race in America* (New York: Routledge, 1993), 3.

5. Ibid., 14.

6. Ibid., 30.

7. Janet Adshead-Lansdale and June Layson, eds., *Dance History: An Introduction* (London and New York: Routledge, 1994), 5.

8. Ibid., 4–5.

9. Ibid., 7–9.

10. Francis Sparshott, "How Can I Know What Dancing Is?" in *Primum Philosopasi* (Warszawa: Oficyna NauKova, 1993), 156.

11. Ibid., 157.

12. Cornell West, *Keeping Faith,* 20.

13. Ibid., 25.

14. Richard Buckle, ed., *Katherine Dunham, Her Dancers, Singers, Musicians* (London: Ballet Publications, Ltd., 1949), ix.

15. Cornell West, *Keeping Faith,* 16.

16. John Martin, *John Martin's Book of the Dance* (New York: Tudor Publishing Company, 1963), 178.

17. Joyce Aschenbrenner, *Katherine Dunham: Reflections on the Social and Political Contexts of Afro-American Dance* (New York: Congress on Research in Dance Inc., 1981), 3.

18. Ibid., 4.

19. Ibid., 44.

20. Ibid., 5.

21. Cornell West, *Keeping Faith,* 27.

22. Ibid., 29.

23. Adshead-Lansdale and Layson, *Dance History,* 11.

24. Ibid., 12–13.

REFERENCES

Adshead-Lansdale, Janet, and June Layson, eds. *Dance History: An Introduction.* London and New York: Routledge, 1994.

Aschenbrenner, Joyce. *Katherine Dunham: Reflections on the Social and Political Contexts of Afro-American Dance.* New York: Congress on Research in Dance, Inc., 1981.

Banes, Sally. *Writing Dancing in the Age of Postmodernism.* Hanover and London: Wesleyan University Press/University Press of New England, 1994.

Dixon Gottschild, Brenda. *Digging the Africanist Presence in American Performance: Dance and Other Contexts.* Westport, Conn.: Greenwood Press, 1996.

Emery, Lynne Fauley. *Black Dance from 1619 to Today.* Princeton, N.J.: Princeton Book Company, 1988.

Fichter, Nancy Smith. "Diversity and Multicultural Concerns: Their Impact on the Preparation of Dance Professionals." Paper presented at the National Association of Schools of Dance (NASD) annual meeting, Dallas, Texas, 1992.

Goler, Veta. "Dancing Herself: Choreography, Autobiography, and the Expression of the Black Woman Self in the Work of Dianne McIntyre, Blondell Cummings, and Jawole Willa Jo Zollar." Ph.D. dissertation, Emory University, 1994.

Malone, Jacqui. *Steppin' on the Blues.* Urbana and Chicago: University of Illinois Press, 1996.

Perpener, John. "The Seminal Years of Black Concert Dance." Ph.D. dissertation, New York University, 1992.

———. "African American Dance and Sociological Positivism During the 1930s and 1940s." *Studies in Dance History* 5, no. 1 (spring 1994): 23–29.

Sparshott, Francis. "How Can I Know What Dancing Is?" In *Primum Philosopasi.* Warszawa: Oficyna NauKova, 1993.

West, Cornell. *Keeping Faith: Philosophy and Race in America.* New York and London: Routledge, 1993.

UNIFIED FIELD POSTSCRIPT

Sondra Horton Fraleigh and Penelope Hanstein

Arrange the Stage

SWING FROM THE ROPE that hangs from the grid, holding the loop at the end. Since we first began to understand it as more than taps and steps or swinging from ropes, more than glitter and goo, more than skipping or running in the breeze (holding our mothers' curtains aloft), more than leaping in splits or tangling ourselves around other bodies, more than contact or giving and taking weight, even more than pulsing with drumming or floating with butoh-white shadow bodies, DANCE HAS BECOME A FIELD, more than its descriptive parts, yet all of them, still more.

Its identity is nevertheless composed through A FIELD OF DIFFERENCE —different ways of moving, expressing, and being-possible- in-the-world, even being-beyond-this-world, entranced.

❁

A field of grain
    ripens in the sun, its
        virtual body shines.

A field is bounded, if not by territorial markers by our sight (as we drink in the land) or (in the case of dance) our insight. The modern/postmodern "field question" has been highly focussed on what might qualify as art—or more roundly stated—what are aesthetic phenomena? The dance field continues to stretch its scope and inquiry as though it were a foreign language that would presume to give us back our own (without prejudice). Its questions are limited only by our soundings and namings of movement: body, expression, spirit, and form.

> Social/
> psychological/
> cultural/natural/
> machine-white-striped pants
> /orgasmic pleasure/ to which
> postindustrial technologies may
> well outlive courtly couples cantering.

❀

Virtuality is a nervy concept. In service of perception, Susanne Langer isolates it from the actual. But what happens as latent powers—the inherent virtues of herbs, for instance—become actual? What happens—as in the dance—when potentiality becomes potent?

❀

As we summarize our evolving understandings of dance, our actual dances and evolving modes of inquiry are creating a field of participation and studies of interest in the academies where DANCE ENTERS into disciplines of more historically established fields. In the academy, someone in the English Department is offering a course on "Dance as Narrative." Now she comes to our concerts and parties, and we share our love of dance and language.

Will those of us who teach, study, and practice the states of movement and mind that we have named *dance* sustain a contiguous field, or splinter into separate disciplines as our respective methodologies become more specialized? Will dance become defined and appropriated by other disciplines? We would argue for retaining some cohesive strategies that embrace a unified field of diverse studies based on a broad interpretation of the term *dance*.

Dance is something we do, also a way of studying ourselves:

a way of knowing
that splits
and altogether handles
fire,
that this line is visible
but largely absent,

motionless,
yet more persuasive
in its own trail.

There can be no touching up,
now-free running and jumping skyward.

Reclined bodies fly painfully across the floor.
Three dancers ripple time.
Why Do they move this way?

CONTRIBUTORS

Shelley C. Berg is an associate professor and chair of the Dance Division at Southern Methodist University. Her book, *Le Sacre du printemps: Seven Productions from Nijinsky to Martha Graham*, was published by UMI Research Press in 1988. A two-part article on the work of Japanese dancer/actress Sada Yacco was recently published in *Dance Chronicle*. She is a member of the board of directors of the Society of Dance History Scholars and the editorial board of *Studies in Dance History*.

Mary Alice Brennan, Ph.D., CMA, is a professor of dance at the University of Wisconsin-Madison. Her research articles on creativity in dance and the movement analysis of dance style have appeared in publications such as the *Journal of Creative Behavior, Research Quarterly of Exercise and Sport, Perceptual Motor Skills, Dance: Selected Research,* and *Dance and Technology.* She was the 1985 National Dance Association Scholar and a 1989 and 1995 Fulbright Scholar to India. Her ongoing research is the study of dance style in *bharatanatyam* Indian classical dance in collaboration with Dr. Parul Shah, Baroda, India.

Steven J. Chatfield, Ph.D., is associate professor in the Department of Dance at the University of Oregon, Eugene, where he is director of graduate studies and coordinator of the graduate Dance Science Program. His ongoing research involves dance in education, and neural science and somatics in dance. Previously, Steven served on the dance faculty at the University of Hawaii, Manoa (1986–1989); was executive director of Verve Dance Co. Inc., Boulder, Colorado (1979–1986); and toured internationally with the Nancy Spanier Dance Theatre of Colorado Inc. (1976–1980). During the past fifteen years he has received various awards to support scientific research in dance, choreography and touring, and curriculum development. Current research involves measurement of motor control changes resulting from select movement and somatic training practices.

Jane C. Desmond, Ph.D., is associate professor of American studies and women's studies at the University of Iowa. Formerly a professional modern dancer and choreographer, she has also worked in film. She is the editor of *Meaning in Motion: New Cultural Studies of Dance* (Duke University Press, 1997) and the author of *Staging Tourism: Bodies on Display from Waikiki to Sea World* (forthcoming, University of Chicago Press). Her articles have appeared in *Signs, Women and Performance, Cultural Critique,* and *TDR,* among others.

Sondra Horton Fraleigh chairs the Department of Dance at the State University of New York, Brockport, and is the author of *Dance and the Lived Body* and many articles on dance and movement, philosophy, and cognitive development. She has served as president of the Congress on Research in Dance and is Faculty Exchange Scholar for the State University of New York. Her innovative choreography has been seen on tour in America, Germany, and Japan. She directs the Core*Star Institute for Somatic Studies.

Joan D. Frosch is director of the Center for World Arts at the University of Florida, where she is associate professor of dance and assistant chair of the Department of Theatre and Dance. A dance ethnographer and certified movement analyst, her research focuses on the use of dance as a catalyst for social change among diverse West African and United States populations. Her collaborative ethnographic projects have attracted extensive funding and honors, including the Eli Lilly Fellowship.

Jill Green, Ph.D., conducts research and teaches at the University of North Carolina at Greensboro. Her research interests include somatics and body studies, dance education, qualitative research, and feminist research and pedagogy. She was awarded an honorable mention by the American Educational Research Association for her dissertation about somatic postpositivist inquiry. Her work has been published in a number of journals including *Impulse, Journal of Physical Recreation and Dance,* and *Journal of Interdisciplinary Research in Physical Education.*

Penelope Hanstein is professor and director for dance at Texas Woman's University and for several summers has been a visiting professor at Teacher's College, Columbia University. She has written many articles on the nature of art making in dance and choreography theory, was named the 1995 National Dance Association Scholar, and is a past president of the Congress on Research in Dance.

Dr. Joann McNamara is an associate professor of dance at Eastern Michigan University, where she serves as dance program coordinator. She trained in modern dance with Aaron Osborne, June Watanabe, Gus Solomons Jr., and in ballet with Mia Slavinska. As a choreographer she often works with the combination of text and movement; her award-winning dance, *Pigeons,* was presented at the Paul Baker Writers' Conference in Dallas, Texas. She has performed in the works of numerous choreographers including the reconstruction of Doris Humphrey's *Passacaglia* with the Utah Repertory Dance Theatre. She has served as dance critic for the *Ann Arbor News* and has presented papers at the National Congress on Research in Dance, American Dance Guild, National Dance Association, and the Association for Integrative Studies.

John O. Perpener III, Ph.D., is an associate professor in the Department of Dance at the University of Illinois, Urbana-Champaign, where he teaches dance history. He has had articles and book reviews on African American dance published in *Dance Research Journal* and *Studies in Dance History.* His forthcoming book, *The Seminal Years of African-American Concert Dance,* will be published by the University of Illinois Press. He is also a consultant for *Free to Dance,* a video series on the history of African American dance that is being produced by the American Dance Festival.

Susan W. Stinson, Ed.D., is professor and Head of Dance at the University of North Carolina at Greensboro, where she teaches courses in dance education and research.

Her scholarly work has been published in a number of journals, including *Dance Research Journal; Design for Arts in Education; Impulse; J.O.P.E.R.D.; Journal of Curriculum Theorizing; Women in Performance; Journal of Curriculum and Supervision;* and *Educational Theory.* For the past ten years, her research has focused on how young people interpret their experiences in dance education. She was selected as the 1994 Scholar by the National Dance Association.

INDEX

Aalten, Anna, 319
Abdulai, Ibrahim, 266–67
Abernethy, Bruce, 129; on paradigm shifts, 131; on revolutionary science, 130
Action Profiling, 297, 300; development of, 304n58
Adair, Christy, 108
Adshead, Janet, 212
aesthetic intention, 193–94
aesthetics, 188–213 passim; defined by Baumgarten, 204
African American dance: concert dance, 343; research in, 335–49 passim
Alderson, Evan, 314
Alexander, Arsène, 237
Alexander, Christopher, 191
Ali Khan, Nusrat Fateh, 191
Althusser, Louis, 316
American Anthropological Association, 269
American Dance Guild, 262
Anderson, Benedict, 18
animation. See computer animatior
Annual Review of Anthropology, 254
Anzaldua, Gloria, Borderlands/La Frontera, 312
Archer, Kenneth, 239, 240, 241
Aristotle, 204, 205
Arkist, Sandy, 260–61
Art Deco, 240, 241
Art Nouveau, 233, 234, 236, 237
Aschenbrenner, Joyce, 345–47; study of Dunham by, 345–46
Ashton, Frederick, 239–44

Bacon, Francis, 127–28
Bakhtin, Mikhail, 202–03
Balanchine, George, 204, 218n36, 293; and African American culture, 227; Agon, 293; Apollo, 227; compared to Massine, 240; Cotillion, 239; The Four Tempera-ments, 227

ballet, 5, 9, 13; Daly on, 313; deconstruction-ist research on, 112; in historical context, 340–41; as object of experimental design, 140–42; use of Choreutics to analyze, 295
Banes, Sally: Dancing Women, 206; Writing Dance in the Age of Postmodernism, 227
Bann, Stephen, 228
Bartenieff, Irmgard, 289
Bartenieff Fundamentals, 286
Bates, Barry, 150
Bateson, Gregory, 252
Battersby, Martin, 237; The World of Art Nouveau, 234
Baumgarten, Alexander Gottlieb, 204
Baure, Jaime, 46
Bausch, Pina, 203
Beauvoir, Simone de, The Second Sex, 207, 311–12
Beck, Jill, 239
Becker, Svea, 295
behavioral research, 295–97
Benesh Notation, 266, 268, 285
Bentz, Valerie Malhotra, 167, 176
Bernard, Claude, 130–31
Bernstein, Penny, 300
Bing, Siegfried, 234
Bishko, Leslie, 301
Bissel, Robyn, 293
Blacking, John, 267–68
Blum, Odette, 292
Blumenfeld-Jones, Donald, 108, 112
Boas, Franz, 251
Boas, Franziska, 251–52, 254
Bobath, Karl and Berta, 151
Bond, Karen, 65, 296
Bopp, Mary, 30
Borg, Walter R., 41
Bourdieu, Pierre, 314–15, 314
Bournonville, Auguste, 293
Boyce, Johanna, Ties That Bind 2, 323
Bradley, Buddy, 227, 241–42

hermeneutics, viii–ix, 162–82 passim: defined by Gadamer, 171; as flexible paradigm, 171; as interpretation theory, 163; phenomenological, 163–64; positivistic, 163

Herskovits, Melville J., 252

High Yellow, 242

Hirsch, E. D., 163

historiography: dance, x, 225–44 passim; as mode of inquiry, 42–43, 44

history, 135

Hodson, Millicent, 239, 240, 241

Holloway, Wendy, 314

Holm, Hanya, 218*n*36

Holt, Claire, 252

Hong-Joe, Christina, 75–77

hooks, bell, 312

Huberman, Michael, 97

human subjects review, 55–56

Humphrey, Doris, 229, 294, 295

Husserl, Edmund, 4, 163, 166, 167, 178: and *noema,* 169; and witness, 211

Hyerle, David, 59*n*22

hypothesis, in proposal, 48, 51–52

independent variable, 134, 135, 136, 137

induction, 128, 129

inductive research, 68

informed consent, 55

Institutional Review Board (IRB), 55–56

instrumentation, 135, 136

intention, 8, 189–96

International Council of Kinetography Laban, 287

interpretation, 189–93, 202–03

interpretive research, 43, 100–04

intrinsic dance, 14–16

IRB. *See* Institutional Review Board

isokinetic dynamometers, 139

japonisme, 233, 234, 236

Jeschke, Claudia, 293

Joffrey Ballet, 239, 240

Jones, Bill T., 323–24

Jordan, Stephanie, 293

Judson Church Dance Theatre, 162, 172

Jürgensen, Knud, 293

Kaeppler, Adrienne L., 66, 67, 250, 261: on "choreology," 257; on dance ethnography, 249; on early study of dance in culture,

251; fieldwork of, 254–55; on influence of Kurath's work, 254; and *kinemes,* 290; on Kurath, 273*n*25; and *morphokines,* 290; and 1972 CORD conference, 255

Kagan, Elizabeth, 295

Kahn, Gustave, 238

Kant, Immanuel, 204, 211

Kasai, Akira, 197

Kawakami, Otojiro, 230, 233, 238

Keali'inohomoku, Joann, 6, 250, 261: on dance and the church, 12–13; on dance ethnology, 257; on dance rituals, 14; and ethnic dance, 253; and Kurath notation system, 290–91; and 1972 CORD conference, 255; and work of Kurath, 254

Kelso, J. A. Scott, 132, 151

Keppel, Geoffrey, 150, 152, 153

Kestenberg, Judith, 296

Kestenberg Movement Profile, 296, 299–300

kinemes, 290

Kinetography Laban, 285, 286

King, Linda, 8

Kinneavy, James, 179

Kirkendall, Donald T., 141

Kleist, Henrich von, 201–02

Kliebard, H. M., 75

Koestler, Arthur, 131

Kolodney, Annette, 312

Koritz, Amy, 317

Kram, Mark, 139

Krasnow, Donna, 153

Kuhn, Thomas S., 129, 203

Kurath, Gertrude Prokosch, 252–55, 273*n*25, 290–91

Kvale, Steinar, 97

Laage, Joan, 34, 65, 203–04

Laban, Rudolf, 218*n*36, 288–89, 297: Choreutics, 295; effort theory, 63; Labanalysis, 101; Movement Analysis, 64

Labananalysis. *See* Laban Movement Analysis

Laban-Bartieff Institute of Movement Studies, 289, 299

Laban Movement Analysis (LMA), 64, 222*n*76, 285, 288–89, 299–300: and computer coding, 298; described, 286; Ness and, 264; used to describe Graham's work, 294–95; use in ethnography, 262

Labanotation, 266, 268, 285, 286–88, 289, 292: borrowed by Kurath, 290–91; Kagan